THE GENIUS OF
VENICE

1500-1600

EDITED BY JANE MARTINEAU
AND CHARLES HOPE

ROYAL ACADEMY OF ARTS LONDON 1983

Catalogue published in association with

WEIDENFELD AND NICOLSON LONDON

GENERAL INFORMATION

DATES OF EXHIBITION
25 November 1983 – 11 March 1984
(closed 24, 25 December)

PRICES OF ADMISSION
Full price £3.50.
Sunday mornings £2.00.
Students, pensioners, disabled, registered unemployed,
parties of more than ten people £2.00.
Pre-booked parties of students in full-time education,
including accompanying members of staff, and
children under the age of 18, £1.00.

BUFFET RESTAURANT WITH LICENSED BAR
Open daily.
Access to the Restaurant is from the Ground Floor, Entrance Hall.

Invalids may use their own wheeled chairs or obtain the use of one
without charge by previous arrangement. Applications should be
made to Reception for the necessary authority.

Visitors are required to deposit all miscellaneous items other than
handbags with the attendant at the Cloakroom in the Entrance Hall.
The other attendants are strictly forbidden to take charge of anything.

George Weidenfeld and Nicolson Limited
91 Clapham High Street, London SW4 7TA

Set in Monophoto Poliphilus, Blado and Sabon and printed by
BAS Printers Limited, Over Wallop, Hampshire
Colour separations by Newsele Litho Limited, Italy
Colour printed in Italy by Printers Srl for L.E.G.O., Vicenza

CONTENTS

PATRONS AND COMMITTEES

Her Majesty The Queen

Il Presidente della Repubblica Italiana,
Sandro Pertini

SPONSOR'S PREFACE

The Sea Containers Group and its member company, Venice Simplon-Orient-Express Ltd., are honoured to be sponsors of the Genius of Venice exhibition. Our connections with Italy include ownership of the Hotel Cipriani in Venice, and, as Sir Hugh Casson said at the press conference for the exhibition, we own a Michelangelo – the Villa San Michele in Fiesole (Florence) which has a Michelangelo façade. Our Venice Simplon-Orient-Express train to Venice and Florence has stimulated tourism from Britain and other countries to Venice and perhaps indirectly created new interest in the art of the Veneto, particularly in painting and sculpture of the sixteenth century – the region's greatest period for such art forms. We're told that the exhibition is the most important display of Italian art outside Italy for more than 50 years and the most important such display of Venetian art ever. No wonder we're pleased to be associated with such an important event! We hope that you, once having seen the exhibition, share our enthusiasm and give full marks to the Royal Academy for having mounted such a tour de force, and we hope as well one day to welcome you aboard our train or to one of our hotels.

James B. Sherwood
President, The Sea Containers Group

like diverting the spice trade from its Levantine outlets, and of the loss to the Turks in 1503 of two of Venice's most valued colony-ports in south-west Greece, Methoni and Koroni.

Yet by 1517 the *terraferma* empire had been recovered, by the 1520s the spice trade, though smaller in volume, had become as profitable as before, and the merchant convoys had adapted to a longer rhythm that carried them from Corfu to Crete with little regret for the lost ports-of-call. Tested on all fronts, Venice settled into the golden age of its culture with a more loyal subject population (for alien rule had proved harsher than the republic's) and a confidence not only higher than ever but buttressed by the amazed, if sometimes grudging, admiration of other states; 'celebrated by all'.

For Venice itself, unlike Milan or Florence or Rome, had never surrendered to siege during the wars of Italy that had begun in 1494 and only petered out in 1530; it had preserved its 'inviolate liberty'. If we look around the peninsula in that latter year the contrast justifies amazement. Milan and Milanese Lombardy had become a Spanish protectorate, the Kingdom of Naples and Sicily a Spanish colony. Florence had just had to surrender to an Imperial army. The Papacy fluttered uneasily between dependence on Spain and France. Genoa was a Habsburg satellite. The territorial pretensions of Mantua and Ferrara had been cut back to a pained provincialism. The Italian states, for so long contemptuous of the foreign 'barbarians', were now forced to pay homage to them, but not Venice.

Moreover, Venice had suffered no violent changes in its form of government. Indeed its republican constitution scarcely changed between the closing of the membership of the Great Council (Cat. H3) in 1297 and the republic's fall to Napoleon Bonaparte in 1797. And none of the few changes that did take place occurred during the Wars of Italy. Compared with Venice's great rival republic, Florence, the contrast is striking. In 1494 Florence exiled the Medici family, who for four generations had fairly tactfully directed the republic's fortunes, and adopted a more representative form of constitution. In 1512, with the aid of a Spanish army, the Medici returned. In 1527 they were exiled again, only to come back, with the help of another foreign army, in 1530, this time to rule as hereditary dukes and grand dukes.

Venice's survival as the only powerful republic in Europe was due, as a host of commentators were moved to admit, to 'the divine institutions of the republic'. They took their cue, it is true, from Venice itself, many of whose laws began 'this well ordered republic . . .', but the admiration was genuine. Venice seemed to have acquired a monopoly of that rarest of Renaissance commodities, political stability. How was it achieved?

The base of the constitution was provided by the Great Council. With some 2,000 members – too unwieldy to conduct day-to-day business – it was primarily the reservoir whence individuals were chosen to sit for short periods (lest they acquire too much power) on smaller councils. Of these the most important were the Senate, the chief policy-forming organ, some 200 strong, the College, which formulated the Senate's business and then saw to its execution, and the Council of Ten (usually, in fact, a body of 25 or so) which was responsible for state security and the handling of confidential diplomacy. Chairman of all these bodies was the doge, elected for life, but usually at an advanced age, through

a procedure elaborately devised to protect the post from self-seeking or party-supported ambition. Only a titular head of state, and denied political initiative, he was, according to his personality, potentially influential largely because of his enduring presence in bodies whose membership was constantly changing.

The secret, however, lay only partly within the constitutional machinery; it also depended on the character of a governing class unique in Europe. Its members, though they referred to themselves as '*nobeli*', were not nobles in the sense of being primarily attached to landownership and having a natural antipathy to central government. The Venetian patriciate contained no disturbing 'feudal' elements; it had defined itself through a shared success in commerce and the administration of the empire overseas. By 1325 it was a caste closed, save by hereditary right, to anyone, however rich he became, whose name was not then inscribed in the Golden Book. Unlike Florence, whose political processes were bedevilled by the absorption into the ruling class of territorial magnates and newly-rich families, such rivalries as there were between Venetian patricians did little to hinder the processes of government, and the Renaissance patriciate as a whole shared a strong sense of putting the interests of the state above their own. There were, of course, individual exceptions, but on the whole, and especially after the gaining of the land empire had doubled the caste's administrative and diplomatic responsibilities, the class that had an absolute monopoly of power had an automatic loyalty to the system that permitted it. 'The immortal virtue of its nobles': this was not just empty rhetoric.

Observers of sixteenth-century Venice, noting the grave decorum of the patricians and the sober relish with which they wore their patrician robes (as in the majority of their portraits), were also amazed by a social harmony which, within a population of some 145,000, allowed power to be wielded by so few. Of the social dissensions, let alone outright revolts, that characterised the other European states, Venice seemed (and, comparatively speaking, was) miraculously free.

It is natural for wealth to seek the prestige and protection of political rank as well. But on the whole the patriciate's commercial and fiscal system was seen to favour the rich non-patricians equally, and they avoided the expense and long absences from business involved in embassies, naval commands and governorships of subject cities which, together with council attendance when in Venice, were among the 'costs' of patrician status. The rich *cittadini*, as they were called, who comprised some seven to ten per cent of the population, provided, moreover, the government's civil service: from accountants and code-breakers to secretaries of the Senate and the Ten and the head of the service, the Chancellor himself ('the doge of the non-nobles', as a contemporary dubbed him), those *cittadini* who did not devote themselves to commerce or banking became identified with the values and purposes of the patricians they served and advised. The administration of the great charitable institutions, the *scuole*, like those of the Carità and San Rocco, for whom Titian and Tintoretto worked, was, too, in their hands, and their boards, like the major secretaryships, provided an informal honours system that acted as a palliative to blocked political ambition.

As for the vast majority of craftsmen, boatmen, shop-fig. 3 Matteo Pagan *Procession of the Doge* (Cat. H2)

keepers, labourers and servants, nowhere in Europe did they expect power; in Venice they were kept from the violent expression of grievances by reasonably full employment (an island city could deter job-seeking immigrants), a guild system whose complaints were considered sympathetically by government, and institutions, like the *scuole*, which cared with some adequacy for those who became too sick or old to work. Commoners too were represented in those great civic processions (fig. 3) which gave living form to the ideological notion that every section of the community had a part to play in 'the city which with eternal concord . . . has eclipsed the example and fame of all other republics'.

One such procession took place each St. Mark's day, 25 April, ending in the Basilica – the chapel of both St. Mark and the Doge – and thereby binding every social sector to re-commitment to the idea that the Evangelist (to whom on a visit to the then uninhabited Venice an angel had appeared and said '*Pax tibi, Marce* . . . Peace be with you Mark; this is where your body will be laid to rest') was the heavenly guarantor of the republic's special destiny: to endure and prosper, and to offer justice, liberty from outside interference and peace to its subjects.

No other Renaissance state used its patron saint to political purpose so effectively; wherever Venice ruled, there was, on pillar or plaque, St. Mark, not just to symbolise the republic's presence, but to license it. For in the illumination prefacing the Libro d'Oro of Doge Andrea Gritti (Cat. H6) the Evangelist holds out not his own book but a compilation of the laws of Venice that the doge must swear to obey, and which were, in a sense, those of the saint himself.

Together with the figure of St. Mark, or his lion with the open book quoting the angel's prophecy, the other themes that played a major role in Venetian political iconography were Justice and Peace (eg. Cat. H8), with Peace stressed all the more when, after its recovery of the mainland empire, Venice came to renounce expansion and proclaim the doctrine of a neutrality armed not just with the navy but with new fortifications round its cities (Cat. H16), a standing army of 9,000 men and a militia force of perhaps 40,000. That recovery confirmed at last the patriciate's preference for its land over its maritime empire. Its subjects, by collaborating in the expulsion of their foreign masters, had given Venice a vote of confidence, and this led, through increased land purchases and villa-building by Venetians, and through the coming and going of civic embassies and of petitions and their replies, to a steady closening of the personal ties between the *terraferma* and the capital, and an increased colouring of the former's cultural life by the art that was changing so rapidly and so wonderfully on the lagoon. How far that influence crossed, as land purchases hardly did, the river Mincio, which figured so largely in Venetian strategic thinking, whether it reached Bergamo and Brescia, for instance,

is one of the questions to which this exhibition hopes to stimulate an answer.

Just how far the imaginative change from an instinct to stress the sea and the east rather than the land and the west went, can be seen from the lack of shock when, in its struggle against the Turks of 1570–73, the republic won the Battle of Lepanto (Cat. 142, H19) but lost the war, being forced to give up Cyprus. Venice's medieval maritime enemies had been, after all, weak: an unsteady Byzantine Empire, and a trade rival, Genoa, operating from a base even further from the Levant than Venice's own. But from 1503 the Turk became an aggressive Mediterranean presence, as voracious for space by sea as on land. Venice had the role of 'defender of the Faith' forced upon it, but shouldered the extra costs of the garrisons and strengthened fortifications (Cat. H16, H17 and H18) that made uneasy coexistence possible, in a spirit of profit and habit rather than of crusade. To continue to think of Venice in the sixteenth century as 'a maritime republic' illuminates neither its psychology nor its culture.

Yet it was the continued presence of empire both by sea and land that gave force to the Myth of Venice, the image, that is, of Venice as a Renaissance Utopia: perfectly governed by a wise and selfless ruling class through a rationally balanced constitution; lacking in party or social tensions; and therefore so stable as to be able, against all the odds, to remain inviolate and independent. The image ignored flaws of character and system. So it has been dubbed a myth. But the glamour of empire diverted attention from the flaws, and when other countries fell to debating the merits of republican as against monarchical rule – in mid-seventeenth century England and Holland, and, later in the century, when constitutions were being proposed for Pennsylvania and New Jersey – the Venetian model was cited because it was offered by an equal. Other king-less polities could not compare. There was no Myth of Lucca, or Genoa, or of the Swiss Confederation.

But nowhere, of course, was the myth, and the confidence it fed, more potent than in the imagination of the Venetians themselves and of those who were drawn to work among them. One such immigrant, Pietro Aretino, the friend of Titian and one of the few writers anxious and able to articulate his feelings about art, in a letter of 1530 to Andrea Gritti praised 'the liberty of this great state.'

'So let us bow before her', he went on, 'and let us offer prayers on her behalf to God, whose benign Majesty . . . has willed that Venice shall rival the world itself in its eternal life – that world which is astounded that nature has placed her in so incredible a site, and that Heaven has been so generous to her in its gifts that she outshines in her nobility, magnificence, riches, palaces, churches, pious foundations, virtues, councils, empire, fame and glory, any other city that there ever was.'

PATRONAGE IN VENICE

J. M. Fletcher

In 1537 Titian's friend Pietro Aretino wrote to the architect and sculptor Jacopo Sansovino, warning him against returning to Rome, which he had left during the Sack ten years before. How could he contemplate exchanging the security of Venice, where he had even been given a house by the State, for the dangers of Rome, or Venetian senators for courtier prelates? Aretino was hardly an objective observer, but his letter raises two issues that deeply affected artistic patronage in Venice: the stability and safety of the city, and the absence of a court. A third factor of equal importance – wealth – is stressed in a short guide-book to Venice published in 1561 by Sansovino's son Francesco. This took the form of a dialogue between a visitor and his Venetian guide, who at one point boasted that there were more pictures there than in the rest of Italy put together. To this the visitor replied: 'As you are the richest men in Italy, it is right and proper that you should also have more beautiful things than other people, for artists go where money flows and where people are plump and prosperous.'

Art is naturally tied to the economy; and Venetian art was bought with the ducat which, like today's dollar, was a highly respected international currency. One of Sansovino's most important commissions in Venice was to build a bigger Mint, and we can see in Tintoretto's *Santa Giustina and the Treasurers* (Cat. 110) magistrates who show their money bags to the Madonna. In their wills Venetians tell us how much they paid for their art: Giuliano Zancarol, a patron of Bellini, who gave 50 ducats for a picture of Christ, boasted that he has never minded how much he spent 'so long as it is beautiful.'[1] Gabriel Vendramin, one of the day's leading

fig. 4 Venice's Mainland Possessions in the Sixteenth Century

connoisseurs who owned Giorgione's *Tempesta* (fig. 5) looked back on years of hard labour in the family firm which had earned him the collection that had brought 'a little rest and quiet' to his soul.

The absence of a court meant that Venice lacked the influence on taste of a single dominant family, as occurred in sixteenth-century Florence, but this was to some extent balanced by the ideology of the State and its leading members, in the emphasis on the continuity of institutions and in the constant proclamation of Venice's wealth and power. In these respects, it is often hard to distinguish between public and private patronage; between the activities of the government and other quasi-independent corporate bodies. As we consider the different types of patron – official, corporate and private – we shall see how this inter-relationship constantly came into play.

The State was not only a considerable patron in its own right, it also set the pattern for other types of patronage and in some cases exerted a direct or indirect control on individual initiatives. Its direct activity might involve the commissioning or purchase of works of art as diplomatic gifts, for example paintings by Bellini or Titian; but much more important was the construction and embellishment of government buildings such as the Fondaco dei Tedeschi (the warehouse leased to the German merchants; fig. 8), which was decorated with frescoes by Giorgione and Titian. This was evidently a relatively unprestigious commission, since it was given to comparatively young and untried artists. By contrast, most of the paintings in the Doge's Palace itself were by the foremost painters in the city. Thus the replacement of the celebrated and politically very significant cycle of canvases in the Sala del Gran Consiglio was entrusted first to Gentile Bellini together with his brother Giovanni and Alvise Vivarini, and later to Titian, Tintoretto and Veronese. Such jobs were eagerly sought by artists, not least because payment often took the form of lucrative sinecures, as well as perks such as free studio space, assistants paid by the State, and, in the case of Giovanni Bellini, exemption from guild control. Once in government service, artists could also act as sub-patrons in finding jobs for pupils and protégés. They also tended to abuse their position, so that Titian took no less than 25 years to execute a single picture. After about 1550 government interest in completing the decoration of the Palace seems to have increased, and after two disastrous fires, in 1574 and 1577, a major campaign was undertaken to replace the destroyed paintings in the minimum time. By then, it was evidently unthinkable that parts of the walls of the Palace should be without their painted adornment.

In granting individual commissions the personal role of the doge was seldom of great importance. It was customary for each to commission his own portrait, and during the sixteenth century it was expected that he would also order a votive painting, showing himself together with various saints; but some doges did not bother to do so. Only a few, in fact, such as the long-reigning Andrea Gritti, who did much to promote the careers of Titian and Sansovino, can be considered as major patrons in their own right. In general the Venetian government discouraged personality cults, and State patronage worked on a consensus system through a series of government departments which often awarded commissions by competition. This had the effect of allowing the Venetian nobility (the only class with political power)

fig. 5 Giorgione *Tempesta* (Gallerie dell'Accademia, Venice)

an opportunity to learn about art while serving in departments with responsibilities for public works, while patricians who already enjoyed a reputation as art experts were able to develop their expertise through frequent co-option to special boards formed to supervise important projects. From such a position a prominent politician such as Marcantonio Barbaro could promote the ideas and career of his favourite architect Palladio, thus reinforcing that subtle interaction between the public and private sectors which is a distinguishing feature of artistic patronage in Venice.

Moving down the social scale, another important source of patronage was the lay confraternities, the Scuole, which were divided into Grandi and Piccole, large and small. By the sixteenth century these organisations, originally founded as flagellant companies, had been largely transformed into mutual benefit societies with special responsibilities for charitable activities. By then the patronage of the Scuole Grandi had become so lavish that they were criticised for diverting funds from charity to art, for building assembly halls as big as ballrooms, for decorating the façades of their buildings with harpies (fig. 9) and for their over-elaborate processional floats.[2] In their commissions for paintings the Scuole tended to follow the example of the government in the decoration of the Doge's Palace, both in the practice of adorning their buildings with cycles of vast canvases and elaborate painted ceilings, and in the choice of artists who had already proved themselves in government service. This was true particularly of the Scuola di San Marco, which was favoured by top civil servants, and which employed the Bellini brothers and later Tintoretto. The latter was also responsible for virtually the entire decoration of the Scuola di S. Rocco, but in this case his employment may have been due in part to the fact that his father was a silk dyer and that this Scuola fig. 6 J. Sansovino *Tommaso Rangone* (S. Giuliano, Venice)

had a high proportion of textile workers and *tintori* on its books. This type of commission was not necessarily very lucrative, but the artists were generally admitted to membership of the relevant Scuola, sometimes, as in the case of Gentile Bellini, rising to key positions on the governing board. Tintoretto was given a life salary and a place on the board at S. Rocco. The Scuole also provided down-and-out painters with almshouses, and encouraged the successful with grants to help them marry off their daughters.

The government exercised a general supervisory role over the Scuole, and its permission was required, for example, when they needed to suspend their charitable activities in order to pay for their lavish headquarters. In the actual granting of commissions, the Scuole in theory exercised corporate patronage, but in practice the taste of the Guardian and management committee could be decisive. At San Marco there was Domenico di Piero, a rich jeweller who sold cameos to the Medici, and Tommaso Rangone, a distinguished patron of Sansovino, Vittoria and Tintoretto, while San Rocco had Martino d'Anna, of Flemish merchant stock, whose family had patronised Titian and whose palace façade was decorated by Pordenone (Cat. D43). In 1525 the board of the small Scuola di S. Pietro Martire asked the government to overrule the majority who wanted to order an altarpiece from someone 'who is not up to the job'. They offered to pay for the picture out of their own pockets, and in the petition, which was signed by Palma Vecchio, they insisted that the task must be done by 'one of the most pre-eminent in the said art'. The final outcome was Titian's spectacularly avant-garde *Death of St. Peter Martyr* (see fig. 14).[3]

Another important branch of corporate patronage was

that of the religious orders. These varied enormously in social and intellectual tone, taste and wealth. Tales of monkish and nunnish philistinism are legion. For example, nuns cancelled a commission to Veronese, seduced by the miniaturist technique of a visiting Fleming;[4] and the Prior of the Frari thought the figures in Titian's *Assumption* (fig. 18) too big. But several orders displayed sophisticated artistic as well as musical taste: thus in the fifteenth century the intellectual Camaldolese at San Michele in Isola and the aristocratic nuns at San Zaccaria were innovative architectural patrons; Veronese received his great opportunity from the Jeronymite Prior of S. Sebastiano, a fellow-countryman from Verona, while Lotto developed a close relationship with the Dominicans at SS. Giovanni e Paolo, where he painted portraits of friendly monks dressed up as their patron saints, and reduced the price of *S. Antonino Distributing Alms* by 30 ducats on the understanding that the monks would pay for his funeral.

A distinctive feature of Venetian religious patronage was the role of community feeling within parishes, which was strengthened by the fact that non-noble householders elected their own parish priests. These could then truly represent the artistic wishes of the parishioners, by petitioning the government for grants to their churches and by organising public subscriptions for new altarpieces. Several priests personally paid for outstanding works of art. Thus Sebastiano's organ doors (Cat. 95, 96) and Veronese's altarpiece for S. Pantalon (Cat. 147) were financed either by or through priests. But in the decoration of churches private initiatives by laymen were also important, and the majority of altarpieces were commissioned by individual patrons as a focus for masses in memoriam. On other occasions, a picture which the patron had kept at home during his lifetime would be bequeathed to his funerary chapel at his death.

Private patronage was often subject to State control. This was most obviously the case in matters involving the public image of Venice. In 1535, for example, two commissioners were appointed by the government to look into the city's embellishment, and the State also intervened to prevent private individuals from commemorating themselves in politically sensitive areas such as Piazza San Marco. Rangone (Cat. S39), who fancied a statue of himself on the façade of S. Geminiano on the Piazza, was side-tracked to a less prominent position on the façade of S. Giuliano (fig. 6). The activities of private patrons might also be affected by sumptuary laws, which could limit expenditure on interior decoration as well as on clothes and parties.[6] But Venetian private collections were certainly a source of civic pride. In his guidebook of 1581 Francesco Sansovino devoted a whole section to them, with special mention given to the Grimani and Foscari collections of antique sculpture, to the Priulis' paintings by Palma Vecchio and to the works by Bellini, Giorgione and Titian owned by Gabriel Vendramin; and important state visitors were often shown such private collections as well as the Treasury of San Marco.

In the fifteenth century virtually all pictures in private hands were religious subjects on panel, and most belonged to the type of Madonna and Child compositions made popu-

lar by Bellini and his workshop. But already some Venetians were showing an interest in the antique. As early as the 1440s Cyriac of Ancona met a Venetian sea-captain who kept a collection of ancient cameos in his cabin;[7] but at this date an interest in ancient art did not necessarily indicate a taste for modern art. After showing the Venetian humanist Ermolao Barbaro the Medici Palace collection in 1490, Piero de' Medici concluded that he did not 'understand much about sculpture', although he was interested in the age of the medals.[8] By the 1520s attitudes had changed, and antiquarian and aesthetic interests had come together. Giorgione was one of the first artists to work almost exclusively for connoisseurs, extending the narrow range of subject matter to include new picture types such as landscapes, reclining nudes, and ambiguous semi-portraits of beautiful boys and girls. It is clear from Michiel's descriptions that competitive collecting accelerated connoisseurship, sharpened the interest in provenance, and encouraged an appreciation for drawings, especially those that could be related to paintings[9]. The point is forcibly made in Lotto's *Portrait of Andrea Odoni* (Cat. 46), in which this connoisseur who owned better pictures than sculptures, including works by Titian, Palma Vecchio and Savoldo, is shown handling an antique statuette, a clear allusion to his more intellectually respectable collection of antiques. From Lotto's picture we would never guess that he also owned a bronze puppy, petrified snakes and a dried chameleon.

fig. 7 G. Bellini *Virgin and Child with Saints and Pietro Priuli* (Kunstmuseum, Düsseldorf)

The prestige of antique art is probably one reason why in the early decades of the sixteenth century several Venetians seem to have been trying to inject classical imagery and classical style into their modern art. In 1501, for example, Cardinal Zen asked that his tomb should be 'as antique as possible'. By 1523 the government Procurators ordering a statue of the Magdalene from Bartolomeo Bon insisted that he use a classical style for drapery and hair.[10] Nor was such taste confined to sculpture, for in 1506 Dürer complained that the Venetians criticised his work because it was not '*antigisch* and so not good'.

In general it is easier to relate subjects rather than styles to patrons. Monks could feast their eyes on supper scenes by Veronese, while members of confraternities dedicated to the sacrament might meditate on the eucharist assisted by Tintoretto's Last Suppers and Washings of Feet (Cat. 101). Thus a Mystic Marriage of St. Catherine would make an ideal gift for a nun, but was also popular with newly-weds such as Lotto's patron Messer Marsilio (Cat. 44). Again, Odoni, who made money from customs duties on wine, had paintings of Bacchus and Ceres, goddess of plenty, on the façade of his house. He also followed the common Venetian habits of displaying a *Reclining Venus* in his bedroom and having his portrait painted. This last form of patronage had a perennial attraction for the Venetians, and on his first visit to Venice in 1541 Vasari was particularly impressed by patrician portrait collections going back four or five generations.

Pride in family often went hand in hand with a wider sense of obligation to the city and the State. Thus Vasari saw a *Supper at Emmaus* by Titian on show in the Doge's Palace, a present to the Republic by its owner who thought it deserved to be seen in a public place; and in 1555 a notary left another painting by Titian, an *Annunciation*, to the Scuola di S. Rocco, with the request that it should be prominently displayed. In 1528 Cardinal Grimani bequeathed not only his library, but also his paintings by Bosch and his classical sculpture to the State, while Andrea Loredan, who may have commissioned Sebastiano's *Judgement of Solomon* (Cat. 97), stipulated that his pictures should be kept together in his inalienable palace both for the 'decoration of the house' and for '*la patria*'.[11]

Venetian patrons, like Venetian art, came in different styles. The extrovert and flamboyant Rangone ordered that the model for S. Giuliano – the church which he had paid to renovate – should be carried in his funeral procession, but the secretive and humble Pietro Priuli insisted that his arms should not appear in his funeral chapel at S. Michele. Their contrasting styles are reflected in their donor portraits: Sansovino's Rangone (fig. 6), a nouveau riche from Ravenna, sits proudly elevated on the façade of S. Giuliano accompanied by a tri-lingual inscription testifying to his learning and generosity. Bellini's Procurator Priuli (fig. 7) kneels devoutly in an old-fashioned triptych wearing the old-fashioned hat (the *capuzzo*) that earned him his nickname.

The last word may be given to Giovanni Cornaro, a friend of Sanmicheli and one of a line of great patrons, for in his will of 1551 he demonstrates all the characteristics of an outstanding Venetian patron – pride in rank and family, business acumen and a love of beauty. Worried lest the art treasures of his late brother, and in particular a set of tapestries showing the life of Scipio Cornelio, from whom the family claimed descent, should be lost to Venice through sale to Rome 'where they are known', he urged his sons to preserve them and to keep them together, for not only were they 'beautiful and delicate', but also 'noble objects and worthy of princes'.[12]

1] Paoletti 1893, I, p. 112. Zancarol, who collected classical art, was a close friend of Tullio Lombardo.
2] Caravia 1541, sig. D r-Fiii r. For Caravia see Logan 1972, pp. 204–05.
3] Ludwig 1905, p. 69.
4] Ridolfi, ed. von Hadeln, 1914–24, I, pp. 328–29.
5] Prodi 1972, pp. 419–20.
6] Bistort 1912.
7] Ashmole 1957, p. 39.

8] Roscoe 1796, Appendix LXXXI, pp. 96–97.
9] Fletcher 1981, pp. 457–67, 602–08.
10] Paoletti 1893, p. 282.
11] Puppi and Olivato Puppi 1977, pp. 222–23.
12] Venice, Archivio di Stato, Sez. Notarile, Testamenti (A. Marsilio), Busta 1209, no. 492. I plan to publish an article in collaboration with Susan Connell on the implications of this document.

PATRONAGE ON
THE VENETIAN MAINLAND

Lionello Puppi

It is by no means easy to provide a brief but clear outline of the trends of patronage in the Venetian mainland territories during the sixteenth century, since we have to take account of a complex network of motives and aspirations, some of which actually contradict one another. Nevertheless, if one accepts that such patronage reflects above all a distinctive sense of mission on the part of the aristocracy, which was attempting to re-establish its position and adapt itself to the new circumstances brought about by the political and military crisis of the years around 1500, then it is possible to discern a coherent and plausible pattern.

The rout of Agnadello in 1509 had aroused real fears that the extinction of Venice was imminent. 'The affairs of the Venetian Republic', wrote Guicciardini, 'were plummeting with immense and almost awesome speed, with disaster continually heaped upon disaster, all hopeful proposals coming to nothing, and without the slightest sign to encourage even the hope that, having lost so great an empire, the people might at least preserve their liberty.' In fact, thanks largely to the loyalty of the rural and urban populace, and despite the widespread treachery of the provincial aristocracy, the Republic managed to survive the period of greatest threat and was soon on the path to recovery. Her prestige was increased by the fact that she had retained her independence while the rest of Italy had fallen under foreign domination, a fate made all the more painful because the concept of Italian liberty retained its appeal as an intellectual ideal.

Writing in 1535, but presumably recording his thoughts in 1509, Guicciardini himself notes that in the period of most acute danger, many people, 'reflecting more soberly upon the state of affairs, and upon how vile and disastrous was the reduction of all Italy into a state of enslavement to foreigners, felt extreme distress that so great a city, so ancient a seat of liberty, the glory of the name of Italy throughout the world, should fall into such complete extinction'. This reaction reflects primarily the self-awareness and pride of the more perceptive among the Venetians themselves. But by the time Guicciardini was writing, a new version of the myth of Venice had been born. The Republic now saw itself as a state whose power – by then established on a European scale – was based not on its maritime activities in the Mediterranean, but on its mainland possessions.

The price for Venice's revival was a decision not to expand the city's territory beyond the areas it had conquered in the fifteenth century. 'They had realised', observed the French Resident Guillaume Pellicier in 1542, 'that for the well-being and consideration of the State it would be best not to become embroiled in matters of war with anybody, but to seek and maintain peace with everyone'. In more specific terms, the Venetians had to strengthen their institutions and reorganise their approach to their subject territories through a marriage of public initiative and private interest. In doing so, the Republic was once again claiming to be the model of an 'administration which is certainly most worthy to be examined and judged, and regarded with no less admiration in our own day than were those of the Spartans and Romans in ancient times', as the Florentine Donato Giannotti wrote in 1526. The comparison with Rome was also stressed by Sabellico: 'In sacredness of laws, in equity of justice and goodness, and in other even nobler ordinances the affairs of Venice, when compared with those of Rome, will not appear as fated to be inferior but as very much superior now that they have been renewed.' Another Venetian, Contarini, made much the same point when he wrote that 'There have been republics which openly tried to gain mastery over the whole of Italy and which . . . far surpassed the Venetian Republic in empire, territory and military glory; however, there is none which, in its institutions, laws directed towards the good, and happiness, can be compared to this republic of ours.' And in a similar vein Bodin was to proclaim that Venice, Athens and Rome were 'the most illustrious republics which have ever existed under popular rule', and to explain that although 'the most sacred laws' were administered by the aristocracy, the Venetian system was built upon a 'harmonious proportion which has made her the fairest and most flourishing of republics'.

In the last analysis, this is the theme of Utopia realised, a society brought into being and maintained by the type of man whom Palladio was to call 'the great Republican gentleman' or 'the gentleman of great splendour and ease', and whose civic role, social position and self-awareness rested upon the preservation of the status quo. Priuli, in his own way, already had a premonition of this when he wrote: 'In this hallowed city of Venice, it used to be merchants who were despised and vilified by all, and they received few honours, so that many merchants likewise used their money to buy possessions and other things so as to live off the income. And this was the ruin of Venice', because eventually 'when the Venetian nobles and citizens had become rich, they wanted to celebrate their success, and live and attend and give themselves up to pleasure and delight and to the green of the countryside on the mainland, with many other amusements, so abandoning navigation and seafaring, which were more vexatious and arduous'.

These developments created the need for a new approach to economic organisation and artistic expression. 'If I may ask', pleads Daniele Barbaro, 'I ask and ask again (that) my fellow-countrymen . . . should remember that, since they have both riches and the power to win honour by their achievements, they should take steps also to ensure that they are not deficient in intellect and knowledge; they will succeed in this only when they bring themselves to realise that they do not know what in fact they do not know, nor can ever know without practice, hard work and science. And if they believe that the traditions in their workshops are of necessity incomparably skilled, they greatly deceive themselves, for in fact they are extremely faulty and bad traditions.' But to establish and preserve the new enterprise, to produce a tangible representation of the myth of Venice and the renewal of her empire, the exercise of 'practice, hard work and science' had to be firmly grounded in the 'true beauty and grace of the Ancients'.

The artists of the Veneto, wrote Pietro Bembo in 1525, 'within the narrow confines of their drawings, portray the forms of beautiful antique figures in marble and sometimes bronze which are lying around or are preserved and treasured publicly and in private, and the arches, baths, theatres and various other buildings which still stand in certain places there; then, when they plan to execute some new work, they examine those models, and, seeking to produce likenesses of them with artifice, they believe their labours will earn them the more praise the more nearly they manage to make their works resemble the ancient ones; so they work, aware that the ancient objects approach the perfection of art more closely than do those of more recent times'. Here, indeed, was a genuine manifesto for classicism, which acquired a topical resonance because of the prevailing ideological climate, however remote from reality this may have been.

Essential features of this reality were the adoption by the aristocracy in the mainland cities of a system of investment economy similar to that of the Venetian patriciate, and the fact that in these years membership of the city councils was increasingly restricted to the nobility. At the same time their traditional antagonism to Venice, mollified by the concession of a limited degree of administrative autonomy, found its only outlet at the level of municipal prestige. Moreover, the language in which such assertions were expressed was itself derived from the programme elaborated by the Venetians to proclaim the renewal of their empire. Now that political rivalry was tamed, punished and rendered unthinkable, it was replaced by a confrontation of ideas, a cultural challenge. By presenting the city as superior in its foundation or destiny, by exalting its glorious history and employing the rhetorical tools of humanism, this challenge would advance the city's claim to civic primacy, which would then be illustrated by its notable achievements in the present. This process of self-glorification involved the rediscovery and updating of the 'true beauty and grace of the Ancients', for which each city was a repository, inasmuch as it was a custodian of antique remains – the very treasures, incidentally, which Venice herself lacked. The spate of municipal eulogies which appeared in these years, therefore, was not so much a revival of the obsolete medieval *laudatio*, as a reflection, modelled on examples from the classics and the humanists, of the real tensions in the historical situation. To mention an analogy in another sphere, there is also unmistakable and significant evidence that cartography was subject to similar pressures, for producers of local maps were eager to invest the bare record of topographical data with symbolic allusions.

Patronage is above all an urban phenomenon, and even though it evolved through a combination of factors too complex and intricate to be reduced to a single rigid scheme, the feature of particular interest here is the element of cultural challenge. On the one hand, it is necessary to consider the initiatives taken by the citizen body as a whole, as represented in its communal councils and magistracies, and by the aristocrats as a distinct class in each city, or by those groups who acted collectively in their role as members of academies. On the other hand, it is equally important not to ignore the distinct, though complementary, impulse to promote the self-glorification of individuals, families and dynasties, a type of initiative in which the Venetian patricians resident on the mainland also participated. This kind of patronage, of course, often involved religious commissions for churches and other sacred buildings. It also encompassed the appearance of the collector, and particularly, though not exclusively, the collector of antiques, whose activity was intended both to provide a basis and a stimulus for the creation of works of art and to celebrate the city's claim to a 'magnificence' superior to that of Venice. It is therefore no accident that in the *Book of the Courtier* Baldassare Castiglione assigns to Ludovico Canossa, a Veronese – not, one should note, Venetian – nobleman active in several spheres of patronage associated with the notion of cultural challenge, the statement that the perfect gentleman 'should be able to judge the excellence of statues both ancient and modern, of vases, buildings, medals, cornices, intaglios and the like'.

A final element to be taken into account in this intricate pattern is the role of Venice herself. Although the Republic, interested in the orderly administration of her mainland heritage rather than in the creation of a monolithic national unity, came to allow the cities considerable freedom of action in the exercise of a cultural rivalry based on municipal pride, she reserved the right to set up, in places appropriate to the expression of her own political authority and rule, the symbols of St. Mark and the kind of unified architectural and artistic complexes that would demonstrate to the city the immutable presence of the 'Republic of the Venetians'. This brought into play the component of Venetian self-awareness discussed at the beginning of this essay.

In the space available it is impossible to justify fully and in detail, case by case, the reconstruction of the history of patronage on the mainland that has just been outlined. Taking the example of Verona, however, one can see the relationship between the execution of the public programme to recreate an antique classicism considered to be the city's birthright, and the care lavished by leading members of the aristocracy on their private collections. The public enterprise had already been inaugurated in the fifteenth century by Mantegna's altarpieces for S. Zeno and S. Maria in Organo, then continued with Falconetto's paintings of the *Triumphs of Caesar* on the façades of major buildings, and finally concluded when the Loggia del Consiglio was crowned with statues representing the five greatest citizens of Verona in antiquity. In short, it was a programme of civic glorification. Meanwhile, in the sumptuous settings of their family residences, which were thus explicitly identified as authentic *hospitia Musarum*, abodes of the Muses, the nobility were assembling outstanding collections, which demonstrated both an antiquarian fervour and a personal taste for contemporary art of an unusually wide-ranging and sophisticated kind. In the case of Vicenza, too, it is evident that there were close links between the corporate initiatives taken by the aristocracy, acting either as a ruling elite or as a council of 'Olympians' in the Academy, in the erection of those monuments – from the Basilica to the Theatre – which expressed their corporate identity, and the private activities of the Porto, Chiericati, Thiene and Valmarana families, and above all of Giangiorgio Trissino (see Cat. 33), with his meeting-place for the Academicians at Cricoli, and of Girolamo Gualdo, who constructed the magnificent garden at Pusterla. Here at Vicenza the Republic also played its part, with commissions to Titian and Paris Bordone for frescoes celebrating its 'most sacred laws' in the Palace of Justice.

Without dwelling on other cities, such as Brescia and Treviso, we should at this point take into account a further effect of this kind of patronage. Although it did not exclude the employment of artists, even outstanding ones, based in Venice and working in a strictly Venetian idiom, it did in time stimulate lively activity on the part of competent local craftsmen, thus fostering an iconographic and stylistic renewal in the various provincial centres, each of which had already developed its own distinctive characteristics.

Padua affords a good example of this phenomenon, and especially noteworthy are the activities of Alvise Cornaro. It is clear from contemporary evidence that the leading craftsmen responsible for the sculptural and pictorial decoration of his two buildings, the Loggia and the Odeo, were the Paduans Tiziano Minio and Domenico Campagnola; and it has also been shown that the plan of the Odeo recalls the studio of Marcus Terentius Varro in his villa at Cassino, as reconstructed in a drawing by Giuliano da Sangallo, while the design of the Loggia depends on information provided by Serlio about the Villa Madama, itself a re-creation of Pliny's Villa Laurentina. In the very years in which the palace for the city council was being completed as an expression of the corporate identity of the Paduan aristocracy, Cornaro's two buildings constitute an analogous enterprise by a private individual. By openly recalling ancient Rome, his scheme also shows his desire to glorify himself as he takes on the task of encapsulating in a unified image the foundations of 'Paduanness' itself, the *Patavinitas* which was here proclaimed as the modern expression of an ancient – and therefore superior – destiny embracing the 'noble city of Padua'. The decoration too evokes the classical world, drawing on a wealth of information provided by Padua's zealous antiquarian collectors, and incorporating, in the abundant use of grotesques, an explicit reference to the Domus Aurea. Classical influences were also transmitted by way of Raphael, whose drawings, according to Michiel, were used by the artists – another example of the stimulus supplied by the passion for collecting. Cornaro's activities even extended to religious art, for he must have been one of the guiding spirits in the planning of the sculptural decoration for the shrine of St. Anthony, which was conceived as an evocation of the 'principles and formulae' of Roman imperial sculpture.

It was no accident that the craftsmen employed by Alvise Cornaro came to form the nucleus of a Paduan School, which, although sometimes augmented by artists from elsewhere, was consistently and coherently to reflect the Paduan ideology of the ancient primacy of the city of Antenor and Livy. The same ideology also lay behind the private commissions of other local patrons, from the house of Marco Mantova Benavides (another splendid 'abode of the Muses' and a temple to the art of rhetoric, which the patron practised) to the residences of the other leading families of Padua and of the Venetians who had settled there, and finally to the buildings owned by the religious organisations, which for the most part were controlled by the aristocracy. Nor did the Venetian government hesitate to draw on this ideology when it restored the Palazzo dei Capitani, 'the hall [which had once been] the ornament of the city' built on the site of the old palace of the Signoria. Here it commissioned a series of frescoes showing 'illustrious men and emperors' (the so-called 'Giants') to commemorate the tribute paid by Petrarch to the greatness of Padua.

Among those responsible for the iconographic programme for this project was Alessandro Maggi, 'the greatest historian of antiquity' in Padua, whose house was designed in imitation of Livy's. Maggi also worked on the programme for the triumphal entry of Bona Sforza in 1556; and here State patronage and the corporate patronage of the local aristocracy came together, in a collaboration between the artists of Padua and the official architect of Venice, Michele Sanmicheli. This enterprise stands as a unique but highly significant illustration of the extreme complexity of the historical situation we have been examining, for it reveals a remarkable phenomenon: the city moderated its challenge to the Venetian myth of imperial renewal while it reconciled, at the civic level, the ancient glory of Padua and the present greatness of the Republic.

ARCHITECTURE

Howard Burns

'In this most noble city of Venice', wrote Serlio in 1537, 'it is the custom to build in a way which is very different from that of all the other cities of Italy.'[1] In Venice buildings rested on oak piles which were driven, tightly packed, into the mud of the lagoon. Symmetrical layouts were desirable, so that structures could settle evenly 'and the walls take the load of the roof equally'.[2] Beam ceilings, with a one-to-one relation between the beams and the spaces between them, were safer and stronger than vaults (which could easily crack) for they had a certain elasticity, and tied the walls together. Wood, however, was costly (timber was also needed for shipbuilding) and its use increased the risk of fire. Fires in Venice were much commoner than elsewhere, and were the main reason for architectural renovation.[3]

Brick was the basic building material. Brickwork lies behind the stone veneers of costly buildings, and was employed with elegance and expertise by Palladio in the Convento della Carità (now the Accademia) and in his two great churches. Building stone was brought by sea from the Istrian coast: Istrian stone weathers well and can take a polish like that of marble.[4] In ordinary houses it was used at water level, for door and window surrounds and for cornices. Stone details were often ordered from the masons in standard shapes and sizes, and their repetition throughout the city gives Venice its attractive visual unity. Important structures were usually faced in Istrian stone, which can be cut easily into large columns or carved into ornate capitals and mouldings. Marbles, often coloured, were used in the most splendid projects, like Sansovino's Loggetta, or the Sala delle Quattro Porte in the Doge's Palace. The red stone of Verona was employed for chimney pieces, and for the red and white chequered pavements of churches.

The environment determined the layout of houses and palaces. Serlio writes that 'as Venice is very densely populated the available sites are restricted and have to be laid out with discretion, and there is not space . . . for great courtyards and many gardens'.[5] He also points out how most of a building's light needs to come from the main façade. In palaces this was on a canal or *campo*. Given security from invasion and Venice's renowned political stability, palaces and public buildings could have their facades pierced by more windows and *loggie* than was the case in Florence, where the traditional palace was a miniature stronghold, a protection against summer heat and the risk of tumult.

Even great houses in Venice are without a central *cortile* and tend to be deep and narrow in plan, with only a small courtyard at the back. Through the centre runs a hall, which on the upper floors served 'for receiving relatives at the time of weddings, and for holding banquets and parties'.[6] These central halls are lit by the group of large windows which one sees in the middle of Venetian façades. The side rooms (unlike the halls) had fireplaces so that 'when one gets up, one has the fireplace to hand'.[7] In palaces these rooms were adorned with hangings, paintings and gilded ceilings, though in terms of function they were rather grand bed-sitters. Rooms could not always be lit from the outside, so that light wells often had to be inserted. Expensive foundations and lack of space made it usual to construct two living floors above the damp ground floor. Between the ground floor and the first floor there was a mezzanine, used for servants, nannies, the small children and kitchens, and sometimes also by the owners themselves, as these low rooms would be cosier in winter.[8]

The cheaper housing developments of Venice anticipate the housing schemes of modern times.[9] A standard living unit of a few rooms was repeated on several floors and sometimes horizontally along the length of a block. A project by Palladio survives for a development of this sort, with pairs of apartments sharing access to a little courtyard with a well. Palladio shows his familiarity not only with Venetian housing, but also with Venetian ways of obtaining drinking water: the little circle which he draws in the outside walls are the pipes which conveyed rain water from the roof to the wells.[10] Rain water was also collected in the *campi* where it was filtered before reaching the public well.

The environment limited architects' choices: little flexibility was possible in planning palaces, and even churches were usually rebuilt on old sites. But despite these limitations, and the fact that Venetian patrons and *proti* (salaried architects and surveyors of works) were usually old (as in the Kremlin, only the old reached the top) Venetian architecture was vigorously innovative. Influential and cultured statesmen pushed for architectural change, and bypassed the local architectural hierarchy by invitations to gifted outsiders: the Florentine Jacopo Sansovino (1486–1570) came up from Rome; the Veronese architect Michele Sanmicheli (1484–1559) was also trained in Rome; Andrea Palladio (1508–1580) had worked in Vicenza.

Scamozzi observes that 'Venice has a great number of master builders and craftsmen in the building trades . . . for as the city is very large and populous, . . . and full of wealth, a very large number of buildings are always being built or rebuilt.'[11] A large group of patricians possessed vast fortunes, and the city's palaces impressed foreigners, not only by their size, but by what seemed, even to sophisticated Italians, an incredible profusion of carved stonework. 'He that will row through the Grand Canal', wrote William Thomas in 1549, 'and mark well the fronts of the houses on both sides shall see them more like the dwellings of princes than private men.'[12]

In the century after 1494 circumstances often placed the Venetian establishment with its back to the wall. In the field of architecture, as elsewhere, the response was generally rapid and effective. The worst of these crises was that of 1509, and the rethinking and reorganisation which followed had consequences not only for military and administrative policy, but also for architecture. There was a general renewal of the fortifications of the State, which from 1529 employed Sanmicheli as a military architect. In this capacity he designed the marvellous Porta Nuova and Porta Palio in Verona, and the gleaming and majestic fortress of Sant'Andrea al Lido, which guards one of the sea approaches to the city. He also designed the huge Palazzo Grimani on the Grand Canal.[13]

The technocratic bias of statesmen like Andrea Gritti (Doge from 1523 to 1538) had wide implications for architecture. It went with a recognition of the importance of prestige building and urban renovation as a means of impressing foreigners, of hinting at the wealth, know-how and determination of the Republic, and of boosting morale in a period when plague, famine and the Turks were constant menaces. Already in 1496 the diarist Malipiero recorded that 'a beginning was made this month on making the foundations of the Clock-tower ... and it will cost around 6,000 ducats. And although the building of the Palace has been somewhat suspended because of the Naples war, nevertheless, so that the city should not seem entirely without money, a start was made on this work.'[14] The need to avoid loss of face (and sometimes loss of state revenues) led to the rapid rebuilding of important buildings destroyed by fire: the Doge's Palace in 1483, the Scuola Grande di San Marco in 1485, the Fondaco dei Tedeschi in 1505 (fig. 8), and, most disastrous of all, the Rialto area, burnt down in 1514.[15] In each case the opportunity was taken to rebuild in a more impressive and functional way. The Fondaco, which served as warehouse, customs office, and hostel for the German merchants, had its plan regularised: from a central loggia one passes into a square arcaded courtyard. To compensate for the plain detailing, imposed by the Senate for reasons of economy, the exterior was decorated with frescoes by Giorgione and Titian.[16] The State also acted quickly after the fires of 1574 and 1577 which gutted the finest rooms in the Doge's Palace. But the final decision to rebuild the rickety wooden bridge at Rialto in stone was continually postponed. The technical problem of spanning the Grand Canal was considerable, but the real reason for lack of action was the cost. The present bridge (1588–91), designed by Antonio da Ponte using a single great arch (rather than the three arches favoured by Palladio and Scamozzi), cost 245,537 ducats; 16 bays of the Library had cost 28,000 ducats.[17]

The boasted similarities between modern Venetians and ancient Romans had, by the 1480s, encouraged the adoption of an *all'antica* style. It was characterised by ornate detail, and by free-standing columns, often raised on pedestals, as in Tullio Lombardo's Vendramin monument (c. 1493) and on the façade of the Palazzo Loredan Vendramin Calergi (begun 1502, completed 1509), which is usually attributed to Codussi (d. 1504).[18] Here for the first time a scheme of columns and pilasters was applied to a Venetian palace façade. By 1509 many leading patricians had become familiar with the architectural taste of Rome and Florence. Some, like Bernardo Bembo, had visited these cities as ambassa-

fig. 8 Fondaco dei Tedeschi, Venice; façade
(rebuilt after the fire of 1505)

dors; and the presence in Rome of Venetian cardinals from leading families increased contacts between the two centres. Venetian interest in Vitruvius had been stimulated by the much-read antiquarian romance, the *Hypnerotomachia Poliphili* (1499), and by the employment of the famous engineer and Vitruvian scholar Fra Giocondo, at a salary only slightly less than the ducat a day which he had demanded as 'I have to spend money on books and on the construction of various inventions, in which all my pleasure lies.'[19] With the publication of Fra Giocondo's illustrated Vitruvius (1511), of Serlio's architectural books (1537ff) of Daniele Barbaro's translation of Vitruvius (1556), illustrated by Palladio, and Palladio's own *Quattro Libri* (1570), Venice became the main centre for architectural publishing.

Antique influence is also evident in the church of S. Salvatore begun in 1507 after designs by Giorgio Spavento (Tullio Lombardo designed the details). This has a central nave vaulted with an alternation of domes and barrel vaults, and the main order, raised on high pedestals, anticipates the interior of Palladio's S. Giorgio. The war years (1509–17) and their aftermath saw a decline in building activity. The reconstruction of the Rialto (1520–22) was dictated by necessity; so too was the rebuilding by the Procurators of St. Mark's, who owned all the properties around the Piazza and fig. 9 Scuola di San Rocco, Venice; façade by Scarpagnino

fig. 10 J. Sansovino, Marciana Library, Venice

the Piazzetta, of the houses on the north side of the Piazza, again after a fire, 'in order to make it very beautiful for the glory of the city . . . in spite of the ear'[20] (fig. 12). In 1515 work began on the Scuola di S. Rocco, which was finished in 1549. The plan, with a columned lobby below, grand stairs, and an assembly hall and committee room above, follows the usual scheme for Scuole. What distinguished S. Rocco, and led the Scuola to be attacked for spending on display what should have been spent on charity, was the lavishness of the workmanship and decoration, which later included Tintoretto's famous paintings.[21] The façade, designed by Antonio Scarpagnino, is particularly extravagant, with its fluted columns, figured capitals, inlays of coloured stone, and little animals, including an elephant, on the plinths.

Scarpagnino's façade was probably meant to be 'antique', but it represents a taste which outside Venice was already outmoded. In Rome, Bramante had evolved a style not based on a profusion of bizarre motifs, but on formulae for the orders derived from a study of Vitruvius and the antiquities. Each order was seen as having a distinct personality, and as being appropriate for certain types of building. In the 1520s this approach had been introduced to Verona by Sanmicheli and to Padua by Falconetto. In 1528 Sebastiano Serlio, who had studied in Rome under Peruzzi, published engravings of the orders, which he followed up with his book on the subject (1537).[22] The new taste, favoured by Doge Gritti and other members of the political elite, and backed by influential intellectuals like Aretino and Pietro Bembo, was above all reflected in Sansovino's work. He had arrived in Venice in 1527, and in 1529 was appointed *proto* to the Procurators. For them he designed the Library (begun 1537, fig. 10), which Palladio called 'the most rich and ornate edifice that perhaps was ever built from the time of the ancients'.[23] It transformed the centre of Venice, not only by its majestic presence, but by setting the principal buildings in new relations to one another. Originally the huge campanile was hemmed in on two sides; by setting the corner of the Library back from the campanile Sansovino made the Piazza wider and even more impressive, and made it possible to see the Palace from the end opposite San Marco. He gave the Library only two storeys, Doric and Ionic, so that it should not rival the Doge's Palace in height, or seem too tall and narrow. Every detail plays its part in the composition, which is carefully thought out both for the frontal and raking views, and in relation to the Palace opposite. The larger number of columns on the upper level (the scheme of smaller columns carrying an arch is derived from the Roman arch at Aquino) balance those of the Palace's upper *loggie*, the balconies echo its balustrades, and even the oval windows in the frieze answer the roundels of the gothic tracery. One has only to change certain details in one's imagination to see how sure was the touch of the Florentine architect: the whole composition would be weakened if the little blocks in the balusters were removed – they reinforce a whole series of other chunky forms.

Sansovino held his position till his death at the age of 84: his reputation was only momentarily dented by the collapse of one bay of the Library in 1545. He responded fluently and competently to tasks as different as that of designing S. Francesco della Vigna, a church for Observant Franciscans dedicated to austerity; the Zecca (Mint), constructed with-fig. 11 A. Palladio, S. Giorgio Maggiore, Venice

fig. 12 Procuratie Vecchie, Venice

out wood and with a suitably robust façade; the vast new palace for the Corner family; and the handsome, low-budget New Buildings at Rialto, constructed by the State as a source of rental income. But by 1560 a group of younger, highly educated patricians, just beginning to get to the top, seem to have regarded Sansovino as a brilliant reformer of Venetian architecture but as too unsystematic in his approach. For those who sought not only artistic flair and technical skill, but also an architecture based on principles and precise antique models, the great architect was now Palladio, who had made his name in Vicenza and had already designed numbers of villas for prominent Venetians.[24] In 1554 he had been turned down for the post of *proto* to the Salt Magistrates (responsible for public works), but through the Barbaro brothers and other patrician supporters he obtained a series of important Ventian ecclesiastical commissions. Then in the 1570s it was Palladio who was asked to design the votive church of the Redentore (1577–92), decided on by the Senate at the height of the 1575–77 plague, and to guide much of the restoration of the Doge's Palace after the fires of 1574 and 1577. His proposal to rebuild the Palace in his own style was rejected, despite Marcantonio Barbaro's eloquent support.[25] That Palladio should make such a proposal at all indicates something of the radicalism and disdain for local decorative traditions which distinguishes him from Sansovino, who always delighted in fusing Venetian and antique elements with the best in central Italian architecture.

Palladio's church of S. Giorgio Maggiore (fig. 11), designed in 1565, is perhaps his greatest masterpiece. He broke with Venetian tradition by creating a church which was brilliantly lit, finished in the interior in Istrian stone and brick covered in stone coloured plaster. The plan and elevation skilfully distinguish between different spaces and functions. The details are sensitively scaled to the whole: the overall effect is one of an extraordinary beauty and fitness. The order seems to grow up like a tree through the pedestals to the column bases, by way of flowing mouldings, to terminate in the capitals and entablature. The pilasters of the smaller order, which taper gently like columns, contribute to this organic, growing character.

The elimination of the public debt in the 1580s and 1590s brought with it the completion of the Redentore and the spanning of the Grand Canal by the new stone bridge.[26] Further palaces were constructed, most notably the handsome Palazzo Balbi (1582–90) designed by Alessandro Vittoria.[27] Palladio's old friends Marcantonio Barbaro and Jacomo Contarini outlived him, and continued to be regular members of official building committees. They transferred their support to another Vicentine, Vincenzo Scamozzi, who completed the Library and began the rebuilding of the south side of the Piazza.[28] The century thus ended, as it had begun, with intense building activity, which had never totally ceased despite war, plague and foreign threats.

The motives for building in sixteenth-century Venice were mixed: a desire to impress foreigners and to show them that Venice was not bankrupt or beaten, especially when this was near to being the truth; the necessity of replacing buildings destroyed by fire; the desire of very rich semi-public institutions like the Scuole and the great families to make a prominent mark; and a real love of architecture. The patronage of the Procurators, the Scuole and rich patricians cannot be considered as entirely autonomous: it was guided and controlled, like everything else, from the upper levels of the political establishment. Thus it was the State which partly subsidised the rebuilding of the Scuola di San Marco, which decided on the stair design at the Scuola di S. Rocco, and which put up 30,000 ducats for the rebuilding of Palazzo Corner.[29] All this was in line with the wording of a Senate resolution of 1535, with its perception of the role of effort and policy in the creation of Venice: 'our ancestors have always striven and been vigilant so as to ... provide this city with most beautiful temples, private buildings and spacious squares, so that from a wild and uncultivated refuge ... it has grown, been ornamented and constructed so as to become the most beautiful and illustrious city which at present exists in the world'.[30]

1] Serlio, IV, 1619, fol. 153v. On Venetian architecture in general see Paoletti, 1893; Heydenreich and Lotz 1974; Trincanato and Franzoi 1971; Howard 1980; Puppi (ed.) 1980.

2] Palladio, I, 1570, p. 52. On building techniques see Howard 1980, pp. 55–60; Sansovino 1663, pp. 381–83; Rusconi 1590; Fontana 1978.

3] Scamozzi 1615, Parte Seconda, p. 319.

4] For Palladio on bricks see Zorzi 1967, p. 89. On Istrian stone see Sansovino, 1663, p. 383; Scamozzi, 1615, Parte Seconda, p. 204.

5] Serlio, IV, 1619, fol. 153v.

6] Scamozzi, 1615, Parte Prima, pp. 242–43.

7] Sansovino, 1663, pp. 383–84.

8] Scamozzi, 1615, Parte Prima, p. 243.

9] Trincanato 1948; Schulz 1982.

10] London 1975, pp. 152–53 (Burns); cf. Sansovino 1663, p. 382.

11] Scamozzi 1615, Parte Prima, p. 86.

12] Thomas 1963, p. 65.

13] Gazzola 1960; Gallo, 1960; Puppi, 1971.

14] Malipiero, ed. Gar and Sagredo, 1843–44, p. 699.

15] Cessi and Alberti 1934, pp. 83–114.

16] Dazzi, Brunetti and Gerbino, 1941.

17] Cessi and Alberti 1934, pp. 171–223; Zorzi 1967, pp. 223–63; London 1975, pp. 123–28 (Burns); Maschio 1980, pp. 119–29; Lewis 1981; Burns 1979, pp. 119–20.

18] Puppi and Olivato Puppi, esp. pp. 221–26.

19] Dazzi 1939–40, pp. 876–80.

20] Howard 1980, p. 129.

21] Paoletti 1893, I, pp. 123–27; Malsburg 1976; Sohm 1978 (1981); Sohm 1978.

22] Dinsmoor 1942; Howard 1973.

23] Palladio, I, 1570, p. 5. On Sansovino see Tafuri 1969 and 1972; Howard 1975; Foscari and Tafuri 1983.

24] On Palladio see Magrini 1845; Zorzi 1959, 1965, 1967, 1969; Ackerman 1966; Puppi 1973 and 1975; London 1975 (Burns); Howard 1980; Lewis 1981; Foscari and Tafuri 1983, pp. 131ff.

25] London 1975, pp. 155–60 (Burns); Olivato, in Venice 1980, p. 102; Lewis 1981, pp. 204–05.

26] On Venetian public finance see Lane 1973, pp. 325–26.

27] Bassi 1976, pp. 124–30.

28] Barbieri 1952; Howard 1974; Howard 1975, p. 26.

29] Sohm 1978 (1981), p. 286; Sohm 1978, p. 148; Gallo 1960, p. 114; Howard 1975, pp. 132–46.

30] Zorzi 1967, p. 247.

ALTARPIECES

Terisio Pignatti

The purpose of this essay is to examine the development of the Venetian altarpiece as a compositional type during the sixteenth century, and in particular to show how this tradition was modified by the major artists of the period. For a variety of reasons this is by no means an easy task. Firstly, the period in question, spanning as it does the early Renaissance, the High Renaissance, Mannerism and the beginnings of the Baroque, was marked by radical changes in artistic theory, principles of composition and forms of expression. Secondly, within the orbit of Venetian painting there existed local schools with their own traditions and standards; and there was an especially marked discrepancy in quality between the products of Venice itself and those of the provincial centres of the mainland. Finally, it is often difficult to accommodate the very original and idiosyncratic contributions of the greatest masters within a rigid scheme of development. Nevertheless it is possible to discern some kind of pattern, whose origins can be traced back to the last quarter of the fifteenth century. At that time there emerged a distinctive formula for Venetian altarpieces, which was subsequently transformed in ways that can be seen in the present exhibition.

A starting point is provided by the visit which Giovanni Bellini must have made to Pesaro in connection with the commission for the grandiose *Coronation of the Virgin* (Museo Civico, Pesaro). This picture, which was almost certainly painted some time between 1471 and 1474, is radically different from an altarpiece which Bellini himself had painted about 1464 for the church of SS. Giovanni e Paolo in Venice. There he had remained faithful to the archaic formula of the polyptych, a scheme which continued to retain a certain popularity until the very end of the century, especially in the provinces. But in the Pesaro altarpiece the ornate frame of carved and gilded wood, enriched with a painted *Pietà* and 15 smaller pictures in the predella and uprights, surrounds a single large square panel which is treated as a unified space with a central vanishing-point. Within this space Christ and the Virgin are shown on an elaborate marble throne, flanked by four saints whose arrangement is analogous to an architectural niche, an impression accentuated by the pattern of foreshortened tiles on the floor. In its luminosity as much as in its architectonic grandeur this painting seems to reflect Bellini's direct experience of Piero della Francesca's altarpiece for the church of S. Bernardino in Urbino (now in the Brera, Milan), which dates from just this period.

Soon after his return to Venice, Bellini received a fresh impetus to follow the path on which Piero had set him, with the arrival in 1475 of another artist of exceptional originality, Antonello da Messina. In his altarpiece for the church of S. Cassiano in Venice (partly preserved in Vienna) Antonello showed the Virgin and saints framed by an architectural niche, much as Piero had done; but here for the first time the Virgin was placed on a high central throne, thus creating a stronger formal relationship between the figures and their setting. This scheme re-appeared, probably about 1487, in Bellini's *S. Giobbe Altarpiece* (Accademia, Venice), where the painted architecture was directly linked to the real architecture of the frame, giving the illusion of a chapel opening directly out of the church. The arrangement at S. Giobbe was to be further elaborated in 1510 by Carpaccio, whose *Presentation of the Virgin* (Accademia, Venice), painted for the altar immediately opposite Bellini's picture, provided a close counterpart to it.

At S. Giobbe Bellini gave the Venetian altarpiece the basic form which it was to retain well into the sixteenth century. He himself used a similar scheme in the church of S. Zaccaria in 1505 (fig. 20), and it was also adopted by lesser artists, for example by Alvise Vivarini, and by Cima in his altarpiece at Conegliano. Of course, each master modified the formula according to his own stylistic preferences; Bellini created diffuse chromatic harmonies by using subtle glazes, while Vivarini and Cima preferred clear smooth surfaces modelled by the harder light of the midday sun. In many altarpieces of these years we also find signs of a new pictorial interest in the natural world. Among works of the fifteenth century, this is true of Montagna's *Nativity* (Museo Civico, Vicenza) and soon after 1500 of Bellini's *Baptism of Christ* in Vicenza. But it was not until 1505 at S. Zaccaria that he created standard form of architectural structure in a landscape, establishing a formula that was to persist in Cima's work right up to his *St. Peter Enthroned* of 1516 (Brera, Milan). The most radical innovation in the process of combining the traditional scheme of the altarpiece with landscape, however, was taken by a younger artist who had emerged from the school of Bellini, namely Giorgione, in his picture at Castelfranco (fig. 13), painted about 1504.

In this masterpiece Giorgione profoundly modified the hieratic conception of the altarpiece established by Bellini, introducing a new kind of naturalism both in the setting and in the figures, which was to have a lasting importance throughout the sixteenth century. In its basic composition it may reflect the influence of Emilian artists such as Costa and Francia, but no less relevant was the contemporary intellectual climate in and around Venice, as manifested both in the interest in physical phenomena fostered by the study of Aristotle at Padua and in the arcadian poetry of Pietro Bembo, who is known to have been an admirer of Giorgione.

The freedom of expression and composition thus initiated by Giorgione soon found a widespread response among his reality of everyday existence to enter the sacred realm of the Virgin and saints.

In his *Assumption of the Virgin* (fig. 19), painted for the church of the Frari between 1516 and 1518, Titian's pre-occupation with sensual beauty and truth to nature even troubled the sensibilities of his Franciscan patrons. But his work was soon publicly acclaimed, and later Lodovico Dolce was to compare it to the masterpieces of Raphael and Michelangelo. Then in 1526, while he was still enjoying this success, Titian provided another picture for the same church, the *Pesaro Madonna*. Here again the real world is strongly in evidence, in the form of six members of the Pesaro family kneeling before a high podium on which are grouped the Madonna and saints. The composition is strikingly original, since the conventional frontal presentation is replaced by an oblique arrangement which emphasises the ascending movement towards the redeeming Virgin. In both these pictures a hitherto static type of design is transformed by dynamic movement and brilliant colour. This novel approach, which was to be Titian's greatest contribution to the tradition of the Venetian altarpiece, is still more evident in the most famous painting he ever produced, the *Death of St. Peter Martyr* (see fig. 14), which was installed in the church of SS. Giovanni e Paolo in 1530 and destroyed by fire in 1867.

The achievements of the other artists active in this period, both in Venice and on the mainland, are inevitably less significant. Probably the most influential of these lesser masters was Palma Vecchio, whose use of rich, sumptuous colour reveals a clear debt to Titian. He is particularly associated with a distinctive type of horizontal composition showing the Virgin with saints and donors in a landscape. The slightly pedestrian tone of his work, as well as his popularity in the provinces, contributed to the diffusion of this formula in the Venetian territory in Lombardy, where it exerted a certain influence on such painters as Previtali, Cariani and Licinio. There are links also between Palma and Lotto, especially during the latter's residence in Bergamo, where he developed an increasingly naturalistic style in which the emotions of the figures were echoed in the setting. Outstanding examples are the two great altarpieces of 1521, for S. Bernardino and Santo Spirito, in both of which Lotto used a formal scheme derived ultimately from Giorgione, but enriched by his personal experience of the work of Raphael. His profound sensitivity to the real world around him remained an important factor in his paintings of the 1530s for patrons in the Marches, such as the altarpieces at Jesi and Ancona (Cat. 49–50, 51). The ideals of another notable artist of this generation, Paris Bordone, place him somewhere between Palma and Lotto, at least in his earlier years; but he was more interested in colour than composition.

It is less easy to fit the altarpieces produced in other provincial cities into the pattern of development centred on Venice. Thus the major figures of the early sixteenth century in Verona, Cavazzola and Caroto, belong essentially to a tradition going back to Mantegna. The Brescian Romanino, by contrast, was at first more closely linked to the Venetians, for example in the altarpiece he painted in 1513 for the church of S. Giustina in Padua (now in the Museo Civico); but after he returned home his style became more naturalistic, under the influence of Leonardo's followers. The work of the other Brescians – Savoldo, Moretto and Moroni – shows a similar compromise between the aristocratic ideals

fig. 13 Giorgione, Castelfranco Altarpiece
(S. Liberale, Castelfranco)

contemporaries, for example in Sebastiano's asymmetrically organised altarpiece for the church of S. Giovanni Crisostomo of 1510–11, although in this instance the example of the Florentine Fra Bartolomeo, who was in Venice in 1508, may also have been relevant. The clearest signs of Giorgione's importance, however, can be seen in the greater prominence given to landscape, especially by the aged Bellini in such works as the *St. Jerome* of 1513 (San Giovanni Crisostomo, Venice), the *Virgin and Eight Saints* of the same year (Murano) and the *Deposition of Christ* of 1515 (Accademia, Venice).

At about this time an equally revolutionary approach to religious painting in Venice was initiated by Titian, who emerged as an independent master around 1510. In a work of this period, the *Virgin and Child with St. Anthony and St. Roch* (Cat. 34), he was still deeply influenced by Giorgione, but in his picture of *Jacopo Pesaro Presented to St. Peter* (Cat. 113) he transformed the traditional altarpiece into a celebration, on a human rather than a celestial level, of a great Venetian family. The powerful realism of the figures probably reflects the impact made on the young artist by Dürer's *Madonna of the Rosegarlands* (Národní Gallerie, Prague), painted in Venice in 1506. In this masterpiece, which was a landmark in the development of Venetian naturalistic painting, Dürer had included portraits of the Pope and the Emperor as well as other contemporaries, thus allowing the fig. 14 Martino Rota *Death of St. Peter Martyr*; engraving after the altarpiece by Titian formerly in SS. Giovanni e Paolo, Venice, destroyed by fire in 1867

of Venice and the realism of Lombardy. In the formal structure of their altarpieces they were often indebted to Venetian models, particularly to Palma and Lotto, but there was a greater emphasis on narrative content and, increasingly, a typically mannerist preciosity, as in Moroni's *Mystic Marriage of St. Catherine* of about 1570 (Cat. 67).

From the mid-1530s and more decisively after 1540 a new aesthetic ideal was taking root in Venice, derived from the Mannerism of Tuscany and Rome, which was superimposed on the traditional local idiom. At the time the contrast between these two approaches was seen in terms of 'buon disegno', the central Italian preoccupation with form, and Venetian 'colore', associated particularly with Titian. The effect on Titian's own work is immediately apparent, for example in his *St. John the Baptist* of about 1540 (Cat. 119), in which his concern for 'painterly painting' was subordinated to an assertion of Michelangelesque plasticity. Under the impact of Mannerism the Venetians soon abandoned the harmonious geometrical structures on which their painting had been based, as well as fidelity to nature and the unity

of time and space. Instead, their work became more unrealistic, more overtly dramatic and expressive. Even Titian adapted his style to this new conception of religious art, notably in his two versions of the *Martyrdom of St. Lawrence*, the first completed in 1559 (Gesuiti, Venice), the second in 1567 (Escorial).

A significant precursor of this development was Pordenone, whose altarpiece for the church of S. Giovanni Elemosinario in Venice (Cat. 78), painted about 1535, already shows mannerist features, both in the crowded and unnatural composition and in the rhythmic energy of the poses. But the most extraordinary manifestations of the new compositional structures appear in the paintings of Tintoretto, beginning around 1540. His *Christ Among the Doctors* (Cat. 99), for example, seems quite unrelated to any religious art produced in Venice up to that time. Another important innovator was Andrea Schiavone, who was largely responsible for introducing the sinuous figurative idiom of Parmigianino. He also played a major role in establishing a new type of composition in which figures and events are expressions of forms and feelings rather than geometrical images in an architectonic framework. Pictures such as his *Adoration of the Magi* (Cat. 89) of about 1547, or the *Adoration of the Shepherds* painted by his follower Mariscalchi around 1560 (Cat. 57), with their closely packed, highly agitated compositions, seem to anticipate the dynamism of the Baroque. The same is true of virtually the whole of Tintoretto's *oeuvre*, in terms both of the intense movement which pervades all the figures and of the dramatic nocturnal illumination, with the emphasis on broken highlights.

In the second half of the century several other artists were moving in the same direction, notably Jacopo Bassano and Palma Giovane, who approached the eclecticism of the Baroque, particularly in his figures, as for example in the *Pietà* of about 1611 (Cat. 71). Bassano, however, perhaps because he was brought up in the provinces, often seems to have been readier to revive compositional schemes more in keeping with the local traditions of the altarpiece. Particularly in his early works this was manifested by his choice of architectural motifs, and later by his arrangement of figures and by his adoption of a central vanishing-point, as in the *Adoration of the Shepherds* of around 1570 (Cat. 9).

The most serious attempt to reassert the distinctively Venetian approach to the altarpiece, however, was made by Paolo Veronese. In an early work such as his painting of 1551 for S. Francesco della Vigna in Venice (Cat. 133), he based his design directly in Titian's *Pesaro Madonna*. Later he tried to achieve a new equilibrium primarily through compositions based on a harmonious pattern of colours, for example in the altarpiece now in the Chrysler Collection, of 1562 (Cat. 135), or in the one he painted for S. Sebastiano around 1565. In such pictures the iconographic content is conveyed by brilliantly coloured figures arranged in the foreground, and by a highly refined draughtsmanship which gives his flowing forms a superhuman beauty. No painter better demonstrates how the intensely vital artistic culture of Venice was able to reject imported aesthetic ideals and once more assert the typically Venetian concern with chromaticism.

PORTRAITS

Lino Moretti

Portrait painting developed at an early date in Venice. Soon after 1339 Paolo Veneziano painted the portrait of the defunct Doge Francesco Dandolo together with his wife, who was still alive, over Dandolo's tomb in the Sala del Capitolo of the Frari. The figures are on the same scale as their patron saints (a very unusual feature for the period) and the faces appear to be authentic portraits, even if the style still follows the conventions of Byzantine painting.

In the reign of Doge Marco Dandolo (1365–68), a remarkable series of commemorative portraits of doges was started in the Sala del Maggior Consiglio in the Doge's Palace.[1] These portraits, which were destroyed in the fire of 1577, constituted a complete portrait gallery of heads of state painted by the greatest artists of each generation, from Guariento to Tintoretto. Between 1408 and 1422, in the same room, Gentile da Fabriano and Pisanello frescoed episodes from Venetian history (substituting an earlier cycle) and it seems likely that they introduced portraits into these scenes, particularly into that of the reconciliation of Frederick Barbarossa with the pope. Gentile was appreciated as a portrait painter in the early sixteenth century, when Antonio Pasqualino bought two 'very lifelike' portraits by him, and Michiel speaks of Gentile as if he were famous.[2]

The first independent portraits date from the second half of the fifteenth century. In Lazzaro Bastiani's *Portrait of Doge Foscari* (Museo Correr) the sitter is shown in profile, a format derived from Roman coins. Gentile Bellini was a distinguished portrait painter and was sent to Constantinople to paint the portrait of Mahomed II. Several portraits of doges were saved from a fire in the ducal apartments in 1483, and some by Bastiani (possibly the same ones) were recorded in 1581 as formerly in the Collegio of the 25. Perhaps these included the fragmentary portrait of Antonio Venier and Michele Steno shown seated in conversation (Museo Correr).[3]

In 1474 it was decided to substitute the historical frescoes in the Sala del Maggior Consiglio with paintings on canvas. This undertaking took almost a century to complete, only to be destroyed in the fire of 1577: Gentile and Giovanni Bellini, Alvise Vivarini, Carpaccio, Pordenone, Titian, Veronese and Tintoretto all contributed to the decoration. As well as Venetian patricians, famous Italian men of letters and poets were portrayed in these scenes; the list of names takes up a good four pages in Sansovino's *Venetia Città Nobilissima*.

This example was followed by the *scuole*, the lay confraternities run by merchants and citizens excluded from politics because they were not of noble blood (Venetian nobles were barred from entry to the *scuole* after 1500). In the fifteenth century members of the confraternities had been painted kneeling at the feet of their patron saints, as in Bartolommeo Vivarini's polyptych in S. Maria Formosa (1474) and the one he painted for S. Ambrogio (1477; Accademia, Venice). But when the *scuole* established their own premises, the members decorated the assembly halls with large canvases in which the members were portrayed participating in episodes from the life of a saint (Carpaccio's *St. Ursula Cycle*; Accademia) or witnessing miraculous events which took place in the city (cycle for the Scuola di S. Giovanni Evangelista by Gentile Bellini and others; Accademia). During this period there was a vast growth in the number of individual portraits, which were by now fashionable both with the patricians and the merchant classes.

Antonello da Messina's presence in Venice (1475–76) marked a turning point in the development of Venetian portraiture. His sharp perception of character, revealed in the slight curve of the lips or eyes, is combined with a remarkable sense of volume and depth, while his intense light effects were derived from the work of the Netherlandish artist Petrus Christus. The words of St. Jerome fit his portrait style perfectly: 'the face is the mirror of the spirit, and the silent eyes reveal the secrets of the spirit'. Giovanni Bellini immediately recognised the value of Antonello's compositional methods, but Bellini's instinctive habit of 'thinking in paint' was not accompanied by such a marked interest in the idiosyncrasies of the sitter's character, as can be seen in his masterpiece of abstraction, the enigmatic *Portrait of Doge Loredan* (National Gallery, London). The markedly three-dimensional quality of the figure, created by Bellini's use of light, underlines the relationship between painted portraits and contemporary Venetian sculpture.

According to Vasari, Giorgione also painted a portrait of Doge Loredan, but this official painting has been lost, and the identity of sitters in Giorgione's surviving portraits is either uncertain or unknown. Instead of concentrating on the individual's physical characteristics, Giorgione either portrayed their state of mind or emphasised one aspect of their personality. The lighting is usually shadowy, and these portraits were almost certainly designed to be displayed in the intimacy of '*studioli*', among books, curios, statues, and other collector's items. After the Venetian defeat at the rout of Agnadello in 1509, when the very existence of Venice seemed threatened, it was fashionable to cultivate the melancholy illusion that '*litteris servabitur orbis*' (the world will be saved by culture). The dark tonality and lack of outline of Giorgione's portraits are the artistic equivalents of the fleeting psychological glimpse we are afforded of the sitters, whose lips do not express character (as in Antonello's paintings) but are sealed, as if concealing a secret. Often the sitters are placed behind a parapet, and their hands are an important expressive element in the portrait. Objects with an emblematic significance and books are often included to emphasise the sitter's humanist culture and poetic sensitivity.

By the beginning of the sixteenth century portraits, apart from recording a sitter's appearance for posterity, had become status symbols. By painting portraits the artist defeated both time and death: Bernardino Licinio inscribed on the portrait of his brother's family (Cat. 41) that the painter 'prolongs life for them with their image, and his own with his art'.

Vincenzo Catena, a colleague of Giorgione's with connections in humanist circles, developed Bellini's schemes in his portraits, but adapted them to the taste of the High Renaissance. Palma Vecchio adopted the broad forms and fresh colour of Titian's youthful style, but rather than stressing the individuality of his sitters he tended to paint generalised ideal types, as is evident in his portraits of men and of voluptuous, blond women decked in luxurious clothes. Portraits of women became increasingly common during the sixteenth century; not only beauties were painted, but also solid citizens and women of a certain age.

The Bergamasque Bernardino Licinio was a follower of Giorgione, though for his portraits he developed a homely manner that suited his clients, who were often of modest stock. Paris Bordone was a pupil of Titian's, but also imitated Giorgione in his youth. In his *Presentation of the Ring to the Doge* (Accademia, Venice), painted for the Scuola di San Marco, he included a remarkable group portrait of dignitaries, each one highly individualised. But despite this he does not appear to have received any official portrait commissions.

Lorenzo Lotto remains apart from his contemporaries. In his youth in Venice he painted several portraits remarkable for their freshness, which retain something of the spirit of Alvise Vivarini and Dürer. Thereafter his restless spirit led him to Rome, to the Marche, and to Bergamo. His sitters seem to take on his own somewhat pensive, melancholic and God-fearing temperament. His figures are positioned obliquely, their heads slightly tilted; often his portraits have religious overtones; amulets, religious medallions, emblems and rose petals (an allusion to the brevity of life) are included; even the oblique lighting evokes a sense of transience. In spirit these portraits are very far from the assurance of the 'humanist' portraits of the beginning of the century: Lotto seems to oscillate between despising the base and vain qualities of earthly life and yearning for a return to simple Christian virtues. It is therefore understandable that he was never asked to paint the portrait of a doge or any other official, and that he himself preferred to paint portraits of married couples, even if they were a little unrefined and provincial; such commissions could inspire him to produce more poetic images, and to express sincere human emotions.

When Giorgione died in 1510, Titian, who must have been barely 20 at the time, was already a successful painter. From 1513 he secured several official commissions, and between 1521 and 1554 he painted the portraits of six doges in the Sala del Maggior Consiglio. Titian's sitters occupy space with greater confidence, and take up more of the canvas than in earlier portraits. Whereas Giorgione's portraits never exceeded the half-length, portraits now began to expand downwards well below the waist. At the same time full-length portraits first appeared in Italy (although not in

Venice). These were derived from German portraits and were soon extremely popular in Italian courts. There were only two precedents for this format in Italian painting: one by Carpaccio of 1510 (Lugano) and the other by Moretto of 1526 (National Gallery, London).

Wilde pointed out a fundamental characteristic of Titian's portraiture: from early in his career 'history painting exerted a fruitful influence on portraiture: motives and methods which had been invented for monumental compositions were drawn upon to enrich and transform the portrait'. In addition 'both public and artists in the Cinquecento looked for a kind of likeness different from what the previous century understood by this word. . . . The new likeness is intended to give not only the social position of the sitter, but also his character and the whole of his personality. This involves his status and rank, his profession, the power he wields and the position he holds'.[4] Titian's portraits, with their chromatic intensity, exuberant outbursts of colour, high rhetoric, ingenious compositional schemes and lucid and unrelenting psychological and moral understanding always enrich our intellectual experience.

It was customary for each doge to commission a votive painting of himself with the Madonna and some chosen saints to be placed in the Collegio or the Senate (eg. Catena's painting of Doge Loredan of *c.* 1505; Museo Correr). By the middle of the century the cult of personality had become so strong that it was accepted that the magistrates would also commission votive paintings for their offices. The Provveditori al Sale who held office between 1552 and 1553 placed a large votive painting of themselves with the Virgin in their rooms at the Rialto: before that date it had been customary to commission pictures of their patron saints which only included their coat of arms. The Provveditori were followed by the Camerlenghi (Chamberlains), another group of financial magistrates of the Rialto, and later the practice was adopted by officials at the Doge's Palace (the Avogaria and Censori). Whereas temporary and collegiate magistracies commissioned group portraits, the Procurators, dignitaries inferior only to the doge, had their own individual portraits in their rooms.

The artist who had, in effect, a monopoly of these official portrait commissions was the inexhaustable Jacopo Tintoretto. In addition to public portraits, he, assisted by his workshop, produced portraits of magistrates, senators and sea captains for their private residences. Even far less important officials would have their portrait painted, and the popularity of this type of portraiture demonstrates the extent to which Venetians identified with these official images of themselves and their society.

Tintoretto focussed attention on the face and hands of his sitters – the most revealing features – whilst the rest of the figure would be only summarily sketched; often he would repeat the same composition and lighting for different sitters; hence the obvious similarity between his portraits. Their success is proof that Tintoretto was the ideal interpreter of society at a time when the Renaissance conception of the individual was being superseded by a more conformist Counter-Reformation stereotype. To understand the change that took place in 30 years one only has to compare the *Portrait of Ottaviano Grimani* (Vienna), painted in 1541 by Licinio, which is still humanist in spirit, to Grimani's official portrait in the uniform of a Procurator painted in Tintoretto's workshop in 1571 (Accademia, Venice).

In contrast, Paolo Veronese rarely painted official portraits, although in about 1562 he did execute a painting including eminent contemporary Venetians (now destroyed) in the Sala del Maggior Consiglio. His style of portraiture was unsuitable for official portraits; his luminous painting and harsh colour harmonies appealed to a very different clientele, to rich merchants and the landed aristocracy (who perhaps, like Doge Alvise 1 Mocenigo, despised the commerce which had created the wealth of Venice) and to the gentry of the *terraferma*. Veronese's style was ideally suited to represent the aristocratic ideals of these individuals who, because of their great wealth, could easily imitate the customs of the nobility. It was natural, therefore, for Sir Philip Sidney, who modelled his behaviour on Castiglione's *Book of the Courtier*, to choose Veronese to paint his portrait (now lost) when he went to Venice.

Pope-Hennessy remarked that Veronese '... was not a face-painter like Tintoretto, and his independent portraits are more decorative and more opulent. But more often than not, once the head is excised from its setting, it looks nerveless and a little dull. Analysis was alien to the cast of Veronese's mind. Yet when his heads are animated, they shed much of their flaccidity and take on a new liveliness'. This is true of the portrait of the parish priest of S. Pantalon, Bartolomeo Borghi, shown holding the dead boy in the altarpiece from his church (Cat. 147): 'there is nothing ostentatious or rhetorical about this image; it shows the priest in the role he played in life, his features stamped with pastoral solicitude'.[5]

During the sixteenth century Brescia and Bergamo, two Lombard cities under Venetian rule, produced artists who combined Venetian colour with Lombard realism. Girolamo Savoldo, a Brescian who spent many years in Venice, was a complex artistic personality. His austere, intense and pensive portraits with a restricted range of colours combine a slightly Giorgionesque mood with the intimacy of the Flemish style.

Alessandro Bonvicino, called Moretto, worked exclusively in Brescia and its environs, portraying the provincial aristocracy. He was influenced by Lotto and Savoldo, yet preserved the silvery tonalities of earlier Lombard painters, despite the occasional hint of Titianesque colour. The decoration of a room in the Palazzo Martinengo, Padernello (1543) with the portraits of eight noblewomen who look out on a landscape which apparently represents the family estate is indicative of the feudal society for which Moretto worked.

It is not clear exactly how Giovanni Battista Moroni, a Bergamasque pupil and collaborator of Moretto, came to know Titian's portraits; in any case, he adapted Titian's compositions to a different end: that of producing 'natural' portraits, as they were dubbed by Titian (who evidently had a very different conception of portraiture). Moroni's clients were the *jeunesse dorée*: city swells, country landowners and soldiers, who, following courtly conventions, would commission full-length portraits. They were acutely self-conscious, obsessed by their appearance, and their portraits are ostentatiously adorned with emblems and mottos in Latin or Spanish. It seems likely that Veronese knew these portraits. Moroni painted Venetian patricians who owned property in the provinces, but he also portrayed less exalted individuals, such as *The Tailor* (National Gallery, London); his sitters appear to have been caught unawares, and in their expressions reveal both their character and their idea of their position in society.

It is significant that for centuries many of Moroni's finest portraits (such as Cat. 66) were ascribed to Titian. Although we can see today the differences in their approach, we can also see not only that both artists, working at different ends of the Venetian domain, nonetheless shared basic assumptions about the role of art as a means of ennobling and recording the society of their day, but also that both of them exploited to the full the technical mastery in the handling of paint that was the special glory of the Venetian school.

1] Sanuto 1733, col. 664
2] Frimmel 1888, p. 78
3] Gallo 1943, p. 47, no. 2
4] Wilde 1974, p. 224
5] Pope-Hennessy 1966, pp. 287, 289

SELECT BIBLIOGRAPHY

Burckhardt 1898, (*Das Porträt in der Malerei*); Castelnuovo 1966; Pope-Hennessy 1966; Rearick 1981; Zeri 1976[2]

'POESIE' AND PAINTED ALLEGORIES

Charles Hope

In October 1510, very shortly after the death of Giorgione, Isabella d'Este wrote to a friend in Venice asking him to acquire 'a picture of a night', which she thought had been left in the artist's studio. Isabella's letter suggests that she did not know much about Giorgione; and what mattered to her about the painting was evidently not the subject, but the fact that it was of a type very unusual in Venetian art up to that time, a night scene. In fact, Giorgione's work seems to have been novel in two ways: he not only initiated a new manner of painting, rejecting the hard outlines of Bellini and his followers in favour of a softer style more suited to the representation of nature, he also seems to have been the first artist in the city whose output consisted predominantly of non-religious subjects for private collectors.

In attempting to account for these innovations, scholars have often speculated about the possible influence on Giorgione of contemporary literature and philosophy, something for which there is virtually no evidence in the surviving historical sources. But even granted that this high culture might have had some relevance for the subject-matter of his paintings, it is by no means clear why it should have prompted him to adopt a new style – a common enough phenomenon, after all, in the history of art. It is likely that the style came first, and that the subjects were then chosen to display its potential to the full, because in other respects these seem to have little in common with one another. One of the paintings recorded by his near-contemporary Marcantonio Michiel illustrated a traditional religious theme, St. Jerome

in the desert, which he then transformed by giving it a moonlit setting; another, *Aeneas and Anchises in the Underworld*, was taken from a familiar literary text, and this too was evidently a night scene; a third, the *Venus* (Dresden), was based on the legacy of classical mythology; while the *Tempesta* (fig. 5), which Michiel described simply as 'the small landscape on canvas with the storm, with the gypsy and the soldier', seems entirely enigmatic. Even now no one knows whether this is a representation of an obscure legend, a learned allegory, or just a picturesque landscape.

The best evidence, perhaps, that Giorgione's pictures were not particularly esoteric in their meaning is provided by the fact that while his stylistic innovations were widely adopted, the distinguishing feature of virtually all Venetian non-religious painting in the first half of the sixteenth century is the lack of learned or literary content. At the least, this suggests that most patrons in Venice at this period did not think that the subject-matter of paintings in private houses necessarily ought to be erudite. Titian's closest approach to Giorgione in both style and content, the *Three Ages of Man* (Edinburgh), is an allegory, to be sure, but of a transparently simple and rather commonplace kind; and even his so-called *Sacred and Profane Love* (Villa Borghese, Rome), which in the past has been considered a learned painting *par excellence*, based on abstruse ideas of neoplatonism, may have been a perfectly straightforward celebration of a marriage, showing the bride with Venus.

Many of the non-religious paintings of this period, in fact,

fig. 15 Titian *Venus of Urbino* (Gallerie degli Uffizi, Florence)

[35]

fig. 16 Titian *The Rape of Europa* (Isabella Stewart Gardner Museum, Boston, Mass.)

are virtually without conventional anecdotal content, no-tably the pictures of beautiful women produced by Palma Vecchio (Cat. 74), Titian and others. This was a type of painting that goes back to Giorgione himself; and it even includes Titian's so-called *Venus of Urbino* (fig. 15), which is almost certainly a representation of a mortal woman in a contemporary setting, not a goddess. The picture was des-cribed in 1538 by its first owner simply as 'the naked woman'; and the same phrase was used in 1598 by a man writing to the Duke of Urbino to ask for a copy. Evidently embarrassed by this request, the Duke asked that he should not be identified as the owner, and explained that he only kept this 'lascivious work' in his collection because it was by Titian; but he did not suggest that the painting actually belonged to the respectable genre of mythology. Even com-positions by Venetian artists with several figures were often surprisingly unspecific in their subject-matter. Palma Vecchio's painting in Vienna (Cat. 77), for example, is often called *Diana and Callisto*, since art historians are accus-tomed to give pictures precise titles of this kind. But there is nothing in the composition to indicate the presence of Diana, and it seems just to show a group of nymphs bathing.

A picture such as Palma's would probably not have been acceptable to the Duke of Ferrara, Alfonso d'Este, who between 1518 and 1525 commissioned a series of Bacchana-lian pictures from Titian, including the famous *Bacchus and Ariadne* (fig. 18). These were to decorate his study, and they were meant to be explicitly *all'antica* in both style and con-tent; indeed, the subjects were largely based on descriptions of lost classical paintings. But when the Duke, who was evi-dently unaware of the casual attitude of Venetian artists to erudite subject-matter, commissioned the first painting in the series, Bellini's *Feast of the Gods* (National Gallery of Art, Washington), he did not bother to provide the artist with

detailed instructions. This was understandable, because Alfonso simply wanted an illustration of a familiar episode from Ovid, the story of Lotis and Priapus. Unfortunately, the notion of classical authenticity meant nothing to Bellini, and he painted instead a mediaeval version of the legend which was readily available in a printed Italian paraphrase of the *Metamorphoses*. This was a popular subject in Venice, and may also have been used by Giorgione. But after Bellini's picture was finished, it had to be changed to satisfy Alfonso's requirements; and when Titian was first employed on the project he was given a specific text to follow.

In general, authentically classical subject-matter was almost always important to patrons elsewhere in Italy. The *Venus of Urbino* is exceptional in this respect; and when Titian supplied further pictures of reclining naked women to his non-Venetian patrons, he gave the figures the attri-butes of Venus or Danäe. The painting of *Danae* (Prado, Madrid) which he sent to Philip II of Spain in about 1550 encouraged the king to commission a whole series of mytho-logies based on Ovidian themes, which are among the artist's greatest and most influential works (fig. 16). Although some scholars have tried to argue that these were allegorical in intent, there is nothing in the many surviving documents about them to support this kind of reading. The term which Titian himself applied to them, *poesie*, makes it clear that they were meant to be regarded in the same way as poetry, in this case ancient poetry; and here it was the way in which the artist recounted the familiar myths, not some hidden meaning, that really mattered. This is made abundantly clear by a long eulogistic description of one of these pictures, *Venus and Adonis*, written by Titian's friend Lodovico Dolce in 1554 or 1555.

By this period there already existed in Venice, as in the rest of Italy, a quite distinct and developed pictorial language fig. 17 Tintoretto *Bacchus and Ariadne* (Doge's Palace, Venice)

for allegory very different from the kind of imagery that we find in Philip's paintings. Its basis was the use of individual figures to personify abstract qualities such as vices and virtues. This was a very old tradition in Italy, but at about this time new fashions in the decoration of public buildings and triumphal entries had led to a great expansion in the repertoire of such personifications. In Venice the earliest elaborate surviving examples are the ceilings painted by Veronese and his collaborators in the Doge's Palace, particularly those in the rooms of the Council of Ten, executed between 1553 and 1556 on the basis of a slightly incoherent programme devised by Daniele Barbaro, and the one in the Sala del Collegio, dating from about 1575–78. They include personifications very similar in character to those found in Florence and Rome in these years, but often with a less learned choice of attributes. Veronese's figure of *Industria*, for example, is not based on an erudite text, as one would expect in central Italy, but on a woodcut in a printed book, Marcolini's *Le Sorti*, which showed a woman sewing, with some ants beside her. Veronese retained the sewing-basket, but because ants would not have been visible in a ceiling painting he replaced them with a spider making a web, an equally self-evident symbol of industriousness, but one that contradicts the interpretation of the spider's web given in the most authoritative contemporary source, Valeriano's *Hieroglyphica*, where it is said to signify 'useless labour', a reading that can hardly have been meant in the context of the Doge's Palace.

Mixed in with such figures were the familiar classical gods, who were also to be understood as personifications – Mars representing military power, Neptune rule over the sea, and so on. Any intelligent observer, of course, would have understood that these figures were included for allegorical reasons, whereas in Titian's *Venus and Adonis*, for example, the goddess was merely the protagonist of a tragic and touching story. And it is the context, above all, that also makes it clear that a series of mythological themes painted in 1577–78 by Tintoretto for the Atrio Quadrato in the Doge's Palace, and now in the Anticollegio, were to be read as political allegories. These even include one of the subjects that Titian had painted for the Duke of Ferrara half a century earlier, *Bacchus and Ariadne*. But whereas Titian had shown the god's sudden encounter with Ariadne (fig. 18), Tintoretto depicted their marriage, with Venus crowning the bride with stars. Here Ariadne personifies Venice, born on the seashore and made immortal by divine favour (fig. 17).

Venetian painted allegories from the second half of the sixteenth century were to be of great importance for later artists throughout Europe; much more so, indeed, than works of this type by their contemporaries elsewhere in Italy. This was not so much because of their content – since in this respect Venetian programmes were distinctive only in their relative incompetence – as of their style, the way in which the great painters were able to make such abstractions plausible. Tintoretto's mythological allegories in the Doge's Palace, for example, were a major source for several of Ruben's most outstanding works, such as the *Consequences of War* (Palazzo Pitti, Florence); and the Flemish artist also retained an interest in the work of Veronese throughout his career. But the Bacchanals and *poesie* of Titian and later imitations by Veronese (Cat. 145, 146) were even more important for the seventeenth century, since they virtually created a new genre of painting. Indeed, it is one of the paradoxes of the history of art that the European vision of classical mythology was mainly established not in Rome, where the visible remains of antiquity were all around, but in Venice, and above all by Titian in his paintings for the Duke of Ferrara and the King of Spain.

THE HISTORIANS OF VENETIAN PAINTING

Charles Hope

The familiar outline of the history of Renaissance art, indeed the very idea of the rebirth of the visual arts, was first established by Giorgio Vasari, whose *Lives of the Most Excellent Painters, Sculptors and Architects* was published in Florence in 1550, with a second and much expanded edition appearing in 1568. Vasari divided his text chronologically into three sections. The first was devoted to the period before 1400, initiated in painting by Cimabue and Giotto, the second to the fifteenth century, when artists, particularly in Florence, learnt how to represent the natural world in a realistic way, and the third to the modern age, when the achievements of the ancients were matched and then surpassed, above all by Michelangelo and Raphael. This scheme gave pride of place to Florence and Rome, and its durability reflects Vasari's brilliance in creating a coherent history of developments in and around those cities. He knew much less about Venice and northern Italy, but his influence on later historians of Venetian art has been equally inescapable.

Everything that Vasari said about Venice in his first edition was based on recollections of a visit he had made to the city in 1541–42, before he had seriously begun collecting material for his book. As he described it, the development of painting there followed the pattern of central Italy, with the major figure of the fifteenth century Giovanni Bellini and the initiator of the modern style Giorgione, whose role was analogous to that of Leonardo da Vinci in Florence. According to Vasari, Giorgione was the first to reject the dry, hard and laboured style of Bellini, softening the outlines of his forms, introducing dark shadows and giving his pictures 'a formidable movement'; and these innovations were soon adopted by a much greater painter, Titian. In the 1550 edition Vasari had very little to say about Titian, because Michelangelo was the only living artist to be given a biography of his own. But he was scarcely more informative about dead Venetian masters, apart from Bellini and Giorgione. For the fifteenth century he did little more than provide a list of names, the most prominent being that of Carpaccio, with whom, surprisingly, he associated the sixteenth-century Brescians Moretto and Romanino; and among the moderns he mentioned only Palma Vecchio, Lotto and Pordenone, together with a few painters in Verona. For Vasari, in fact, Venetian painting was of no more than marginal interest.

While preparing his second edition he made a very brief trip through northern Italy in 1566, stopping in Venice for less than a week. During his stay he assiduously visited churches and public buildings, making notes about the pictures he saw, but he did very little to remedy his ignorance about the Venetian cities on the mainland. Although he now included extensive material on painters still alive, Vasari added only two biographies of Venetians. One was inevitably devoted to Titian, then the most famous artist in Europe, the other to the mediocre Battista Franco, who had spent most of his career in central Italy. Other artists were also mentioned, but often without being given the prominence they deserved, for example Bonifazio, Schiavone and Jacopo Bassano. Vasari was a little more informative about Paris Bordone, but otherwise he provided a comprehensive account of the work of only two Venetian painters, both of the younger generation, namely Tintoretto and Veronese.

Given his very limited knowledge of Venice, it is not surprising that in 1568 Vasari did not really try to recount the recent history of Venetian art, but simply recorded what he had seen. His own tastes and preconceptions would in any case have made it difficult for him to have done much more. For Vasari, good art was primarily concerned with the idealised human figure, and it was necessarily based on *disegno*, the use of drawings to elaborate and perfect formal inventions conceived in the mind. *Disegno*, in fact, was the foundation of all the visual arts, and its greatest exponent was Michelangelo. But in Venice preparatory drawings were never as important in the creative process as they were in central Italy. Moreover, by the 1560s it was a commonplace that the outstanding quality of Venetian painting was *colorito*, the actual business of applying paint to canvas, which was a craft skill primarily concerned with the imitation of nature rather than an intellectual activity. Since Vasari's history of art was essentially a history of *disegno*, he therefore could not readily accommodate the Venetians in his scheme. Indeed, he regarded them as fundamentally misguided.

In his treatment of Venetian art, Vasari repeatedly returned to this theme. The revolution wrought by Giorgione, as he described it, was a new approach to *colorito* which allowed a more perfect imitation of nature. Similarly, Titian was characterised as an artist unrivalled in *colorito* but prevented from achieving supreme excellence because he did not recognise the importance of drawing. Palma Vecchio, too, was dismissed as an imitator of nature, whereas Schiavone, whose debt to Parmigianino, whom Vasari admired, was too evident to be missed, had for this reason 'sometimes produced good things by accident'. Tintoretto and Veronese presented a much greater problem, since Vasari was well aware of their exceptional talent. He could find nothing to criticise in the work of Veronese, but adopted a slightly patronising tone, calling him 'Paolino', implying that he was little more than a beginner and relegating his paintings to the biography of the architect Sanmicheli. Vasari's comments on Tintoretto were for the most part equally positive, and included many of his favourite terms of praise – rapid, resolute, capricious, extravagant, stupendous. But he also complained that the artist did not give enough attention to perfecting his inventions and he deplored the lack of finish in his paintings. Vasari, in fact, always suspected that the bravura, sketchy type of brushwork favoured by so many Venetian artists was a means of concealing deficiencies in *disegno*.

What is missing from Vasari's text is any adequate explanation of how the Venetians of the later sixteenth century came to paint as well as they did. One might therefore have expected that this task would have been undertaken by one of the local writers on painting in the next century, Carlo Ridolfi and Marco Boschini. Ridolfi, indeed, set out to amplify Vasari's account and bring it up to date, publishing in 1648 a collection of biographies of the painters of the Venetian State, thus making explicit the geographical delineation of Venetian art already implied by his predecessor. Unfortunately, he had none of Vasari's gifts as a historian, and confined himself to describing pictures and recounting anecdotes without giving his material any coherent shape. Boschini, whose most important book appeared in 1660, was more perceptive; but his purpose was to challenge Vasari's critical standpoint, not his history. In particular, he denied the pre-eminence of *disegno*, arguing that this merely provided the painter with his framework, which he could only transform into great art by means of *colorito*, as the Venetians had been the first to recognise. Thus Boschini gave added authority to Vasari's contention that Venetian art was primarily concerned with *colorito*, at the same time greatly exaggerating the role of Giorgione, about whose work he knew almost nothing.

Boschini's greatest strength was in his recognition of the crucial importance of Venice for artists of the seventeenth century, an influence that involved not just *colorito*, but also figures and compositions of a kind very different from those used by the Mannerists of central Italy, such as Vasari. By his day this was generally admitted, but it did not lead to a substantial reconsideration of the history of Italian painting as a whole. Thus for Bellori, in 1672, the history of art was still centred on Florence and Rome, so that he could say without any incongruity that the Carracci had revived the dead art of painting in the 1580s, then adding a few pages later that this had happened after Annibale Carracci had met Tintoretto, Veronese and Jacopo Bassano in Venice, all of them very much alive. A less parochial view was first expressed in print in Modena in 1657 by Francesco Scanelli, who divided Italian painting into different 'schools'. The first was the Tuscan school, which reached its highest point in Raphael and then entered a catastrophic decline in the work of the Mannerists; the second was the school of the Venetian State, brought to perfection by Titian and maintained there by Veronese; the third was the Lombard school, whose greatest figure was Correggio. For Scanelli, as to some degree for Bellori, seventeenth-century painting was derived from these three sources, but in the first instance from Venice and Lombardy.

The notion of distinct schools, which inevitably underlined the differences between the Venetians and the despised Mannerists, was given its most intelligent statement by Luigi Lanzi in 1795. But rather than treating Venetian art as a single tradition he fragmented it still further into various sub-schools, headed respectively by Giorgione, Titian, Tintoretto, Jacopo Bassano and Veronese. By his time local antiquarians had begun to discover documents about Renaissance artists, and this enterprise became increasingly important in the nineteenth century. But even now, because of the evidence that has survived, we know much more about painting in Florence and Rome than in Venice, especially before 1550. Thus dates ranging over a decade or more are proposed even for major pictures by Titian, while no two scholars can agree about the attribution or precise chronology of paintings by Giorgione.

The art historian obviously not only has to establish who painted what, and when, but also to create a coherent pattern from this data, to place each artist in a wider context. In dealing with sixteenth-century Venice, scholars have been greatly influenced by the early historians. Thus it is generally agreed that Giorgione brought about a major change in the local tradition, introducing a new kind of naturalism based on a distinctive type of *colorito*; while to explain subsequent developments it is now customary to apply a historical scheme similar to that of Florence and Rome, where a 'classic' High Renaissance was supposedly replaced by the more overtly anti-naturalistic style of Mannerism. In Venice this change is usually said to have taken the form of a 'Mannerist crisis' around 1540, when the placid course of Giorgionesque naturalism was rudely interrupted by the introduction of formal elements from central Italy. Such borrowings permanently enriched the language of Venetian painting, but in the second half of the century a renewed assertion of the traditional concerns with naturalism and *colorito* led to a new 'classic' synthesis in the work of Titian, Tintoretto, Veronese and Jacopo Bassano.

This scheme has the merit of taking into account the manifest debt of many Venetians to their contemporaries elsewhere in Italy, as well as challenging the idea, common since the nineteenth century, that their art was largely hedonistic. But in several respects it seems inadequate. In particular, it involves a gross oversimplification of the situation before 1540, when the variety of styles current in Venice and on the mainland was greater than at any other period. To characterise Titian, Lotto, Palma Vecchio, Bordone, Bonifazio, Savoldo and Pordenone as naturalistic followers of Giorgione is to say very little about them, especially as the term naturalism is derived from Vasari, who used not to define a quality these artists possessed, but ones they lacked, namely a knowledge of the antique and an appreciation of *disegno*. Moreover, even Vasari recognised that this deficiency was only relative, as his enthusiastic comments on works by Titian and even Pordenone make clear. Neither of these painters was indifferent to developments elsewhere in Italy, and in Titian's case contemporary art in Florence and Rome was an important influence from the outset of his career. Against this background the Mannerist crisis, whose principal manifestation was the use of motifs derived from prints after artists such as Parmigianino and Michelangelo by a group of younger painters, notably Tintoretto, Schiavone and Bassano, was simply an extension of a practice already existing in Venice. To show that something new was involved one would have to argue that these painters believed that there was a fundamental stylistic distinction between Mannerism and the art of the High Renaissance. But there is no evidence that anyone in Venice, or indeed elsewhere, then thought this to be the case. Nor is there any indication that attitudes in Venice changed significantly later in the century, let alone that there was any general reassertion of local ideals current before 1540. From this period only the work of Titian had a continuing relevance, while Tintoretto remained faithful to the idiom of Michelangelo, and Veronese created a personal style which included elements from Raphael, Giulio Romano, Parmigianino and the antique.

Rather than seeing the development of Venetian painting in terms of a pattern borrowed from elsewhere, it makes more sense to consider the local situation. For the first four decades of the century, unfortunately, the evidence about the attitudes of artists and patrons is very fragmentary. But it is clear at least that Giorgione's innovations in technique led to a decisive break with the hard, linear manner of Bellini and his followers, and that from about 1510, when Giorgione died, virtually all the younger artists abandoned the traditional conventions for figures and compositions, and introduced a greater sense of movement, larger forms and less symmetrical designs. Titian seems to have been the main innovator in this respect, but several other Venetians showed notable independence and originality, particularly Lotto. Today he seems an eccentric outsider, since his style has very little in common with the ideals of the High Renaissance in central Italy, but this does not seem to have been held against him by his patrons, who had no universally accepted standard, such as the antique, against which to judge new types of painting.

From the 1530s, however, conventions for figures and compositions ultimately derived from central Italy were increasingly adopted by Venetian artists, and from the early 1540s several of them, notably Tintoretto, Schiavone and then Titian, began to use a more open type of brushwork. It can be no accident that these developments coincided with a growth in critical and theoretical writing about art, which owed much to the criticism of rhetoric and poetry. This phenomenon also occurred in Florence and Rome, but its first important manifestation was in Venice, in the letters of Titian's friend Pietro Aretino. Common to all this literature was the tendency to divide the activity of the painter into various categories, such as *disegno*, *colorito* and invention, and to place a high premium on such qualities as grace, facility and decorum. At the same time, a few outstanding artists were constantly invoked as ideal models, above all Raphael and Michelangelo, but also younger painters like

Parmigianino and Salviati. In most respects the critical standards proposed in Venice were no different from those current in central Italy; but there it was constantly emphasised that the basis of all art was *disegno*, whereas the Venetians attached as much importance to *colorito* and always included its foremost exponent, Titian, in the canon of great artists. In other words, within a generally accepted group of assumptions about the nature of art, which can loosely be summarised as the advocacy of a self-conscious stylishness, there were crucial differences in emphasis, reflecting diverse local traditions. For the artists of central Italy, the new criticism led to a codification of existing practice, whereas in Venice it had a more positive effect: not only were the painters encouraged to draw on a wider range of models, but also the presence and continuing activity of Titian sanctioned further innovation on the part of his younger contemporaries. As a result, in Florence and Rome we find an increasingly stereotyped form of Mannerism, while the Venetians took a different path. Even the most overtly Mannerist among them, Tintoretto and Schiavone, never adopted a working method based on elaborate preparatory drawings, but were the very artists who displayed the most extreme virtuosity in their brushwork; and Vasari was surely right in seeing the relatively loose and seemingly spontaneous handling of Titian's later paintings, particularly those for Philip II, as a prodigious demonstration of skill, rather than as mere naturalism (fig. 16). Even Bassano can be fitted into this framework of ideas; for the unidealised style of his late work is precisely appropriate to his chosen subject-matter.

Considered in these terms, it is possible to see painting in Venice, especially from the 1530s, as the most notable part of a wider Italian development. It is also easy to understand why only in the Veneto was the Mannerism of central Italy not adopted wholesale, except by a few painters of the second rank. Venice, after all, was one of the wealthiest and most stable cities of the peninsula, at least twice as populous as Florence or Rome, with an outstanding indigenous artistic tradition and a network of subject towns which were a constant source of new talent and a rich market for pictures. The present exhibition provides a unique opportunity to appreciate the strength of that tradition, which made Venice in the second half of the sixteenth century the pre-eminent centre of painting not only in Italy, but in the whole of Europe.

TITIAN AND VENETIAN COLOUR

John Steer

'Michelangelo for form and Titian for colour': this well-worn dichotomy, which originated in the Cinquecento itself, has recently been thrown into disarray by the discovery, as a result of cleaning, of the brilliance and subtlety of colour in Michelangelo's frescoes; and no-one who saw the many-splendoured display of variegated colour in the early six-teenth-century Florentine paintings in the Medici exhibitions of 1980 could doubt the importance of colour, or at least of colours, to central Italian artists. If this exhibition were of Florentine rather than Venetian sixteenth-century paint-ings the colours would be brighter, more variegated in hue and altogether more dazzling than what we see before us. Why then the importance given, from Vasari onwards, to Venetian colour?

In considering this question there are two difficulties. The first is an almost complete lack of information about what Venetian artists, and in particular Titian, actually thought about colour, if indeed they thought about it theoretically at all. From his writings it can be deduced that the Florentine Leon Battista Alberti, the author of the major fifteenth-century treatise on painting, did not have a conception of colour as a constituent of visual experience which could be applied to what happened in Venice in the first three decades of the sixteenth century. Venetian writers of the mid-century, particularly Pino and Dolce, were moving somewhat hap-hazardly towards an understanding of the role of colour in vision, based on their observations of what actually took place in Venetian painting at that time. But even their think-ing is very tentative and certainly does not constitute a coher-ent theory.

The second difficulty, which they did not face, is that the colour of Venetian paintings, which is more vulnerable than that of Florentine paintings because of the complexity of their paint structure, has often been radically changed and distorted by time. The favourite Venetian green, a copper resinate, tends to turn brown or even black, thereby robbing paintings of a fundamental colour dimension. The process is, alas, irreversible, and in the beautifully cleaned *St. John the Baptist* by Titian (Cat. 119) the marvellous blues are no longer matched, as they were intended to be, by an equal range and intensity of greens.

With this in mind we can nonetheless discover in Venetian colour, as it developed in the hands of Titian in the first two decades of the sixteenth century, three main tendencies: firstly, a severe limitation in the actual number of hues, which very much contrasts with the emphasis on variety in Florentine painting; secondly, a tendency to choose the pur-est hues in their richest and most saturated state; thirdly, the intention to arrange them in overall harmonies that are both simpler and more sophisticated than the mere balancing

of bright, contrasting colours that had gone before. These tendencies are remarkable in themselves, but they have their basis in a more fundamental change of which they are an expression. They depend on what amounts to a new mode of vision, which may be loosely described as 'perceptual' and still more loosely as 'realistic', a term applied by Titian's contemporaries, who saw in his handling of light and colour a way of recording in paint a sense of living reality not achieved before.

This new mode of vision is related to the theory of percep-tion – going back to antiquity, but alien to Alberti and the Florentine School – which takes colours as the primary and essential constituents of visual experience and considers them – rather than outlines – as the primary building blocks in our conception of form. Whether or not this view was theoretically understood by Venetian artists at the beginning of the century, and most likely it was not, it is certain that in the work of Giovanni Bellini from the 1490s onwards a change takes place that asserts this principle. Johannes Wilde compared the structure of Bellini's *Baptism* of 1500–01 in S. Corona, Vicenza, which is built up of patches of colour directly observed from nature, to that of a painting by Cézanne. This method, more boldly applied, is taken up by the early Titian and can be seen for example in *Jacopo Pesaro Presented to St. Peter* (Cat. 113).

Here the scene is built up without outline, in patches of colour, which stand for the form itself, its local colour and the modification of colour by light. So all the elements in the painting are integrated into a single system, in which the beauty of individual hues, so central to the Florentine tra-dition, is subordinated to an overall system of values drawn from the relationship of the colours to each other, and arising directly from the artist's perceptual experience of nature. It is the act of seeing the world in terms of colour that now forms the basis for painting; and it is because this aspect of visual experience is, by being translated into painting, here for the first time fully articulated, that the paintings convey to us, as they did to contemporaries, so intense a vibration of life. Titian in this very early work and, in a more deve-loped way, in the paintings which follow it, was making dis-coveries about the role of colour in vision that added a new dimension to European art.

But the system of colour which Titian evolved in the years between 1510 and 1520 owes its force and its subsequent influence not only to its direct relationship with visual exper-ience, but also to his power of organising that experience in ways which were to become norms for the future of paint-ing throughout Europe. The votive painting from Antwerp (Cat. 113) still includes a bright grass green and a soft warm brown, but the palette of what may be termed the 'classic paintings' of the next decade, *Noli Me Tangere* (National Gallery, London) for example, and the *Assumption of the Virgin* in the Frari (fig. 19), depends on the sonorous accord of only three main colours: red, blue and green. The combination of richness and intensity of hue which Titian achieves in the individual colours is made possible by his use of the oil medium, but his desire to present these primary hues at such a level of saturated intensity and his way of putting them together is an aesthetic choice. Thus Titian limits his colours in order to bring them into a new kind of accord. 'The colourisation of which Titian was the originator', Theodore Hetzer wrote in German in 1935, 'is characterised by the fact that its fidelity to nature is bound up with an arrangement of colours which in its independent character displays the internal order of the world and its associations, relationships and connections'.

We may not wish to express ourselves so metaphysically, but in practice our experience of the essential rightness of Titian's colour harmonies confirms what Hetzer says, and shows that Titian achieves through colour a harmonious but active balance of opposing forces in a manner strictly comparable to what Raphael achieved through form. Moreover, in the attitude towards colour that the Renaissance inherited from antiquity and the Middle Ages there was material for a theoretical explanation of what Titian did.

The idea that all colours may be calibrated on a scale between black and white and have, according to their mixture of hue and tone, relative weights comparable to tones in music, is found in Aristotle. It justifies the view, proposed incidentally with regard to Venetian painting by Constable, that the harmony of colours has an intellectual as well as a sensuous base. It is also worth noting that Aristotle in *De Sensu*, among several somewhat contradictory theories about colour, described the primary colours which complete what we call the colour circle as red, blue and green, regarding yellow not as a colour in itself but as a constituent of light, an idea not incompatible with Titian's practice between 1510 and 1520. In his paintings of this decade, yellow as a local hue seems to be largely excluded: it only re-emerges in the robe of St. Peter in the *Pesaro Madonna* in the Frari painted between 1519 and 1526. Strong as the yellows are, in, for example, the *Assumption of the Virgin* (fig. 19), they stand for light.

But Titian, whose style and practice always varied enormously according to the nature of the commission, could not long be limited by the classically pure formulae of his early years; and the introduction of further pigments and hues, especially the orange realgar and the yellow orpiment, which play such an important role in, for example, the *Bacchus and Ariadne* (fig. 18) is, during the 1520s and 1530s, part of a decorative tendency natural to an artist brought up with the Byzantine heritage of the Pala d'Oro. Indeed, it is characteristic of Titian's approach to colour at this time that he handles pigments, especially the deeply saturated ultramarine of his skies and mountains, as precious materials in themselves, so that the colours in his court paintings, of which the *Bacchus and Ariadne*, painted for Alfonso d'Este, is an example, have the surface richness of an enamel.

It was the special wizardry of Titian in these years to retain the individual brilliance of a hue and yet relate it tonally to the whole. Differently formulated, the same skilful balance is present in the work of another artist of Titian's generation, Lorenzo Lotto, whose greatness as a colourist is especially revealed in this exhibition. Habit and tradition lead us, wrongly I think, to regard Lotto as an eccentric artist. But his understanding of the interaction of colour and light is hardly less than that of Titian, and can lead to effects as visually sophisticated as the overall sense of marine atmosphere in the great *St. Christopher, St. Roch and St. Sebastian* of the mid-1530s (Cat. 52). Here the muffled pinks and mauves of St. Roch are wonderfully related to the surrounding tones of aqueous grey-blue, and the scarlet and yellow of St. Christopher provide a clarion call of explosive colour in the centre of the composition. Expression rather than decoration is always the driving force behind Lotto's colour, and this is again superbly shown in the *Visitation* (Cat. 50). Here the hues are not decoratively balanced as they would be in Titian or Veronese, but create a tenderly moving contrast in the imbalance between the bright colours of the youthful Virgin and her attendants coming in from the right, and the muted violets and blues of the old people, Zacharias and St. Elizabeth, on the left.

A transformation in the handling of colour, in particular, in its relation to tone, is one of the chief developments in Venetian painting in the 1540s, the decade in which not only the younger generation of artists, but also the middle-aged Titian responded to the new developments in central Italian art. But whereas the new forms in Venetian art of the period can often be directly attributed to the influence of central Italy, this cannot be so with colour. What took place was a largely indigenous development which seems to have happened almost simultaneously among a number of younger and older artists. It can be studied in Andrea Schiavone's *Adoration of the Magi* (Cat. 89), probably datable to *c.* 1547. Here the intensity of the individual hues is so muted that the drama and movement of the painting depends not on the colours themselves, but on the interplay of warm and cool tones to which the colours are subordinate, an interplay which, in Schiavone's fluent painterly style, weaves like a knot of writhing snakes over the whole surface of the painting. Of course not all painting of the 1540s and 1550s is so concerned with chiaroscuro, but what we find almost universally is a movement away from the pure, primary colours of the classic phase towards much more complex systems of harmonies and dissonances built from mixed hues. These are often highly individual in character, and usually emerge from a darkened background. In a way this development can be seen as a parallel in Venetian terms to the complexities of the 'maniera' style of the mid-century in central Italian art; and from paintings in this exhibition it is possible to study this development in the sharp, rather acidulated hues and silvery tonality adopted by Jacopo Bassano (Cat. 8, 9) at this period, and also in some of the works of Tintoretto.

Tintoretto is not a great colourist, although he often uses exciting, even bizarre, colours. But his approach to colour is indicative of a general tendency at this time, because he detaches it from the direct relation to visual experience which it had in the hands of Titian, and makes it one element in a bravura system of picture-making as varied and inventive as any in the history of art. Although in the deeply moving late *Deposition* (Cat. 112) silvery colour and fluent trails of paint are set against the circumambient darkness, they remain sharply separated from their surroundings, and their character is expressive rather than realistic: only very rarely fig. 18 Titian *Bacchus and Ariadne* (National Gallery, London)

in Tintoretto do we find that reality of space and air which is fundamental, as will be suggested in a moment, to the late work of Jacopo Bassano and Titian.

Veronese also started from the principle of picture-making, but for him relationships of colour were, as they were not for Tintoretto, the fundamental constituent in his compositions. Although there is no evidence that he used any new pigments, Veronese's method of mixing and combining hues achieved a new level of decorative and expressive sophistication. But what is of particular interest here is the way in which in his late work he re-integrated this system of colour with a new understanding of chiaroscuro and related it more directly to visual experience. A superb example is the altarpiece from S. Pantalon (Cat. 147), in which the saint emerges from darkness into light, and all the colour values are related to the light and shade in such a way that they establish precisely the reality of the space in which the figures move.

Veronese's painting was made in 1587, but this development had been anticipated by Jacopo Bassano and Titian. In the work of Bassano it can be illustrated by the altarpiece of *St. Martin and the Beggar* (Cat. 10) or by the tiny *Susanna and the Elders* (Cat. 11). In the latter the distant buildings seem suspended in crepuscular twilight and in both the figures are evoked by what seem to be the final flashes of the dying light out of the thickening atmosphere. This vision is based on the artist's actual experience of the behaviour of colours in semi-darkness, and it is to this that the paintings owe their intensity and truth.

In two great late works by Titian (Cat. 130, 132) light and colour seem to emerge only with difficulty out of the surrounding darkness, but from his struggle to describe this phenomenon as precisely as possible, a reality of space and air is established so certain that it is almost tangible. Colour plays a part, but it is handled in a different way in each of the paintings. In the *Tarquin and Lucretia* (Cat. 130), an easel painting, broken areas of local colour are retained as part of the painting's close claustrophobic focus; in the *Flaying of Marsyas* (Cat. 132) it is not individual colours that tell, but an all-over emanation of broken touches, evoking a greenish-gold, that is spattered, appropriately to the theme, with reds like splotches of blood. Vision and expression are here so much one that they cannot, even for the purposes of discussion, be separated. But it can, I think, be said that in these paintings Titian's intense struggle to grasp in paint, through tone and colour, the physical realities of the scene is a fundamental part of their meaning.

For Titian as a colourist see:
T. Hetzer, *Tizian, Geschichte seiner Farbe*, Frankfurt, 1935; 2nd edition 1948

For colour in the Italian Renaissance in general see:
M. Barasch, *Light and Color in the Italian Renaissance Theory of Art*, New York, 1978
(including references to Dolce, Pino and other primary sources)

J. Gavel, *Colour: A study of its position in the Art Theory of the Quattrocento and Cinquecento*, Stockholm Studies in the History of Art, 32, Stockholm, 1979 (with useful material on classical writings on colour)

For Florentine colour in particular, but with further fundamental discussion of general value, see:
J. Shearman, *Andrea del Sarto*, Oxford, 1965, and ibid 'Leonardo's Colour and Chiaroscuro', *Zeitschrift für Kunstgeschichte*, XXV, 1962, pp. 13–47

CONSERVATION, RESTORATION, AND NEW FINDINGS

Francesco Valcanover

In recent years there has been increasing co-operation between academic and artistic institutions on the one hand, and scientific and technical laboratories on the the other. This has had a very beneficial effect on the practice of conservation and restoration, in that the danger of works of art suffering irreversible damage at the hands of ignorant or arrogant restorers has now been largely eliminated. The role of the restorer today is two-fold: to preserve the fabric of a painting or sculpture, and to recover, as far as possible, the unity of its original appearance. That these aims are now to a great degree being achieved owes much to the rigorous and objective guidelines formulated by the Istituto del Restauro in Rome.

As a result of the exceptionally severe flooding (the *acqua alta*) of 4 November 1966, the Soprintendenza ai Beni Artistici e Storici of Venice had to undertake a very wide-ranging programme of restoration, which has been supported by the increased financial aid made available by the Italian State and by the Municipality of Venice, as well as by countless contributions from private individuals both in Italy and abroad. This programme is based on a new conservation policy, which closely reflects the ideals and practice of the Istituto del Restauro in Rome. Whereas in the past there was an elitist and haphazard approach, in that only works of the highest quality were restored, now there is a systematic plan, based on research carried out in 1968 and financed by UNESCO, to conserve all the works of art of the historic centre of Venice and the islands.

In order to fulfil these ambitious aims, an effective organisation has been created, which works in close collaboration with the Soprintendenza ai Beni Ambientali e Architettonici, and which makes use of the latest scientific innovations and methods of conservation. Its task is to preserve not only panels, canvases, frescoes and sculptures, but also the buildings in which they are housed – in other words the entire artistic and historical wealth of Venice. One need only glance at successive issues of *Arte Veneta* to understand the scale and importance of this undertaking, which has already rescued more than 30 architectural complexes from centuries of neglect, and halted the deterioration of at least 50 pictorial cycles and numerous works of sculpture. Naturally the study of Venetian painting, and in particular that of its greatest period, the sixteenth century, has benefited enormously from this impressive campaign.

Just a few examples of the restoration work recently carried out in Venice will give an idea of what has been achieved. Giovanni Bellini's three important altarpieces for the churches of S. Pietro Martire, Murano (1488), S. Zaccaria (1505; fig. 20) and S. Giovanni Crisostomo (1513) have once again been revealed in their full glory after the removal of large areas of repaint and thick layers of varnish. As a result, we can now appreciate how Bellini's style evolved continuously throughout his career, from his early interest in the work of Andrea Mantegna, Piero della Francesca and Antonello da Messina to his intensely poetic late manner. In his last years indeed, he, together with Titian, anticipated and then surpassed the 'new style' of Giorgione. Another painter who drew on much the same fifteenth-century sources as Bellini was Carpaccio, but he was also indebted to the artists of Ferrara, as has become all the more evident now that the restoration of the *St. Ursula Cycle* (Accademia, Venice) is under way.

Restoration has also contributed significantly to our understanding of the development of Venetian painting in the first decades of the sixteenth century. Thus the confrontation between Giorgione's restored fresco of a female nude from the façade of the Fondaco dei Tedeschi (now in the Galleria Franchetti, Ca d'Oro) with the surviving fragments of Titian's frescoes from the same building, which were discovered in 1967, has enabled us to see the vast stylistic differences between the two artists that already existed in 1508. At that date Titian's work was imbued with a classicism equal to that of Raphael and Michelangelo, and it has little in common with Giorgione's contemplative sensibility and essentially naturalistic approach.

In the opinion of the present writer, the evidence of these frescoes from the Fondaco makes it clear that such paintings as the *Fête Champetre* (Louvre) and *Christ and the Adulteress* (Cat. 35) cannot be by Giorgione, as is still sometimes proposed, but must instead be by Titian. In these years, as the two organ shutters from S. Bartolomeo (Cat. 95, 96) especially restored for this exhibition demonstrate, Giorgione's most faithful follower in Venice was Sebastiano del Piombo, who left for Rome in 1511.

Our understanding of Titian's development after the death of Giorgione has also been increased through the restoration of his paintings in Venice. Thus we can appreciate better than ever before the extraordinary novelty of the *Assumption of the Virgin* of 1518 (fig. 19; Frari), which, with its sumptuous colouring, heroic forms and remarkable depiction of emotions, introduced a new type of altarpiece to Venice; while the composition of the *Pesaro Altarpiece*, finished in 1526 for the same church, seems to anticipate the Baroque style of the next century. A third important work which has benefited from the removal of earlier inaccurate restorations is the *Presentation of the Virgin* (Accademia), completed in 1538; and another aspect of Titian's style, his debt to Michelangelo and the mannerists, can be now seen in the vibrantly coloured *St. John the Baptist* (Cat. 119).

A careful analysis of these paintings, which were pro-

fig. 18 Titian *The Assumption of the Virgin* (S. Maria Gloriosa
dei Frari, Venice)

fig. 19 Giovanni Bellini, San Zaccaria Altarpiece (S. Zaccaria,
Venice)

foundly influential for Venetian artists such as Palma Vecchio and Paris Bordone, makes it clear that the development of painting on the *terraferma* during the first half of the sixteenth century was very different. Savoldo, for example, seems to have been largely indifferent to many of the innovations of Giorgione and Titian. The removal of a murky layer of repaint and oxidised varnish from his *St. Anthony and St. Paul* (Accademia) has not only revealed a signature and a date, probably 1520, but also established that Savoldo looked principally to the rigorously formal style of Tuscany, to northern artists such as Hugo van der Goes and Dürer, and to the tradition of Lombard realism initiated by Foppa. Another artist working in Venice who was indebted to the

Lombards was Lotto, as, for example, in two paintings of 1528, the *Portrait of a Young Man* (Accademia) and the Carmine altarpiece, both of which have recently been cleaned. In the brilliant clarity of the colours, the tension of the compositions and the delicate characterisation, these have little in common with the contemporary works of Titian and his immediate followers.

Like Lotto, Pordenone spent much of his career on the *terraferma*, and the cleaning of his small altarpiece from S. Giovanni Elemosinario (Cat. 78) of *c.* 1535 has shown that even in Venice he too was less influenced by Titian than was hitherto supposed. The crowded composition, discordant lighting and strident colour revealed by the removal of the old varnish, indicate that his stylistic ideals were very different from those of his rival.

By 1550 Titian must have been aware that there were other artists who were no less original but even more gifted than Pordenone working in Venice. Tintoretto's *Miracle of the Slave* (Accademia, Venice), painted in 1548 for the Scuola

Grande di San Marco, was considered, before its restoration in 1966, to be an example of the most 'Titianesque' phase of his early, unsettled style. Today, however, it is clear that in this, his first public commission, Tintoretto's own artistic language was already established. The picture anticipates the characteristics of his mature style: the dynamic compositions, the virtuosity of his handling of paint, the provocative colour schemes and the violent sensation of tension created by his use of highlights. The extraordinary development of Tintoretto's sensibility and the formal means by which he expressed it are particularly apparent in several works that have recently been restored: the three canvases for the Scuola della SS. Trinità (Accademia, Venice), the organ shutters and other paintings in the chancel of S. Maria dell'Orto, and above all, the magnificent cycle of paintings for the Scuola Grande di S. Rocco. It is clear that Tintoretto refused all studio assistance for this last great undertaking, and we can observe that the evolution of his mature style falls into three distinct phases corresponding to the work in the Sala dell'Albergo (1564–67), the Sala Superiore (1576–81) and the Sala Terrena (1582–87).

Like Tintoretto, Paolo Veronese was trained in the mannerist tradition, but the mood of his paintings, which seem so perfectly to celebrate the optimism of sixteenth-century Venetian life, has little in common with the ambiguities and tensions commonly associated with mannerism. However, after the restoration of some of Veronese's pictures it is possible to see that in his choice of intense colours and his use of harsh highlights he remained faithful to his origins in Verona, even though he used these devices to new ends, for example in such works as the *Holy Family with St. John the Baptist, St. Anthony Abbot and St. Catherine* of *c.* 1551 (Cat. 133), the great decorative cycle in the church of S. Sebastiano, the magnificent *Feast in the House of Levi* (1573; Accademia, Venice), and the *Allegory of the Battle of Lepanto* of *c.* 1578 (Cat. 142), whose autograph status now seems beyond dispute. Finally, the San Pantalon altarpiece of 1587 (Cat. 147), which has been restored especially for this exhibition, is entirely typical of Veronese's late style: no longer joyously serene in spirit, but instead characterised by an almost lyrical melancholy, perfectly matched by the soft colouring and the subtle, shimmering lighting.

While Tintoretto and Veronese developed their individual styles, Titian advanced in sublime isolation. The restoration of *St. James the Apostle* (San Leo), and especially of the *Martyrdom of St. Lawrence* (Gesuiti) has revealed the incredible subtlety of Titian's late 'chromatic alchemy'. The *St. Lawrence* begun in 1548 but only finished in 1559, must be one of the most tragic and awesome of all sixteenth-century paintings. Titian's very personal style can also be recognised in the autograph parts of the votive painting of *Faith Adored by Doge Grimani* (Sala delle Quattro Porte, Doge's Palace), notably in such details as the figure of St. Mark, the warrior with the helmet, and the view of the basin of San Marco.

The restoration of Titian's intensely moving *Pietà* (Accademia, Venice), which is now in progress, is revealing the unique qualities of his late style, in which forms are created through an elaborate network of blended tones and fiery highlights. This phase, in which colour is submerged in mysterious shade and paintings appear to be unfinished ('*non finito*'), prefigures, and perhaps even surpasses, the late style of Rembrandt. Titian's contemporaries were unable to comprehend his late works, and the art dealer Niccolo Stoppio judged him both harshly and naively; he believed that the artist's weakened physical condition had impaired his creative genius.

While the restoration programme begun in 1966 has contributed to a greater understanding of these masterpieces of sixteenth-century painting, it has been equally important for the understanding of the minor painters of the century, particularly the later mannerist artists such as Palma Giovane, Pietro Malombra, Leonardo Corona, Antonio Vassillacchi, and Andrea Vicentino. Much of the recent research on these artists, which was published in the exhibition catalogue *Da Tiziano a El Greco: per la Storia del Manierismo a Venezia* (1981), has been stimulated by the re-emergence of paintings which were hitherto almost invisible.

The restoration of the decorative canvases in the Sala del Maggior Consiglio in the Doge's Palace, including the enormous *Paradise* designed by Tintoretto and executed by his workshop under Domenico Tintoretto between 1588 and 1592 (see Cat. 111), is still in progress. This campaign has, in particular, increased our knowledge of the importance of the workshop in the execution of the large-scale official decorative cycles undertaken by Tintoretto and Veronese in the Palace.

The restorers have been concerned not only with paintings and frescoes, but also with sculptures, notably those in the Galleria Giorgio Franchetti at the Ca d'Oro, including masterpieces such as the bronze reliefs by Camelio, Riccio (Cat. S15), and Tullio Lombardo. In several cases traces of the original gilding have been revealed. Amongst the many works in marble, a few should be mentioned: the extraordinary *Double Portrait* by Tullio Lombardo (incredibly, its autograph status was recently questioned), the group of portrait busts by Alessandro Vittoria, and Sansovino's masterpiece, the *Madonna and Child with Angels*.

Statues and carved decorations on the exterior of buildings have also been restored. Obviously sculpture of the thirteenth, fourteenth and fifteenth centuries has taken precedence, since it was most urgently in need of preservation; but some of the greatest sixteenth-century masterpieces have also been restored. These include the Loggetta in Piazza San Marco by Sansovino (fig. 26), the bronzes by Antonio Lombardo and Paolo Savin in the Zen Chapel, San Marco, and those by Tiziano Minio, Desiderio da Firenze and Francesco Segala on the font in the Baptistery of San Marco. Here too, the programme of conservation and restoration can be seen not as a short-sighted gesture in response to an immediate crisis, but rather as an undertaking of permanent cultural importance, carried out in the awareness of the profound importance of art for us all.

VENETIAN SIXTEENTH-CENTURY PAINTING – THE LEGACY

Francis Haskell

The heirs to the great flowering of Venetian art surveyed in this exhibition were to be found not in Venice itself (where talent declined precipitously at the end of the sixteenth century) but in Amsterdam, Antwerp and Madrid; Rome, Paris and London. Caravaggio and Annibale Carracci; Rubens, Van Dyck and Rembrandt; Poussin and Velázquez – these geniuses, whose example inspired and dominated European painting for some 250 years, as they still preside over our real and imaginary museums, drew much of their sustenance from Venetian painting, which thus moved from the borders of Italian art (to which Vasari wished to consign it) to the very centre. Some of these painters actually visited Venice itself, but some did not; for during the course of the seventeenth century Venetian pictures spread to cities throughout Europe. When the young Rembrandt was urged to go to Italy to improve his style, he claimed that there was no point in doing so, because it was easier to see Italian art concentrated in Amsterdam than to travel from town to town in Italy itself. We will see that this claim was not wholly unreasonable.

The process had begun in the lifetimes of some of the masters shown here. By the middle of the 1530s Titian had not only painted a famous portrait of the Emperor Charles V, but had also been invited to Spain to paint his wife and son. After some hesitation Titian declined to make the journey, but his pictures did so in increasingly large numbers, for members of the Habsburg court became by far his most important patrons, and it was for them that he painted some of his supreme masterpieces. Francis I of France was also

fig. 21 Teniers the Younger *The Archduke Leopold Wilhelm's Picture Gallery* (Kunsthistorisches Museum, Vienna)

fig. 22 Teniers the Younger after Giorgione *The Finding of Paris* (Princes Gate Collection, Courtauld Institute Galleries, London)

painted by Titian (who had to make use of a medal to obtain a likeness, as he never saw the King) and tried unsuccessfully to attract the artist to his court; but on the whole it was the art of Florence and Rome rather than of Venice that was patronised and collected at Fontainebleau.

Tintoretto and Veronese were less widely known outside Italy than was Titian, though it seems that after 1576 some of Veronese's most splendid pictures were painted for the collection of the Emperor Rudolph II in Prague; and one can assume that his portrait of the young Sir Philip Sidney (now lost) must have attracted attention in England as Sidney's fame grew ever brighter.

At the very end of the sixteenth century there occurred the first major dispersal of Venetian pictures from their original destination. In 1598 Ferrara fell into the hands of the Papacy, and *The Feast of the Gods* by Bellini (and Titian), together with Titian's *Andrians*, *Bacchus and Ariadne* (fig. 18) and *Worship of Venus*, all of which had been painted for a special room in the castle of Alfonso d'Este, were taken to Rome. Their impact was not seriously felt for a generation, but thereafter it can hardly be exaggerated. In the 1620s Poussin was only the greatest among a number of leading artists in Rome who agreed that 'Titian never executed anything more gay, charming and beautiful, since art and nature are presented together with the greatest delicacy in every part'; and we constantly find beautiful echoes of these *Bacchanals* by Titian both in Poussin's own works and in those of other seventeenth-century painters – nowhere more so than in the wonderful transcriptions (in Stockholm) made by Rubens (at some uncertain place and date) of *The Andrians* and *The Worship of Venus*.

To the great distress of Italian artists, in 1638–39 these

two paintings by Titian were sent to Spain, where the reign of Philip IV (1621–65) saw an astonishing accumulation of pictures by all the greatest Venetian masters. When Velázquez arrived in Madrid in 1624 he could already have seen the supreme group of Titians which had been assembled by Charles V and Philip II, and we are told that when Rubens paid his second visit there in 1628 he copied every Titian in the royal collection. Three years later Velázquez paid his first visit to Italy, during the course of which he apparently brought back to Spain further Venetian pictures (including a Bassano), and throughout this period others were arriving to enrich the collections of the King and his courtiers. It was in 1650, however, that Velázquez paid a second visit to Italy, for the specific purpose of buying works of art for Philip IV, and acquired masterpieces by Tintoretto and Veronese.

By then great pictures by these and other Venetian artists could also be seen elsewhere in Europe. During the sixteenth century the Gonzaga rulers of Mantua had been among the most active patrons of Venetian painters, and when in the 1620s their collections were sold to Charles I, London could almost rival the riches of Madrid in this field; for Lord Arundel, the Duke of Buckingham and other noblemen were also building up magnificent collections of paintings, among which Venetian works were given special prominence. The overwhelming majority of these were to leave England for ever during the Commonwealth, but the impact they made can happily still be seen in the portraits and very rare mythologies painted in England by Van Dyck (who himself owned some superb Venetian pictures, including Titian's *Vendramin Family*, now in the National Gallery, London).

While Charles I was still (just) alive, another great collection of Venetian (and other) paintings was broken up when Prague was looted by Swedish troops in 1648. Masterpieces by Veronese were sent to Queen Christina in Stockholm, and when a few years later she abdicated and began her travels through Europe she was able to add to them Titians of superlative quality. These pictures were eventually installed in her palace in Rome, and although much admired they did not, alas, stimulate the painters there as fruitfully as Titian's *Bacchanals* from Ferrara had done a generation earlier. Only one artist of real quality, Pier Francesco Mola, took full advantage of this new opportunity to study the finest Venetian art at leisure; and early in the eighteenth century the Queen's pictures once more resumed their travels – this time to France.

The dispersal of the collections of Charles I, the Duke of Buckingham and other English noblemen following the defeat of the Royalists in the Civil War brought more great Venetian pictures on to the market than ever before – or since; and many of the most famous museums in Europe still owe their principal holdings in the field to this extraordinary sale. Philip IV of Spain (who years earlier had presented Charles I with his first Titian) did well out of the occasion. And it is now that, for the first time, significant numbers of major pictures by Venetian artists came to Paris – though they were for the most part bought by a German banker who was acting on behalf of the Italian Cardinal (Mazarin), who was the effective ruler of France.

But it was the Low Countries that – temporarily – benefited most from the downfall of Charles I. For many years Amsterdam had been the centre of the European art trade, and outstanding Italian pictures were bought and sold there. It was this that prompted Rembrandt to claim that it was no longer necessary to go to Italy to study Italian art – and to be able to justify that arrogant claim by the marvellous use to which he put the opportunities open to him. Major Venetian pictures featured prominently in the private cabinets that were assembled in the city, and in 1648 the earliest (and most important) book devoted to the Lives of the Venetian Painters was dedicated to two brothers in Amsterdam who were building up a superb collection there: it is not unreasonable to think of these volumes as constituting, at least in part, an elaborate sale catalogue. And when Lord Arundel's pictures were transferred from London to Holland as the Civil War drew near, there were among them many attributed to Giorgione, Titian, Tintoretto and Veronese.

In the Habsburg Netherlands (which today constitute much of Belgium) Venetian pictures were equally accessible. Rubens himself had for a time owned a fine collection in Antwerp. He was not alone, and when in 1646 the Archduke Leopold Wilhelm, son of the Emperor Ferdinand II, was made Governor General of the provinces, he established in Brussels one of the greatest of all European collections of paintings, most of which are now in Vienna. For the lover of Venetian art his collection is the most evocative of all those built up in the seventeenth century, for, in his enthusiasm to make his treasures widely known, the Archduke instructed his chief curator, the painter David Teniers the Younger, to paint a number of views of his gallery (fig. 21). Even though the arrangement of what is to be seen in them may not be entirely accurate, these captivating views allow us to gaze at his pictures with the collector himself and his courtiers. We can see the ranks of Giorgiones and Titians and Tintorettos, some of them supreme masterpieces, some of them the unworthy recipients of optimistic attributions – and some sold from English collections. Moreover, not satisfied with this, the Archduke commissioned an illustrated catalogue of his collection (one of the very first ever to be produced), and in order to assist the engravers who were engaged on the task Teniers himself painted small copies on panel of some of the most admired works. A group of these panels can still be seen in the Princes Gate Collection (fig. 22), and through them (and others now scattered throughout the world) we can get a remarkable impression of the appeal made by Venetian painters of the Renaissance to the artists and amateurs of the seventeenth century – and also an invaluable record of the appearance of pictures that are now lost.

Venetian paintings continued to leave first Venice, then Italy, and then Europe; but by the second half of the seventeenth century superb examples were already to be seen in most centres where great new art was being produced. The impact made by such painting was by no means always welcomed by theorists. But to art lovers it may well seem to have been the one artistic influence that has been invariably beneficial.

32 Carpaccio *The Lion of St. Mark (detail)*

32 Carpaccio *The Lion of St. Mark*

35 Circle of Giorgione, attributed to Titian *Christ and the Adulteress*

36 Circle of Giorgione, attributed to Titian *Head of a Soldier* (fragment from *Christ and the Adulteress*)

34 Circle of Giorgione, attributed to Titian *Virgin and Child with St. Anthony and St. Roch*

113 Titian *Jacopo Pesaro Presented to St. Peter by Pope Alexander VI*

97 Sebastiano del Piombo *The Judgement of Solomon (detail)*

97 Sebastiano del Piombo *The Judgement of Solomon (detail)*

25 Cariani *The Lutenist*

37 Circle of Giorgione, attributed to Vittore Belliniano *Portrait of a Young Man*

26 Cariani *Allegory of a Venetian Victory*

27 Cariani *Courtesans and Gentlemen* (*Seven Members of the Albani Family*)

29 Cariani *Portrait of Giovan Antonio Caravaggi*

29 Cariani *Portrait of Giovan Antonio Caravaggi (detail)*

75 Palma Vecchio *Lady with a Lute*

114 Titian *Salome*

74 Palma Vecchio *Nymph in a Landscape*

77 Palma Vecchio *Nymphs Bathing*

76 Palma Vecchio *Mars, Venus and Cupid*

14 Bonifazio de' Pitati *Lot and his Daughters*

20 Bordone *Perseus Armed by Mercury and Minerva*

17 Bordone *Two Lovers*

22 Bordone *Family Group*

84 Savoldo *The Rest on the Flight into Egypt*

87 Savoldo *Virgin and Child with Two Donors*

85 Savoldo *Shepherd with a Flute*

86 Savoldo *Tobias and the Angel*

39 Girolamo da Treviso *Hagar and the Angel*

38 Girolamo da Treviso *Isaac Blessing Jacob*

40 Girolamo da Treviso *Sleeping Venus*

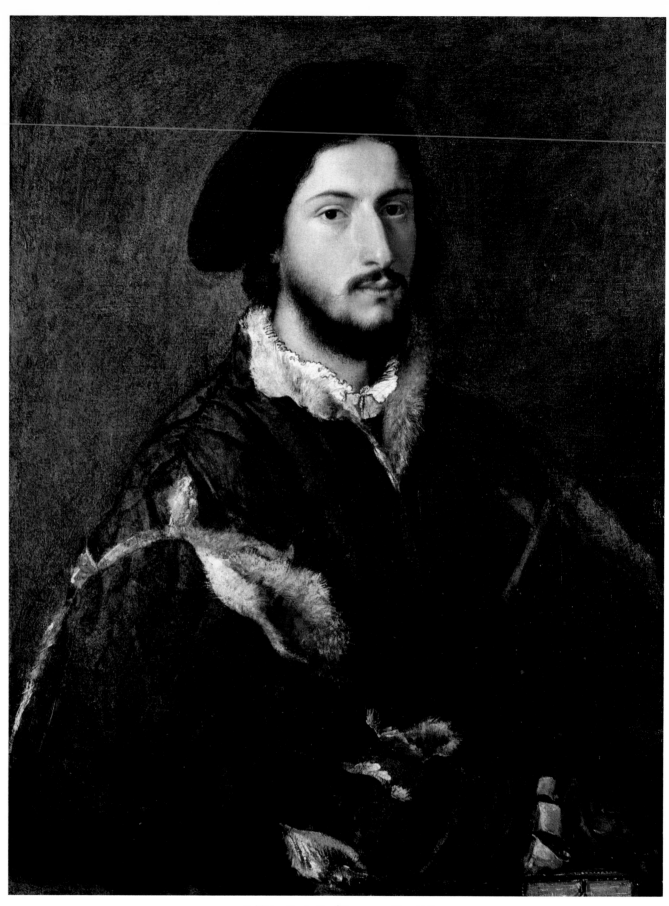

118 Titian *Portrait of Tommaso Mosti (?)*

116 Titian *Portrait of a Man*

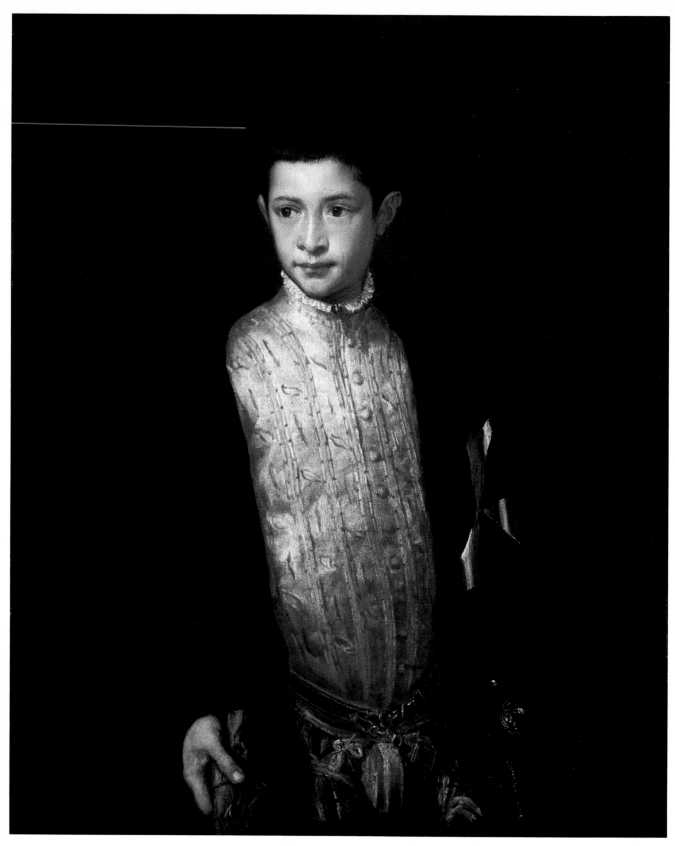

121 Titian *Portrait of Ranuccio Farnese as a Knight of Malta*

117 Titian *Portrait of a Man (called the Physician Parma)*

123 Titian *Portrait of a Knight with a Clock*

129 Titian *Portrait of a Man with a Palm (Antonio Palma?)*

130 Titian *Tarquin and Lucretia*

127 Titian *The Entombment*

128 Titian *Boy with Dogs*

122 Titian *Portrait of Francesco Savorgnan della Torre (?)*

45 Lotto *The Mystic Marriage of St. Catherine with St. Jerome, St. Anthony Abbot and other Saints*

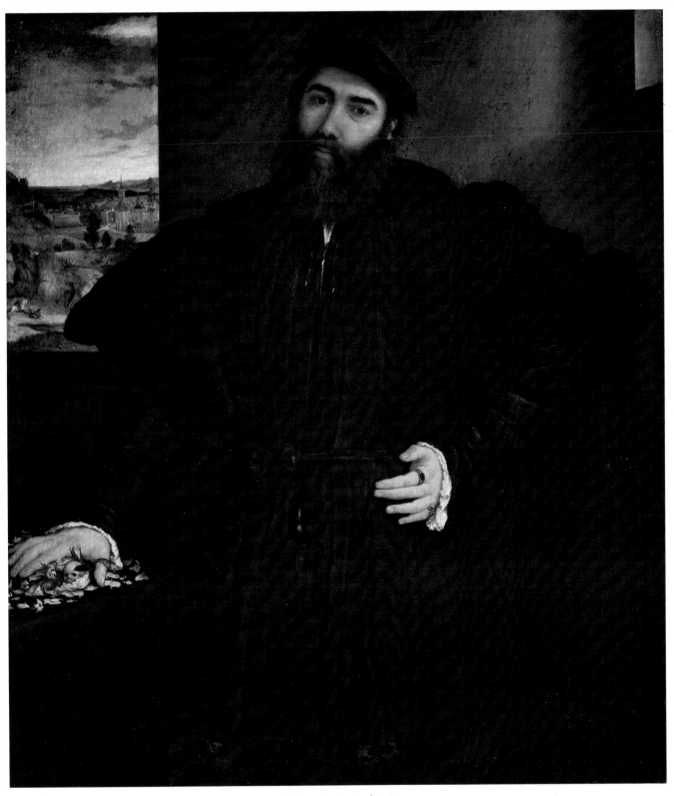

48 Lotto *Portrait of a Man*

47 Lotto *The Annunciation*

49 Lotto *The Annunciation*

50 Lotto *The Visitation*

46 Lotto *Portrait of Andrea Odoni*

54 Lotto *Portrait of Laura da Pola*

52 Lotto *St. Christopher, St. Roch and St. Sebastian (detail)*

52 Lotto *St. Christopher, St. Roch and St. Sebastian*

81 Romanino *Virgin and Child Crowned by Two Angels*

82 Romanino *The Mystic Marriage of St. Catherine with St. Lawrence, St. Ursula and St. Angela Merici*

60 Attributed to Moretto *Portrait of a Young Woman*

58 Moretto *Portrait of a Man*

59 Moretto *Ecce Homo with an Angel*

VENISTI CATHERINA
VT DESPONDERERIS
IMMORTALI SPONSO
CHRISTO

IO:BAP:MORONVS·P

67 Moroni *The Mystic Marriage of St. Catherine*

61 Moroni *Portrait of Gian Lodovico Madruzzo*

125 Titian *Portrait of Cristoforo Madruzzo, Cardinal and Bishop of Trent*

41 Licinio *Portrait of Arrigo Licinio and his Family*

62 Moroni *Portrait of Gian Gerolamo Grumelli* ('*Il Cavaliere in Rosa*')

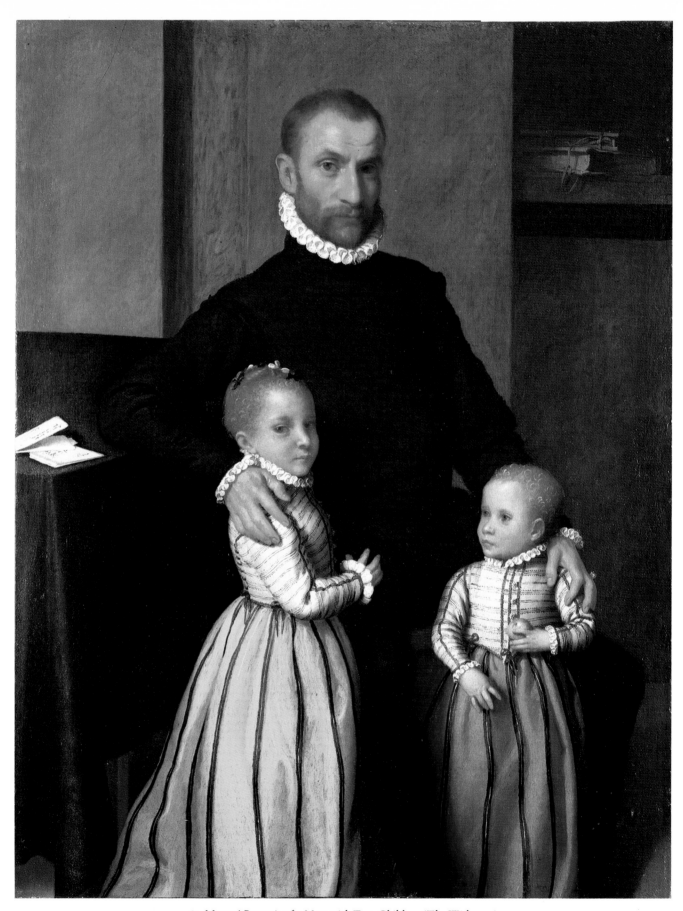

63 Moroni *Portrait of a Man with Two Children (The Widower)*

65 Moroni *Portrait of an Old Man with a Book*

1 Jacopo Bassano *The Flight into Egypt*

3 Jacopo Bassano *Rest on the Flight into Egypt*

5 Jacopo Bassano *The Adoration of the Shepherds*

4 Jacopo Bassano *Christ on the Way to Calvary*

7 Jacopo Bassano *St. Giustina Enthroned with St. Sebastian, St. Anthony Abbot and St. Roch*

[112]

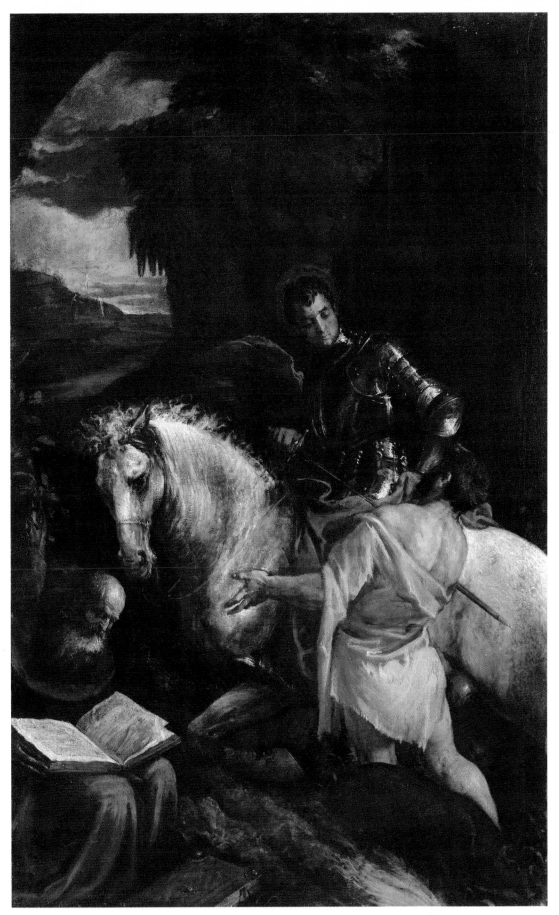

10 Jacopo Bassano *St. Martin and the Beggar with St. Anthony Abbot*

8 Jacopo Bassano *Jacob's Journey*

89 Schiavone *The Adoration of the Magi*

92 Schiavone *The Annunciation (Angel of the Annunciation)*

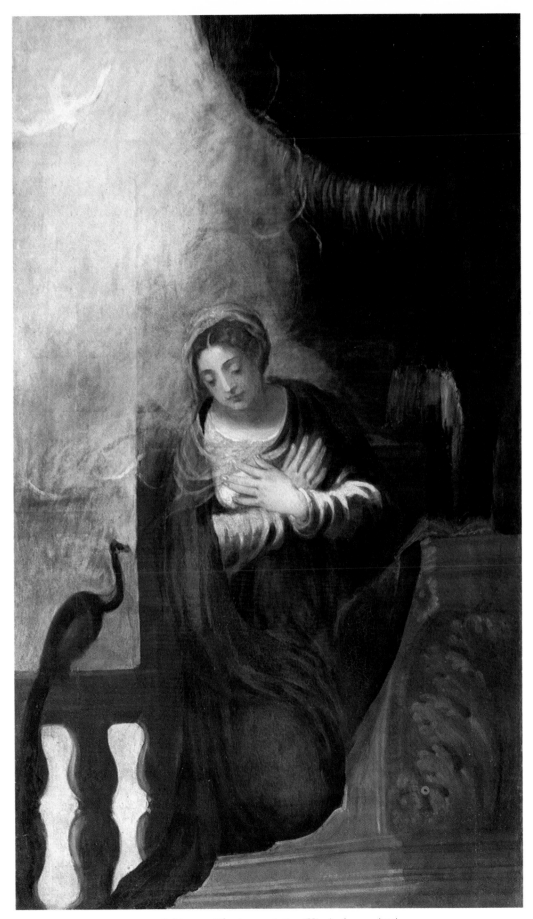

93 Schiavone *The Annunciation (Virgin Annunciate)*

94 Schiavone *Christ Before Herod*

57 Pietro de Mariscalchi *The Adoration of the Shepherds (Madonna della Misericordia)*

98 Sustris *Venus*

99 Jacopo Tintoretto *Christ Among the Doctors*

106 Jacopo Tintoretto *The Finding of Moses*

105 Jacopo Tintoretto *Judith and Holofernes*

100 Jacopo Tintoretto *Apollo and Marsyas*

101 Jacopo Tintoretto *The Washing of Feet (detail)*

107 Jacopo Tintoretto *Pietà*

110 Jacopo and Domenico Tintoretto *Santa Giustina and the Treasurers*

109 Jacopo Tintoretto *Portrait of an Elderly Senator*

111 Jacopo Tintoretto *Modello for 'Paradise'*

136 Veronese *The Miracle of St. Barnabas*

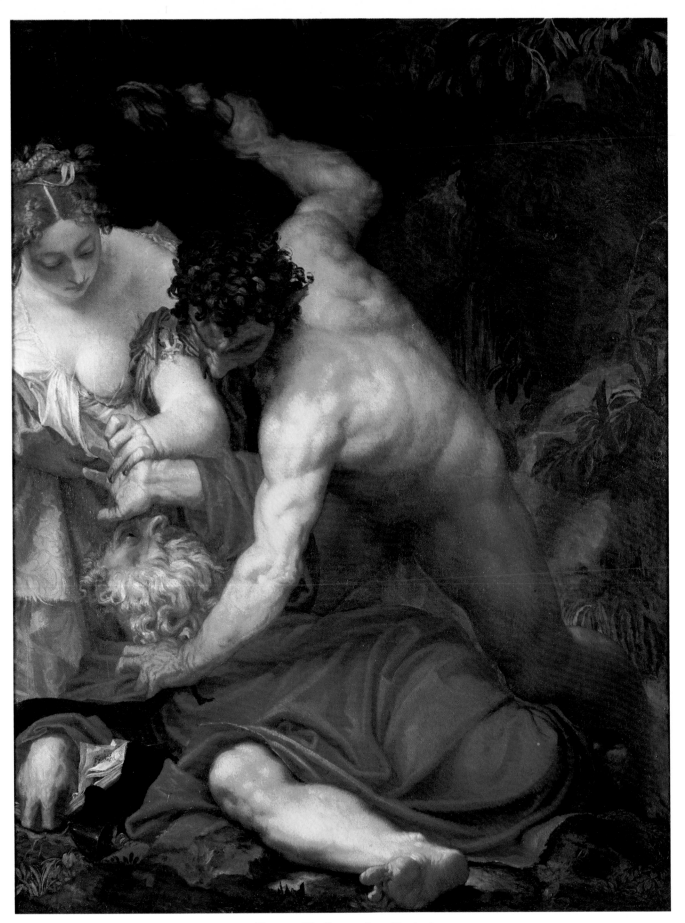

134 Veronese *The Temptation of St. Anthony*

143 Veronese *The Resurrection of Christ*

135 Veronese *Virgin and Child Appearing to St. Anthony and St. Paul*

145 Veronese *Venus and Adonis*

146 Veronese *Cephalus and Procris*

138 Veronese *Portrait of a Woman*

141 Veronese *Portrait of a Member of the Soranzo Family*

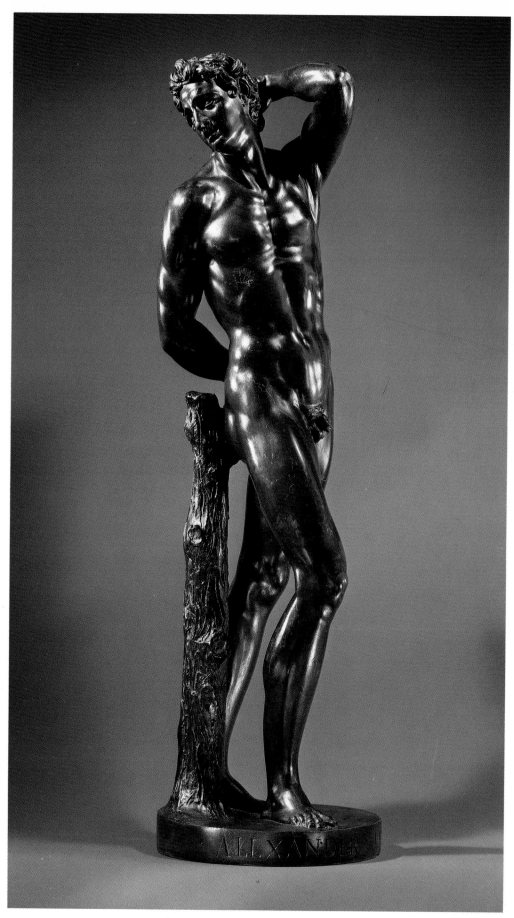

S37 Vittoria *St. Sebastian (Marsyas?)*

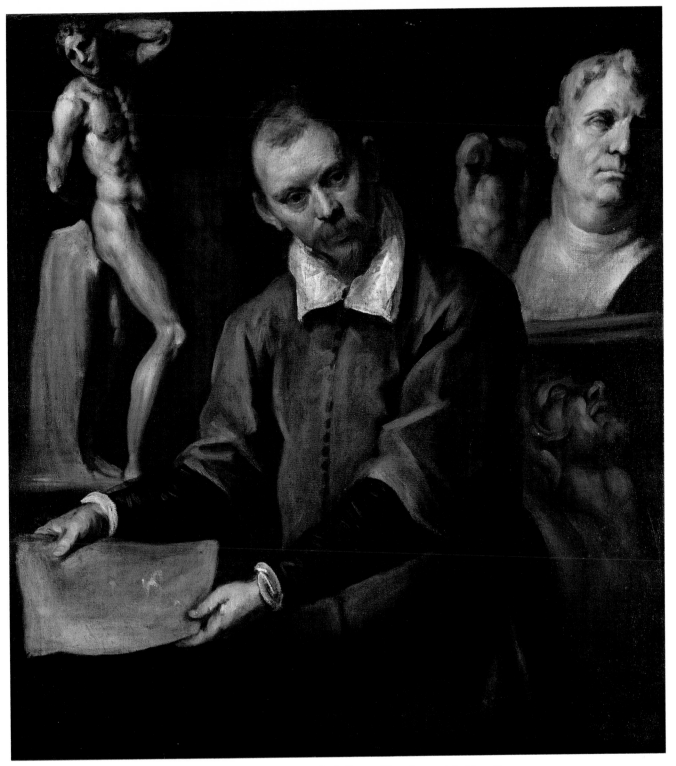

70 Palma Giovane *Portrait of a Collector (Bartolomeo della Nave?)*

NVDA VENVS A DIDAS EXPRE ME CMAS

S13 Mosca *Venus Anadyomene*

59 A. Lombardo *Philoctetes*

S29 J. Sansovino *The Annunciation*

S19 Riccio *Curete Milking the Goat Amalthea* (*The Nourishment of Jupiter*)

S5 Cattaneo *Lazzaro Bonamico*

THE CATALOGUE

Jacopo da Ponte, called
Jacopo Bassano

Bassano c. 1510 – Bassano 1592

Jacopo da Ponte (or dal Ponte; Rigon 1978, p. 174) was the son of Francesco, a mediocre painter of the Vicentine school. He was brought up near the Ponte Vecchio on the Brenta canal in the heart of the town of Bassano (Rigon 1980). The bridge was rebuilt on various occasions, most significantly by Andrea Palladio in 1570. By 1535, following a stay in Venice, Jacopo's personal style had emerged. At first he was influenced by Bonifazio de' Pitati and Titian, but prints also played an important part in the formation of his style, including the work of northern artists such as Dürer, Barthel and Sebald Beham, and also prints after paintings by Raphael and Salviati. These encouraged the mannerist elements in his style which became increasingly evident in the works of the late 1530s, such as the paintings for the Sala dell'Udienza and the Sala del Consiglio Communale (all now in the Museo Civico, Bassano), and the frescoes on the façade of the Palazzo Dal Corno (after 1538), the altarpiece of Borso, dated 1538, the *Martyrdom of St. Catherine* (Museo Civico, Bassano), the *Portrait of a Man of Letters* (Cat. 2), the *Christ amongst the Doctors* (Ashmolean Museum, Oxford) and the *Adoration of the Magi* (Edinburgh).

After 1540–42 Bassano was deeply influenced by Parmigianino, as can be seen in *The Flight into Egypt* (Pasadena), the *Adoration of the Shepherds* (Cat. 5), *The Rest on the Flight into Egypt* (Cat. 3), and the *Christ on the Way to Calvary* (Cat. 4). During the 1550s his extremely personal mannerist style and his exotic and sumptuous use of colour were fully developed. Masterpieces of this date include the *Decollation of St. John the Baptist* (Copenhagen), *Dives and Lazarus* (Cleveland), the *St. John the Baptist* of 1558 (Bassano), the *Adoration of the Magi* (Vienna), and the *St. Giustina Enthroned* (Cat. 7). Between 1545 and 1560 Bassano held an important position in Venetian painting; despite the fact that he worked in a small provincial town he was, together with Veronese and Tintoretto, one of the most influential painters in the Veneto apart from Titian. Although a pastoral element had always been present in his work, during the 1560s he combined a highly elaborate and artificial style with natural detail observed from nature as can be seen in *Jacob's Journey* (Cat. 8), and the *Adoration of the Shepherds* of 1568 (Cat. 9).

For many years it was thought that Jacopo ceased to paint after 1580 because in a letter from Jacopo's son, Francesco Bassano the Younger, to Niccolò Gaddi of 1581, Francesco said his father was unable to draw as he was losing his sight. However, during recent restoration, dates have been revealed on several paintings, most notably the date 1585 on the *Susanna and the Elders* (Cat. 11). A more careful analysis of the so-called 'genre' works of the 1580s, previously thought to have been shop productions, has revealed that they are the work of Jacopo (Ballarin 1966; Rearick 1967 and 1968; Pallucchini 1982). He was evidently active until the very end of his life, and, while preserving his own idiom and style, was profoundly influenced by Titian after the latter's death in 1576.

L.M.

1
The Flight into Egypt

183 × 198 cm
Signed: *Jacobus/a ponte*; below: the remains of an inscription, now obliterated
Museo Civico, Bassano del Grappa (no. 6)
[*repr. in colour on p. 108*]

This is Jacopo Bassano's first masterpiece; its composition seems to be derived from Giotto's fresco of the *Flight into Egypt* (Cappella degli Scrovegni, Padua) while the Virgin and Child appear to be taken from Titian's frescoed lunette in the Doge's Palace which is dated 1523. In 1775 Verci claimed that he could read the date 1534 on the painting, and Paroli transcribed the signature as '*Jacobus a ponte pingebat 1534*' (c. 1830, MS catalogue of paintings in the Sala della Congregazione Municipale, Bassano). But Arslan, who claimed that the inscription must have been illegible even before Paroli's day, believed that the work was later than the three canvases of the Sala del Consiglio – certainly later than that with the Soranzo coat of arms – and dated the picture 1535–36 (Arslan 1931). Longhi (1948) has rightly discerned that this work combines the old-fashioned style Jacopo would have learnt from his father with that of the more modern Bonifazio de' Pitati. This would suggest that the date of 1534 is correct, as Smirnova (1976) and Pallucchini (1982) believe.

L.M.

PROVENANCE
S. Girolamo, Bassano del Grappa; 1780, when the church was suppressed, passed to the Municipality; 1840 Museo Civico

EXHIBITIONS
Venice 1945, no. 107; Lausanne 1947, no. 58; Bassano 1952, no. 12; Venice 1957, no. 5

REFERENCES
Magagnato and Passamani 1978, p. 19; Pallucchini 1982², p. 17; Smirnova 1976

2
Portrait of a Man of Letters

76.2 × 65.7 cm
Signed on the letter on the left: *Jac. A. Ponte Bassanensis F. in Venetiis*
Brooks Memorial Gallery, Memphis, Tennessee; Gift of the Samuel H. Kress Foundation (61.208)

This is the only signed portrait by Jacopo Bassano, and the inscription states that it was painted in Venice. The identity of the sitter is unknown, but details such as one hand resting on an open book and a glove held in the other are derived from Lorenzo Lotto's portraits. The oriental carpet covering the table appears in several other paintings by Bassano including the *Madonna and Child with St. Anthony Abbot and St. Martin Abbot* (Alte Pinakothek, Munich, originally from Rasai, near Feltre), and the *Christ amongst the Doctors* (Ashmolean Museum, Oxford), as well as the *Dives and Lazarus* (Cleveland) and the

2

Decollation of St. John the Baptist (Copenhagen). It is likely that this rug was in Jacopo's house, or more probably in his studio, and may have been there since his youth; he continued to paint it until the 1550s. The versimilitude with which it is painted is typical of Jacopo's treatment of 'still-life' objects, which are often found in his paintings. The sitter appears to be distracted and unaware of the painter's presence. This is characteristic of Jacopo's naturalistic approach to his subjects; he was always a humble, yet subtle, observer of reality. It is generally agreed that the work can be dated *c.* 1540.

L.M.

PROVENANCE
Private collection, England; 1950 Samuel H. Kress Collection

EXHIBITION
Venice 1957, Portraits no. 2

REFERENCES
Arslan 1960, I, p. 46; II, fig. 26; Berenson 1952, pl. 95; 1957, I, p. 19; Pallucchini 1982², pl. 7; Washington 1951, pp. 124–25 (W. Suida); Zampetti 1958, p. 19, pl. LXXIV

3
Rest on the Flight into Egypt

118 × 158 cm
Pinacoteca Ambrosiana, Milan (no. 40)
[*repr. in colour on p. 109*]

This painting of the late 1540s is of fundamental importance in Jacopo's *oeuvre*. At this date he was still

influenced by Parmigianino; although some elements in the painting are observed from nature and emphasised by particularly strong colouring, the composition creates a restless sensation. It is crammed with incident and the figures are inextricably interlocked with one another; it almost seems as if the paint is trapped between the complex contours of the design, which is masterly (such total control of composition only reappeared in Jacopo's work of 1558–68). It is painted in a rich impasto in which warm tones predominate, so that there are no stark contrasts between the strident colours and the burnt earth pigments. The painting was formerly attributed to Titian.

L.M.

PROVENANCE
Cardinal Federigo Borromeo; 1618 donated by him to the Ambrosiana

REFERENCES
Falchetti 1969, pp. 262ff, with bibliography; Pallucchini 1982², pl. 15

4
Christ on the Way to Calvary

146 × 133 cm
The Earl of Bradford
[*repr. in colour on p. 111*]

Stylistically this work can be dated around 1545–50. Compared to the *Christ on the Way to Calvary* (Fitzwilliam Museum, Cambridge) which is almost contemporary, the figures, which are based on prints of recent Roman paintings, are more explicitly mannerist in style and may have been influenced by Schiavone. This is also true of the *Christ on the Way to Calvary* in Budapest which, according to the present writer, dates from just before 1550. The crowded composition of this painting is unlikely to have been deliberate, but is probably due to the painting having been cut on the left-hand side. As a result, the figures are thrust into the foreground, and the somewhat mannerist confusion of the composition is accentuated. In many respects the painting is closest to the *Decollation of St. John the Baptist* (Copenhagen), although the latter work is probably slightly later in date. Ballarin supported this view and has convincingly argued that an engraving of 1519 of Raphael's *Lo Spasimo di Sicilia* (Prado, Madrid) must have been known to several Venetian mannerists – including Sustris, Schiavone and Jacopo Bassano – and influenced their work.

L.M.

PROVENANCE
Probably acquired in Venice for Gerrit Reynst (died 1658) of Amsterdam; donated to Charles II as part of the gift of the States of Holland (listed as Jacopo Bassano); 1688 James II inventory, listed amongst the pictures in custody of Catherine of Braganza (died 1705); between 1721 and 1727 Viscount Torrington; by descent to the Earls of Bradford

EXHIBITIONS
London 1960, no. 64

REFERENCES
Ballarin 1967, p. 98; Mahon 1950, p. 15, no. 15

5

The Adoration of the Shepherds

139.5 × 219 cm
Her Majesty The Queen
[*repr. in colour on p. 110*]

The view of the countryside of Bassano with Monte Grappa rising in the background is almost identical to that in *Rest on the Flight into Egypt* (Cat. 3), the *Good Samaritan* (Royal Collection), and the *Trinity* (Angarano). Stylistically this painting is closest to another *Adoration of the Shepherds* (Giusti del Giardino Coll., Verona) in which the classical ruins derived from Dürer also recur (as they do in the *Adoration of the Magi*, Edinburgh). The combination of observed reality in the landscape and classical motifs copied from prints is typical of Jacopo's work. There is a great contrast between Jacopo's pastoral scenes with 'antique' ruins and the almost contemporary studies of classical architecture by Andrea Palladio; Jacopo's dilapidated columns, broken arches and walls are purely decorative. It is generally agreed that the painting dates from the late 1540s, although Pallucchini (1982) and others place it after the *Adoration* in the Giusti del Giardino Collection. The present author suggests that it is close in date to the *Adoration of the Magi* (Edinburgh) and earlier than the Giusti del Giardino painting.

This work can probably be identified with the 'Nativity of Christ per Bassano' in Charles I's collection, which was valued at £35 in 1649, and should not be confused with a 'Birth of Christ with Four Shepherds' attributed to Tintoretto which was bought for the King's collection in 1637. Later it was attributed to Palma Vecchio, but was re-ascribed to Jacopo by Crowe and Cavalcaselle, who believed it was an early work coming between the *Adoration of the Magi* (Edinburgh) and the *Rest on the Flight into Egypt* (Cat. 3).

L.M.

PROVENANCE
1649 probably collection of Charles I, 'The Nativity of Christ per Bassano'; 1649 sold to De Critz; probably James II, George III, Hampton Court (as Palma Vecchio)

EXHIBITIONS
1822 British Institution, no. 120 (?); 1868 Leeds, no. 99; London 1946, no. 204; Venice 1957, no. 20; London 1964, no. 21; Montreal 1967, no. 183

REFERENCES
Crowe and Cavalcaselle 1871; Pallucchini 1982², pl. 13; Shearman 1983, no. 16, pp. 21–23 with full bibliography

6

Two Hunting Dogs

85 × 126 cm
Gallerie degli Uffizi, Florence (no. 965)

This painting is virtually unique in sixteenth-century art in that it is a study of two dogs painted for their own sakes, and not a fragment cut out of a larger picture; this is clear

6

from the composition, which places the animals on the main diagonals. The classical architecture in the background frequently occurs in Jacopo's work; here it acts as a frame to the view of Bassano dominated by Monte Grappa, leaving no space for figures except for the two most unusual protagonists. Ballarin (1964) drew attention to another slightly smaller painting (61 × 79.5 cm) of two dogs formerly in the collection of the Duke of Bedford: stylistically that painting is close to the *Rest on the Flight into Egypt* (Cat. 3), and can be dated 1546–47. He correctly dated the Uffizi *Dogs* to 1555, relating it to the *Dives and Lazarus* (Cleveland). The *Two Hunting Dogs* belongs to the most mannerist phase of Jacopo's career; here, typically, he emphasises the unpretentious simplicity of his subject matter.

Although this work has been somewhat neglected in the past, it is extremely important in Jacopo's *oeuvre* (Ballarin 1964). It is almost universally attributed to Jacopo; only Arslan has suggested Leandro Bassano as the author.

L.M.

PROVENANCE
1663 Cardinal Giovan Carlo de' Medici; 1668 Cardinal Leopoldo de' Medici (attributed to Titian); 1675 Uffizi

REFERENCES
Arslan 1960, p. 340; Ballarin 1964, pp. 55–61, 62–67; Florence 1978, no. 46

7

St. Giustina Enthroned with St. Sebastian, St. Anthony Abbot and St. Roch

170 × 112 cm
Parish Church, Enego; on deposit at the Museo Civico, Bassano del Grappa
[*repr. in colour on p. 112*]

This was originally part of a series of paintings which decorated the Arcipretale (the priest's residence) of one of the seven municipalities of the Altopiano of Asiago. The decoration included a fresco cycle which is now lost. Verci (1775) placed the *St. Giustina* in Jacopo's third period when he was deeply influenced by Parmigianino; it can be dated shortly before 1560 (Magagnato 1952, Shearman 1976, Pallucchini 1982). Ballarin (1969) has pointed out the connection between this altarpiece and the drawing of *Diana in the Clouds* (D1) and observed that they are both deeply influenced by Veronese's work at Palazzo Trevisan, Murano, after *c.* 1557. The silvery colours of this small altarpiece suggest a return to Jacopo's early mannerist style; however, the mint greens, silvery whites, and translucent violets are treated more subtly than in his earlier style, with shimmering mother-of-pearl effects on the saint's bodice, and vivid highlights on St. Roch's tunic. This magical, delicate use of light is developed even more in *Jacob's Journey* (Cat. 8).

L.M.

PROVENANCE
Arcipretale, Asiago; Parish Church, Enego, on deposit at the Museo Civico, Bassano de Grappa

REFERENCES
Ballarin 1973, pp. 105, 108; Magagnato 1952, pp. 42–43; Pallucchini 1977–78, p. 48; Pallucchini 1982², p. 34; Sgarbi 1980, p. 59; Smirnova 1976; Verci 1775, p. 105

8

Jacob's Journey

127.8 × 183.5 cm
Her Majesty The Queen
[*repr. in colour on p. 114*]

On 8 September 1649 this painting was valued at £50 and attributed to 'Bassano in his first manner'. It has always been greatly admired, as the many copies indicate (Shearman 1983). In 1853 it was attributed to Leandro, but recently it has not only been ascribed to Jacopo but also considered to be one of the few 'pastoral' scenes which is entirely autograph. The dating of this important work is contentious: Arslan and Rearick dated it 1565, Bettini suggested 1568, Zampetti and Ballarin place it in the late 1550s, and Pallucchini believed it to be after 1562, probably closer to 1565.

The subject of the painting is uncertain. Zampetti has suggested that it represents Abraham's Journey rather than that of Jacob, but Shearman and the present writer prefer Jacob as the protagonist. A date of *c.* 1560 seems appropriate; it can be compared to the *Adoration of the Magi* (Vienna), and the *Parable of the Good Sower* (Thyssen Collection, Lugano). This is one of Jacopo's earliest pastoral scenes; stylistically there are still mannerist elements, and, as in the *St. Giustina* (Cat. 7), he demonstrates his extraordinary control of rich colours and complex light effects.

PROVENANCE
Charles I; 1650 sold to Willet; recovered at the Restoration; Charles II inventory

EXHIBITIONS
1831 British Institution, no. 100 (as Leandro Bassano); 1868 Leeds, no. 68 (as Jacopo); London 1946, no. 275; London 1960, no. 11

REFERENCES
Pallucchini 1982², pl. 28; Shearman 1983, no. 19, pp. 25–27 with full bibliography

9

Adoration of the Shepherds with St. Victor and St. Corona (The Nativity of S. Giuseppe)

240 × 151 cm
Museo Civico, Bassano del Grappa (no. 17)

This is one of only two paintings by Jacopo which is documented; it was placed on the high altar of S. Giuseppe, Bassano, on 18 December 1568 (Gerola). The other documented work is the *St. John the Baptist* (Museo Civico, Bassano) which was installed in the Chapel of S. Giovanni, S. Francesco, Bassano on 28 December 1558 (Sartori). In the ten years between these two fundamental works Jacopo's mannerist traits fell away; the evolution of his style between the late 1550s and the mid-1560s can be traced in this exhibition from the *St. Giustina Enthroned* (Cat. 7), and *Jacob's Journey* (Cat. 8). Another *Adoration* (Palazzo Barberini, Rome), probably immediately precedes the present work; however, in the earlier picture the format is horizontal, whereas here it is based on two interlocking

9

[149]

triangles, and the figures are situated around a horizontal circular plane (Verci). So the composition, which appears to be natural and spontaneous, is in fact subtly contrived.

The painting was frequently copied from the eighteenth century onwards; it has always been considered one of Bassano's best pastoral scenes.

L.M.

PROVENANCE
S. Giuseppe, Bassano; 1859 when the church was closed
transferred to the Museum

EXHIBITIONS
Venice 1945, no. 60; Venice 1946, no. 257; Lausanne 1947, no. 60;
Bassano 1952, no. 25; Venice 1957, no. 55

REFERENCES
Gerola 1906, p. 110; Magagnato and Passamani 1978, p. 27;
Pallucchini 1982², pl. 33; Sartori 1958, p. 20; Verci 1775, p. 53

10
St. Martin and the Beggar with St. Anthony Abbot

165 × 105 cm
Museo Civico, Bassano del Grappa (no. 25)
[*repr. in colour on p. 113*]

This small altarpiece is one of the few works of the 1570s and 1580s from Jacopo's studio which is entirely autograph: this can be deduced from the contract of 1580 for a painting of *St. Apollonia and St. Agatha* in which Jacopo was requested to paint the altarpiece in a similar

way to that of 'St. Martin in the church of St. Catherine'. From this it would seem that the altarpiece was still considered a novelty, at least among the works Jacopo painted for the town of Bassano.

In this work there is no hint of Jacopo's 'genre' – or pastoral style – which he adopted in the very last years of his life. Like the slightly earlier *Baptism of St. Lucilla* (Museo Civico, Bassano) of 1574–75, Bassano here exaggerated the contrasts of light and shade of the twilight scene; but the reflection of the light on the drapery and the armour is closer to the harsh colouring of the *Nativity* formerly in the church of S. Giuseppe, Bassano (Cat. 9) than to the nocturnal scenes of Jacopo's last years, when he fell under the influence of Titian's late style.

L.M.

PROVENANCE
Church of S. Caterina, Bassano; 1785 donated to the museum by
Commendatore Giuseppe Remondini (Advisory Acts;
Archivio Comunale, Bassano)

EXHIBITIONS
Venice 1945, no. 113; Bassano 1952, no. 28; Venice 1957, no. 82

REFERENCES
Ballarin 1966, p. 114; Magagnato and Passamani 1978, pp. 28–29;
Pallucchini 1982², pl. 32

11
Susanna and the Elders

86 × 127 cm
Inscribed lower right: *J. B. f. 1585*
Musée des Beaux-Arts, Nîmes

11

The date 1585 emerged on the painting when it was cleaned in 1965–66 (Shearman, Rosenberg, Ballarin). Previously it had been read as 1572 (Pallucchini 1944), 1576 or 1579 (Berenson 1957), or 1571 (Bettini 1933 and Rosenberg 1965). This new date is particularly revealing because previously a letter of Jacopo's son, Francesco, had been taken to imply that after 1581 Jacopo gave up painting. So the *Susanna and the Elders* was painted about five years after *St. Martin and the Beggar* (Cat. 10), and can be related stylistically to the *Diana and Acteon* (Chicago), as Pallucchini and Zampetti noted. From the mid-1580s Jacopo painted a series of dream-like nocturnal scenes influenced by Titian's late work which in some respects anticipate the luminous quality of Rembrandt's paintings (Rosenberg 1965); they possess an extraordinarily inventive freedom in their approach to their subject matter.

It is unlikely that the painting has been cut on the left, as has been suggested. The composition is based on crossed diagonals, with the old man's face in the centre, and the wall of Susanna's bath dividing the painting in half.

L.M.

PROVENANCE
Gower Collection (no. 580); 1875 Musée des Beaux-Arts, Nîmes

EXHIBITIONS
Amsterdam 1953, no. 2; Bordeaux 1953, no. 56; Venice 1957, no. 59; Paris 1965–66, no. 33 (Rosenberg, with full bibliography); Nice 1979, no. 2 (with full bibliography)

REFERENCES
Ballarin 1965, p. 239; Berenson 1957, I, p. 19; Bettini 1933, pp. 92–93; Pallucchini 1944, II, p. 38; Pallucchini 1959, p. 266; Pallucchini 1982², pl. 37; Shearman 1966, p. 67; Zampetti 1964, I, pp. 231–32

Bonifazio de' Pitati

Verona 1487–Venice 1553

Bonifazio de' Pitati was born in Verona in 1487 and lived there until 1505. He is first recorded in Venice in 1528, but he must have been there earlier, between 1515 and 1528, absorbing the influence of Giorgione, Titian and Palma Vecchio, and producing his first works. Some of Bonifazio's paintings dating from before 1530, such as *St. Mark Enthroned* (Corbolone), the *Sacra Conversazione* (Palazzo Pitti, Florence, no. 84), *The Rest on the Flight into Egypt* (Pinacoteca Ambrosiana, Milan) and the *Sacra Conversazione* (San Francisco, ex-Farrer Coll.), show his ability to rework characteristically Venetian compositions and colouring while also making use of what he had learnt from the contemporary paintings of Savoldo and Lotto.

In 1529 Bonifazio began work on the decoration of the Palazzo dei Camerlenghi at the Rialto, which took him and his collaborators about 20 years to complete; in 1530 he became a member of the *Fraglia* (the Venetian painters' guild). His mature style combined elements derived from both Raphael and Pordenone; his distinctive approach to narrative and his robust colour sense can be seen in *The Judgement of Solomon* of 1533, and in the *Massacre of the Innocents* (both Accademia, Venice). Around 1540 a more meditative tone enters his paintings. It is most evident in

Dives and Lazarus (Accademia): in this work the landscape setting (close to those of Tintoretto) is combined with a restless decorative tension, which is even more evident in the later *Finding of Moses* (Brera, Milan) and which has affinities with the style of Paris Bordone.

Apart from his biblical subjects (in which narrative is combined with moralising overtones) and numerous *sacre conversazioni*, Bonifazio is famous for his many small panel paintings of historical, mythological and allegorical subjects that were made to decorate *cassoni* (marriage chests), headboards and other furniture. In these he displayed a seemingly inexhaustible imagination and miniaturistic attention to detail, and continued to develop his figurative ideas, in the last decade of his life adopting mannerist traits evident in elongated figures that show the influence of Schiavone and Parmigianino.

Bonifazio died on 19 October 1553 (parish records of S. Ermagora) after a long illness; he was married but childless. The scarcity of documentation and of signed and dated paintings, together with the enormous output of Bonifazio's studio, have made an evaluation of his work very difficult.

S.S.

REFERENCES
Faggin 1963, pp. 79–95; Ludwig 1901, pp. 61–78, 180–200; Ludwig 1902, pp. 36–66; Westphal 1931, with full bibliography

12
The Rest on the Flight into Egypt

109.9 × 170.8 cm
Art Gallery of South Australia, Adelaide

First recorded in 1854, when it was in the collection of Sir Archibald Campbell and attributed to Palma Vecchio, this painting was recognised by Westphal as a late work of Bonifazio's, stylistically close to the Bridgewater painting that she dated c. 1545–47. Faggin suggested it was by Domenico Biondo, a painter in Bonifazio's circle.

The relaxed and balanced composition is a fine example of Bonifazio's interpretation of the theme of the *sacra conversazione*, derived from Palma Vecchio's paintings of serene encounters between elegantly attired saints in the open air. Bonifazio emphasises the narrative content of the picture; the main story (*St. Matthew*, II, 14, with the addition of the Miracle of the Palm from Voragine's *Golden Legend*) is set in the foreground. In the background, on the left a young friar witnesses the scene, whilst on the right the landscape abruptly falls away into the distance. The unusually marked plasticity of the figures – especially of the playing children, who appear almost to break out of the painting – and the intense emotional bond between the Virgin and Child seem to reflect the influence of the work of Raphael, presumably known to Bonifazio through prints. The soft handling of colour which is characteristic of Bonifazio, the inclusion of details, such as the shepherd with a donkey, painted with a few rapid brush strokes, and the treatment of the spotted and stippled foliage make it likely that this beautiful picture dates from the late 1520s.

S.S.

PROVENANCE
Sir Archibald Campbell; 1947 Colnaghi's sale; Art Gallery of South
Australia, Morgan Thomas Bequest

REFERENCES
Berenson 1957, I, p. 41; Faggin 1963, p. 95; Gaston 1977, pp. 36–41;
Waagen 1854, III, p. 293; Westphal 1931, pp. 74, 76, 152

13

La Madonna dei Sartori
(Virgin of the Tailors)

130 × 149 cm
Inscribed bottom right centre on the second step of the throne:
BONIF. / ACIO.F.;
dated on the first step of the throne in a scroll
M.D.XXXIII. / ADI.VIIII. / .NOVĒB.
Gallerie dell'Accademia, Venice (no. 1305)

The painting comes from the main altar in the Scuola dei
Sartori (the Confraternity of Tailors), which was situated
near the Campo dei Gesuiti; Boschini saw it there and said
it was by Bonifazio. The identification of Sant'Omobono,
patron saint of tailors, and the large pair of scissors resting
on the step provide further confirmation of its provenance.

Since this is Bonifazio's only work that is signed and
dated (1533), it is fundamental to any evaluation of his art.
Although the composition follows the traditional altarpiece
format (Bellini's influence is especially evident in the
colonnaded niche in the background and in the overall
symmetry of the composition), Bonifazio was also
influenced by Palma Vecchio and, in terms of colour, by
Titian. The painting reflects his concern with the

organisation of the figures in space, and his use of more
monumental forms shows his precocious awareness of the
mannerist style, even though the influence of Parmigianino
and the Tuscans had barely reached Venice by this date. A
narrative element is introduced through the inclusion of the
beggar to whom Sant'Omobono gives alms. The pauper's
pose is highly complex, yet he is observed objectively, a
comparatively new development in Venetian art
(Pallucchini 1950). This mature work illustrates Bonifazio's
taste for rich and brilliant colours, and shows the
development of his style towards a more flexible and lively
narrative, which nevertheless always avoids dramatic
excesses.

S.S.

PROVENANCE
Scuola dei Sartori; during the Napoleonic wars confiscated and chosen for
the Royal Palace; 1945 transferred to the Gallerie dell'Accademia

REFERENCES
Freedberg 1971, p. 231; Moschini Marconi 1962, pp. 31–32, with full
bibliography; Perissa 1981, p. 109; Sgarbi 1981, p. 55

14

Lot and his Daughters

125.5 × 167.5 cm
Chrysler Museum, Norfolk, Virginia, Gift of Walter P. Chrysler, Jr.
(in memory of Della Viola Forker Chrysler)
[repr. in colour on p. 68]

The painting, ascribed almost unanimously to Bonifazio –
although it has also been attributed to Cariani (Troche

12

13

1934) – was probably painted around 1545. It combines several characteristically Venetian painting conventions. The approach to narrative is derived from Carpaccio: the entire story (*Genesis*, IX, 1–36), including the burning of Sodom and Gomorrah and the flight of Lot and his family, is used as a background to the central scene of the drunkenness of Lot and the incestuous designs of his daughters. The broad landscape setting derives from Giorgione, while the figures recall Palma Vecchio, and the daughter sitting in the foreground with a slightly apprehensive expression is close to Lotto. The subtle, decorative poses of the daughters have much in common with Paris Bordone's mannerist style, especially in the elaborate drapery, on which the light plays and is reflected in changing hues.

There is a strong moralistic and didactic flavour to the work, which is also an allegory of the conflict between *voluptas* and *virtus*. The women play a dual role in the painting: one holds a mirror, symbol of prudence but also of wisdom, and, in a wider sense, of intellectual knowledge, virtues diametrically opposed to the sterility of worldly pleasure. The theme of *voluptas* versus *virtus* is further enforced by the two playful putti: one wears a mask, an allusion to the dichotomy between truth and falsehood.

S.S.

PROVENANCE
Sir Coutts Lindsey, London; Arthur Ruck, Albemarle Agency Ltd., London; Giuseppe Bellesi, Florence; 1954 Julius Weitzner, New York; Walter P. Chrysler Junior, New York; presented by Walter P. Chrysler Junior to the Chrysler Museum

EXHIBITIONS
Portland 1956, no. 24; New York 1963, no. 7; Norfolk 1967–68, no. 8

REFERENCES
Berenson 1957, I, p. 43; Suida Manning 1956, p. 26; Suida 1954, pp. 159–60; Troche 1934, pp. 117, 123; Willard 1956, p. 47

Paris Bordone

Treviso 1500–Venice 1571

Born in Treviso, Bordone was in Venice by 1518 and probably trained there with Titian, whose influence was fundamental to Bordone's early style (see Cat. 15 and Cat. 17). During the 1530s he developed a more complex and articulated manner, as, for example, in the *Portrait of Nicolaus Korbler* dated 1532 (Liechtenstein Gemäldegalerie, Vaduz). *The Presentation of the Ring to the Doge* for the Scuola Grande di San Marco (Accademia, Venice), commissioned in 1533–35, shows Bordone's preference for architectural settings, derived probably from Serlio's architectural designs. Vasari stated that Bordone went to the court of François I at Fontainebleau in 1538, but this has been questioned by some later writers. His overtly erotic, mannerist style of the 1540s may have been inspired by this possible contact with the School of Fontainebleau.

Around 1540 Bordone was working in Augsburg for the Fugger family, and soon afterwards he was probably in Milan (Vasari), painting altarpieces (S. Maria sopra Celso) as well as a series of cabinet paintings of mythological and allegorical subjects. He continued to produce these throughout the 1540s and 1550s (*Mars and Venus in Vulcan's Net*, Dahlem Museum, Berlin; *Bathsheba*,

Cologne); evidently they appealed greatly to Bordone's wealthy clientele and contributed to his success. Outstanding examples of these cabinet paintings are two paintings of Bathsheba (Kunsthalle, Hamburg; Walters Art Gallery, Baltimore), the allegories in Leningrad (Cat. 21), Vienna, and Cat. 20. Several of Bordone's religious works, such as *The Baptism of Christ* (Cat. 23), and *The Annunciation* (Musée des Beaux-Arts, Caen) are also overtly mannerist in style.

Bordone was also a most successful portrait painter; the intimacy of his later portraits appears to reflect the influence of Lotto. After working in Treviso in 1557–58, he possibly went to France in 1559 to work at the court of François II (Orlandi; Federici); there he painted *The Battle of the Gladiators* (Kunsthistorisches Museum, Vienna) and the *Tibertine Sibyl* (ex-Mazarin Coll., now in the Hermitage, Leningrad (Formicheva 1971). He appears to have been influenced by the Second School of Fontainebleau, but the problem of the exact date of Bordone's visit to France, 1538 or 1559 (or whether, perhaps, he made two journeys there), is still unresolved. By 1565 Bordone is again recorded in Venice where, according to Vasari, he was one of the most famous artists of his day. He died in Venice in 1571.

G.M.C.

REFERENCES

Federici 1803, II, pp. 41–42; Formicheva 1971, p. 152; Orlandi 1753, pp. 410ff; Vasari (ed. Milanesi), VII, pp 461–66

15

16

15
The Mystic Marriage of St. Catherine

149 × 260 cm
Doria Collection, Genoa

Ridolfi (1648) described a painting that would seem to match this one (although he failed to mention St. Joseph) in Leopoldo de'Medici's collection in Florence. There is another version in the Museum of Fine Arts, Boston.

This is one of Bordone's most successful early works and, given its similarities with the altarpiece in the Galleria Tadini, Lovere, it can be dated *c.* 1525. The bosky landscape, sumptuous colouring and vivid presentation of the main figures, who are linked together both emotionally and by gesture, are obviously derived from Titian's *sacre conversazioni* of 1510–20, and it seems to confirm Vasari's statement that Bordone trained in Titian's workshop. Certain motifs and figures are particularly Titianesque – the gesture of the infant Christ towards St. Joseph for instance, that of the Virgin towards St. John, and, above all, the magnificent St. Catherine, who recalls female figures in Titian's early works. But the clearly defined quality of the drawing is typical of Bordone and very different from Titian's style, which would explain why Ridolfi likened the painting in the Medici Collection to Palma Vecchio. Bonicatti (1964), however, detected an affinity between Bordone's work and that of Savoldo of the same date.

G. M. C.

PROVENANCE
By 1846 Doria Collection

EXHIBITIONS
Genoa 1946, no. 54 (Morassi)

REFERENCES
Berenson 1957, I, p. 46; Bonicatti 1964[1], p. 250; Canova 1964, pp. 7, 101, with bibliography; Morassi 1946, p. 54; Pallucchini 1946, p. 148; Ridolfi 1648, I, p. 233; Suida 1906, p. 143

16
St. Jerome in a Landscape

70.2 × 87 cm
Philadelphia Museum of Art, John G. Johnson Collection
(no. 206)

The splendid landscape that forms the most important part of the composition is closely related to the one in *The Mystic Marriage of St. Catherine* (Cat. 15), which would suggest that the painting dates from the early 1520s. The gentle undulation of the open green hills, the warm light bathing the scene, the lush treatment of the leafy branches and the inclusion of a shepherd and his sheep grazing in the pasture, while a dragon appears to scare the solitary passer-by, are all motifs deriving from Titian. In particular, St. Jerome's contorted, twisting movement recalls the 'difficult' poses used by Titian, particularly in the allegories made for Alfonso d'Este between 1518 and 1525. In the view of the present writer, the treatment of the figures in this painting is particularly close to that of the *Apollo and Ariadne* (Seminario Patriarcale, Venice), which is also attributed to Bordone (Canova 1964; Bonicatti 1964).

G. M. C.

PROVENANCE
By 1851 in the Leuchtenberg Collection, Munich; 1896 Leuchtenberg
Collection, St. Petersburg; by 1905 Johnson Collection

REFERENCES
Berenson 1957, I, p. 48; Bonicatti 1964¹; pp. 249ff; Canova 1964,
pp. 14–15, 98, with bibliography; Fredericksen and Zeri 1972, p. 32;
Harck 1896, p. 430, no. 34; Philadelphia 1941, p. 13; Reinach 1918, p. 569;
Sweeny 1966, p. 114

17

Two Lovers

95 × 80 cm
Pinacoteca di Brera, Milan (no. 105)
[*repr. in colour on p. 70*]

This is the earliest example of one of the erotic themes that later became a standard part of Bordone's repertoire; such paintings were evidently intended for rich Venetian connoisseurs. It can be dated *c.* 1525, and shows the influence of Titian on Bordone during the early part of his career.

In fact, while the woman's pose recalls that of Titian's *Young Woman at the Mirror* (Musée du Louvre, Paris) of 1515, the composition seems to be derived from the fascinating *Love Scene* (Casa Buonarotti, Florence), thought by some scholars to have been inspired by a lost work by Titian of about 1515 (Pallucchini 1952–53; Berenson, 1957; Valcanover 1960, 1969) and by others to be autograph (Suida 1933; Ballarin 1970–71). The affinities between the *Two Lovers* and the Florentine painting, of which other versions exist, are so striking that the latter has even been attributed to Bordone. However, if the painting is examined closely, the differences in style become evident: the picture in Florence is marked by rich, painterly brushwork and vibrant colour whereas Bordone's treatment of the scene is far more stylised and dull. The lyricism and sensuality of the master's prototype has been replaced by a banal scene of seduction, which is expressed by the ambiguous offer of a gift to the woman.

G.M.C.

PROVENANCE
1890 acquired from the Pinetti family, Milan, by the Pinacoteca di Brera

EXHIBITIONS
London 1930, no. 175; Venice 1955, no. 134

REFERENCES
Berenson 1932, p. 431; Canova 1964, p. 107, with full bibliography;
Ricci 1907, pp. 228, 287

18

Knight in Armour

91.4 × 76.2 cm
Inscribed with fragments of verse on the tournament favour;
later inscription on the back: CAROLUS V. PAR BORDONE F.
North Carolina Museum of Art, Raleigh, purchased with funds
from the State of North Carolina (no. 52.9.148)

This is clearly not a portrait of the Emperor Charles v, as the inscription on the back suggests; it probably shows an eminent member of one of the Italian courts during the reign of Charles v when the Spanish dominated Italy. He is ostentatiously dressed in full armour. Perhaps the inscriptions on the tournament favour (a ribbon worn by a knight to indicate his loyalty to a lady) could shed some light on his identity; it is extremely unusual to find such a favour illustrated in a portrait, although some actual favours have survived in the Imperial Armoury in Vienna (information from A. V. B. Norman).

The monumentality and balance of the composition, together with the chromatic harmony of the painting, emphasises its similarities to Titian's court portraits during the early phases of his mature style (Pignatti 1979). This would suggest that the work may be a little earlier than 1540–45, the date originally proposed by the present writer.

G.M.C.

PROVENANCE
Archduke of Tuscany (?); 1838 Sir Abraham Hume (as Pordenone); 1851
Viscount Alford; by 1854 Earl Brownlow, Llandoff, Weybridge-on-Thames; Arthur L. Nicholson, Llandoff, Weybridge-on-Thames; 18 May
1933 Anderson Galleries, New York sale (lot 22)

EXHIBITIONS
Portland 1956, Los Angeles 1979–80, no. 24

REFERENCES
Bailo and Biscaro 1900, p. 131, no. 41; Berenson 1897, p. 87; Berenson
1957, I, p. 48; Canova 1964, p. 110; Fredericksen and Zeri 1972, p. 32;
Pignatti 1979, p. 82, no. 24; Valentiner 1956¹, p. 77, no. 178; Valentiner
1956², p. 40; Venturi 1925–34, IX, iii, p. 1032

18

19

19
Portrait of a Man Holding a Letter

110 × 84 cm
Galleria di Palazzo Rosso, Genoa (no. 98)

This painting probably shows a young lover who is
separated from his lady; he holds a letter which the lady,
seen in the background under a loggia, is either receiving
or sending by messenger.

As the painting is documented in the Brignole Collection
from the eighteenth century, it is possible to identify it with
the 'Portrait of Ottaviano Grimaldi of Genoa', said by
Vasari (1568) to have been sent from Venice to Genoa
together with a portrait of a 'Wanton Lady'. Vasari's
statement has also been used to suggest that this painting
is the pendant of the *Portrait of a Young Woman* in the
National Gallery, London (Bailo and Biscaro 1900; Canova
1964); almost identical in size and with similar architecture
in the background as well as a melancholic young man; it
was said traditionally to have come from Genoa. Gould
doubts the identification, pointing out that Ridolfi (1648),
who was perhaps only paraphrasing Vasari's text, talked of
a nude Venus. He believes that the pendant of the National
Gallery *Portrait of a Young Woman* is probably the *Portrait
of a Cavalier* (Uffizi, Florence), which was obviously made
to commemorate a betrothal and which also has a similar
architectural background, with a lady and a little cupid
hovering above.

The three portraits seem to date from the 1540s, both

stylistically and in the costume of the sitters (Gould 1959;
Canova 1964). Their theme is that of problematic love,
which was very popular in portraiture at that date and often
illustrated by Paris Bordone: he portrays the themes of
falling in love, betrothal, estrangement and conjugal love,
as in the *Family Group* (Cat. 22). His partiality for subjects
dealing with intimate sentiments, and the inclusion of
symbolic motifs and still-life details such as the ring,
brooches and the small wreath of carnations – a symbol of
love – in the *Portrait of a Cavalier* in Florence, might
suggest that Bordone was developing a sensitivity akin to
that of Lotto.

G.M.C.

PROVENANCE
From at least 1756 Brignole Sale Collection, Palazzo Rosso; 1874 property
of the Comune of Genoa

REFERENCES
Alizieri 1875, p. 165; Bailo and Biscaro 1900, pp. 52–53, 82, 124, no. 27;
Berenson 1894, p. 91; Berenson 1932, p. 130; Berenson 1957, I, p. 46;
Burckhardt 1907, p. 982; Canova 1964, p. 100; Gould 1959, p. 23; Grosso
1909, p. 70; Grosso 1932, p. 38; Jacobsen 1896, pp. 92, 94; Jacobsen 1911,
p. 198; Suida 1906, p. 143; Venturi 1925–34, IX, iii, pp. 1010, 1032

20
Perseus Armed by Mercury and Minerva

100.3 × 153.7 cm
Signed indistinctly: *Paradis Bordono*
Birmingham Museum of Art, Birmingham, Alabama, (no. 61117;
Samuel H. Kress Collection K 1631)
[*repr. in colour on p. 69*]

This is one of a group of mythological works in Bordone's
mature style. The subject is probably Perseus before his
battle with the Medusa. He is being armed by Mercury and
Minerva: Mercury offers him the helmet of Hades, which
made him invisible, and Minerva gives him her burnished
shield, which acted as a mirror in which Medusa's head was
reflected so that Perseus did not have to look at her directly.
With these divine gifts the warrior's success was assured.
The painting also illustrates the invincibility of strength and
valour if these qualities are accompanied by shrewdness and
wisdom. In both style and subject matter it is close to
Bordone's *Mars and Venus in Vulcan's Net*, painted for
Carlo da Rho in Milan (Dahlem Museum, Berlin), which,
like the present work, combines a menacing atmosphere and
bellicose subject with a delicately balanced composition.

It has been suggested that Bordone worked in Milan in
the early 1540s, and in this case the painting, which has been
dated to either 1535–45 (Longhi, Suida, Seymour) or the
1550s (Canova, Shapley), could quite reasonably be dated
between 1545 and 1555. The treatment of the figures is
similar to that in *The Baptism of Christ* (Cat. 23), although
there they are set in a wider spatial composition.

This painting is closest to *Thetis and Vulcan* (Kress Coll.,
University of Missouri, Columbia), to *Venus, Flora, Cupid
and Mars* (Cat. 21) and *Mars Disarmed by Cupid*
(Kunsthistorisches Museum, Vienna). The last two
illustrate anti-martial themes in a light-hearted manner.

G.M.C.

PROVENANCE
Edward Solly, London; sold 8 May 1847 Christie's, London (no. 17),
bought by Captain Barrett; by 1868 Cook Collection, Richmond; Contini-
Bonacossi Collection; 1949 Samuel H. Kress Collection, New York;
by 1959 Birmingham Museum of Art

EXHIBITIONS
Leeds 1868, no. 51; Tulsa 1900; Washington 1961–62, no. 10

REFERENCES
Canova 1961, p. 88; Canova 1964, p. 75, with bibliography; Fredericksen
and Zeri 1972, p. 32; Seymour 1961, pp. 121–26, 207–08; Shapley 1973,
pp. 36–37; Suida 1959, p. 8

21
Venus, Flora, Cupid and Mars

108 × 129 cm
Signed on the lower left: PARIS BORDON F
The State Hermitage Museum, Leningrad (no. 163)

This is one of a series of paintings of mythological or
allegorical scenes produced by Bordone in the 1540s and
1550s. The subject appears to be a celebration of the
triumph of the pacifying virtues of love over the brutal force
of arms. Flora is the goddess of virginal love and Venus the
goddess of fertile love; Cupid hovers overhead crowning
Venus and showering Flora with flowers, and the two
goddesses serenely cross hands, exchanging flowers. Mars,
in contrast, is almost hidden in the background.

A precedent for this work, both stylistically and
iconographically, is the *Bathsheba* painted in Milan
(Wallraf-Richartz Museum, Cologne), which is
characterised by the same rather self-conscious erudition
and a mannerist type of female beauty – sensual, yet cold
and artificial. The painting can probably be dated 1545–55
if the hypothesis that Bordone was in Milan in the early
1540s is correct. The theme of Venus being crowned by
Cupid was used by Lotto in the *Toilet of Venus* of *c.* 1540
(private coll., Bergamo) and it is likely that Bordone
imitated that motif, which he also used in *Daphnis and
Chloe* (National Gallery, London).

G.M.C.

21

PROVENANCE
Between 1774 and 1783 entered the Hermitage

EXHIBITIONS
Göteborg 1968, p. 5; Milan 1976, no. 4; Moscow 1982, no. 8

REFERENCES
Berenson 1957, I, p. 460; Canova 1961, p. 88; Vsvevolozhskaja 1982,
p. 264, no. 62–63; Hermitage catalogue 1976, pp. 78–79

22
Family Group

119.4 × 150 cm
Signed: O. PARIDIS BORDON
The Trustees of the Chatsworth Settlement, Chatsworth,
Derbyshire (no. 52)
[*repr. in colour on p. 71*]

This group family portrait, imbued with a sense of
affectionate intimacy, shows the profound influence of
Lotto on Bordone. The two artists must have met in Venice
between 1545 and 1549; in October 1548 Bordone valued
three portraits painted by Lotto for Francesco Cavalli, a
dyer who lived in S. Stae, Venice (Zampetti 1969). It is
possible that they met even earlier since Lotto was in Venice
between 1540 and 1542 and in Treviso (where Bordone had
many interests) between 1542 and 1545. Furthermore, both
artists were friends and business associates of Francesco
Beccaruzzi, the painter from Conegliano, during the 1540s.

This painting, which has been restored for the exhibition,
is close in style to Lotto's *Family Group* (National Gallery,
London), which can plausibly be identified as a portrait of
Giovanni dalla Volta with his wife and children, painted in
Venice in 1546–47 (Gould 1975). However, the muted
colours of Bordone's painting, reminiscent of Tintoretto,
suggest that it dates from the late 1540s. It is likely that
Lotto's influence also stimulated the more intimate quality
of some of Bordone's mature portraits, such as the *Portrait
of a Knight* (Uffizi, Florence) and the *Portrait of a Man
Holding a Letter* (Cat. 19). When the present painting was
in the collection of Jan Six it was listed as 'Paris Bordone,
his wife and daughter', probably because the man holds an
apple, the attribute of Paris.

G.M.C.

PROVENANCE
23 Oct 1651 sold by the Commonwealth to Houghton and others; 6 April
1702 Jan Six sale, Amsterdam;
Sir Gregory Page (as Titian); 2 June 1813 John Willet;
Willet Sale (as Titian);
G. J. Cholmondeley Sale; bought by the 6th Duke of Devonshire

EXHIBITIONS
British Institution 1821, no. 124 (as Titian); London 1950–51, no. 234 (as
The Family of the Painter ?)

REFERENCES
Berenson 1957, I, p. 45; Canova 1964, p. 76; Gould 1975, pp. 134–35;
Zampetti 1969, p. 60

23

23
The Baptism of Christ

175 × 202 cm
Pinacoteca di Brera, Milan (no. 107)

This painting, which is conceived in an unusually grandiose manner, is important for our understanding of the development of Bordone's style during the late 1540s. The striking monumentality and the exaggerated twisting of the two nude figures in the foreground are overtly mannerist, and it is difficult to imagine that they could have been painted without the example of Titian's *St. John the Baptist* (Cat. 119) and his paintings of 1541–44, now in the Salute. Consequently it seems reasonable to suggest a date of 1544 for the present picture. The complexity of the influences on Bordone is demonstrated in the Baptist's group of followers: thus, for example, the figure of the man putting on his trousers is loosely derived from one of the bathers in Michelangelo's cartoon of the *Battle of Cascina*, which Bordone probably knew from a print. The marvellous landscape, although still in the Venetian tradition, is imbued with a rather pale light that makes it unusually attractive.

A 'Salvatore al Giordano' by Bordone was recorded by Ridolfi (1648) in the house of Bernardo Giunti in Venice. An earlier example of this subject, with the figure of an angel instead of the bathers, is in the National Gallery, Washington (Shapley 1979, p. 77), and there also exists a preparatory drawing for the figure of Christ, or another similar figure, in the Uffizi, Florence (Tietze and Tietze Conrat 1944, no. 396).

G.M.C.

PROVENANCE
1650 bequeathed by Cardinal Cesare Monti to the Archbishop's Residence in Milan; from 1811 Pinacoteca di Brera

REFERENCES
Berenson 1957, I, p. 47; Canova 1964, p. 106, with bibliography; Latuada 1737, I, p. 78

Domenico Brusasorci
Verona c. 1516–Verona 1567

Domenico Riccio, called Brusasorci, was the son of Andrea Riccio, a painter whose family came from Chiavenna. He is recorded in the census of Sant' Andrea in Verona and he was probably born around 1516. He seems to have been influenced less by his Lombard origins than by the mannerist style which reached Verona through the influence of both the Roman and Venetian Schools (Magagnato 1968). He was the foremost Veronese artist of the generation before that of Paolo Veronese. His earliest works probably date from 1545–50 (eg. *The Virgin with SS Sebastian, Roch, Monica, Augustine and two Donors*, Sant' Euphemia; the frescoes in the Muletta Chapel, S. Maria in Organo; a fresco cycle for the Casa di Fiorio della Sera, now in the Museo degli Affreschi, Verona). Together with Paolo Veronese, Paolo Farinati and Battista del Moro, Brusasorci was commissioned by Cardinal Ercole Gonzaga to paint one of a group of altarpieces for the Chapel of the Sacrament in Mantua Cathedral; his subject was *St. Margaret* (see also Cat. 134). He frescoed a *Fall of the Giants* (1555) in Palladio's Palazzo Iseppo da Porto, Vicenza, which shows his evident admiration for Giulio Romano's fresco of the same subject in Palazzo del Te, Mantua. There were also many paintings by Titian in Mantua at this time which would explain his influence on the *Portrait of Pase Guarienti* (Cat. 24).

From 1558 he worked with Battista Zelotti and the stucco-worker Bartolomeo Ridolfi on the decoration of the Sala dello Zodiaco in the Palazzo Chiericati, Vicenza. Once again in Verona, he painted the *Portrait of Bonuccio Moscardo* (c. 1561; Museo di Castelvecchio, Verona), and the vast cycle of 108 portraits of bishops interspersed with landscapes in the Salone of the Bishop's Residence at Verona, dated 1566. The *Martyrdom of St. Barbara* (S. Barbara, Mantua) dates from 1564.

Domenico died on 30 March 1567; his sons Giambattista and Felice were both artists, and the latter became the foremost Veronese painter in the early seventeenth century. Domenico was also gifted musically and was one of the founder members of the Accademia Filarmonica of Verona.

L.M.

REFERENCES
Magagnato 1968, p. 180

24
Portrait of Pase Guarienti

204 × 116 cm
Inscribed on the pedestal on the left: PASIUS GUARIENTUS / GUGLIELMI UTRIUSQ / IURIS DOCTORIS / FILIUS CENTU / CATAPHRACTORU / EQUITUM / GUBERNATOR / MDLVI
Museo di Castelvecchio, Verona (no. 267)

Pase Guarienti is portrayed in splendid armour as a commander of heavy cavalry. The armour was probably made in Brescia around 1550 (Boccia 1967, and forthcoming catalogue of armour at Castelvecchio, Verona), and the

24

slightly later *Giovanni da Castaldo* (linked with Titian's stay in Augsburg), and finally the *Portrait of Prince Philip of Spain*, usually dated 1551 (Prado, Madrid). In all these portraits the brushwork carefully follows the form of the armour, animates it, and by means of flashing highlights gives it depth. Brusasorci followed this technique and thereby created a monumental portrait, one of the most unusual of the sixteenth century in Verona. Two paintings (both now in the Museo di Castelvecchio, Verona), the *Portrait of a Bishop*, and the *Madonna and Child with SS Ursula and Catherine*, have been attributed to Brusasorci; they probably date from immediately after his visit to Mantua in 1552.

L.M.

PROVENANCE
Guarienti Collection

REFERENCES
Ballarin 1971, p. 110; Boccia 1967, p. 332; Marinelli 1980; Pignatti 1976, I, p. 219, Cat. A375; Verona 1980, p. 309 (Brognara Salazzari); p. 208, Cat. VIII, 7, note 1 (Marinelli)

Giovanni Cariani

Fuipiano val Imagna (?) *c.* 1485 – Venice after 1547

Cariani was probably born in the region of Bergamo, but he was trained in Venice (where he is recorded from 1509), first in Giovanni Bellini's workshop and then in the circle of Giorgione. The rediscovery of his lost altarpiece for Lonno, dated 1514 (Pallucchini 1982), and research by Ballarin (1968) have contributed to our understanding of his youthful style. Cariani was indebted to Bellini for his compositional schemes, but he also showed a precocious predilection for the themes of Giorgione that is evident in such works as *The Concert* (Warsaw) and *The Lutenist* (Cat. 25), and his use of warm colours, conception of landscape and delicate tonality show that he fully assimilated the early styles of both Titian and Sebastiano del Piombo.

A visit to Bergamo seems to have been of great importance for the development of Cariani's style: in 1517 he went there to paint the *Madonna and Saints* for S. Gottardo. This altarpiece, like other contemporary works such as *Judith* (ex-Neeld Coll.), was still conceived in the Venetian style, its bright colours and spatial conception reminiscent of Palma Vecchio; but soon afterwards other influences appear – those of Lotto, who was in Bergamo from 1512, and the Brescian painter Romanino, who was working in Cremona.

Cariani's finest qualities are revealed in a series of altarpieces for Crema that include *The Resurrection of Christ with St. Jerome and St. John the Baptist* (Cat. 28), *The Adoration of the Shepherds* (ex-Sackville Coll.), and a splendid group of portraits: *Courtesans and Gentlemen* (Cat. 27), *Giovanni Benedetto Caravaggi* (Cat. 30), *Francesco Albani* (National Gallery, London), *Giovan Antonio Caravaggi* (Cat. 29), *La Schiavona* (Accademia Carrara, Bergamo) and *The Musician* (Huntingdon Museum), all of which were painted within the space of a few years. To his Venetian sense of colour

painting is invaluable as a record of the armour of a mid-sixteenth-century Venetian knight. The sitter belonged to the S. Quirico branch of the noble Guarienti family which at that date was engaged in building a new residence at Bra'dei Filippini (Brognara Salazzari 1980). Pase, the son of Guglielmo Guarienti, was born in 1500 and died some time after 1563. He was a bachelor and left his fortune to his nephews. The portrait was in the Guarienti family collection until it was donated to the museum.

The problem of its attribution is still unresolved. Traditionally the Guarienti family attributed it to Veronese, a view accepted by Avena, von Hadeln, Fiocco and Berenson; but Tea (1920) suggested that it was by Caroto, and Coletti proposed Domenico Brusasorci; this was accepted by Arslan, the present writer, Ballarin and Pignatti. Recently Marinelli (1980) has suggested it is the work of Battista del Moro.

The precedent for the work must be three famous portraits of men in armour by Titian: the equestrian *Portrait of Charles* V (Prado, Madrid) dated 1548, the

Cariani now added a Lombard feeling for realism and light, and some of his works from this period – for example, *The Concert* (Heinemann Coll., Lugano) – foreshadow Caravaggio. Some frescoes by him have recently been discovered in the Citadel of Bergamo.

In 1523 Cariani returned to Venice. *The Madonna of the Doves* (Bergamo Cathedral), *The Visitation* (Kunsthistorisches Museum, Vienna), and *La Madonna Cucitrice* (Cat. 31) probably date from this period. In Bergamo again between 1528 and 1530, he painted the *Locatello Triptych* and the *Invention of the Cross* (Accademia Carrara, Bergamo). These cheerful, rustic scenes are very close to Palma Vecchio in style. The last years of his life are obscure; he lived in Venice and painted very little, and there is a visible decline in the quality of his works. His religious paintings of these years, such as the *Sacra Conversazione* (National Gallery, London), are less remarkable than his portraits (Oslo, Bergamo, Strasbourg), which are tinged with an air of melancholy and sometimes show a knowledge of German art (eg. the *Woman of Nuremberg*, dated 1536; Kunsthistorisches Museum, Vienna). This is also evident in a few small, lively, religious subjects, such as *The Way to Calvary* (Ambrosiana, Milan).

F.R.

REFERENCES
Ballarin 1968¹, pp. 242–44; Pallucchini 1982¹

25
The Lutenist

71 × 65 cm
Musée des Beaux-Arts, Strasbourg (no. 236)
[*repr. in colour on p. 58*]

Now unanimously attributed to Cariani, *The Lutenist* is central to an understanding of both the relationship between Cariani and Giorgione and the intellectual climate of Venice in the sixteenth century. Cariani's choice of a musical theme, which reappears in *The Violinist* (Dijon) recently re-ascribed to him and *The Concert* (Heinemann Coll., Lugano) presupposes an allegorical and intellectualised conception of music in the spirit of the works of Giorgione (Bonicatti 1964). Music is a dream-like interlude in reality, a moment of reverie reserved only for a small circle of intellectuals.

However, although in its theme and, possibly, its ideological intent, the painting is Giorgionesque, in its technique it is much closer to Titian: the coarse treatment of the face, constructed in flat planes with particular attention paid to the individual features, is utterly different from Giorgione's portraits. Cariani probably painted *The Lutenist* in Venice (where it originally came from); it shows the first manifestations of a more naturalistic style, which finally blossomed in the *Courtesans and Gentlemen* (Cat. 27). Here he begins to move away from the Giorgionesque expression of noble melancholy (still evident in the Warsaw *Concert*) towards the visualisation of the sensation of immediate enjoyment created by the sound of music (as in *The Concert*, Heinemann Coll., Lugano), or

the sensation of drowsiness induced by a concert (*Musicians*, Accademia Carrara, Bergamo). Cariani abandons the subtle intellectual approach he had absorbed from his masters and instead heightens the emotive content of the image by directly expressing the sentiment of the lutenist, which is echoed in the stormy landscape opening out behind the decorative leafy screen.

F.R.

PROVENANCE
Private Collection, Venice; *c.* 1890 acquired by Bode for the Musée des Beaux-Arts

EXHIBITIONS
Paris 1935, no. 85; Venice 1955, no. 98; Paris 1965–66, no. 62

REFERENCES
Baldass 1929, p. 105; Bonicatti 1964¹, p. 88; Gallina 1954, p. 64; Haug 1926, p. 13; Haug 1938, p. 143; Mariacher 1975, pp. 64, 293; Pallucchini and Rossi 1983, forthcoming publication, with full bibliography; Troche 1934, p. 103; L. Venturi 1913, p. 235; A. Venturi 1925–34, IX, iii, p. 460; Zampetti 1955, p. 206

26
Allegory of a Venetian Victory

120 × 204 cm
Mario Lanfranchi, Rome
[*repr. in colour on p. 60*]

This painting, first noticed by Bassi-Rathgeb (1952, p. 39), has recently been researched by Sgarbi, who has confirmed its attribution to Cariani and studied its iconography. The theme of the painting is the contrast between Venice at peace, seen on the left of the picture, and the scene of war depicted on the right. In the centre is the figure of Fortune, or Chance, who will guarantee the peace of the city; she is accompanied by two figures symbolising nature and music.

The theme is typically Giorgionesque, but it has been carefully adapted to function as an allegorical celebration of a military victory. Sgarbi has suggested that this took place between the Peace of Cambrai (1512) and that of Noyon (1516), and has dated the painting between 1512 and 1515. However, the rounded, opulent figures and the lush landscape, both derived from Palma Vecchio, are often found in slightly later works by Cariani, such as the *S. Gottardo Altarpiece* dated 1518 (Brera, Milan), and it is more likely that he painted this allegory just before his visit to Bergamo. In certain respects the artist remained faithful to his training: the composition of the painting and the inclusion of a nude female were inspired by Titian's *Sacred and Profane Love*. However, the work also reveals knowledge of Savoldo's earliest Venetian paintings, such as *The Temptation of St. Anthony* (private coll., New York): the setting is very similar and both works share the detailed treatment of the leafy branches that is reminiscent of Flemish art, the vivid rendering of storm clouds and smoke over the burning city, the cold colouring and billowing forms of the drapery. Cariani's numerous contacts with the Brescian painter would therefore seem to have started early in his career; this work seems to anticipate the profound effect the Lombard school was to have on his later style.

F.R.

PROVENANCE
Castello Dentico di Frasso, Conversano (Bari); Manzolin, Rome;
1978 Mario Lanfranchi, Rome

REFERENCES
Mariacher 1975, p. 291, no. 46; Pallucchini and Rossi 1983, forthcoming
publication, with full bibliography; Sgarbi 1982, pp. 6–8

EXHIBITIONS
Bergamo 1799; Bergamo 1870; Bergamo 1875, no. 37; Lausanne 1947,
no. 43; Zurich 1948, no. 735

REFERENCES
Baldass 1929, p. 93; Crowe and Cavalcaselle 1871, II, p. 549;
Formicheva 1979, p. 163; Gallina 1954, pp. 65ff; Morelli 1891, p. 35;
Pallucchini 1966, p. 90; Pallucchini and Rossi 1983, forthcoming
publication with full bibliography; Safarik 1972, p. 527; Tassi 1973, I,
p. 38; Troche 1934, pp. 99ff; Venturi 1925–34, IX, iii, p. 465

27

Courtesans and Gentlemen (Seven Members of the Albani Family)

117 × 117 cm
Signed and dated: IŌ. CARIANVS. BGOMEVS. M.D.XVIIII
Private Collection, Bergamo
[repr. in colour on p. 61]

The traditional title for this painting is untenable, as the seven figures cannot be identified with any sixteenth-century members of the Albani family; nor do they resemble any portraits of the various members of the family. In fact, the painting probably represents the meeting of a group of gentlemen and some courtesans with their procuress. This is evident from the distinctive grouping of the figures, the showy, immodest dress of the women and certain symbolic attributes in the painting that have hitherto been overlooked: the mirror representing vanity, the squirrel symbolising parsimony, greed and lust, and the procuress's feather fan, which is a typical attribute of a courtesan.

The recognition of this painting as a profane representation of mercenary love emphasises the parallel between it and The Concert in the Heinemann Collection, Lugano (Pallucchini and Rossi 1983). Both works were inspired by the artist's desire to give a naturalistic treatment to a theme derived from Giorgione: in The Concert the theme is music, here it is a certain type of love. Cariani, however, concentrated not on the exalted sentiment behind such a theme, but rather on the physical presence of the figures, an approach that was typical of the Lombard school. To create this impression he used a composition based on diagonally intersecting blocks, which emphasise the spatial depth of the painting without sacrificing the expressive quality of the areas of colour in the background. The painting also displays a sensitivity to naturalistic elements, which was probably the result of Cariani's knowledge of the work of Lotto and Savoldo.

In many ways this painting contains some of the most innovative and remarkable pictorial solutions created by a painter of the new Venetian-Lombard school; this is true of details like the woman dressed in white who appears to lean out beyond the frame into 'real' space, the men who are lined up, one behind the other, in a psychological and emotional pecking order, and finally, the mirror, which isolates and reflects a minute fragment of reality.

F.R.

PROVENANCE
Albani family, Bergamo; Roncalli di Montorio Collection

28

The Resurrection of Christ with St. Jerome and St. John the Baptist

208 × 170 cm
Signed on the lower left: IOANES/CAR/IAN/VS/P.;
inscribed on the scroll along the bottom of the painting:
OCTAVIANVS VIC. EQVES. MDXX
Pinacoteca di Brera, Milan

This painting, signed and dated 1520, was commissioned by Ottaviano Vimercati, a member of the City Council of Crema and one of the chief figures in the defence of the city against the French. Vimercati died in 1520 and the painting was made for the altar of the family chapel in S. Pietro, Crema.

Although this Resurrection is one of Cariani's most important works, it has generally been considered to be a provincial, unrefined variation of a Venetian devotional type of painting, popularised by Bellini and already outmoded, with the addition of some Lombard realistic elements. It was formerly thought to be earlier than the Palmesque S. Gottardo Altarpiece (Accademia Carrara, Bergamo). But since the discovery that the S. Gottardo Altarpiece was commissioned in 1517 and delivered in January 1519, the order of the two paintings has been reversed, so that the Resurrection can now be seen as a work in which Cariani revived and elaborated a Bellinesque theme. The same is true of other contemporary works, such as the Baglioni Madonna (Accademia Carrara, Bergamo) and the Virgin with St. Peter (Galleria Borghese, Rome).

Although the 'apsidal' distribution of the saints is a rather archaic device, here it animates the composition, the monumentality of which is emphasised by the solid figures, whose forms are defined by light and by the open setting. The landscape is no longer a mere backdrop, but an integral and expressive part of the design that is reminiscent of Moretto, conceived in a blaze of flashing lights, evocative and mysterious, similar to works by Romanino and Altobello Meloni. The use of 'natural' light, as in The Concert (Heinemann Coll., Lugano) or Courtesans and Gentlemen (Cat. 27), shows Cariani to be a remarkably realistic painter: in the portraits of the patrons, for example, he invests the figures with a psychological awareness that is close to Lotto, but envelops them in a brilliant light, which enhances the plasticity of their forms and creates an equilibrium in the composition.

F.R.

28

PROVENANCE
S. Pietro, Crema; Palazzo Vimercati, Crema; Conte Antonio Marazzi,
Milan; Conte Paolo Gerli, Villa Gaeta, Milan; 1957 presented to the
Pinacoteca di Brera

EXHIBITIONS
London 1930, no. 354; Zurich 1948, no. 733

REFERENCES
Baldass 1929, pp. 93 ff; Gallina 1954, pp. 66 ff; Grohn 1968, p. 311;
Mariacher 1975, p. 290, no. 40; Morelli 1886, p. 154; Pallucchini and Rossi
1983, forthcoming publication, with full bibliography; Safarik 1972,
p. 527; Troche 1934, p. 106, no. 26; Venturi 1925–34, IX, iii, p. 448

29

Portrait of Giovan Antonio Caravaggi

93.5 × 93.7 cm
Inscribed on the left on a white scroll: ĪO.CARIANVS. /DE BVSIS BGO
/ MESIS P.X.T; on the letter: .ĪO.ANT.I / CAR. (CAN)
(the last letters are indistinct)
National Gallery of Canada, Ottawa (no. 3568)
[*repr. in colour in p. 62; detail on p. 63*]

On the left of the painting there is a coat of arms, a black eagle on a gold ground above a horse-drawn chariot on a silver ground, which is identical to that in the *Portrait of Giovanni Benedetto Caravaggi* (Cat. 30). Mariacher (1975) believed that this was a portrait of the same sitter some 20 years later, but the man shown here – whose hair is blond, not white – is in fact Giovan Antonio Caravaggio, the elder brother of Giovanni Benedetto, who also lived in Crema and was probably a magistrate. The painting would seem to be closely connected with the other Caravaggi portrait of *c.* 1522, and it is unlikely that it dates from 1525–30 as Jarvis suggested (1957).

The two portraits almost seem to be a pair, given the symmetry of the poses, the continuity of the landscape backgrounds and the inclusion of the symbols of each brother's profession – the large book for the philosopher and doctor, Giovanni Benedetto, and the writing paraphernalia, parchment and seals for the magistrate Giovan Antonio. However, the slight difference in scale between the two portraits suggests that they are not exactly contemporary: the present painting seems a little earlier. The sharpness of the brushwork in the face and landscape recalls the portrait of Ottaviano Vimercati in *The Resurrection of Christ* (Cat. 28), while the Palmesque motif of the laurel bush was first used by Cariani in an earlier *Judith* (private coll., Milan). The coarse, angular qualities of the figure and the intense concentration of the sitter's face and gestures, qualities that are not present in the milder, more introverted Giovanni Benedetto, were emphasised by the artist.

F.R.

PROVENANCE
Marchesa Serra, Sampierdarena (Genoa); 1905 Adolph Thiem, San Remo; Knoedler & Co. New York; 1928 National Gallery of Canada

EXHIBITIONS
New York 1926, no. 1; London 1930, no. 382; Montreal 1949, no. 30; Los Angeles 1979, no. 15

REFERENCES
Gallina 1954, p. 40; Grohn 1968, p. 310; Hubbard 1956, p. 146; Jarvis 1957, p. 11; Mariacher 1975, p. 50; Pallucchini and Rossi 1983, forthcoming publication, with full bibliography; Troche 1934, p. 110, no. 45; Venturi 1925–34, IX, iii, p. 466

30

Portrait of Giovanni Benedetto Caravaggi

82 × 82 cm
Inscribed on the right:
IO.BENED. CARRAVAG.S/PHILOS.S ET MEDICVS/AC
STUDY PATAVINI/RECTOR ET LECTOR;
a little lower:
JOANIS/CARIANI/.P
Pinacoteca dell'Accademia Carrara, Bergamo (no. 675/74)

The coat of arms above the inscription on the right of the painting (a black eagle on a gold ground and a horse-drawn chariot on a silver ground) has been identified as that of Giovanni Benedetto Caravaggi from Crema. He was born in 1485, graduated in medicine and philosophy in Padua in 1507 and died some time after 1555 (Pallucchini and Rossi 1983). This portrait was probably painted in Bergamo *c.* 1522, just before Cariani returned to Venice.

30

31

Of all Cariani's works, this painting has most often been associated with Lotto, who was also in Bergamo at this period. Certainly, both the sitter's expression and the inclusion of realistic details such as the open book are similar to Lotto's portraits. But the compact, geometric spatial construction is close to that of earlier works by Cariani, such as *Courtesans and Gentlemen* (Cat. 27). The doctor holds out his arm as if he were measuring space and the drapery is arranged in sharp, dihedral folds. The treatment of the face and clothing is delicate and the phosphorescent lighting of the grand, yet simple, landscape was obviously influenced by Titian, as were the recently rediscovered frescoes in the Citadel of Bergamo, dated 1521. This portrait should not, therefore, be considered a mere imitation of Lotto's style, but rather an attempt by Cariani to introduce into his fundamentally Venetian and Titianesque language a new conception of a portrait, more direct in presentation yet more subtle psychologically, like those he had seen in Lombardy.

F.R.

PROVENANCE
Crema; before 1833 Conte Lochis; 1859 Gallerie dell'Accademia Carrara

REFERENCES
Baldass 1929, p. 105; Crowe and Cavalcaselle 1871, II, p. 551; Gallina 1954, pp. 72ff; Mariacher 1975, p. 286, no. 14; Pallucchini and Rossi 1983, forthcoming publication, with full bibliography; Phillips 1913, pp. 158ff; Troche 1934, p. 116; Venturi 1925–34, IX, iii, p. 445

31

La Madonna Cucitrice (The Seamstress Madonna)

168 × 164 cm
Galleria Nazionale di Palazzo Barberini, Rome (no. 830)

The ostensible subject of this painting is the Christ Child and Infant St. John playing while the Madonna and St. Elizabeth look on, but it is probable that a symbolic meaning was also intended by the artist. The Madonna sits in front of a rose bush, beneath which are two quails, and St. Elizabeth leans against a lime tree before which two rabbits play. Both roses and quails were traditional symbols of virginity, while the lime tree and rabbits symbolised fertility; this can be read as an allusion to the two aspects of motherhood, the human and the divine, and can be interpreted as an unusual representation of the Immaculate Conception.

The painting is generally considered to date from the end of Cariani's career, probably from his second Venetian period (1524–1528), and until recently had been associated with the *Virgin with St. Anthony Abbot* (Alte Pinakothek, Munich). But the Munich painting has rightly been re-ascribed to Lambert Sustris (Pallucchini 1982), which makes it easier to define the distinctive characteristics of *La Madonna Cucitrice*. It is unusual in that it represents a fusion between a Venetian and a Lombard style. On the one hand, the typology of the Virgin and the plump infants, the bushes with their broad, pointed leaves and the extensive landscape show the influence of Palma Vecchio, which is also evident in works such as *The Madonna of the Doves* (Bergamo Cathderal) and *The Visitation* (Kunsthistorisches Museum, Vienna), both of which date from the mid-1520s. On the other hand, details such as the rabbits playing in the shade, the marvellous still life of the untidy sewing basket – no wonder Venturi thought of Moretto – together with the domestic, pastoral air of the scene, are closer to the unaffected realism that had influenced Cariani during his time in Bergamo.

F.R.

PROVENANCE
Torlonia family; 1892 presented to the Galleria Nazionale

EXHIBITIONS
London 1930, no. 337

REFERENCES
Baldass 1929, p. 100; Di Carpegna 1964, p. 24; Gallina 1954, p. 85; Mariacher 1975, p. 293; Pallucchini 1944, p. 38; Pallucchini 1982¹, p. 338ff; Pallucchini and Rossi 1983, forthcoming publication, with full bibliography; Troche 1934, p. 112; Venturi 1925–34, IX, iii, p. 446

Vittore Carpaccio

Venice 1460/65 – Venice 1525/26

The artist's name in Venetian dialect was Scarpazza; a considerable number of his works bear the Latin signature *Carpathius*: hence the Italian form Carpaccio. Except for a possible early visit to Rome, Carpaccio seems to have spent his entire career in his native city. His training is uncertain, but obvious formative influences include those of Gentile and Giovanni Bellini, and Antonello da Messina. Carpaccio is best known for his cycles of lively and festive narrative paintings, four of which survive almost complete (cf. Cat. D11, D12 and D13); he also made individual contributions to cycles involving other artists, including the most prestigious of all, that for the Sala del Maggior Consiglio in the Doge's Palace, destroyed by fire in 1577.

In accordance with Venetian tradition, his narrative paintings often include views of identifiable places (Cat. 32) and figures identifiable as portraits (Cat. D13). To judge from contemporary literary evidence, Carpaccio also enjoyed considerable fame as a portrait painter, mainly in the normal bust-length format. Although much of his best work was done before *c.* 1505, he remained capable of producing works of great charm and originality, and it is only his work after *c.* 1520 that shows an uninterrupted decline in quality. As a specialist in cyclical narratives rather than devotional altarpieces, Carpaccio was one of the first Venetian painters to use canvas more regularly and naturally than panel. His priming was often thin, barely hiding the roughness of the weave, and his handling of paint is normally sketchy and vivacious, anticipating sixteenth-century developments in its bold touches of pure colour.

P.H.

REFERENCES
Lauts 1962, with full bibliography up to 1960; Muraro 1966

32
The Lion of St. Mark

130 × 368 cm
Inscribed on the left:
Victor Carpathius/A.D./M.D. XVI; on the book:
PAX/TIBI/MAR/CE E/VAN/GELI/STA/MEVS
Doge's Palace, Venice
[*repr. in colour on pp. 50–51; detail on p. 49*]

As the traditional emblem of the Evangelist St. Mark, the winged lion also symbolised the Venetian State, which since the ninth century had acknowledged the saint as its special protector. According to pious legend, the Evangelist's body was stolen from Moslem Alexandria by Venetian sailors and brought to Venice in 829, and divine sanction was given to its final resting place in the words quoted on the book: '*Pax tibi Marce Evangelista meus*' ('Peace unto you, Mark my Evangelist'). The possession of so sacred a relic was felt to endow the city with a quasi-apostolic status, while the winged lion aptly symbolised both the formidable power and the pacific intentions of the Most Serene Republic.

Carpaccio followed a well-established iconographical pattern in his representation of the lion, but characteristic of the artist himself was the inclusion in the left background of an accurate view of the Piazzetta di San Marco, as seen from the island of S. Giorgio Maggiore. To the left of the lion's head is the Doge's Palace, the seat of the Venetian government; next to it is the basilica of San Marco, the state church and shrine of the Evangelist; then comes the recently completed clock-tower, with its own winged lion in the upper tier; and to the far left is the campanile of San Marco, with the winged lion again visible on the attic storey. The original pyramidal spire at the very top had been destroyed by lightning in 1489, and its replacement, including the gilded angel set on its apex, was completed only a year or two before 1516, the date of Carpaccio's picture. Moored alongside the Piazzetta is a state barge; the ships emerging from the Arsenal on the far right allude to Venetian dominion of the seas. The painting was apparently intended to adorn the wall of a government office; the five escutcheons at the lower edge (belonging respectively to the Balbi or Zorzi, Dandolo or Gritti, Manolesso, Bragadin and Foscarini families) probably refer to the five officers who commissioned it.

P.H.

PROVENANCE
Palazzo dei Camerlenghi, Rialto

EXHIBITIONS
Venice 1963, no. 60

REFERENCES
Lauts 1962, pp. 40, 249; Molmenti and Ludwig 1907, p. 215; Muraro 1966, pp. CCX–CCXII

Vincenzo Catena

Venice (?) *c.* 1478/89 – Venice 1531

There is no record of either the place or date of Catena's birth; it is probable that he was born around 1480 in Venice, where he worked throughout his life. He is first mentioned in the inscription on the back of Giorgione's *Laura* in Vienna, dated 1 June 1506, where Giorgione is described as his '*Cholega*'. This association is surprising, since his earlier signed paintings show him to have been a rather naive follower of Giovanni Bellini, with no understanding of Giorgionesque innovations. He appears from his various wills to have been a man of some means and also to have had friends in Venetian humanist circles, including Antonio di Marsilio and Giovanni Battista Egnazio, and it may be that they encouraged Catena to support Giorgione before the latter artist had achieved official or widespread recognition. The connection with Giorgione is confirmed by the revelation, made evident by x-rays, that underneath Giorgione's *Self-portrait* (Brunswick) there is a Virgin and Child of a type which frequently recurs in Catena's work, and which was apparently his own invention.

Some years after Giorgione's death, Catena began to develop a style which was a sort of simplified revival of Giorgione's manner, and by 1520 he created a minor masterpiece in this vein in his *Martyrdom of St. Christina* in the church of S. Maria Mater Domini in Venice. He repeated this success at the same time (or a little later) in *The Adoration of the Shepherds* (Metropolitan Museum, New York). In portraiture he developed from a purely Bellinesque type of bust portrait to such works as the *Trissino* (Cat. 33), which recall, even if at a long remove, such works of Giorgione as the male portraits in the Dahlem Museum, Berlin and in Budapest (Cat. 37).

G.R.

REFERENCES
Robertson 1954

33
Portrait of Giangiorgio Trissino

72.5 × 63.5 cm
Musée du Louvre, Paris (no. 1252B)

The picture is neither signed nor documented and was formerly ascribed to Giovanni Bellini, but the attribution to Catena, first advanced by von Hadeln, is entirely convincing. Giangiorgio Trissino of Vicenza was a well-known scholar and author of the first classical Italian tragedy, the *Sofonisba*, and an epic poem, *Italia Liberata dai Goti*. He was the first patron of Andrea Palladio. The portrait came from the Trissino family as a likeness of Giangiorgio by Giovanni Bellini: the attribution is no longer tenable, but the identification is probably correct. On stylistic grounds one would judge that it dates from about 1527, when Trissino would have been 47.

G.R.

33

PROVENANCE
Trissino family, Vicenza; by 1912 collection of Baron Schlicting; 1915 bequeathed by Baron Schlicting to the Musée du Louvre

REFERENCES
Robertson 1954, pp. 12, 35, 67; von Hadeln in Thieme-Becker, VI, 1912, p. 182

Giorgio da Castelfranco, called

Giorgione

Castelfranco 1478(?) – Venice 1510

Giorgione has been acknowledged ever since his lifetime as a great artist and as a figure of capital importance in the evolution of Venetian – even of Western – painting. Yet there are few Renaissance artists of whom we have less certain factual knowledge.

We know from documents that he painted a canvas for the audience chamber of the Council of Ten in the Doge's Palace in 1507–08, and frescoes on the main façade of the Fondaco dei Tedeschi in 1508. We know from correspondence between Isabella d'Este and Taddeo Albano, her representative in Venice, that he died in October 1510 of the plague. And both sources call him Zorzo (or Zorzi) da Castelfranco, thus indicating his place of origin.

Vasari, writing 40 years later in 1550 – and then again, more fully, in 1568 – supplied further information, the accuracy of which is less certain. In the two editions of his *Lives of the Artists*, Vasari tells us that the artist was born in 1477 (1550 edition) or 1478 (1568 edition) and died in his 34th year; that he was called, from the greatness of both his person and his spirit, Giorgione (Big George); that he was of humble family but, because he played the lute and sang 'so divinely', was accepted into the society of noble persons; that he studied initially 'with the Bellini' but later, having seen works by Leonardo, painted differently and in a way that was new not only for Venice but for all Italy; that he 'willingly taught with love what he knew'; and that he left, to lessen the loss implicit in his death, 'two excellent disciples' (*due eccellenti suoi creati*), Sebastiano del Piombo and Titian, the second of whom not only equalled but surpassed him. Vasari also enumerated paintings by Giorgione, but demonstrated thereby that the attributional confusions and disputes surrounding the master's *œuvre* were already well under way by the mid-sixteenth century.

An earlier and more reliable source for attributions to Giorgione are the notes of Marcantonio Michiel (dated between 1525 and 1543) on works of art in Venetian collections. Michiel, who was one of the 'noble persons' spoken of by Vasari and who could therefore have known Giorgione personally, mentioned 16 paintings by Giorgione, and his ascriptions are usually taken to have a quasi-documentary status. Of those 16 paintings, however, only three can quite certainly be identified with works now extant: the *Three Philosophers* in Vienna (finished, says Michiel, by Sebastiano), the *Sleeping Venus* in Dresden (finished, says Michiel, by Titian) and the *Tempesta* in Venice (fig. 5).

In addition, the *Laura* in Vienna is identified as Giorgione's by a circumstantial sixteenth-century inscription (and by its resemblances to the previous three works), the *Terris Portrait* in San Diego by a more fragmentary sixteenth-century inscription (and, again, by its style), and the *Madonna Enthroned* in Castelfranco (fig. 13) by its location in the cathedral of Giorgione's home town and, again, by its style. A semi-effaced remnant of Giorgione's Fondaco frescoes – approximately half of a female nude – is preserved in the Accademia in Venice.

These seven works constitute a nucleus of paintings which can be considered to be almost certainly by Giorgione. To them a nearly unanimous consensus of scholars has added three more: the *Portrait of a Young Man* (or *Giustiniani Portrait*) in the Dahlem Museum, Berlin; the *Judith* in Leningrad; and – though only relatively recently – the *Col Tempo* (Accademia, Venice). And perhaps the *Self-portrait* in Brunswick can now be thought of as approaching that status.

The many other paintings that have been ascribed to Giorgione, including some exceedingly famous and beautiful works, must be considered subject to dispute – a state of affairs to which the catalogue entries below testify. What is not disputed, and never has been, is the importance of this immensely gifted artist's contribution to a distinctively Venetian way of seeing and painting. The impact of that contribution is plain in the work of his immediate followers and seems by no means to be exhausted even now.

F.L.R.

REFERENCES

Morelli 1800 (Michiel); Pignatti 1971, with full bibliography; Richter 1937, with full bibliography; Vasari 1550 (Giorgione); Vasari 1568 (Giorgione, Titian, Sebastiano Viniziano, Bordone).

Circle of Giorgione
Attributed to Titian

34
Virgin and Child with St. Anthony and St. Roch

92 × 133 cm
Museo del Prado, Madrid
[*repr. in colour on p. 54*]

This picture was first recorded in the sacristy of the Escorial in 1657, with an attribution, very possibly due to Velázquez, to 'Bordonon'. This has been variously interpreted as signifying Pordenone, Bordone, and Giorgione ('Zorzon'; Baldass 1964). In 1871, Cavalcaselle attributed it to Francesco Vecellio, in 1893 Morelli to Giorgione. Schmidt suggested the young Titian in 1908, a view now accepted by most writers. Some, however, including Richter, Berenson, Baldass and Heinz, believe it is a work by Giorgione. Wilde (1974) declined to decide between the two.

All writers, to whomever they ascribe this small *sacra conversazione*, agree on its great beauty and high quality, and most writers date it around 1510. Wilde (1933) noted the very close similarity of motif between this painting and Domenico Mancini's signed and dated *Virgin Enthroned with an Angel* of 1511, a similarity which encompasses both the general configuration of the Virgin and details of her elaborately worked sleeve and veil. (The Mancini painting elaborates them still further.) This is generally taken to preclude a date after 1511 for the present painting; in fact, it need not do so were one to postulate either that the *Virgin and Child* depended on the much larger Mancini altarpiece rather than vice versa, or that Mancini was the author of both paintings – a theory which, rather surprisingly, no one has yet propounded. The quality of Mancini's Lendinara altarpiece is such as not absolutely to exclude either possibility, and the possibility that Mancini was author of both paintings especially should not be dismissed without consideration, for the present painting is not altogether typical for either Titian or Giorgione, and there are elements of paint handling and (compare Mancini's angel and the Christ Child in the present painting) of type, as well as of motif, that link the two paintings.

In the end, though, the present writer must side with the majority view that this is a work by the young Titian, acknowledging the often cited points of contact with such others works as the *Gipsy Madonna* (Kunsthistorisches Museum, Vienna) and the *Noli Me Tangere* (National Gallery, London), and acknowledging also that, although the exquisiteness of this small-scale picture is not in Titian's usual vein, it is not beyond his range, as occasional later paintings like the *Madonna of the Rabbit* (Louvre) demonstrate.

The connections with Giorgione's accepted work are principally with the Castelfranco altarpiece (fig. 13). These are visible in such general features as the generous spacing of the figures and also in more specific reminiscences: the Franciscan saint seems a free variation on his Castelfranco counterpart and the Virgin still closer to hers – in the arrangement of her mantle and veil, the placement of her knees, the relationship between her figure and the brocaded backcloth, her pointed oval face, and her downcast eyes and pensive, introspective look. Even the Virgin, however, differs from the Castelfranco Virgin in the delicate linearity of her features and the discreet sumptousness of her dimpled fabrics – both features that can be duplicated in early works by Titian, but not in Giorgione's certain works. And the *farouche* St. Roch seems, in his active and purposeful character, positively anti-Giorgionesque; in his pose, almost a premonition of such figures as the famous *St. Sebastian* from Titian's Brescia altarpiece of 1522. (The pose seems also, perhaps, related to that of the Baptist in Sebastiano's S. Giovanni Crisostomo altarpiece of 1510.)

This picture seems, then, to be a work by Titian in Giorgione's mode, in which his individual temperament and style are already in evidence. As such, it need not, in the view of this writer, be dated quite as late as the currently conventional *c*. 1510. The painting is unfinished, lacking the final surface layer of pigment in the Virgin's mantle and the lower part of the landscape, as well as in portions of the St. Anthony.

F.L.R.

PROVENANCE
c. 1650 presented by the Duke of Medina de las Torres to Philip IV of Spain; 1657 the Escorial

REFERENCES
Baldass 1964, p. 156; Crowe and Cavalcaselle 1871, II, p. 292; Freedberg 1975, p. 146; Gronau 1908, p. 425; Justi 1908, p. 140; Longhi 1927³, p. 218; Morelli 1893, p. 216; Pallucchini 1978, p. 27; Pignatti 1971, p. 126; Richter 1937, p. 228; Schmidt 1908, p. 115; L. Venturi 1913, p. 134; Wethey 1969, p. 174; Wilde 1933, p. 99; Wilde 1974, p. 118; Zampetti 1968, p. 94

Circle of Giorgione
Attributed to Titian

35

Christ and the Adulteress

139.2 × 181.7 cm
Glasgow Art Gallery and Museum
[*repr. in colour on p. 52*]

The first certain reference to this painting occurs in the 1689 inventory of the collection of Queen Christina of Sweden, in which it was attributed to Giorgione. Several earlier seventeenth-century references to paintings of this subject by Giorgione must refer to more than one work, and hence cannot certainly be associated with this one.

A copy often thought to be by Cariani (fig. 23) shows that the picture has been cut down on the right, excising most of a standing male figure, and also, less substantially, at the bottom; the standing figure's head and shoulders survive as a fragment (Cat. 36).

In 1945, Tietze-Conrat proposed – on the basis of the uncanonical outdoor setting and other unprecedented features – a re-identification of this subject as *Daniel and Susanna*, thereby connecting the painting with a contract between Alvise de Sesti and Giorgione, first mentioned by Urbani de Gheltof in 1869 and published by Molmenti in 1878, in which Giorgione undertook to furnish Alvise with four paintings of deeds of Daniel. The contract has disappeared and many scholars suspect it of being a fabrication by Urbani (others such exist); Hendy (1954) argued the contrary view, and, indeed, the action, personnel

fig. 23 Follower of Titian *Christ and the Adulteress* (Pinacoteca dell'Accademia Carrara, Bergamo)

and setting do fit the apocryphal subject rather better than they do the New Testament one. Most scholars have nonetheless preferred the traditional identification, chiefly because restoration established that the male protagonist wore a cruciform halo (Ruhemann 1955). Pallucchini is an exception, as was Wilde, and the present writer would also wonder whether Daniel might be portrayed here as a prefiguration of Christ.

Few Giorgionesque paintings have been more hotly disputed as regards their authorship. The old ascription to Giorgione was questioned in 1871 by Cavalcaselle, who inclined toward Cariani; Lionello Venturi (1913) preferred Sebastiano del Piombo and Adolfo Venturi (1928) Romanino; in 1927 Longhi proposed Titian and he has been followed in this by perhaps the majority of scholars, both then and later. Zampetti (1955, 1958) thought of Mancini, perhaps copying a lost Titian; Richter (1937) hypothesised a collaboration between Giorgione and Titian, and Wilde (1974) suggested a Giorgione design largely executed by his studio. The difficulty of the attributional problem can be judged not only from the multiplicity of proposals, but also from the fact that several great scholars have changed their minds on the question: Lionello Venturi, for example, who proposed Sebastiano in 1913 and Giorgione in 1954, or Berenson, who in the course of a long career gave the painting successively to Cariani, Sebastiano, Titian and Giorgione.

Since 1955 the question seems to have narrowed down, for most scholars, to 'Titian, or Giorgione?' The majority answer 'Titian'; they include Gamba, Pallucchini, Valcanover, Baldass and Heinz, Morassi, Pignatti and Freedberg. A distinguished minority hold to Giorgione; they include Robertson, in part Wilde (see above), Wethey and Anderson.

Both parties, interestingly, date the painting within a year or two of 1510. For Giorgione's proponents, the work's principal *point d'appui* would be his frescoes of 1508 on the Fondaco dei Tedeschi, as known fragmentarily in engravings and as described by the sources; for Titian's partisans, the essential connection would be with *his* Fondaco frescoes (also 1508, and similarly known) and, even more, with his frescoes in the Scuola del Santo in Padua, dated 1511.

For the present writer the dilemma can be summed up as follows: the painting fits quite well with what the sources tell us of the character of Giorgione's Fondaco frescoes, and with Vasari's description (in his life of Titian) of the more advanced style that Giorgione arrived at 'circa 1507'. There are also tempting possibilities of documentary connections – with the four canvases of the deeds of Daniel mentioned above (if, indeed, the document in question is not spurious) or, alternatively, as Wilde suggested, with the canvas commissioned by the Council of Ten for their new audience hall in 1508. (His suggestion was presumably based on the size of the painting and the suitability of its subject – in either identification – to a site associated with the administration of justice. Hirst recently argued against this connection.)

On the other hand, it is less easy to associate this work with any of Giorgione's *surviving* paintings; indeed, the only ones of comparable size, the *Three Philosophers* and the Castelfranco altarpiece (fig. 13), are very different in

character. And to this writer's eye there are many telling likenesses – in types, colour, composition, landscape elements, boldly gleaming surfaces – with Titian's Padua frescoes, and also with other works associated with Titian's early career, for example the *Gipsy Madonna* and *Jacopo Pesaro Presented to St. Peter* (Cat. 113).

For this writer, then, the likeliest solution would be that the picture is one of those of which Vasari speaks in the passage following his description of Giorgione's style cited above: '[Titian] adopted [Giorgione's] manner, imitating . . . his works so well that his paintings were sometimes confused with, and believed works by, Giorgione.'

Three supplementary observations might finally be made. First, the date of the painting would seem to be less close to the Padua frescoes of 1511 than many writers have placed it; here the painter still appears in some ways a kind of 'primitive' genius. Second, Richter's view of the painting as a work of collaboration between Giorgione and Titian remains one worth considering. Third, Zampetti's idea that Domenico Mancini might have had something to do with this painting perhaps deserves more attention than it has received: there are real affinities between this picture and Domenico's signed Lendinara *Madonna* of 1511 in some types and in the handling of fabrics. To this writer these seem best explained as derivations on Domenico's part.

F.L.R.

PROVENANCE
Possibly the *Adultera* attributed to Giorgione in 1661 inventory of Gio. Vincenza Imperiale; 1689 Queen Christina of Sweden; Orleans Collection; McLellan Collection

EXHIBITIONS
London 1893, no. 119; London 1909–10, no. 85; London 1930, no. 162; London 1950–51, no. 214; London 1953; Venice 1955, no. 47; London 1980, no. 11

REFERENCES
Baldass 1964, p. 169; Berenson 1894, p. 99; Castelfranco 1978 (Anderson), p. 73; Crowe and Cavalcaselle 1871, II, p. 547; Freedberg 1975, p. 138; Gamba 1954, p. 174; Hendy 1954, p. 157; Hirst 1981, p. 20, note 93; Longhi 1927³, p. 218; Molmenti 1878, p. 17; Pallucchini 1955, p. 13; Pallucchini 1978, p. 28; Pignatti 1971, p. 122, no. A.16; Richter 1937, p. 219; Robertson 1955, p. 176; Ruhemann 1955, p. 278; Tietze-Conrat 1945, p. 189; A. Venturi 1925–34, IX, iii, p. 812; L. Venturi 1913, p. 157; Wethey 1969, p. 168, no. X-4; Wilde 1974, pp. 115, 120; Zampetti 1968, p. 94, no. 34

Circle of Giorgione
Attributed to Titian

36

Head of a Soldier (?)

47 × 40.6 cm
Glasgow Art Gallery and Museum
[*repr. in colour on p. 53*]

This is an excised fragment of the upper right portion of the painting of *Christ and the Adulteress* (Cat. 35). It was first identified by Berenson (1928). As Richter and Pignatti noted, Titianesque characteristics are especially evident in this fragment and in the portions of the whole that originally adjoined it: one might cite the piratical three-quarters profile and the bright blue Dolomitic crags, neither of which can be paralleled in works securely attributed to Giorgione.

F.L.R.

PROVENANCE
Queen Christina of Sweden (?); 1928 Paul Sachs; 1962 Mrs D. M. Alnatt 1962; 30 June 1971, acquired by the Glasgow Art Gallery at Sotheby's

EXHIBITIONS
Cambridge, Mass. 1953; Cleveland 1956–57; London 1980, no. 12

REFERENCES
See Cat. 35, with special reference to Berenson 1928

Circle of Giorgione
Attributed to Vittore Belliniano

37

Portrait of a Young Man

72.5 × 54 cm
Szépművészeti Muzeum, Budapest
Inscribed on the parapet: ANTONIVS. BROKARDVS MAR . . .
[*repr. in colour on p. 59*]

The subject has been variously identified as Antonio Brocardo (on the basis of a seemingly later inscription on the parapet, now half-effaced) and Vittore or Vincenzo Cappello of Treviso (on the basis of the images, inset in the parapet, of a hat inscribed with a v and a three-faced woman; *cappello* meaning hat and *tre viso* three face[s].) Both identifications are speculative, but the latter, suggested by Jacobs, is tempting.

The painting was first attributed to Giorgione in 1884 by Thausing, whose ascription has been endorsed by a sizeable segment of later opinion, although sometimes with reservations. The majority of scholars, however – especially within the past 30 years – have preferred to seek an alternative author. Among those that have been suggested are Pordenone, Licinio, Cariani, Titian and, most often, an anonymous Giorgionesque painter.

X-rays have shown that at one stage a window opening on clouds and mountains impinged on the upper left corner of the picture, and that the young man's gaze was directed upward towards it. Vague traces of landscape can still be detected behind the neutral background in that quadrant. The revisions seem, however, to have been made largely (at least) by the artist himself. Gould noted in 1978 that this painting shared an unusual *craquelure* pattern with the *Tramonto* (National Gallery, London) – for Gould a possible Giorgione – but also with a few other unrelated paintings. The picture's surface gives evidence of some abrasion and retouching.

This portrait in its present form is obviously close in type to several that have been credibly ascribed to Giorgione, notably the *Portrait of a Young Man* (or *Giustiniani Portrait*) in the Dahlem Museum, Berlin and (minus their special iconographic features) the *Col Tempo* (Accademia, Venice) and the *Self-portrait as David* (Brunswick). The

more expansive forms and more overt sentiment of this portrait, as compared with that in Berlin, would suggest a somewhat later date. Indeed, certain scholars have proposed dating it well into the second or even the third decade of the sixteenth century – in other words, after Giorgione's death. For this writer, a date very much after 1510 would seem, on the basis both of style and of such factors as format, costume and coiffure, unfeasible. The most likely date is perhaps c. 1507–c. 1512.

This *Portrait of a Young Man* is in many ways an epitome of the Giorgionesque portrait – in its colouristic infusion of austerity with richness, in its atmospheric qualities, in its evocation through gesture and gaze of an inward emotion arising from contemplation or self-communion, an emotion whose outward manifestations are understated and seemingly involuntary. It epitomises these qualities, moreover, with a subtlety and conviction that have impelled many scholars to consider it a Giorgione.

One should also note, however, that even in mood this portrait is more romantically single-minded, less ambivalent than those given to Giorgione by consensus or by documentation. And, at least in its current condition, it evinces few, if any, of the more specific earmarks of Giorgione's personal execution in morphology or in the handling of paint. 'Nor', as Pignatti puts it, 'does an attribution to the well-known artists of Giorgione's circle, like Cariani or Pordenone or . . . Titian really seem possible.' Nonetheless, one is reluctant to consign a painting of this quality and individuality to the limbo of 'anonymous follower of Giorgione'.

It would therefore seem premature, in the present state of our knowledge, to foreclose absolutely the possibility of an attribution to Giorgione. And this writer would tentatively proffer another possibility, which has not hitherto been entertained: that this portrait might conceivably be by Vittore Belliniano.

Vittore is an artist now known by very few works, but the one portrait by him that this writer knows in the original, the *Kneeling Man in a Landscape* signed and dated 1518, in Bergamo, shows him to be, in matters of technique and tone, a close and highly perceptive follower of Giorgione. Further, it shows very specific analogies with this painting: in the thin pigment and diffused, almost ethereal textures; in the austere colour scheme, setting a figure in black against a landscape dominated by autumnal browns; in the almost colourless flesh tones, lacking in the ruddy undertones usual for Giorgione; in some aspects of physiognomy and pose (the latter especially with the Budapest portrait's initial version); and in the romantic sensibility evident in the whole.

F.L.R.

PROVENANCE
Before 1863 János László Pyrker, Patriarch of Aquileia

EXHIBITIONS
London 1930, no. 155; Paris 1935, no. 192

REFERENCES
Castelfranco 1978 (Anderson), p. 73; Castelfranco 1979 (Ballarin), p. 236; Castelfranco 1979 (Gould), p. 254; Gronau 1908, p. 430; Jacobs quoted in Gronau 1908, p. 431; Kakay 1960, p. 320; Pigler 1968, p. 264, with full bibliography; Pignatti 1971, p. 118; Richter 1937, p. 211; Thausing 1884, p. 313; L. Venturi 1913, p. 256; Zampetti 1968, p. 98

Girolamo da Treviso

Treviso c. 1498 – Boulogne 1544

According to Vasari (1550), Girolamo da Treviso died in 1544 aged 46. He is first mentioned in a document of 3 November 1523 referring to a commission for a lost altarpiece for the Confraternity of S. Maria dei Servi, Bologna. As this was a commission of some importance, it is probable that by 1523 Girolamo was already well-known, as indicated by a reference to 'egregius vir magister Hieronymus quondam Thome de Trivisio pictor'.

Girolamo's only works which probably predate 1523 are the large woodcut of Susanna and the Elders of c. 1515 (Venice 1976, no. 10), the two small paintings exhibited here (Cat. 38, 39), The Holy Family with Simeon (Balduina, Padua), the slightly later Female Nude (Kunsthistorisches Museum, Vienna) and the Sleeping Venus (Cat. 40). A series of at least 13 woodcuts depicting Scenes from the Life of Christ after Girolamo's drawings by Francesco De Nanto (an engraver who worked in both Venice and Emilia), date from the early 1520s (Zava Boccazzi 1958).

The Noli Me Tangere (S. Giovanni in Monte, Bologna) must have been painted when Girolamo first arrived in Bologna; it shows the influence of Francia and Costa, while the figure of the Magdalen recalls that of the Virgin in Titian's Annunciation in Treviso Cathedral of c. 1520.

Between late 1525 and May 1526 Girolamo was working in the Guidotti Chapel in S. Petronio, Bologna; the decoration consists of eight grisaille wall-paintings in oil of The Miracles of St. Anthony of Padua, which are signed Hieronimus Tarvisius. This cycle shows the impact of Raphael's classicising Emilian followers on Girolamo, who was 'one of the most eclectic Venetian painters' (Pouncey 1961); he was susceptible to the influence of many Emilian painters, in particular the Ferrarese – Garofalo and Dosso – and Parmigianino. Whilst visiting Genoa in 1527–28 he painted the façade of the Casa Doria (Vasari), and it is probable he was able to see Pordenone's work at Cortemaggiore and Cremona, which influenced his fresco style. In 1531 he was in Venice where he painted an altarpiece (now lost) for S. Salvatore, and frescoed the house of Andrea Odoni (see Cat. 46), also painting frescoes in the Chiesa della Commenda, Faenza, and for S. Sebastiano, Castelbolognese.

The last work Girolamo painted in Italy was probably The Presentation of the Virgin in the Temple with St. Thomas of Canterbury for the chapel of the English students in S. Salvatore, Bologna (Pouncey 1953, 1961); apparently as a result of this commission Girolamo was offered the opportunity to move to England the following year and entered the service of Henry VIII as a military engineer. However, he did not completely abandon painting, as is confirmed by the small Anti-Papal Allegory (Royal Collection) of 1542–44 (Pouncey 1953). Girolamo died on 10 September 1544, during a cannon attack on the besieged city of Boulogne (Vasari, from a letter of Aretino).

G.D.

REFERENCES
Pouncey 1953, pp. 208–11; Pouncey 1961¹, pp. 209–10; Venice 1976², p. 83; Zava Boccazzi 1958, pp. 70–78, with bibliography

38
Isaac Blessing Jacob

55.2 × 73 cm
Oil on canvas, transferred from panel
Monogrammed lower left: HIRTV
Musée des Beaux-Arts, Rouen (inv. no. D 863.1.4)
[repr. in colour on p. 76]

This little painting and its pendant (Cat. 39) were first attributed to Girolamo Rizzo da Santacroce. Berenson suggested an attribution to Moretto, but Coletti (1936) published them as early works of Girolamo di Tommaso da Treviso and linked them stylistically to the Female Nude (Kunsthistorisches Museum, Vienna, no. 2647), the Sleeping Venus, (Cat. 40) and the Noli Me Tangere, Bologna. The Holy Family with Simeon (Balduina, Padua), rediscovered by Fiocco in 1949, was later added to the group. The monogram can be read Hieronymus Tarvisii (or Tarvisius as it is spelt in the Guidotti Chapel, Bologna); it is identical to that on the Sleeping Venus, the Balduina painting and a woodcut of Susanna and the Elders probably dating from c. 1515. The attribution to Girolamo has been generally accepted, but was opposed by Longhi (1940, 1946), who attributed the Sleeping Venus (Cat. 40) and this painting and its pair to Savoldo, despite the monograms. But it is difficult to doubt the attribution to Girolamo, especially since more is now known of his career (Zava Boccazzi 1958) and his eclecticism and stylistic inconsistencies have been recognised. Coletti suggested the pair could be dated 1520, prior to Girolamo's move to Bologna, and certainly they appear to be the work of a young artist. There is a striking contrast between the style and positioning of the figures, which is slightly archaic and reminiscent of Flemish painting, and the up-to-date painterly technique, clearly influenced by Giorgione.

The bare interior, animated only by the light falling through the windows, is unusual amongst Italian paintings of this period. The atmosphere is enhanced by the subtle use of colour, which is highlighted or subdued by the soft light, and there are few dark shadows even on the elaborate folds in the drapery. The landscape becomes a positive element in the composition; the white houses just visible on the distant mountains are obviously Giorgionesque in inspiration.

The resemblance between this work and paintings of old men by Savoldo, together with certain affinities with the work of the Lombard artist Giovanni Agostino da Lodi (pseudo-Boccaccino), explain why it was attributed to the Lombard-Venetian school, and why Moretto and Savoldo have been both suggested as the author.

G.D.

PROVENANCE
Campana Collection, Rome; 1863 bequeathed to the Musée des Beaux-Arts

REFERENCES
Berenson 1957, p. 90; Boschetto 1963, no. 1; Coletti 1936, pp. 174–78; Fiocco 1949², p. 160; Longhi 1940, p. 34; Longhi 1946, p. 63; Nicolle 1927, p. 5; Popovitch 1967, p. 124; Popovitch 1978, p. 147; Zava Boccazzi 1958, pp. 71–75

44

composition; the lighting is organised in a completely different way, based on violent contrasts of light and shade antithetical to the Renaissance ideals of serenity and balance in composition. It might be going too far to see in this work the influence of northern painting, but it is clear that the strange qualities of the painting may reflect Lotto's state of mind at that time, as might also be true of the contemporary frescoes in the Oratory at Trescore. There is an almost mystical intensity in the rapport between the infant Jesus and St. Catherine as she leans towards him with a gesture of extreme gentleness and pathos; movement and forms are accentuated by the intense lighting.

P.Z.

PROVENANCE
In the nineteenth century Palazzo Quirinale, Rome; Galleria Corsini; Palazzo Barberini

EXHIBITIONS
Venice 1953

REFERENCES
Banti and Boschetto 1953, p. 77, no. 63; Caroli 1980, pp. 52–3; Mascherpa 1971, pp. 58–61; Pallucchini and Canova 1975, p. 98, no. 74; Zampetti 1969, p. 260

PROVENANCE
Giovanni and Jacopo van Buren, Antwerp (Ridolfi 1648); also recorded by Tassi (1793); between 1773 and 1783 Castle of Gatchina, St. Petersburg; Hermitage Museum, Leningrad

EXHIBITIONS
Leningrad 1972, no. 351; Milan 1977, no. 13; Washington, Los Angeles, New York 1979, p. 81

REFERENCES
Berenson 1955, pp. 83–84; Hermitage catalogue 1976, p. 108, no. 1447; Mascherpa 1971, pp. 56–57; Palluchini and Canova 1975, p. 98, no. 72; Vsevolojskaia 1982, p. 274, no. 60–61

46
Portrait of Andrea Odoni

104 × 116.6 cm
Signed and dated lower left: *Laurentius lotus/1527*
Her Majesty The Queen (no. 72)
[*repr. in colour on p. 92*]

Michiel saw this portrait in Odoni's house in Venice, and recorded it in his note-book as 'the half-length portrait in oil of M. Andrea contemplating ancient marble fragments, painted by Lorenzo Lotto'. The painting is also mentioned by Vasari (1568).

Andrea Odoni was a renowned Venetian antiquary and collector; he is portrayed here holding a precious statuette in the Egyptian style of Diana of Ephesus, as if displaying it to a fellow connoisseur. Beccati identified some of the pieces scattered in untidy abandon around the collector (Berenson 1955). The fragment on the left is a reproduction of the *Hercules and Antaeus* (Uffizi, Florence) then in the Belvedere courtyard in the Vatican, which Lotto, like many other artists, would certainly have seen during his stay in Rome in 1509. In the right background, there is a small *Hercules*, a female nude and a small putto. In the foreground is a *Venus*, missing its arms and head; and a male head, which appears to be a late Roman piece. As is often the case in Lotto's portraits, the sitter's expression appears to be completely sincere and almost abandoned, if somewhat melancholy, as though the presence of so many tokens of past epochs were a reminder of the transitoriness of human life. It has also been suggested that the prominence given to the statuette of Diana of Ephesus – who was a symbol of Nature or Earth in the Renaissance – symbolises the eternity of Nature in contrast to the transitory quality of Man's achievements, as exemplified by the broken antique fragments (Burckhardt 1911). Lotto used light here both to animate the sitter, to bind him to

45
The Mystic Marriage of St. Catherine with St. Jerome, St. Anthony Abbot and other Saints

98 × 114 cm
Signed and dated: L. LOTUS 1524
Galleria Nazionale di Palazzo Barberini, Rome
[*repr. in colour on p. 88*]

This work was described by Lotto as one of the group of paintings made for Giovanni Casoto in 1524, so it dates from towards the end of the artist's time in Bergamo. Lotto described it thus: 'The painting for the room of Messer Marsilio and in the centre the Madonna with the Child in her arms'. He also describes the saints: 'on the right St. Jerome . . . St. George, St. Sebastian; on the left, St. Catherine, St. Anthony, St. Nicholas of Bari' (Zampetti 1969). So this was a devotional painting made for the same Messer Marsilio who had been painted by Lotto, together with his betrothed wife, in a famous painting of 1523 (Prado, Madrid).

Stylistically this *Mystic Marriage* fits in quite well with the group of works dating from these years, which includes *Messer Marsilio with his Bride*, the *Double Portrait* (Cat. 44) and the *Portrait of Lucina Brembate* (Accademia Carrara, Bergamo). Lotto had already painted another picture of the *Mystic Marriage of St. Catherine* (Cat. 43) in 1523, but this version is more complex and dynamic in his surroundings and to create a psychological tension, as he did in *The Annunciation* (Cat. 47) and the *St. Lucy Altarpiece* completed in 1532 (Jesi).

P.Z.

PROVENANCE

1532 Andrea Odoni's house, Venice; Lucas van Uffelen, Amsterdam; 1639 acquired by Gerard Reynst; 1660 acquired by the state of Holland and presented to Charles II; Whitehall; Windsor; before 1776 Hampton Court

EXHIBITIONS

Venice 1953, no. 67 (Zampetti); Stockholm 1962, no. 81; London 1964, no. 7

REFERENCES

Banti and Boschetto 1953, p. 81; Berenson 1955, p. 131; Burckhardt 1911, pl. 314; Caroli 1974, pp. 235–52; Coletti 1953, pp. 3–16; Mascherpa 1980; Michiel (ed. Frizzoni) 1884, pp. 84ff; Pallucchini and Canova 1975, p. 109, no. 175; Shearman 1983, pp. 144–48; Vasari (ed. Milanesi) 1878–85, v, p. 249

47
The Annunciation

166 × 114 cm
Signed: *L. Lotus*
On deposit at the Pinacoteca Civica, Recanati
[*repr. in colour on p. 90*]

First mentioned in 1601, when Francesco Angelita saw it in the church of S. Maria dei Mercanti, Recanati, in 1894 the painting was judged to be 'very beautiful' by Gianuizzi, who dated it not later than 1526. Berenson suggested 1527/28 and Mascherpa believed it to be a late work, the culmination of a series of quite extraordinary variations on the theme of the Annunciation.

The painting is not dated, but it is signed in italics rather than the lapidary capitals preferred by Lotto in his youth (eg. in the 1508 polyptych); later he abandoned the Latin form and signed himself Lorenzo Lotto, as in the Ancona altarpiece (Cat. 53). In a letter dated 12 August 1527, Lotto wrote that he had abandoned a long planned trip to the Marche, but that he had sent two finished paintings there, 'of which I have not yet received any news, which leaves me rather anxious'. This *Annunciation* may be one of them; the other was probably a triptych for Jesi of which only the two lateral panels survive: *The Angel* and the *Virgin Annunciate* (Pinacoteca Civica, Jesi).

In this *Annunciation* Lotto abandoned the traditional format and instead showed a terrified Virgin visited by an angel who bursts upon her in a blaze of light: the apparition and the light violate the quiet chamber and create total panic and confusion. The young woman, cowering, her hands raised in an expression of fear and awe, turns towards the spectator as if seeking protection and help; the cat, symbol of evil, jumps away from the angel, mewing wildly. This interpretation of the Annunciation breaks completely with the dictates of sixteenth-century iconography. God the Father appears to be about to dive into the room from behind the clouds, adding to the confusion. Evidently the room had been serene and tranquil; the Virgin's domestic habits are indicated by the objects arranged along the shelf, from which hang her

night-cap and towel. The blond, adolescent angel, dressed in an ice-blue robe and with his hair swept back by flight, is the herald of confusion. The light plays a major role, intensifying the rich chromatic symphony of atonal colours in the Virgin's garments. The reds are pinky-blue, and the light insinuates itself between the folds and the facings until it reaches those defenceless and imploring hands.

This painting is in an almost perfect state of preservation, restored and relined by Pellicioli in 1953. Only the face of the angel has lost a few of its glazes after an earlier, more drastic cleaning. The original canvas has a rather handsome lozenge-shaped weave.

P.Z.

PROVENANCE

S. Maria dei Mercanti, Recanati; 1953 deposited at the Pinacoteca Communale, Recanati

EXHIBITIONS

Venice 1953, no. 73; Ancona 1981, no. 73, pp. 310–12 (Zampetti) with full bibliography

REFERENCES

Berenson 1956, p. 71; Caroli 1980 *passim*; Gianuizzi 1894, p. 41; Mascherpa 1980, pp. 112–13; Pallucchini and Canova 1975, pp. 109–10, with bibliography; Zampetti 1953, p. 49

48
Portrait of a Man

118 × 105 cm
Galleria Borghese, Rome
[*repr. in colour on p. 89*]

This portrait was listed in the 1682 inventory of the collection of Olimpia Aldobrandini as 'a painting on canvas portraying Lorenzo Lotto and painted by himself'. Later it was attributed to Pordenone, but Mundler re-ascribed it to Lotto and this has been generally accepted. It is still uncertain whether it is a self-portrait. Della Pergola (1952) compared the severe and introspective figure with the portrait of Lotto in the first edition of Ridolfi (1648) and decided that it was indeed the artist. But it is not easy to make such an identification, because there are several other paintings that have been suggested as self-portraits, including one in the frescoes at Trescore (Cortesi Bosco 1980). The triple portrait in Vienna, which in the past has been suggested as a self-portrait, has recently been identified as a painting of three brothers of the Carpan family, who were jewellers and friends of Lotto.

The composition is bold and severe; the figure stands in a simple setting, looking out as if he wishes to engage the spectator in conversation. His right hand rests on the table on which there are some rose petals and a small skull, both symbols of the ephemeral nature of earthly things and hence of death. In the segment of landscape that can be seen through the window on the left St. George is shown slaying the dragon. The allegorical significance of this scene is uncertain, but if it was intended as a reference to the name of the sitter, then this is obviously not Lotto's self-portrait. The painting is usually dated around 1530.

P.Z.

PROVENANCE
1611 Cardinal Ippolito Aldobrandini; by inheritance to Olimpia Aldobrandini

EXHIBITIONS
Venice 1953, no. 83 (Zampetti)

REFERENCES
Banti Boschetto 1953, p. 84; Caroli 1974, pp. 235–52; Coletti 1953, pp. 3–16; Cortesi Bosco 1980, pp. 124–45; Della Pergola 1952, pp. 187–88; Mascherpa 1980, p. 114; Pallucchini and Canova 1975, no. 197, p. 113, with bibliography

49 & 50
The Annunciation

Lunette, 103 × 152 cm
[repr. in colour on p. 91]

The Visitation

154 × 152 cm
Signed: *L. Lotus . . .*
Pinacoteca Civica, Comune di Jesi
[repr. in colour on p. 91]

These two paintings constitute an altarpiece, the lunette of *The Annunciation* being placed over *The Visitation*. The date is illegible, but it is generally agreed that the altarpiece can be dated 1530–35. Lotto was in the Marche in 1535 and remained there until 1539, and certainly these paintings have stylistic similarities with other works of this period, the last of which is the Cingoli *Madonna of the Rosary* of 1539. In one of the roundels illustrating the mysteries of the life of the Virgin on the Cingoli altarpiece there is a small *Visitation*, compositionally very like this present painting, but set in the open air.

Here the meeting of the Virgin and St. Elizabeth takes place in a homely interior: objects in everyday use are set out along a mantelpiece and the gestures and poses of the figures are those of simple, unsophisticated people. Lotto employed a direct and simple narrative style to illustrate an event of supernatural significance. In fact, the objects on the mantelpiece and the scattered flowers are symbols of the Virgin's divinity. *The Annunciation*, a subject dear to Lotto, is intensely vibrant and imbued with contained spirituality. The Virgin devoutly accepts the Will of God; the atmosphere is very different from the drama of the Recanati *Annunciation* (Cat. 47). In these paintings the shifting light is all important. A preparatory drawing for *The Visitation* was sold at the Hôtel Drouot in 1924, but has since disappeared (Berenson 1955; Canova 1974; Chiappini 1981).

P.Z.

PROVENANCE
Church of the Monte dei Minori, Jesi (Franciscan Observants); 1866 moved to the Pinacoteca Communale, Jesi, when the church was deconsecrated

EXHIBITIONS
Ancona 1950, nos. 63, 64; Venice 1953, no. 801 (Zampetti); Ancona 1981, no. 83, pp. 334–36 (Chiappini), with full bibliography

REFERENCES
Banti and Boschetto 1953, p. 84; Pallucchini and Canova 1975, p. 115; Zampetti 1953, p. 51

51
Virgin and Child in Glory with St. Andrew and St. Jerome

251 × 139 cm
Signed and dated: *L. Lotus 1535*
Private Collection, Rome

This painting was indirectly mentioned by the historian Alessandro Maggiori in 1832: 'In the church of St. Agostino (at Fermo) there was formerly a very beautiful painting by Lorenzo Lotto, which is now in Palazzo Bernetti.' In a guide-book to Fermo of 1864, Curi described the copy that had replaced the original painting on the sacristy altar in Sant'Agostino as 'a good copy of a painting by Carlo Loth, the Bavarian (seventeenth century). The original is in the possession of Count Bernetti.' So Lotto was transformed into Loth (Dania 1967).

The painting was lost for many years, but was traced by the present writer and exhibited at Ancona in 1981. It is of particular interest in that it confirms that Lotto was in the Marche in 1535; this can also be surmised from a small altarpiece by a local painter, Durante Nobili da Caldarola, which is dated 1535 (S. Martino, Caldarola; see Ancona 1981, no. 82) and which is so strongly Lottesque that it is unthinkable that it could have been painted without the example of the master. In fact it seems probable that Lotto actually helped his seventeen-year-old pupil; a comparison of the two works reveals their iconographic and stylistic links.

This altarpiece must have been the first of a group Lotto painted in the Marche between 1535 and 1539; it was followed by those at Ancona (Cat. 53) and Cingoli, the latter completed in 1539. It seems almost to anticipate the directives of the Counter-Reformation in its religious intensity and fervour, while the realism of such details as St. Andrew's dusty feet was later used by Caravaggio. The ascetic expressions of the saints are intensified through Lotto's use of cold, strong colours (unlike any he had used before), and the whole scene is immersed in an all-pervasive luminosity. This work marks a turning-point in Lotto's conception of the devotional image of the Virgin who, instead of being seated on a throne as in earlier *sacre conversazioni*, is here transformed into a celestial vision. Echoes of the painting are still found in Lotto's Sedrina altarpiece of 1542.

P.Z.

PROVENANCE
S. Agostino, Fermo

EXHIBITIONS
Ancona 1981, no. 80, pp. 329–30 (Zampetti), with full bibliography

REFERENCES
Dania 1967, p. 73; Zampetti 1980, p. 52

51

which in fact he never undertook, and in the same year he painted an altarpiece formerly in S. Agostino, Fermo (Cat. 51). It seems quite plausible that the present painting dates from that year or not long afterwards. Certainly there is no documentary evidence that Lotto was in Venice, Treviso or Bergamo at this date, while he appears to have been extremely active in the Marche: in 1532 he delivered the *St. Lucy Altarpiece* to Jesi, while the Fermo altarpiece is dated 1535, the *Madonna of the Rosary* (Cingoli) is of 1539 and the Ancona altarpiece probably dates from 1538. The present painting belongs to the same group, and was probably painted *c.* 1535.

This work, of great chromatic intensity, shows St. Christopher between St. Roch and St. Sebastian. All three saints were invoked for protection against the intermittent outbreaks of plague in the Marche at this time; Lotto himself wrote in one of his Bergamasque letters that epidemics were common throughout Europe during these years. The promontory of land jutting into the sea behind the saints corresponds quite closely to the bay of Ancona seen from the north; it is almost a fragment of real landscape. Trevisani recently suggested that the painting was a copy, but the hypothesis is untenable – not even his quotation of Vasari's reference to the work as a *tavola* (literally a panel, while in fact the painting is on canvas) is valid, since *tavola* was often used instead of *dipinto*, or painting, in the sixteenth century.

P.Z.

PROVENANCE
Church of the Madonna, Loreto; 1834 Palazzo Apostolico, Loreto (Ricci 1834, II, pp. 93–94)

EXHIBITIONS
Ancona 1981, no. 78, p. 326 (Varese), with full bibliography

REFERENCES
Banti and Boschetto 1953, p. 87; Pallucchini and Canova 1975, no. 210; Zampetti 1953, p. 52; Trevisani 1981, p. 388

52
St. Christopher, St. Roch and St. Sebastian

275 × 232 cm
Signed: *Laurentii Loti pictoris opus*
Pinacoteca, Palazzo Apostolico, Loreto
[*repr. in colour on p. 95; detail on p. 94*]

Vasari said that Lotto painted this picture before he finally moved to Loreto: 'He went to the church of the Madonna of Loreto, for which he had already made a painting in oil, which is in a chapel on the right as one enters the church' (Vasari 1568). Ridolfi (1648) stated that it was sent by Lotto from Venice to Loreto. Since the work is not recorded in Lotto's *Libro di Spese*, the note-book he kept from 1538, it seems reasonable to assume that it was painted before this date. In 1535 the painter was in Jesi for a commission,

53
Virgin and Child Enthroned with St. Stephen, St. John the Evangelist, St. Matthias and St. Lawrence

294 × 216 cm
Signed: *Lorenzo Lotto*
Pinacoteca Civica, Ancona

According to Vasari (1568), this altarpiece was in the church of S. Agostino, Ancona. It probably dates from between 1535 and 1539, when Lotto was in the Marche painting the altarpieces at Fermo (1535) and Cingoli; it is with this last altarpiece that this Ancona painting has certain iconographic similarities. It was in Ancona in 1538 that Lotto wrote the first entry in his *Libro di Spese*, and it is possible that this work dates from that same year. This is a work of intense devotional fervour; the harsh,

[181]

penetrating light coming from the left augments the sensation of restless spiritual tension. There is a preparatory drawing for the head of St. Matthias in the British Museum (Cat. D26).

P.Z.

PROVENANCE
S. Agostino, Ancona; in the nineteenth century the church was suppressed and the painting transferred to S. Maria della Piazza; late nineteenth century moved to the Pinacoteca Civica, Ancona; 1925 returned to S. Maria della Piazza; 1940 Palazzo Ducale, Urbino; 1950 Pinacoteca Civica

EXHIBITIONS
Ancona 1950, no. 66; Venice 1953, no. 93; Ancona 1981, no. 84, p. 336 (Zampetti), with full bibliography

REFERENCES
Banti and Boschetto 1953, p. 89; Canova 1975, p. 116; Caroli 1974, pp. 235–52; Zampetti 1953, p. 54

54
Portrait of Laura da Pola

91 × 76 cm
Pinacoteca di Brera, Milan
[repr. in colour on p. 93]

Lotto made the following note in his *Libro di Spese*: 'around the beginning of April 1543: Messer Febbo da Bressa, in Treviso, owes for two life-size half-length portraits of himself and of his lady, Madonna Laura da Pola'. The two portraits were finished in March 1544. The artist also noted that his work 'is worth, between good friends, 40 golden scudi in solid gold'; however, he had to make do with 30, 'and not all in ready money', although he also received 'a pair of large gilded peacocks', suggested in recompense by Messer Febbo. 'And so to keep my word I took as much as he offered.' (Zampetti 1969).

There is no positive proof, but it is generally accepted that the two Brera portraits can be identified as Febbo da Bressa and Laura da Pola, given that they are half-lengths, as Lotto states, and because stylistically they would seem to date from 1543–44. At that time Lotto had settled in Treviso, hoping he would be able to remain there, but in 1545 he left the city and returned to Venice because in Treviso 'I could not earn enough with my art to cover my expenses'. The fact that he had to accept what he considered to be inadequate payment is evidence of his financial difficulties.

Laura, a young woman, kneels at a *prie-dieu*. In her left hand she holds a small book and in her right a fan, which is attached to her belt by a chain. The splendour of her costume is to some extent moderated by her composed and thoughtful expression. Even if the colouring reflects Titian's art, the moral substance of the portrait is entirely Lotto's own. The sitter appears to be meditative and removed from reality. Berenson has rightly pointed out the close relationship between this portrait and the beggar woman, next to the veiled woman in profile, in *St. Anthony Distributing Alms* (SS. Giovanni e Paolo, Venice) of 1542.

P.Z.

PROVENANCE
Baslini Collection; 1860 acquired by the Pinacoteca di Brera

EXHIBITIONS
Venice 1953, no. 97

REFERENCES
Banti and Boschetto 1953, p. 90; Berenson 1955, p. 118; Caroli 1980, pp. 235–52; Pallucchini and Canova 1975, p. 118, no. 237; Zampetti 1953, with full bibliography; Zampetti 1969, p. 56

55
The Presentation of Christ in the Temple

172 × 136.5 cm
Pinacoteca, Palazzo Apostolico, Loreto

This is very probably Lotto's last work, painted in Loreto while he was a lay brother at the Santa Casa, not long before his death in 1556/57. This can be deduced from the fact that the work does not appear in a list of the paintings brought by Lotto from Venice, which were included in the sale he held in the Loggia dei Mercanti at Ancona in 1550. It was seen by Vasari (1568) in the Basilica at Loreto.

It is widely believed that the painting is partly unfinished, and that it owes its sketchiness and the congealed appearance of its dim, dull colours to its incomplete state. The composition is on two levels and derives from Lotto's drawing for *David and Goliath* for the intarsia of the choir stalls of S. Maria Maggiore, Bergamo; the artist obviously had this drawing with him since he noted that it was still present in the Ancona lottery. Subsequently it was lost.

Berenson described this painting as perhaps the most modern work by an Italian Old Master. Lotto, who had taken all his possessions to the shrine at Loreto and renounced his worldly goods and even his free will, perhaps wished to reflect the human condition in this work. Pignatti (1953) suggested that the old man at the open door high on the right might be a self-portrait. The old man acts as a witness to a life endured but enlightened by faith, which provides the only hope for wretched and suffering humanity, represented in the painting by the crowd of men and women gathered around the Christ Child – the symbol of faith, hope and human charity.

P.Z.

PROVENANCE
Santa Casa, Loreto; 1853 moved to the Palazzo Apostolico

EXHIBITIONS
Venice 1953, no. 108; Ancona 1981, no. 138, pp. 460–61 (Varese), with full bibliography

REFERENCES
Berenson 1905, pp. 235–36; Mascherpa 1980, p. 163; Pallucchini and Canova 1975, p. 10, no. 274; Pignatti 1953, p. 181; Zampetti 1953, pp. 38, 58; Zampetti 1980, p. 19

80

REFERENCES
Crowe and Cavalcaselle 1912, I, p. 285; Heinemann 1962, p. 137,
no. s 304; Meyer zur Capellen 1972, p. 73, no. 192; Pallucchini and Rossi
1983, forthcoming publication; Rossi 1979, p. 147; Rossi 1981; Tassi 1793,
I, p. 34; Zampetti 1975, p. 129, no. 12

Girolamo Romanino

Brescia 1484/87 (?) – Brescia 1562

Romanino was trained in the tradition of Foppa and
Bramantino, but early in his career (c. 1508–12) he
assimilated the lessons of Giorgione, Titian and Dürer.

Romanino's most Venetian paintings, full of shimmering
reflected highlights and brilliant colours, date from 1513
onwards. The influence of his friend Melone, and of Lotto,
is evident in the frescoes at Cremona Cathedral and the
paintings in S. Giovanni, Brescia (1521–24). These works
display a distinct originality in approach and composition,
a skilful use of light and colour and a decisive manner of
drawing. Romanino was the most Venetian of the Brescian
painters and the precursor of the move away from Titian's
style (Longhi). He next came into contact with Moretto, but
this influence was already over by 1532, when he was
painting at Trent, his work there displaying an overt
sensuality and realism.

The impact of northern painting and of Pordenone is
apparent in Romanino's frescoes at Pisogne, Breno and
Bienno. These works are relatively free in style, possibly due
to the less exacting requirements of his patrons; his
combination of the Lombard realism with a Venetian use
of colour is sometimes reminiscent of Gothic painting and
sometimes almost proto-baroque.

Romanino's last phase began in 1540: by this time the
exuberant and impulsive quality of his earlier works had
been tempered into a form of mannerism, sometimes dull,
occasionally full of life, and he produced a series of
paintings with complex compositional schemes and
strongly modelled figures in which skilful lighting effects
heightened the sense of drama. He collaborated with his
son-in-law Lattanzio Gambara, who was an associate of the
Campi brothers of Cremona. This Cremona Brescia school
co-existed alongside the more famous, realistic school of
Brescia and Bergamo to which Foppa, Moretto, Moroni,
and later Caravaggio belonged.

G.P.

81

Virgin and Child
Crowned by Two Angels

152 × 110.8 cm
Pia Opera Congrèga della Carità Apostolica, Brescia
[repr. in colour on p. 96]

The Madonna sits enthroned with the Infant Christ
standing on her knee in an apsidal niche surmounted by a
gold mosaic semi-dome; two angels hold a crown over her
head.

Romanino uses this archaic architectural scheme both to
create an intimate, yet sumptuous setting, and enhance the
atmosphere by means of delicate chiaroscuro effects which
mute the colours of the Virgin's silvery cloak and rosy
dress; her solemn and dignified bearing is in the Lombard
tradition. It can be dated c. 1530.

G.P.

PROVENANCE
1743–57 Oratorio di S. Pietro della Casalta; 1855 Annibale Maggi Via

EXHIBITIONS
Brescia 1878, no. 43; Brescia 1904, no. 44; London 1930, no. 724; Brescia
1939, no. 129; Brescia 1965, p. 87, no. 37, with full bibliography

REFERENCES
Boselli 1965, p. 206; Cassa Salvi 1965, pp. 6–7; Cheney 1966, p. 107

82

The Mystic Marriage of St. Catherine with St. Lawrence, St. Ursula and St. Angela Merici

153 × 207.7 cm
Brooks Memorial Gallery, Memphis, gift of the Samuel H. Kress
Foundation (1961.202)
[*repr. in colour on p. 97*]

This painting records the foundation of the Order of the
Orsoline Dimesse by St. Angela Merici in 1535; it probably
dates from that year, or soon after. In the foreground are
the Virgin and Child with St. Catherine kneeling before
them, while St. Lawrence leans against a marble pillar;
behind the Virgin are St. Ursula, holding a standard, and
St. Angela Merici, wearing a nun's habit and kneeling in
prayer. In the background there is the castle at Brescia.

The composed, dignified figures, harmoniously arranged
in a row, are uncharacteristic of Romanino and make this
work exceptional in his *œuvre*; there is no heightened
drama or movement, but instead a strong sense of religious
intimacy. The colour is extremely rich, and the effect of the
highlights on the silk drapery is particularly exquisite, even
if the painting has been over-cleaned. Again, the painting
shows a skilful mixture of the Venetian style, derived from
Titian and Lotto, and that of Lombardy; the silvery cascade
of the Virgin's cloak is reminiscent of Foppa's work, whilst
her figure is stylistically close to Bramantino.

G.P.

PROVENANCE
1760 Maffei Collection; 1871 Erizzo Maffei, Brescia; 1871 Cook
Collection, Richmond; 1948 Kress Collection

EXHIBITIONS
Brescia 1965, no. 59, with full bibliography

REFERENCES
Boselli 1965, p. 208; Bossaglia 1965, II, p. 169; Fredericksen and Zeri 1972,
p. 176; Kossoff 1965, p. 518; Vezzoli 1974, p. 394

83

Christ Carrying the Cross

81 × 72 cm
Private Collection

The subject of Christ carrying the Cross was painted
frequently by north Italian painters, and often by
Romanino. There is a tondo by him of this subject
(Pinacoteca Tosio Martinengo, Brescia) with Christ wearing
a silvery tunic, the composition of which is carefully
constructed to create a peaceful effect. By contrast, the
painting in Hanover and, above all, this work, are both
imbued with a sense of pathos, accentuated by the
exaggerated expression of the figures, the tentative
modelling of the knotted hands and the wrinkled folds in
the drapery. In addition, Romanino has crammed the figure

83

into a small space and used no tonal gradations, passing
abruptly from a bright red to a faded pink, and to the
ashen-coloured flesh of the figure of Christ.

Romanino was deeply influenced by Pordenone and
northern painting at this period (*c.* 1535) as can be seen in
the frescoes in Pisogne and Breno, and in the Asola pulpit.

G.P.

PROVENANCE
1853 Averoldi Collection, Brescia; 1907 Crespi Collection, Milan; 1914
Paris sale; later acquired in Milan by a private collector

EXHIBITIONS
Brescia 1878, no. 33; Brescia 1965, no. 51, with bibliography

REFERENCES
Boselli 1965, p. 208; Cheney 1966, p. 107; Kossoff 1965, p. 518

Giovanni Girolamo Savoldo

Brescia (?) *c.* 1485—Venice after 1548

Savoldo certainly came from Brescia, as may be deduced
less from the phrase '*da Brescia*' always applied to him than
from his lifelong contacts with patrons in the town, but this
is not documented. He first appears in Florence, where he
joined the painters' guild in 1508; later he lived in Venice
from at least 1520 to 1548. Although evidently trusted and
liked by pupils and neighbours (several of the few
documents relating to Savoldo name him as executor of
wills), he was notably unsuccessful in his career. His pupil
Pino observed that his few works brought him little fame,
his only patron being the last Duke of Milan.

Perhaps more than any other artist of his age, Savoldo specialised in paintings of a single figure – when there are two or more, the figures are detached and immobile. The figures often nearly fill the frame, their imposing volume suggesting a quattrocento-like conservatism, and his work shows a traditional duality of mass and void. However, Savoldo's sense of atmosphere, his ability to animate his figures by clothing them in sensuously vivid colours (often large blocks of local hue), and his use of the wide portrait all address his own century's demand for modernity. He thus provides the vibrant age of Titian with heroes of meditative dignity.

The idea of including Savoldo in the Brescian School, along with Foppa, Moretto and Moroni, is made dubious by these artists' preference for grey tonal worlds and humble still-life motifs, so unlike Savoldo's concentration on contrasting blocks of colour and figures. More closely related to the Titian of the phase of *Sacred and Profane Love* and *The Assumption*, Savoldo is no more Brescian than Veronese is Veronese.

C.E.G.

REFERENCES

Berenson 1899, pp. 129ff; Boschetto 1963; Crowe and Cavalcaselle 1912, pp. 308ff; Gilbert 1955; Gilbert 1969; Ortolani 1925, pp. 193ff; Pino 1548, ed. 1946; Vasari (ed. Milanesi) 1878, VI, pp. 507ff; A Venturi 1925–34, IX, iii, pp. 749ff; von Hadeln 1925¹, pp. 72ff

NOTE: THE CHRONOLOGICAL SEQUENCE IS 84, 88, 87, 85, 86.

84

The Rest on the Flight into Egypt

87 × 124 cm
Private Collection, Italy
[*repr. in colour on p. 72*]

This canvas, a favourite size for Savoldo, contains figures painted on a scale unusually small for him. Of 40 surviving pictures, this occurs only in two other versions of the *Rest on the Flight into Egypt*, an *Adoration of the Shepherds*, and his two paintings of *The Temptation of St. Anthony*. While the last theme documents Savoldo's fascination with Flemish painting, the first two, from the infancy of Christ, are those incidents most adaptable to Giorgione's arcadian tone.

This work is perhaps the earliest of the four versions of the subject painted by Savoldo, which may explain the unusually literal dependence on several sources, notably prints. The composition, with all the standard subject matter to one side and a wide vista on the other, follows the formulae of Giulio Campagnola, as in Cat. P9, which, like this painting, includes a view of the Doge's Palace, and Cat. P8 and P11, which also show the figures in shadow before a backdrop.

More generally, the two-sided formula, balancing all the figures against a wide view, is a major Venetian tradition, illustrated by Giovanni Bellini's famous *St. Francis* (Frick Collection, New York) and Giorgione's *Three Philosophers* (Kunsthistorisches Museum, Vienna). A print by Fogolino had Italianised the popular Flemish theme of the Rest on the Flight into Egypt, with its ruined buildings and figure

of Joseph at the well. As to specific details, Benedetto Montagna's *Orpheus* included the buttressed tower – on fire, as it is when Savoldo uses it again in his *St. Catherine* (Pesenti Coll.) – while the Child, shown in perspective lifting Mary's veil, is copied from an engraving by Mabuse.

The date usually given to the painting, *c*. 1520–27, is supported by that of the Mabuse engraving (after 1520) and if indeed this is Savoldo's first version of the theme, by documents of 1527 recording a set of four canvases by him on the theme of the Flight into Egypt. Ridolfi (1648) mentioned a version with Joseph at the well among ruined buildings and the Child at his mother's breast, evidently very close to this one. Savoldo's preference for the subject of the Rest on the Flight, rather than the conventional subject of the Flight itself, demonstrates his liking for still figures; the disjuncture of the environmental motifs from the setting was to remain a problem for him.

C.E.G.

PROVENANCE
By 1869 in Palazzo Albani, Urbino (Burckhardt); thereafter by descent

EXHIBITIONS
Venice 1955, no. 109

REFERENCES
Berenson 1899, pp. 129ff; Boschetto 1963, pls. 51–53; Burckhardt 1869, III, p. 995; Capelli 1950, p. 404; Fiocco 1956, p. 166; Gamba 1939, p. 382; Gamulin 1955, p. 254; Gilbert 1955, pp. 92–94, 183–84; Longhi 1927², p. 75; Nicco Fasola 1940, pp. 62, 67; Ortolani 1925, pp. 171–72; Serra 1924, p. 65; Suida 1935, p. 511; A Venturi 1925–34, IX, iii, pp. 755–56; L. Venturi 1915, p. 206

85

Shepherd with a Flute

97 × 78 cm
Private Collection
[*repr. in colour on p. 74*]

The theme of the musical shepherd is obviously Giorgionesque, a quality reinforced by the passivity (not actually playing the flute) and light (that this is evening is insisted upon by the fact that the sheep have been brought into the fold). Formally, however, it is related to the much more old fashioned Madonnas of Giovanni Bellini, where a solid heroine is contrasted with very distant landscape anecdotes. Savoldo maintains the massive grandeur of the figure with his almost slick large areas of strong local colour and by sharply silhouetting the figure against sky, thus retaining his dualistic quattrocento instinct for the balance of mass and space, as against the tendency in Venice amongst his contemporaries to absorb forms into a luminous unity. In spite of this, he is able to produce a modern mood and give the light an emphatic value by suggesting tremendous depth of air (through the inescapable intricacy of the far away scene) and by the dimming of the hero's face (through the device of the big hat). Conservative techniques for a modern expression are essential to him, nowhere more elegantly achieved than here. The device of silhouetting is splendidly handled to this end in a group of works of this date, about 1525, notably the *Transfiguration* (Uffizi, Florence), where the iconography evokes it, the Brera altarpiece and the

Cleveland *Pietà*. Later it is combined in the *St. Matthew* (New York) with a similar distant busy scene in an even more sophisticated way. The *Shepherd* is one of the few Savoldos that was repeatedly copied; one copy, at Gosford House, was noted by Cavalcaselle and regularly attributed to Savoldo long before the discovery of the original, which then was wrongly reported for a time (first by Longhi) to be the same painting in new ownership.

C.E.G.

PROVENANCE
Duke of Anhalt, Buerlitz; *c.* 1927 sold to Cassirer, Berlin, and thence immediately to Contini, Florence; 1970s sold to the present owner

EXHIBITIONS
Brescia 1939, no. 176; Milan 1953, no. 19; Venice 1955, no. 110

REFERENCES
Boschetto 1963, p. 50; Capelli 1950, p. 412; Gilbert 1955, pp. 83–84, 169–70; Longhi 1927², p. 74; Longhi 1929, p. 288; Suida in Thieme-Becker 1935, p. 511; A. Venturi 1925–34, IX, iii, pp. 766–67

86

Tobias and the Angel

96 × 126 cm
Galleria Borghese, Rome (inv. no. 547)
[*repr. in colour on p. 75*]

In most images of this theme, the angel Raphael is the protagonist. Usually an adult, he often holds the boy Tobias's hand as they walk, or, in another version common at this period, he leans over to help Tobias pull the fish from the water. The seated angel here not only evokes quietude, but also enables the child to be a co-protagonist.

There are a remarkable number of parallels between this painting and the artist's *St. Matthew and the Angel* (Metropolitan Museum, New York), beginning with the shared theme of an angel helping a saintly person, which is not found again in Savoldo's work. The *St. Matthew* is also the same size (to within 3 cm, 93 × 124.4), which is unique among Savoldo's religious works (two portraits measure approximately 91 × 123 cm, but reports of the measurements vary). Since the present painting and the *St. Matthew* were both discovered in central Italy in 1912, it is suggested that they were a pair and had been together until shortly before 1912. Although the lighting is very different, the paintings are similar in other respects: such as the disjuncture of the figures in woolly red and blue robes of high key from the very dark background or the unusual debt in both to figure types of Leonardo. As St. Matthew dominates his angel, the connection would also explain the greater emphasis on Raphael.

As a pair, exceptional in Savoldo's work, they might well then be identified as the two survivors of his 'four paintings of night and fires' reported by Vasari in the Mint at Milan. Matthew, the tax-collector, is the patron of mints; Tobias made his journey to collect money. Mints, which are rarely adorned with pictures, have no settled iconography, so that a planner of one would start with Matthew and then have to work up other harmonizing themes. Savoldo's *Matthew*

as a picture of the mint's Saint, with a night and a fire, indeed matches Vasari's specifications nicely. And the stylistic date most often given to both paintings, in the early 1530s, also matches the information that Savoldo's only long-term patron was a duke of Milan who reigned principally from 1530 to 1535, inasmuch as the mint is a ducal building. Admittedly the Tobias only evokes evening rather than night, and lacks a fire; one would have to presume that Vasari responded to the imagery of the paintings as a group rather than to motifs found in every one, a presumption less awkward when it is noted that in this period there seem not to be sets of paintings where all are nocturnes.

C.E.G.

PROVENANCE
Palazzo Alfani, Perugia; R. Pompili, Tivoli; 1911 Galleria Borghese

EXHIBITIONS
London 1930, no. 123; Paris 1935, no. 188; Brescia 1939, no. 171; Venice 1955, no. 114

REFERENCES
Capelli 1951, pp. 18–20; D'Achiardi 1912, pp. 81–83; Della Pergola 1955, p. 128; Gamba 1939, p. 385; Gilbert 1955, pp. 113–16; Longhi 1927², p. 75; Nicco Fasola 1940, pp. 67–68; Suida in Thieme-Becker 1935, p. 511; A. Venturi 1925–34, IX, iii, p. 771; L. Venturi 1913, pp. 220–21; von Hadeln 1925, p. 78

87

Virgin and Child with Two Donors

102.2 × 139.7 cm
Her Majesty The Queen (no. 235)
[*repr. in colour on p. 73*]

Composing a row of half-length figures is a standard way of bringing them closer to the front of the picture plane and filling the canvas: Giovanni Bellini's classic prototype, with Mary between the two other figures, is followed here. This is a less individual work than most of Savoldo's, and a more standard devotional image of the time, yet there is an elegance in the suspension in shadow of the immobile heavy forms that evokes meditation. The Child is on some sort of crib, which implies that the adults are kneeling, but no other adjustments are made along these lines.

Most remarkable is the single, central action in which the male devotee raises the cloth from the Child and, with a glance towards us, offers him to our view, as well as to the prayerful response of the women. This unveiling, or *revelatio*, is clearly a reference to the distinction between the New Testament's message of salvation from the 'veiled' one of the Old, a distinction achieved by Christ's incarnation. No analogous images are known, other than Savoldo's own variant in Turin (93 × 139 cm), in which instead of the donors we see St. Jerome lifting the cloth and St. Francis in adoration. Since saints seem more plausible in this role, one might infer that the Turin picture was painted earlier and that the donors in the present painting especially asked for the variant. To be sure, as Shearman noted, there is no obvious reason why Jerome should have been shown lifting the cloth, but Shearman's alternative suggestion that this donor might be named Joseph, and so

88

constitute an allusion to Joseph of Arimathea's role in Christ's burial, does not seem to fit the donor's gesture, which is the opposite of shrouding. In contemporary Nativities that have been cited as parallels, it is only Mary who lifts the cloth from Christ, or, as in other Savoldo Nativities, the Infant himself. But as one of the church's great teachers, Jerome might conceivably have been regarded as appropriate for the role of revealing the incarnate Christ to the faithful.

C.E.G.

PROVENANCE
Probably in Charles I's collection (see Gilbert 1955, pp. 173–74, and Shearman 1983, p. 221, for somewhat varied selections of items in inventories of that and later reigns that might match this picture); in James II's collection

EXHIBITIONS
London 1946, no. 223

REFERENCES
Boschetto 1963, pls. 42–43; Crowe and Cavalcaselle 1912, III, p. 316; Gamba 1939, p. 382; Gilbert 1955, pp. 71, 173–74; Longhi 1917, p. 113; Ortolani 1925, p. 172; Shearman 1983, pp. 221–22; A. Venturi 1925–34, IX, iii, p. 756; L. Venturi 1913, p. 221

88

Lady with a Dragon Fur

91 × 123 cm
Pinacoteca Capitolina, Rome (inv. no. 49)

In the 1520s, when the schema of the Venetian Renaissance portrait in its steady expansiveness first permitted the knee-length figure as an option, a few of these are in addition on canvases wider than they are high, a truly bold oddity for the single-figure portrait, which in all ages is unusually invariant. The format was invented by Savoldo and Lotto, but Lotto continued to centre the figure on the canvas (least so in his *Portrait of a Man, c.* 1526 [Accademia, Venice],

where the head is in the centre but not the body). It is one of their ways of linking portraits to other painting, which Lotto also did by introducing vigorous action into his portraits. Savoldo retained the stillness, but, as in *The Rest on the Flight* (Cat. 84), allotted the figure only the left half of the canvas.

The lady has often been identified as St. Margaret (whose attribute is the dragon), but the fur head on a chain, seen also in Lotto's *Lucina Brembate* of 1532, would have been luxury wear in the early sixteenth century. Other costume elements here have inexact analogues between the 1520s and the 1540s; however, the absence of any head-dress, usually restricted to figures in prayer, is strange, and may suggest that the lady is in the very private interior of her house. Surface losses of paint have made it difficult to date the painting; the even, dark tone probably suggests a late date, *c.* 1540, which was preferred by Longhi and others until earlier ones were proposed by Gilbert (*c.* 1523–24) and Boschetto (*c.* 1527–30), on the basis of the relatively linear contours, similar to those in Cat. 87.

The late date of the painting and the fact that it was once called a portrait of Duchess Eleanor of Urbino reflect its remarkable parallels with Titian's portrait of the Duchess of 1536 (Uffizi, Florence): they share specific details, such as the fur head on the chain and the landscape through a window, as well as their general composition. It is natural to think Savoldo followed Titian, and he may well have done, but there is a good deal to be said for the converse view. For Titian this was an unusual project, only his third (surviving) female portrait in 30 years – as against dozens of portraits of men – and of the two preceding pictures, the London *Schiavona* and *Laura de' Dianti* are so unlike in design as to offer no precedent. Titian, like Shakespeare, had no hesitation in borrowing old formulas, even from sources far more humble than this, and patrons (including Eleonora's mother, Isabella d'Este) regarded them with favourable interest.

C.E.G.

PROVENANCE
Cardinal Carlo Pio (1622–89), bought with his other paintings in
Venice, with the aid of Giovanni Bonatti; his great-nephew, Giberto Pio;
1750 acquired by Benedict XIV; Pinacoteca Capitolina, founded by
Benedict XIV; 1767 reported by Venuti in the second gallery, where the Pio
collection was hung (as 'in the manner of Giorgione'); 1871 reported by
Cavalcaselle, rejecting official attribution to Giorgione; for further gallery
history see Pietrangeli 1951

EXHIBITIONS
Brescia 1939, no. 166

REFERENCES
Barbier de Montault 1870, p. 38; Bruno 1978, p. 25; Capelli 1950, p. 410;
Crowe and Cavalcaselle 1912, III, pp. 47, 319; Donovan 1843, III, p. 578;
Gamba 1939, p. 386; Gilbert 1955, pp. 94–96, 185–86; Longhi 1927, p. 75;
Morelli 1893, p. 149; Nicco Fasola 1940, p. 57; Pietrangeli 1951, p. 62;
Righetti 1836, II, p. 15, repr.; Tofanelli 1818, p. 108; A. Venturi 1925–34,
IX, iii p. 781; L. Venturi 1913, p. 22; Venuti 1976, pp. 480, 799

Andrea Meldolla, called
Schiavone

Zara c. 1510/15 – Venice 1563

Andrea Meldolla was born in Zara, Dalmatia (at that time
under Venetian jurisdiction) of a family which had
originally come from Meldolla in the Romagna. Although
the artist's birthdate is unknown, Richardson (1980, p. 16)
has persuasively argued for a date of c. 1510/15; Schiavone
died on 1 December 1563.

The artist's early training and the circumstances of his
establishment in Venice are entirely matters for speculation.
Most likely Schiavone was living in Venice by the late
1530s, and in 1540 he was commissioned by Vasari to paint
a large battle scene, subsequently given to Ottaviano de'
Medici, but now lost. The earliest surviving dated work
by Schiavone is the *Abduction of Helen*, an etching of 1547.
He must have produced etchings throughout his career, for
they constitute a fundamental part of his *oeuvre*. The
influence of Parmigianino is widespread in Schiavone's
prints, paintings and drawings; but other central Italian
artists such as Raphael and Francesco Salviati, and
Venetians such as Giorgione and Titian also affected his art.
In 1548 Pietro Aretino wrote to Schiavone, commenting on
his speed of execution and lack of finish, which evidently
amazed Titian.

In the 1550s Schiavone's work lost some of its more
exaggerated elements and became closer to Venetian
naturalism. The three tondi completed in 1556–57 for the
ceiling of the Libreria Marciana document this
development; they also demonstrate the freedom and
virtuosity of his brushwork. In May 1563 Schiavone was
named an expert witness in the dispute between the
Procurators of San Marco and the Zuccati family of
mosaicists. Some of his late paintings are among his most
arresting and original creations.

D. McT.

REFERENCES
Richardson 1980, with full bibliography

89
The Adoration of the Magi

185 × 222 cm
Pinacoteca Ambrosiana, Milan (inv. no. 198)
[repr. in colour on p. 115]

This agitated and engaging canvas represents Schiavone's
painting at its most imaginative. The contorted and
frequently unanatomical figures have been improbably
compressed into a shallow, frieze-like space, with only the
cloudy sky for a backdrop. Even the Solomonic column
bends as if made of rubber. The colour is reminiscent of
such contemporary Tuscan painters as Vasari, with
dissonant contrasts of wine-red and dull gold, copper-green
and smokey-blue, but the paint itself has been applied with
a verve and indifference to the precise definition of contours
that are singularly Venetian. The result is an animated relief
pattern of skilfully interwoven arabesques looping in and
out of highlight and shadow. Since these features represent
the counterparts, in oil paint, to Schiavone's etching of the
Abduction of Helen, dated 1547, Richardson has proposed
a similar date for this canvas.

While many of the figures are generically
Parmigianesque, the angel with crown and laurel wreath –
an unusual iconographic feature – may reflect the angel
with equally spindly limbs in Francesco Salviati's Corpus
Domini altarpiece (c. 1540). It is also possible that
Schiavone knew Francesco Salviati's drawing of the
Adoration of the Magi (British Museum, London), which
has also been dated to Salviati's Venetian visit of 1539–41
(Cheney 1963).

Nothing is known about the original commission of this
ecstatic epiphany. It is first recorded in the inventory of
Cardinal Federico Borromeo's bequest to the Ambrosiana
in 1618 (Falchetti 1969). The painting was correctly
attributed to Schiavone at that time.

D. McT.

PROVENANCE
Cardinal Federico Borromeo

EXHIBITIONS
Venice 1981, no. 30

REFERENCES
Berenson 1957, I, p. 160; Cheney 1963, p. 348; Falchetti 1969, pp. 252, 291;
Freedberg 1971, pl. 238; Fröhlich-Bum 1913–14, p. 206; Hope 1980, p. 104;
Pallucchini 1944², II, p. IX; Pallucchini 1950, p. 30; Richardson 1980,
pp. 31, 144–45; A. Venturi, 1925–34, IX, iv, 1929, pp. 741–43

90
Diana and Callisto

19 × 49 cm
Musée de Picardie, Amiens (no. 248)

The story of Diana and Callisto is told in Ovid's
Metamorphoses (II, 401–503). Callisto, the daughter of the
King of Arcady, joined the retinue of Diana, but was then
violated by Jupiter. When her companions stopped by a

90

stream to bathe, Callisto refused to join them, in order to conceal her pregnancy. In the painting, Diana, the cruel goddess of Chastity, imperiously orders Callisto to be undressed; her condition is then revealed and she is banished from Diana's retinue. Callisto was eventually transformed by Jupiter into the constellation Ursa Maior.

As Gould observed, the present canvas is listed in the Vivant Denon collection along with two unidentified mythological pictures (of approximately the same height), now in the National Gallery, London. Probably all three were together in the Algarotti collection in the eighteenth century, but nothing is known of their whereabouts before that. Such small-scale representations of figures in a landscape were commonly undertaken in Renaissance Venice as decoration for domestic interiors, frequently for pieces of furniture. Ridolfi mentions that on roundels and cupboards Giorgione had painted stories from Ovid, including this very subject: *Diana con molte Ninfe ignude ad una fonte, che della bella Callisto le violate membra scoprivano*. Because Giorgione's composition is now lost, its relationship with later interpretations of the subject, including Titian's painting of 1559 for Philip II (National Gallery of Scotland, Edinburgh), is impossible to establish. Richardson has dated Schiavone's picture to the late 1540s, and it is conceivable that his *Diana and Callisto* exerted an influence on Titian's picture. Especially relevant are Diana's commanding gesture and the frenzied agitation of the disrobing of Callisto, the two features which Panofsky (1969, p. 160) found most original in Titian's interpretation.

Richardson describes this canvas as 'a happy balance between painterly brilliance and poised, decorative elegance'. While the influence of Parmigianino is generally reflected here, in a particularly refined and delicate vein, the picture also resembles a more painterly and naturalistic reworking of one of Francesco Salviati's ceiling frescoes of 1540 in the Sala di Apollo in the Palazzo Grimani, Venice.

D. McT.

PROVENANCE
Algarotti (?); Vivant Denon; E. and O. Lavalard

EXHIBITIONS
Paris 1965–66, no. 255

REFERENCES
Gould 1959, p. 75; Richardson 1980, pp. 37, 152, with full bibliography; Ridolfi 1648, I, p. 98

91

Sacra Conversazione

122 × 96.5 cm
British Government Art Collection

The Christ Child reaches forward to embrace the young John the Baptist, who is presented by his mother, Elizabeth; Zacharias is further to the right. Behind the Virgin Mary are St. Catherine of Alexandria, Joseph, and an unidentified female figure. Aspects of a Holy Family and the traditional *sacra conversazione* are thus combined, with the figures unconventionally aligned along a diagonal from the right

91

foreground to the left middleground. The subject of the introduction of the Christ Child and John the Baptist, each supported by his kneeling mother, was also treated by Schiavone in an etching (Bartsch 63). Although the scene is clearly set out of doors, the figures are placed in a somewhat dilapidated architectural setting with a richly decorated façade, reminiscent of Jacopo Sansovino's Loggetta (begun in 1537).

Both the elegantly posed figures and the elaborately decorated architecture seem to be viewed through a faint mist, and the landscape vista at the right suggests a night view. Richardson has proposed a date of *c.* 1552–54 for this lovely canvas, which would make it an early instance of a nocturne. As such, it prophesies the increasing vogue for these pictures by such artists as Jacopo Bassano, Paolo Veronese and Palma Giovane in the succeeding decades.

D. McT.

PROVENANCE
Lady D'Abernon

REFERENCES
Berenson 1957, I, p. 161; Richardson 1980, pp. 44–47, 172

92 & 93
The Annunciation

Two canvases, each 272 × 156 cm
S. Pietro, Belluno
[*repr. in colour on p. 116 and p. 117*]

These canvases were formerly the outsides of the organ shutters of the church of S. Pietro, with Schiavone's paintings of St. Peter and St. Paul on the insides; all four paintings now hang separately in the church. The custom of including figurative paintings on the shutters of pipe organs has a long history in Venice and the Veneto. Frequently the figures are shown in an architectural setting, usually in arched openings, as are the saints on the interior of the Belluno shutters (cf. Cat. 95 and 96). The Annunciation may also be set in an arch (as on the shutters by Cosmè Tura in the cathedral of Ferrara), or in an elaborate chamber (as in the shutters ascribed to Giovanni Bellini from S. Maria dei Miracoli, in which SS Peter and Paul appear in separate niches on the inside). But here Schiavone has chosen to minimise architecture and to concentrate on atmospheric conditions and landscape. The descending vaporous cloud that unifies the two canvases and surrounds the dove of the Holy Spirit obliterates the wall behind the Virgin, while the landscape below the angel constitutes one of the most outstanding details in any work by Schiavone. The broken brushwork of trees, hills and twilit sky looks forward to similar treatments of landscape in works by Titian (Richardson 1980). Equally impressive is the vigorous execution of the angel's fluttering draperies and curly hair.

The angel retains much of the gracefulness of Parmigianino's figures and is very close to the same figure in Schiavone's etching of *The Annunciation* (Bartsch 5), whilst the figure of the Virgin approaches that in Titian's lost *Annunciation* of 1536, known through the print by

Caraglio (Richardson 1980). Thus the two major stylistic elements in Schiavone's art – the inventive gracefulness of Parmigianino and the elevated naturalism and painterly handling of Titian – are combined here.

Although these paintings are not mentioned in Ridolfi's life of Schiavone, they are recorded as his works in the accounts of Lucio Doglioni and Florio Miari, local historians. Fiocco dated the canvases to Schiavone's last years, while Richardson has convincingly argued for a date of *c.* 1554–55, just before the tondi in the Libreria Marciana.

D. McT.

EXHIBITIONS
Belluno 1950, nos. 27–28; Los Angeles 1979, no. 28 (the Archangel);
Venice 1981, nos. 32–33

REFERENCES
Berenson 1957, I, p. 159; Doglioni 1780, p. 30; Doglioni 1816, p. 36;
Fiocco 1950, p. 42; Miari 1843, p. 146;
Richardson 1980, pp. 47–48, 154

94
Christ Before Herod

130 × 209 cm
Museo di Capodimonte, Naples (no. 863)
[*repr. in colour on p. 118*]

The original destination of this deeply moving painting is unknown. In subject and composition it is related to a number of similar paintings by Schiavone of Christ before Pilate. According to Ridolfi (1648, p. 251), one version – probably the painting now at Hampton Court – was owned by Jan Reynst, a Dutch resident of Venice, and it is likely that all these pictures were intended for private possession.

In terms of both format and approach to subject matter, these half-length narratives follow works like the canvases depicting Christ and the Adulteress by Titian and Lotto. Usually Christ and another figure have been forced together by the clamorous protestations of the crowd, but in Schiavone's interpretation of this rare subject, taken from *Luke* XXIII, 6–12, the drama has been internalised, the gestures abated and the glances stilled. A number of subsidiary figures merge almost totally with the surrounding deep brown shadow. In this respect, Schiavone's picture compels comparison with Rembrandt's mature work a century later, and, indeed, it is quite possible that the Dutch master had access in Amsterdam to some of Schiavone's paintings (Richardson 1980, p. 68).

Christ Before Herod represents Schiavone's late style at its most eloquent. The gracefulness and the exaggerated contortions of the earlier figures have been replaced by a more uniform naturalism that also extends to the lighting of the scene. The paint has been very freely applied, and drawing, in the central Italian sense, has been largely ignored. What remains most impressive, however, is the pathos of this silent drama. Richardson dates the picture to *c.* 1558–62.

D. McT.

PROVENANCE
1821 Neapolitan Royal Collection

REFERENCES
Richardson 1980, p. 167, with full bibliography

Sebastiano del Piombo

Venice (?) *c.* 1485 – Rome 1547

Vasari, who knew Sebastiano in his later years, states that he was aged 62 when he died in 1547; a birth date of around 1485 is likely to be correct. Early accounts state that the painter became a pupil or associate of Giorgione, and the works of his Venetian years fully substantiate this. Before he left Venice for Rome in 1511, Sebastiano had undertaken three major commissions: the organ shutters for S. Bartolomeo a Rialto (Cat. 95, 96), *The Judgement of Solomon* (Cat. 97) and the high altarpiece of S. Giovanni Crisostomo. A smaller Venetian work, the National Gallery *Salome*, is dated 1510.

The move to Rome brought Sebastiano into contact with a radically different artistic environment dominated by Michelangelo and Raphael and led to a gradual abandonment of the Venetian style. Decisive in effecting a change to more monumental forms and to an increasingly cool range of colour was his friendship with Michelangelo. In the 1510s he produced a number of major altarpieces, including a *Pietà* for Viterbo and the *Raising of Lazarus*, now in the National Gallery, London. Michelangelo had a share in the design of both these works. From the time of his arrival in Rome, Sebastiano established himself as a great portrait painter, producing masterpieces such as the *Ferry Carondelet* (Thyssen Coll., Lugano) and after Raphael's death in 1520 he had scarcely a rival as a portraitist in central Italy. Involved in the Sack of Rome in 1527, he sought refuge in his native Venice, but soon returned to Rome, receiving the office of papal *piombatore* from Pope Clement VII in 1531.

Sebastiano's inactivity as a painter in his later years has been exaggerated, but these late works assume an intensely personal character; often painted on stone supports, they take on an almost crepuscular quality. A late mural altarpiece in this style is in S. Maria del Popolo, Rome.

M.H.

95 *(before restoration)*

96 *(before restoration)*

95 & 96
St. Louis of Toulouse
St. Sinibaldus

Each 293 × 137 cm
S. Bartolomeo a Rialto, Venice

These two canvases formed the interior sides of shutters made to cover the organ (now destroyed) of a church in the commercial centre of Venice at the Rialto. Painted organ shutters, of which a number survive from the fifteenth century, became a highly popular form of Venetian church decoration. SS Louis and Sinibaldus, here depicted in shallow niches crowned by a mosaic semi-dome (a setting recalling those in works of Bellini's circle), were revealed when the shutters were open and the organ in use. Two other saints, Bartholomew and Sebastian, shown standing before a unified architectural setting, decorated the exterior of the shutters.

The paintings are first recorded in print by Scanelli as late as 1657; he ascribed them to Sebastiano, an attribution later endorsed by Boschini. Subsequent attempts to advance alternative attributions, or to argue for Giorgione's involvement in their design, have for the most part wisely been abandoned since the painstaking restoration by Pellicioli in 1940 (Pallucchini 1941).

Our two saints are closer in style to the work of Giorgione than their external counterparts; they share the meditative calm of the figures in Giovanni Bellini's altarpiece in San Zaccaria (Accademia, Venice) and Giorgione's *Three Philosophers* (Kunsthistorisches Museum, Vienna). The profile head of St. Sinibaldus is a personal variation by Sebastiano of the head of the oldest philosopher in the latter painting, carried out in a less broad, more prismatic style. Other features, such as the acute observation of the fall of light, owe more to Giovanni Bellini than to Giorgione, whilst the virtuosity of some passages, for example in St. Louis's cope, are difficult to match in Venetian art of the period.

The shutters were painted *c.* 1508–09 (Nardini 1788) and constitute one of Sebastiano's earliest major commissions. The choice of saints is due to local circumstances: Louis reflects the name of the *vicario* in charge of the church, while the pilgrim Sinibaldus was patron saint of Nuremberg; his presence in S. Bartolomeo a Rialto can probably be explained by the interests of the German colony in Venice (von Erffa 1976). Their rebuilt *Fondaco dei Tedeschi* stood a few paces from the church of S. Bartolomeo, in which Dürer's *Feast of the Rose Garlands* had recently been installed. X-rays of the heads of the saints show minor changes in the painting of St. Sinibaldus and a more significant change in the design of St. Louis, whose head was originally painted on a vertical axis and subsequently shifted to an inclined position.

M.H.

EXHIBITIONS
Venice 1955, nos. 83 and 84

REFERENCES
Hirst 1981, pp. 9–13, with bibliography; Lucco 1980, pp. 92–93;
Pallucchini 1941, pp. 8–12; Wilde 1974, pp. 94–98; von Erffa 1976,
pp. 8–11

97
The Judgement of Solomon

208.3 × 315 cm
The National Trust, Kingston Lacy
[*details repr. in colour on p. 56 and p. 57*]

Imposing in scale and ambitious in its treatment of the scene described in I *Kings*, III, 16–28, this is one of the most important Venetian paintings to have survived from the early sixteenth century. The circumstances of its inception have, however, remained obscure, and the identity of the artist has been much debated. No early mention of the work seems to exist; the first known reference to it is by Ridolfi in 1648, who saw it in the Palazzo Vendramin (a palace built for Andrea Loredan, who had died in 1513). Ridolfi attributed the work to Giorgione, and the painting enjoyed this ascription when acquired by William Bankes on the advice of Byron (see the latter's letter of 26 February 1820). But the enormous number of paintings attributed to Giorgione by Ridolfi gravely weakens his authority. In 1903 Berenson rejected the traditional attribution, seeing in the work the hand of Sebastiano and, although he subsequently changed his mind, his earliest attribution was endorsed by, among others, Longhi and Wilde (Lucco 1980).

The present writer shares this view (Hirst 1981). The design of the architecture can be matched most closely in that of the *all'antica* arch invented by Sebastiano for the exterior of the S. Bartolomeo organ shutters, on which he was probably engaged as early as 1508 (Cat. 95, 96). The receding perspective of the pavement, incised in the gesso ground, has no real parallel in Giorgione's surviving work and the deliberation over spatial construction points to Sebastiano. Whilst the figures are still redolent of Giorgione, their gestures and their individual morphology are most closely paralleled in Sebastiano's other Venetian paintings. Cleaning of the painting has revealed that the figure of the true mother is one of the best preserved areas of the painting, and her features are a paradigm of Sebastiano's ideal of female beauty in his Venetian period. The closest parallels for the style of painting are the external sides of the S. Bartolomeo organ shutters and the S. Giovanni Crisostomo high altarpiece. These comparisons suggest that *The Judgement of Solomon* preceded the Crisostomo altarpiece and may have been begun about 1508, scarcely after 1509.

Never previously exhibited in public, restoration of the painting is still in progress at the time of writing. It has been cleaned of subsequent overpainting, which has confirmed, as was already clear from the absence of the two babies, that the painting was never finished. A different interpretation of the same subject lies beneath the incomplete final paint layer. Figures on a smaller scale, previously just detectable (Hirst 1981), are now more apparent; underdrawing, clearly readable in infra-red photographs, shows that this earlier composition even included a horseman. In all, there were two earlier attempts at the composition, the most obvious being a painted architectural setting with tall lateral tabernacles instead of the basilican interior which was finally adopted. The change shows how radically Venetian painters of the early

97 (*before restoration*)

sixteenth century could alter their compositions on the canvas itself. It also suggests that the artist arrived at his later solution on the advice of someone familiar with the judicial implications of the antique basilican form: the painting has become a more learned one. The position of the earlier tabernacles suggests that the canvas may have been cut by about 40 cm on the left, implying that the final design was planned to be symmetrical. The left edge has no original pigment on the turnover; against this, scrutiny of the canvas during relining has revealed cusping of the material on both lateral edges. Resolution of the question of the painting's original size must await completion of the restoration, but uncertainty over this issue cannot seriously impair our appreciation of one of the masterpieces of Venetian narrative painting.

M.H.

PROVENANCE
Before 1648 Palazzo Vendramin Calergi, Venice; Marescalchi Collection, Bologna; 1820 (?) Bankes Collection, Kingston Lacy

REFERENCES
Hirst 1981, pp. 13–23, with bibliography; Lucco 1980, pp. 91–92, with bibliography; Ridolfi 1648 (ed. von Hadeln), I, p. 102

Lambert Sustris

Amsterdam *c.* 1515 – after 1568

Sustris was born in Amsterdam and trained in Scorel's workshop in Utrecht. He was probably in the Veneto by the late 1530s, most likely in Titian's studio. A document of 1543 states that *Alberthus de Olandis Amsterdam* was in Padua in the company of Gualtieri dall'Alzere (in 1541 Giuseppe Salviati was there too), at which date Padua was undergoing a cultural renaissance inspired by the example of Mantua. In 1542–43 he was commissioned to decorate the Villa dei Vescovi at Luvigliano (Ballarin 1966, 1967, 1968); although Titian's influence is evident in this work, it is also apparent that Sustris had learnt from the Mantuan and Emilian schools.

Sustris was in Augsburg in 1548 with Titian; he returned there in 1552. During these visits Sustris worked mainly as a portrait painter: the *Portrait of William IV the Elder of Waldburg-Trauchburg* (Augsburg, Gallery) dates from his

first stay while the portraits of *Hans Christoff* and *Veronika Völhin* (Alte Pinakothek, Munich) date from his second visit. The *Portrait of Otto Truchsess von Waldburg* in the Castle of Zeil dates from 1553 and the same family also commissioned Sustris to paint *The Baptism of Christ* at Caen (Ballarin, 1962–63 presumes that all Sustris's paintings now in France originally came from Germany).

After this, Sustris probably returned to Venice and was associated with the circle of artists around Tintoretto, but practically nothing is known about the latter part of his life; we can now exclude the possibility (Ballarin 1968) that the payments for the portraits in the Procuratoria de Supra from 1572 and 1584 are connected with Sustris. According to Vasari he was still alive in 1568.

S.M.R.

REFERENCES
Ballarin 1962, pp. 61–81; Ballarin 1962–63, pp. 335–66; Ballarin 1966, pp. 244–49; Ballarin 1967, pp. 77–101; Ballarin 1968², pp. 115–26; Vasari (ed. Milanesi) 1881, VII, p. 588; Venice 1981¹, no. 36

98

Venus

116 × 186 cm
Rijksmuseum, Amsterdam (inv. A3479)
[*repr. in colour on p. 120*]

This painting belongs to a small group of works, securely datable to 1548–52, which includes the *Noli Me Tangere* (Lille) and the *Birth of the Virgin* (formerly in Hanover). These are stylistically close to Titian's work around 1548, but Sustris was also open to a variety of influences, including that of Flemish art (Ballarin 1962).

This *Venus* is a direct reflection of Titian's *Venus of Urbino* (Uffizi, Florence; fig. 15): it has the same composition, with the nude goddess seen in an interior setting and chambermaids leaning over a chest in the background. Sustris has added a musician playing a clavichord and two lovers on the balcony. However, his use of colour is different from Titian's: Sustris defines areas with clear outlines and enhances his fine tonal range and sensitive draughtsmanship with silvery highlights. Although his style is fundamentally dependent on Titian's work, there are diversities which can probably be explained by the influence of Giulio Romano and Paris Bordone. Sustris did not manage to develop an independent style of his own until the *Mars, Venus and Cupid* (Louvre, Paris), in which the delicately wrought composition and subtle eroticism is finely balanced.

S.M.R.

PROVENANCE
Before 1824 acquired by W. Buchanan from the Villa Borghese, Rome; Mr Willett; after 1829 Mr Neeld; 1945 acquired by T. Harris; 1946 Rijksmuseum

EXHIBITIONS
Venice 1981, no. 36

REFERENCES
Ballarin 1962, pp. 64, 67; Ballarin 1967, p. 86; Ballarin 1968², p. 122; Berenson 1957, I, p. 173; Buchanan 1824, I, p. 223; Amsterdam 1961, p. 296; Rijksmuseum 1976, pp. 529–30; Waagen 1854, II, p. 244

Jacopo Robusti, called

Tintoretto

Venice 1519–Venice 1594

Jacopo Robusti, called Il Tintoretto because his father was a dyer by trade, began his artistic career in about 1537. He worked primarily for a Venetian clientèle, both religious and lay patrons, private and State. According to some sources he was, for a brief period, a pupil of Titian, but he was never tied to one master and was variously influenced by the narrative elements of Bonifazio's painting, Pordenone's plasticity and dynamism, the study of copies after Michelangelo's paintings and copies after the antique. He also assimilated Schiavone's Parmigianesque elegance and painterliness and, around 1554–55, Veronese's use of colour and light.

Tintoretto's youthful compositions already show the fundamental elements of his art: an ability to illustrate a narrative, a remarkable sensibility to the spatial and dynamic values of a composition, extreme skill in the use of colour, light and three-dimensional form. The influence of mannerist art is evident in his mature works in his bold chiaroscuro effects. His treatment of narrative subjects is extremely dramatic and seems to involve the observer in the action. In both his religious compositions and his profane paintings, the realistic evocation of settings and figures brings to his subjects a sense of everyday life, making his works immediately accessible on an emotional level.

P.R.

REFERENCES
Pallucchini and Rossi 1982, with full bibliography

99

Christ Among the Doctors

197 × 319 cm
Museo del Duomo, Milan
[repr. in colour on p. 121]

This painting, formerly in the Galleria Arcivescovile in Milan, was traditionally attributed to Tintoretto; this is now universally accepted, as is its dating in the early 1540s.

At the outset of his career Tintoretto was influenced by Pordenone and Michelangelo, as is evident in this painting, which is close to the *Sacra Conversazione* of 1540 (private coll., London) in the dynamic tension of the composition, the vigorous build of some of the figures and the twisted poses, emphasised here by the use of a particularly bright range of colours in which yellow predominates. Details are painted with lively brushstrokes: the ruffled hair of the venerable doctors, the tiny figures fading into the distance and the minute statuette, which glows like a spectre, show that Tintoretto was already assimilating ideas from Schiavone. This becomes increasingly obvious in the works he painted immediately afterwards.

According to Arcangeli, Tintoretto included in the painting a self-portrait (the curly-headed youth by the colonnade in the background to the left, who is watching

his companion reading), a portrait of Titian (the old man on the left leaning on a stick, disdainfully turning his back on Tintoretto) and also, perhaps, one of Michelangelo (the bearded man at the end of the left-hand group), thus alluding to the position Tintoretto had assumed between these two great artists. It is a rather fanciful interpretation, but undoubtedly reflects the influences evident in this work, which formed the basis of the young artist's mannerist style.

P.R.

PROVENANCE
Galleria Arcivescovile, Milan

EXHIBITIONS
Venice 1981[1], p. 150, no. 41 (Rossi)

REFERENCES
Arcangeli 1955, pp. 21–34; Latuada 1737, p. 84; Pallucchini and Rossi 1982, pp. 17–20, 136–37, no. 41, with full bibliography; Torre 1674, p. 394

100

Apollo and Marsyas

137 × 236 cm
Wadsworth Atheneum, Hartford, the Ella Gallup Sumner and
Mary Catlin Sumner Collection (no. 1950. 438)
[repr. in colour on p. 123]

It is generally accepted that this work can be identified with a ceiling painting of *Apollo and Marsyas* painted by Tintoretto, together with another work (now lost) of *Argos and Mercury*, for Aretino's house in Venice, for which Aretino thanked the artist in a letter dated 15 February 1545.

However, the letter lacks the details that might have conclusively identified Aretino's ceiling painting with the present picture. Also, the *Apollo and Marsyas* is unique among Tintoretto's ceiling paintings of the early 1540s: whereas the rest are painted with foreshortened figures to give a *trompe l'oeil* effect when viewed from below (eg. the paintings in the Galleria Estense, Modena), in this picture no foreshortening was used and no modifications were made for its supposed position on a ceiling (Arcangeli 1955; A. Pallucchini 1969, 1982).

However, the fact remains that the date of Aretino's painting – shortly before February 1545, which can be deduced from the letter since Aretino specifically mentions the rapidity of execution – coincides perfectly with the style of *Apollo and Marsyas*. The picture belongs to the end of Tintoretto's youthful phase when he was influenced by Bonifazio (evident in the vivacity of the colour) and, especially, by Schiavone. At this stage the artist was moving away from his small-scale, highly decorative, narrative style towards broader and airier compositions. If the standing figure on the right is a portrait of Aretino, as Schulz convincingly suggested (1968), his presence would of course be consistent with his having commissioned the picture. Given that Aretino came from Tuscany it would have been appropriate for Tintoretto to follow the central Italian practice of *quadri riportati* (ceiling paintings in which the figures are not foreshortened).

P.R.

PROVENANCE
By 1618 possibly in England (Sir Dudley Carlton); Duke of Abercorn, Sir W. Bromley Davenport, London

REFERENCES
Arcangeli 1955, pp. 30–31; A. Pallucchini 1969, pp. 11, 28; R. Pallucchini and Rossi 1982, pp. 25, 143–44, no. 82, with full bibliography; Schulz 1968, pp. 25, 117, no. 46

101

The Washing of Feet

215.5 × 533.3 cm
The Chapter of the Cathedral Church of St. Nicholas,
Newcastle-upon-Tyne
(on loan to the Shipley Art Gallery, Gateshead)
[*detail repr. in colour on p. 124*]

This painting was published as an autograph Tintoretto by Pallucchini (1976), who believes that it is contemporary with, or a little earlier than *The Last Supper* of 1547 in S. Marcuola, Venice. Previously it had been thought to be either a copy of *The Washing of Feet* (Prado, Madrid) or a partly autograph replica of it. It differs from the Prado canvas only in a few background details, which are, however, present in the copy now facing *The Last Supper* in S. Marcuola. From this fact, and other details concerning the provenance of the Prado version, Pallucchini convincingly argued that *The Washing of Feet* in Newcastle (and not the one in the Prado) is the painting originally executed for the Venetian church, and that the copy still in S. Marcuola (Ridolfi 1642, p. 13) had already been substituted for it in the seventeenth century. The Prado version is also autograph and must have been painted shortly afterwards (1547–48).

The painting was cleaned in 1972 and is in a relatively good state of conservation except for a few areas. Tintoretto abandoned some of the fantastic qualities of his earlier works by this stage, and here emphasised the human nature of the event in details like that of the apostle pulling off his companion's stockings, or the conversation between the two apostles seated at the end of the table; the one on the left must certainly be a portrait.

P.R.

PROVENANCE
Alexis Delahante; 2 June 1814 Phillips's sale; H. Baring; 3 June 1814 acquired privately; 1818 presented to the cathedral of St. Nicholas, Newcastle-upon-Tyne, by Sir Matthew White Ridley; 1980 on loan to Shipley Art Gallery

REFERENCES
Borenius 1932, p. 103, note 3 (as a copy); Gould 1959, p. 88 (as a copy); Gould 1975, pp. 258ff; Newton 1952, p. 75 (as a copy); Osmaston 1915, I, p. 54, note 2; II, p. 180 (as perhaps partly autograph); Pallucchini 1976, pp. 81–97; Pallucchini and Rossi 1982, pp. 31–33, 153–54, no. 124

102

The Visitation

250 × 146 cm; originally with an arched top, made up at the sides
Pinacoteca Nazionale, Bologna (inv. 520)

This painting is recorded in the church of S. Pietro Martire, Bologna, in the seventeenth century; it has always been attributed to Tintoretto. The dating, however, is controversial: Venturi (1928, 1929) placed the work at the beginning of the artist's career, and Pittaluga, Tietze and von der Bercken all believe it to be before 1548. But Coletti, Pallucchini and De Vecchi place it in the 1550s, a dating accepted by the present writer.

It reflects on the one hand the artist's early mannerist formation based on the work of Pordenone and Michelangelo, and, on the other, his new sensitivity to landscape, which is found in other works of this decade.

The Virgin and St. Elizabeth dominate the scene, and their meeting is the centre of the painting in both compositional and emotional terms. Their deliberate, measured gestures of greeting are typical of Tintoretto's interpretation of biblical subjects in human terms; it is the

101

102

103

subordinate figures who emphasise the significance of the meeting.

P.R.

PROVENANCE
S. Pietro Martire, Bologna; after the Napoleonic suppressions acquired by the Pinacoteca Nazionale

REFERENCES
Pallucchini and Rossi 1982, p. 160, no. 143, with full bibliography

103

St. Louis, St. George and the Princess

226 × 146 cm; arched top
Gallerie dell'Accademia, Venice (no. 899)

This painting, together with two other canvases representing *St. Andrew and St. Jerome* and the *Virgin and Child with Four Provveditori* (Accademia, Venice), was commissioned for the first Sala del Magistrato del Sale in the Palazzo dei Camerlenghi, where it was recorded as the work of Tintoretto (Ridolfi 1648). It was apparently commissioned by Giorgio Venier and Alvise (Louis) Foscarini, who retired from the Venetian magistracy on 13 November 1551 and 1 May 1552 respectively, and who, as

was customary on retirement, offered a votive painting of their patron saints to the magistracy in which they had held office. The earliest date for the painting is therefore 1552.

The composition is centred around the princess. Her tense and twisted pose, the plasticity of her figure and her heroic scale all reveal Michelangelo's influence. The extreme plasticity of the three figures, the slightly muted colours and the accentuated contrasts between light and shade are paralleled in other contemporary works of Tintoretto in which a mannerist pictorial language is in evidence. There is a school copy in the Royal Collection (Collins-Baker 1929, p. 142, no. 181).

P.R.

PROVENANCE
Palazzo dei Camerlenghi (Sala del Magistrato del Sale); 1777–1937 in the *antichiesetta* of the Doge's Palace

EXHIBITIONS
Paris 1935, no. 455; Venice 1937, no. 11; Rome 1945, no. 36

REFERENCES
Boschini 1664, p. 271; Ludwig 1902, p. 45; Ridolfi 1648, II, p. 58;
Pallucchini and Rossi 1982, pp. 165–66, no. 162, with full bibliography;
Zanetti 1771, p. 153

104
Portrait of a Man

145.5 × 87.5 cm
The Governing Body, Christ Church, Oxford (no. 100)

The attribution of this portrait to Tintoretto, first suggested
by Borenius, has been unanimously accepted. Borenius
considered it to be a very early work of the artist, dating
from the 1540s. Von der Bercken, who placed it between
1544 and 1548, and Byam Shaw both considered the portrait
to be very close to the *Portrait of a Young Man Aged
Twenty-Five* of 1545 (Her Majesty the Queen). Pallucchini,
on the other hand, found it very close to the *Portrait of a
Young Man* dated 1551 (Metropolitan Museum, New
York), and the present writer has dated it *c.* 1553. It is an
early masterpiece comparable to the *Portrait of a Young
Man Aged Thirty-Five* dated 1553 (Kunsthistorisches
Museum, Vienna). The imposing presentation of the sitter
is created by the use of strong chiaroscuro, which also
accentuates the intensity of his glance.

P.R.

PROVENANCE
1765 Guise

EXHIBITIONS
London 1960, no. 85

104

REFERENCES
Borenius 1938, pp. 37–38; Byam Shaw 1976, p. 76; Pallucchini 1950,
pp. 141–42; Pallucchini and Rossi 1982, p. 56; Rossi 1974, pp. 37, 38, 118,
with full bibliography; von der Bercken 1942, p. 119, no. 270

105 & 106
Judith and Holofernes

58 × 119 cm
[*repr. in colour on p. 122*]

The Finding of Moses

56 × 119 cm
Museo del Prado, Madrid (nos. 389 and 396)
[*repr. in colour on p. 122*]

These paintings are from a series of six pictures depicting
biblical stories, which Sánchez Cantón suggested might be
identified with a group of ceiling paintings of stories from
the Old Testament. They were bought for Philip IV in
Venice by Velázquez during his second trip to Italy
(Palomino). According to Palomino, there was an oval
painting in the centre of *The Fall of Manna*, which Sánchez
Cantón identified with a *Purification of the Midianite
Virgins* in the same format. This identification has been
accepted by all but Schulz. Coletti dated the series in the
mid-1550s, when Tintoretto was deeply influenced by
Veronese, and this has been generally accepted.

The influence of Veronese's style is evident in other
works by Tintoretto dating from around 1555, but it is
usually less pronounced than in this series – except in the
case of *The Assumption* in the church of the Gesuiti,
Venice, which was deliberately painted in the manner of
Veronese. Here his influence is combined with Tintoretto's
own characteristics in a particularly felicitous way. These
decorative scenes, fully mannerist in idiom, are imbued with
a particularly Venetian spirit by Tintoretto's use of colour
and light, and the subjects are presented with his usual
narrative verve. Two maidservants flank Pharaoh's
daughter who holds the infant Moses; the group creates a
calculated rhythm of movement. They are dressed in
brilliantly coloured garments which stand out against the
luxuriant foliage in the background, yet the precious
elegance of form is accompanied by an extraordinary
freshness in the treatment of this narrative subject.

P.R.

PROVENANCE
1686 inventory of the Alcázar, Madrid; collection of Isabella Farnese,
La Granja

REFERENCES
Coletti 1940, pp. 14–15; Palomino 1947, p. 911; Pallucchini and Rossi
1982, pp. 50, 171–72, no. 184, 187, with full bibliography; Sánchez Cantón
1949, pp. 640–43; Schulz 1968, pp. 125–26

107
Pietà

108 × 170 cm
Pinacoteca di Brera, Milan (no. 149)
[*repr. in colour on p. 125*]

This painting can be identified with a lunette formerly in the courtyard of the Procuratie, for which Tintoretto was paid in part on 19 February 1563, receiving the balance on 31 July 1571. In 1590 Tintoretto restored the work when it was installed in the interior of the new building by Scamozzi (von Hadeln). Ridolfi recorded the painting in the Procuratia de Supra.

Presumably it was painted soon after 1563, given its similarity to *The Deposition* of 1559–60 (Accademia, Venice); the ample proportions and the pose of the Magdalen are derived from *The Deposition*. The mourners are arranged around the lifeless figure of Christ in a kind of syncopated rhythm; all their eyes turn to him and they seem transfixed by the grief they are suppressing.

P.R.

PROVENANCE
1590 Procuratia de Supra

EXHIBITIONS
London 1930, no. 339; Paris 1935, no. 452; Venice 1937, no. 39

REFERENCES
Ridolfi 1648, II, p. 57; Pallucchini and Rossi 1982, p. 185, no. 246, with full bibliography; von Hadeln 1911¹, pp. 39, 54, 57; von Hadeln 1911², pp. 125, 129; Zanetti 1771, p. 153

108
Portrait of Sebastian Venier

104.5 × 83.5 cm
Kunsthistorisches Museum, Gemäldegalerie, Vienna (no. 694)

The attribution of this portrait to Tintoretto has been generally accepted, although Venturi and von der Bercken thought it was a copy and De Vecchi rejected it altogether. There are many elements which suggest that it is autograph: notably the virtuoso use of light glinting on the armour and creating a shot effect on the cloak, and the vivid view of the Battle of Lepanto (Sebastian Venier was one of the foremost Venetian commanders) are painted with light, rapid touches of colour on the petrol-blue sea. However, some details are rather less impressive, in particular the hands, which are somewhat harshly modelled.

The portrait must have been painted at about the same time as *Sebastian Venier with a Page* (private coll.; cf. Rossi 1974, p. 134, fig. 160), not long after the Battle of Lepanto

108

in 1571. Between November 1571 and 1572, Tintoretto also painted a large scene of the battle for the Sala dello Scrutinio in the Doge's Palace, which was destroyed by fire in 1577 (Rossi 1982, p. 265). The present painting is a typical state portrait intended for public display. It is more conventional in its positioning of the sitter on the canvas than the portrait in the private collection, and appears to be derived from it. Tintoretto succeeded in infusing a touch of freshness into the penetrating characterisation of Venier.

Ridolfi (1648, II, p. 54) recorded two portraits of Venier by Tintoretto in Venetian collections – one 'in the apparel of a general', in the possession of the Barbarigo family, the other belonging to Nicolò Crasso, which, he said, was 'executed with great diligence'. Lacking further details, it is impossible to know whether the Vienna portrait corresponds with either of them.

P.R.

PROVENANCE
Archduke Leopold Wilhelm

REFERENCES
De Vecchi 1970, p. 137, F. 63; Rossi 1974, pp. 64–65, 130, with full bibliography; Venturi 1925–34, IX, iv, pp. 418, 619; von der Bercken 1942, p. 133, no. 560

109
Portrait of an Elderly Senator

84 × 60 cm
National Gallery of Ireland, Dublin (no. 1122)
[*repr. in colour on p. 127*]

This portrait is unanimously attributed to Tintoretto; the dating of *c.* 1570 proposed by Tietze should be advanced slightly to 1575–80, since the painting is so close in style to the three portraits of Marco Grimani (Prado, Madrid, no. 379; Kunsthistorisches Museum, Vienna, no. 700; Royal Collection), which can all be dated 1576–83 (cf. Rossi 1974, pp. 108, 113, 130).

The four portraits all depict old men who held high positions in the Venetian magistracy, and it is possible that, indirectly, they represent the crisis of values in the society which the sitters themselves represented and served. The drawn features, limp hands and stupefied, although still animated, expression of the senator's eyes, reveal almost shockingly his advanced age. His position in the magistracy is no longer a subject for celebration; instead the emphasis is placed on his years of accumulated experience, and his tragic and profound awareness of the imminence of death. Tintoretto has captured a moment in the sitter's existence and endowed it with the dignity, sensibility and human warmth that distinguish his best portraits.

P.R.

PROVENANCE
Cook Collection, Richmond; 1945 F.A. Drey

REFERENCES
Rossi 1974, pp. 71, 104, with full bibliography; Tietze 1948, p. 359

Jacopo and
Domenico Tintoretto

110
Santa Giustina and the Treasurers

216 × 183 cm
Inscribed bottom right: *1580*; below, corresponding to the three coats of arms, the initials M.A. (originally M.Z., wrongly restored as A); A.M.; A.B.
Gallerie dell' Accademia (no. 225); on deposit at the Museo Correr, Venice
[*repr. in colour on p. 126*]

According to Ridolfi (1648), Boschini (1664) and Zanetti (1771), this painting hung in the Palazzo dei Camerlenghi and was attributed to Jacopo Tintoretto. It may have been a pendant to the *St. Mark with Three Treasurers* (Dahlem Museum, Berlin, no. 316).

On the basis of the coats of arms and the initials, the three treasurers have been identified as Marco Giustiniani (Zustinian), Angelo Morosini and Alessandro Badoer – all magistrates who held office in 1580, the date of the painting. The three figures behind the treasurers are clerks; the

inscription *'el nostro fascicolo'* – our documents – (now darkened) which was next to the clerk on the left suggests he was the usher responsible for the Treasury documents.

Mariacher and De Vecchi have suggested that the painting was partly painted by assistants, and certainly there are weak points such as the treasurers' hands, the lifeless glance of the man on the left, a certain forced emphasis in the painting of Santa Giustina – for which a drawing by Jacopo survives (The Hermitage, Leningrad, no. 25641) – and the weak highlighting of the saint's robe. Domenico Tintoretto has been suggested as a collaborator (Rossi). This is a late, routine composition in which Tintoretto's inspiration congealed into the more conventional tones necessary for an official commission.

P.R.

PROVENANCE
Palazzo dei Camerlenghi, first Sala del Magistrato del Sale

REFERENCES
Boschini 1664, p. 226; De Vecchi 1970, pp. 123–24, no. 245 (as Jacopo and assistants); Mariacher 1953, p. 207; Ridolfi 1648, II, p. 58; Rossi 1974, pp. 72, 126; Rossi 1975, p. 41; Pallucchini and Rossi 1982, p. 218, no. 406, with full bibliography (as Jacopo and Domenico Tintoretto); Zanetti 1771, p. 153

Jacopo Tintoretto

111
Modello for 'Paradise'

152.4 × 490.2 cm
Baron Thyssen-Bornemisza Collection, Lugano
[*repr. in colour on pp. 128–29*]

This painting has recently been included in the corpus of Tintoretto's work as the *modello* for the *Paradise* in the Sala del Maggior Consiglio in the Doge's Palace, a vast canvas painted between 1588 and 1592 to replace Guariento's fresco, which was damaged beyond repair in the fire of 1577.

The present *modello* provides a new document in the complex evolution of this work. There is another *modello* (Louvre, Paris), which the present writer believes can be linked to the competition of 1579–80, as a result of which Veronese and Francesco Bassano were chosen to undertake the commission. This *modello* may be linked to a later, undocumented stage of the commission; when Veronese died in 1588, neither he nor Bassano had begun work on the painting and the commission must have been passed on to Tintoretto.

The grandiose conception of the composition seems to have flowed effortlessly from Tintoretto's brush; it must post-date the Louvre *modello* in which the composition was established. Obviously his experience of creating ample, airy, epic canvases in the Scuola di S. Rocco and the Doge's Palace must have contributed to this facility. The present *modello* is closer than the one in Paris to the final canvas, which was painted almost entirely by Domenico Tintoretto, perhaps with help from other assistants. Schulz believes that the two *modelli* could be part of an initial project for the replacement of Guariento's fresco, perhaps dating from around 1564, in which Zuccari may also have been involved. Pallucchini, however, believes that the Louvre *modello* was executed in competition with Zuccari, and that the present work was painted around 1580.

P.R.

EXHIBITIONS
Los Angeles 1979, no. 37

REFERENCES
Pallucchini and Rossi 1982, pp. 98–99, 231–32, no. 461, with full bibliography; Schulz 1980, pp. 112–26

112

The Deposition

288 × 166 cm
S. Giorgio Maggiore, Venice

Recorded in seventeenth-century sources as a work by Tintoretto, *The Deposition* belongs to the very end of the artist's career. Work began on the Cappella dei Morti, where the painting still hangs, in 1592, and two years later 70 ducats were paid for this altarpiece (Cicogna).

Venturi suggested that Tintoretto's son, Domenico, assisted in the execution of the painting, and the present writer agrees that he was involved in a very minor capacity, but overall, the work reveals a sensibility typical of Jacopo, who was still able to create a work of contained dramatic force by using a sombre tonality interrupted by brilliant flashes of light, and by setting the desolate, limp body of Christ against that of the unconscious Virgin in the background.

P.R.

EXHIBITIONS
Venice 1937, no. 74

REFERENCES
Boschini 1664, p. 566; Cicogna 1834, p. 353 (note 270), 385, 388; Ridolfi 1648, II, p. 60; Pallucchini and Rossi 1982, pp. 108–09, 234, no. 468, with full bibliography; Venturi 1925–34, IX, IV, pp. 613, 618

Tiziano Vecellio, called

Titian

Pieve di Cadore *c.* 1480/85 – Venice 1576

Contemporary evidence can be adduced to support a variety of dates between 1473 and 1490 for Titian's birth. Much recent criticism, exemplified by Wethey, favours the latest possible dating, but Panofsky and Hope have argued more convincingly for a date in the first half of the 1480s, which is accepted here. According to Dolce and Vasari, Titian was sent to Venice as a young boy and trained by Gentile and/or Giovanni Bellini, adopting the new manner of Giorgione in about 1507. In 1508 he frescoed the side façade of the Fondaco dei Tedeschi in Venice; in 1516 he was appointed

112

to work in the Sala del Maggior Consiglio in the Doge's Palace and in the same year he began work on the *Assunta* (fig. 19) for the high altar of the Frari. At this time he also began working for Alfonso d'Este, Duke of Ferrara, his first courtly patron outside Venice. From 1523 Titian worked also for Federigo Gonzaga, Marquis and later Duke of Mantua. His *Death of St. Peter Martyr* (see fig. 14), completed for SS. Giovanni e Paolo in Venice in 1530 and widely considered to be his masterpiece, was destroyed by fire in 1867, while the great battlepiece for the Sala del Maggior Consiglio, completed in 1538, suffered a similar fate in 1577. The Emperor Charles V became a major patron after 1532, but Titian also worked for Pope Paul III and other members of the Farnese family, visiting Rome in 1545–46. In 1548 and 1550, he travelled to the Imperial court at Augsburg, and between 1551 and 1554 he was working on the great *Trinity* (also called the *Gloria*) now in the Prado, Madrid, which the Emperor took with him on his retirement to Yuste. In the 1550s Philip II of Spain became Titian's principal patron and received from the artist a splendid series of religious and mythological pictures (fig. 16).

G.R.

REFERENCES
Dolce 1557, pp. 51–52; Hope 1980, pp. 10–11; Panofsky 1969, pp. 176–79; Vasari (ed. Milanesi) 1881, VII, pp. 426–28; Wethey 1969, I, pp. 40–42

113

Jacopo Pesaro Presented to St. Peter by Pope Alexander VI

145 × 183 cm
Inscribed on a tablet: RITRATTO DI VNO DI CA^{sa} PESARO / IN VENETIA CHE FV FATTO / GENERALE DI Sta CHIESA. / TITIANO F.
Musée Royal des Beaux-Arts, Antwerp (no. 357)
[*repr. in colour on p. 55*]

The inscription is clearly not contemporary, but the information it gives seems to be correct, if imprecise. The kneeling figure is certainly Jacopo Pesaro, who was portrayed again by Titian in the *Pesaro Madonna* in the Frari. He was appointed papal legate to command a detachment of galleys against the Turks on 20 April 1502 and won a victory at Santa Maura (Leucadia) on 23 August.

Mather has suggested that the picture must have been painted, or at least commissioned, before the engagement, as it shows no battle, but it seems much more likely that it is an *ex voto* expressing thankfulness for the victory. Crowe and Cavalcaselle thought that it must have been painted before Pope Alexander's death in 1503, since hatred of the Borgias would have prevented his being portrayed later, but Hope has plausibly suggested that it must postdate his death as a living pope would not have been shown standing in the presence of the saint. He also argues that, since Pesaro was absent from Venice from early 1503 until 1506, the picture dates from the latter year. Other authorities, such as Wethey, who accept a late date for Titian's birth, date the whole picture as late as *c*. 1512, Suida even suggesting that the portraits were not finished until about 1520. Others have proposed that the execution of the picture falls into two distinct phases and this has been most fully elaborated by Meyer zur Capellen, who has supported this view with arguments based on supposed differences in the surface appearance of the picture and spatial confusion on its left-hand side, and on discrepancies in the treatment of the head of St. Peter and those of the other two figures revealed by x-rays. The differences of surface and the spatial confusion are not apparent to the present writer, to whom the picture appears a unity, and the admitted discrepancies shown in the x-rays might be explained by the hypothesis that Titian adopted a different approach in his portraits and in the conventional portrayal of a saint.

The composition is certainly the most primitive in Titian's surviving work, perpetuating a familiar scheme of the fifteenth century, and the St. Peter is, in general terms, Bellinesque. In the view of the present writer, the design was made not later than 1506, perhaps earlier, and the picture

was completed later, shortly after Pesaro's return to Venice in that year. The iconography of the pseudo-antique relief decorating the socle of St. Peter's throne, which has some analogies with the grisaille fragments from Titian's part of the decoration of the Fondaco dei Tedeschi, has been studied by Wittkower, who interprets Cupid (on the altar in the centre) as Divine Love, his spiritual character emphasised by the juxtaposition of St. Peter's keys. He shoots at Venus Victrix, the figure next to the corselet, whose portrayal here has special significance since Pesaro was titular bishop of Baffo, the ancient Paphos. The whole relief echoes the theme of the papal victory. It has also been studied by Tressider, who noted stylistic resemblances to the contemporary reliefs of Antonio Lombardo, as well as to antique sources, and further elaborated the iconographical interpretation.

G.R.

PROVENANCE
Presumably commissioned by Jacopo Pesaro, probably for his palace rather than a church; 1623 seen by Van Dyck in Venice; 1639 in the collection of Charles I at Whitehall; 1650 Thomas Bagley; Don Gaspar Henríquez de Cabreras, Duque de Medina de Rioseco; Convent of S. Pascuale, Madrid; Godoy; Príncipe de la Paz; King William of Holland; 1823 donated by King William to the Musée Royal des Beaux-Arts

EXHIBITIONS
London 1930, no. 158 (commemorative catalogue, no. 356); Venice 1935, no. 3

REFERENCES
Crowe and Cavalcaselle 1877, I, pp. 74–79; Hope 1980, pp. 23–26; Mather 1938, pp. 18–19; Meyer zur Capellen 1980, pp. 144–52; Suida 1935, pp. 23–24, 151; Tressider 1979, I, pp. 142–59; Wethey 1969, pp. 152–53; Wittkower 1938–39, pp. 202–03

114

Salome

90 × 72 cm
Galleria Doria-Pamphilj, Rome
[*repr. in colour on p. 65*]

This composition exists in three early versions, of which this is widely accepted as the finest. It was ascribed to Titian in early inventories, but was attributed to Giorgione by the time Crowe and Cavalcaselle wrote. They confidently ascribed it to Pordenone, but Morelli, in rare agreement with von Bode, argued convincingly for Titian's authorship, which has been generally accepted. It is usually dated about 1515, but Hope has noted its dependence on Sebastiano del Piombo's version of the same subject of 1510 (National Gallery, London). He also considers that the model was the same as that used by Giorgione for his *Venus* (Gemäldegalerie, Dresden) and has suggested a date of about 1511.

Panofsky has emphasised the erotic elements in the picture and pointed out that the tradition of Salome's love for the St. John the Baptist goes back at least as far as the twelfth century, when it formed the subject of a Latin poem. The cupid on the keystone of the arch in the background, while emphasising this element, also reflects the widespread use of winged putti as keystone decoration on the arches of public buildings in fifteenth-century Venice (as, for instance, in the Arco Foscari, the Arsenal gateway, the main door of the Scuola Grande di San Marco and the choir arch of S. Giobbe) and this also stresses the official nature of St. John's imprisonment and execution. Panofsky has suggested that the head of the Baptist may be a self-portrait.

G.R.

PROVENANCE
1592 Lucrezia d'Este, Duchess of Urbino (?); 1602 Cardinal Pietro Aldobrandini, Rome; by 1665 Olimpia Aldobrandini-Pamphilj; Giovanni Battista Pamphilj; Galleria Doria-Pamphilj

EXHIBITIONS
London 1930, no. 165 (commentary to no. 359)

REFERENCES
Crowe and Cavalcaselle 1912, III, pp. 29, 178; Hope 1980, p. 32, pl. IV; Morelli 1982, I, p. 307; Panofsky 1969, pp. 20, 42–47; Richter 1937, pp. 227–28; Wethey 1969, pp. 155ff

115
Holy Family with a Shepherd

99 × 137 cm
The National Gallery, London

This is one of the earliest known examples of a type of religious composition that was to become immensely popular in Venice. Slight weaknesses in the drawing of the

Madonna and the fact that she seems too small prompted various scholars from Crowe and Cavalcaselle onwards to question Titian's authorship. But the other names proposed – Lotto, Palma Vecchio and Bordone – are clearly unacceptable, and in the past thirty years the traditional attribution has been unanimously accepted. As with virtually all Titian's early works the precise date is controversial, and proposals range from c. 1510, favoured by the present writer, to c. 1516. The issue cannot be settled until agreement is reached about the authorship of *The Virgin and Child with St. Anthony and St. Roch* (Cat. 34) and *Christ and the Adulteress* (Cat. 35), which, if also by Titian, must both be of around 1510. The present exhibition provides a unique opportunity to compare these two problematic works with a group of undisputed early paintings by Titian, notably the votive picture from Antwerp (Cat. 113), which seems to be the earliest, this *Holy Family* and the *Salome* (Cat. 114), which is surely the latest of the three.

C.H.

PROVENANCE
1693 Palazzo Borghese, Rome; by 1799 acquired by W. Ottley; W. Champion; 1810 acquired by Holwell Carr; 1831 bequeathed to the National Gallery

REFERENCES
Crowe and Cavalcaselle 1877, II, p. 428; Freedberg 1971, p. 95; Gould 1975, pp. 267f; Hope 1980, p. 40 note 19; Pallucchini 1969², pp. 33, 247; Valcanover 1969, p. 99, no. 77; Wethey 1969, pp. 94f, with full bibliography

116

Portrait of a Man

85.6 × 72.5 cm
Her Majesty The Queen (no. 149)
[*repr. in colour on p. 79*]

Traditionally this portrait was said to represent Boccaccio and later Alessandro de' Medici, but neither identification can be supported. Gronau claimed to have seen a copy with an inscription identifying the sitter as the poet Jacopo Sannazaro, and this identification is not irreconcilable with other evidence of Sannazaro's appearance. But if it is intended to represent the poet it must be based on an earlier picture since this portrait cannot have been painted before 1510 when Sannazaro, who was born in 1458, was already in his fifties – much older than the man shown here.

The portrait was ascribed to Titian in Charles II's inventory, and to Giorgione in those of James II and Queen Anne, but Crowe and Cavalcaselle were unable to pronounce on the authorship of the picture in the state in which they saw it. The picture is indeed rubbed and badly damaged, but much of its original quality has been recovered and it has been accepted by recent critics, with the exception of Hetzer and Tietze, as an autograph work. Gronau and Fischel dated it about 1511, but Suida felt 1513–14 to be more appropriate and Ricketts, though he found its dating difficult, associated it with the *Physician Parma* (Cat. 117) and placed it c. 1514–16. More recently Valcanover and Pallucchini have advanced the date to c. 1518–20, but the costume would seem to favour an earlier dating, c. 1511–12.

G.R.

PROVENANCE
Gerrit van Reynst, Amsterdam; 1660 Dutch gift to King Charles II; Whitehall; Kensington Palace; 1834 Hampton Court

EXHIBITIONS
Manchester 1857, no. 256; Leeds 1868, no. 237; London 1872, no. 72; London 1915, no. 18; London 1946, no. 199; London 1960, no. 20; London 1964, no. 22; London 1976; London 1977, no. 23

REFERENCES
Berenson 1894, p. 124; Berenson 1957, p. 186; Collins-Baker 1929, pp. 143–44; Crowe and Cavalcaselle 1877, II, p. 465; Fischel 1911, p. 18; Gronau 1904, pp. 43, 279; Mahon 1950, p. 12; Pallucchini 1969², p. 254; Ricketts 1910, pp. 46, 54; Shearman 1983, pp. 251–52, no. 270, pl. 229; Suida 1935, pp. 33, 153; Valcanover 1969, no. 94; Wethey 1971, p. 138

117

Portrait of a Man (called the Physician Parma)

88 × 75 cm
Kunsthistorisches Museum, Gemäldegalerie, Vienna (no. 708)
[*repr. in colour on p. 81*]

While there is general agreement as to the high quality of this painting, many scholars, notably Crowe and Cavalcaselle, have doubted the attribution to Titian. While there is nothing in the conception to make the composition irreconcilable with Titian's practice around 1510–20, the actual handling seems lighter and more delicate than we would expect from him. Wilde thought that the technique, painted *alla prima* without underpainting, ruled out Titian as the author, and the catalogue of the London exhibition of 1949 stated that 'Titian's authorship of this work . . . can no longer be upheld after the recent cleaning'. Wickhoff attributed the portrait to Domenico Campagnola, and Cook (predictably) to Giorgione, an opinion followed with some reserve by Justi. Hetzer ascribed it to an unknown painter of the first quarter of the century and Tietze omitted it from his catalogue. On the other hand, Morelli, followed by Berenson, Gronau, Suida and, more recently, Baldass, Klauner and Oberhammer, Valcanover, Pallucchini, and Wethey, stood firm for the Titian attribution. The attribution to Giorgione does not really seem possible, and the present author prefers the ascription to Titian, who was capable of great variations of style between contemporary works, rather than an attribution to a second-rate painter like Domenico Campagnola or an unknown artist. In its delicacy of finish the painting may be compared to the *Tribute Money* in the Gemäldegalerie, Dresden or, to a lesser extent, the *Portrait of a Man* in Copenhagen.

The identification of the sitter as Titian's physician, Parma, rests on the assumption that this is the picture described by Ridolfi in the collection of Bartolomeo della Nave in Venice. The description fits well and we know that much of the della Nave collection passed into that of Archduke Leopold Wilhelm, with which this picture came to Vienna, and, although the portrait cannot be identified with any of the items listed in della Nave's collection in the inventory published by Waterhouse from the Hamilton papers, Garas has identified it in another Hamilton inventory. Schupbach has plausibly identified Ridolfi's 'Medico suo detto il Parma' with Gian Giacomo Bartolotti (active 1491–1530), a member of a medical family from Parma who was a doctor with the Venetian fleet in 1505–07 and Prior of the Collegio dei Medici in Venice in 1511 or 1512, and who left a number of writings in manuscript, including a vigorously obscene Macaronic poem. Schupbach also, again plausibly, identifies the same sitter at an earlier age, in Giorgione's *Terris Portrait* in San Diego, California.

Gronau suggested a date of 1511, from a comparison of this portrait with the Padua frescoes, and in this he was followed by Fischel, but Ricketts suggested a later date of c. 1514–16. Wethey suggested 1515–18 and Valcanover as late as 1520. The age difference between the sitters in this and the *Terris Portrait* – if that is of the same sitter – suggest a date towards the end of the second decade. The picture is often linked in discussion with the so-called Sannazaro portrait from the Royal Collection (Cat. 116).

G.R.

PROVENANCE
Collection of Bartolomeo della Nave (?), Venice; by 1659 Archduke Leopold Wilhelm, Brussels; Imperial Collection, Vienna

EXHIBITIONS
London 1930, no. 164 (commentary to cat. no. 360); London 1949², no. 181

REFERENCES
Baldass 1957, pp. 150–52; Berenson 1894, p. 127; Berenson 1957 p. 191;

Cook 1907, p. 148; Fischel 1911, pp. 19, 248; Garas 1967[1], pp. 39–80; Gronau 1904, p. 276; Hetzer cited in Wilde 1928; Justi 1908, II, no. 59; London 1949, p. 72; Morelli 1892, I, p. 308; Oberhammer and Klauner 1960, I, p. 134; Pallucchini 1969, p. 254; Ricketts 1910, p. 46; Ridolfi 1914, I, p. 169; Schupbach 1978, pp. 142ff.; Suida 1935, pp. 33, 152; Valcanover 1960, I, pl. 85; Valcanover 1969, no. 96; Waterhouse 1952, pp. 14–20; Wethey 1971, II, p. 121; Wickhoff 1893, pp. 135–36; Wilde 1928, pp. 231–32, amplified in conversation with the author in 1937

118

Portrait of Tommaso Mosti (?)

85 × 67 cm
Inscribed on back of canvas:
DI.THOMASO. MOSTI. / IN.ETA.DI.ANNI
XXV. L'ANNO. / M.D.XXVI. / THITIANO DA CADORO / PITTORE
Galleria Palatina, Palazzo Pitti, Florence (no. 495)
[repr. in colour on p. 78]

The inscription is old but certainly not contemporary; the picture is on its original canvas and has been neither relined nor transferred. While Berenson, Wethey and others have accepted the date of 1526, the content of the inscription has been challenged as regards both the date and the identification of the sitter. Tommaso Mosti was a Ferrarese courtier intimate with Alfonso d'Este, Duke of Ferrara, but by 1524, at the latest, he had taken holy orders and 1526 is not a year in which Titian is otherwise known to have been in Ferrara. Lazzari suggested that the sitter was Mosti's younger brother Vincenzo and this view has been widely accepted, but, as Wethey has pointed out, this can hardly be the case if we adhere to the date of 1526 and the age of 25 for the sitter, since Vincenzo is known to have distinguished himself at the Battle of Ravenna in 1512. Zecchini (Florence 1978–79) has suggested the possibility of the sitter being the third Mosti brother, Agostino, who was a literary figure and a follower of Ariosto, but if the inscription is to be relied on at all, then it is not very easy to understand how the wrong christian name came to be given.

Some of these difficulties are removed by Hope's suggestion that the date should read 1520, and one can see how a mistake might have arisen if the original inscription – perhaps on the stretcher, which, according to Zecchini, has been renewed – gave the date in arabic figures, as a nought might easily be confused with a six. Hope thinks this picture may be identical with one of an unidentified sitter that Alfonso is known to have commissioned from Titian in that year. He also draws attention to the analogies between this picture and Raphael's Portrait of Castiglione, (Louvre, Paris) which Titian might have seen on a visit to Mantua in 1519. Ricketts associated the picture with Titian's Man with a Glove and Man in Black in the Louvre, dating them about 1520, with which Valcanover agreed. On the other hand, Gronau proposed a date of 1516, which Suida and Tietze accepted, while Hetzer suggested 1515. The association with the Man with a Glove is compelling and suggests that Hope's emendation of the date to 1520 is correct.

G.R.

PROVENANCE
1675 entered the Palazzo Pitti with the collection of Cardinal Leopoldo de'Medici

EXHIBITIONS
Venice 1935, no. 20; Stockholm 1962–63, no. 89; Florence 1978–79, no. 55

REFERENCES
Berenson 1957, I, p. 185; Crowe and Cavalcaselle 1877, I, p. 303; Fischel 1911, pp. 34–35; Gronau 1904, p. 292; Hetzer in Thieme-Becker 1940, p. 161; Hope 1980, pp. 62–64; Lazzari 1951, pp. 185–86; Ricketts 1910, p. 64; Suida 1935, pp. 30–35; Tietze 1936, I, p. 124, II p. 289; Valcanover 1969, no. 95; Wethey 1971, II, pp. 119–20

119

St. John the Baptist

201 × 134 cm
Signed on the stone on which the saint rests his left foot: TICIANVS
Galleria dell'Accademia, Venice (no. 194)

Much praised by early writers, this impressive picture has not commended itself so strongly to more recent critics, who have also disagreed about its dating. It must have been painted before 1557, when Dolce wrote in praise of it, and Crowe and Cavalcaselle seem to have thought it not much earlier. Mayer, on the other hand, proposed a dating before 1533, on the grounds of, first, the spelling of the name in the signature – with a 'c' rather than a second 'T' – and, second, the stylistic resemblance to figures in the Brescia polyptych of 1522. He has been followed recently by Hope, who has dated the picture to 1531 and related it to the lost Death of St. Peter Martyr (see fig. 14). It is true that Titian seems in general to have abandoned spelling his name with a 'c' by the mid-1530s, but we cannot be certain he never reverted to it later, and strong stylistic relationships can be seen with works of the early 1540s, such as The Allocution of Alfonso d'Avalos (Prado, Madrid), The Crowning with Thorns of 1540–42 (Louvre, Paris) and, as Ricketts observed, the Ecce Homo of the following year (Kunsthistorisches Museum, Vienna). Brendel has suggested that the figure derives from the same antique model as the Risen Christ in Urbino of 1542–44, and certainly it is exceptional in Titian's work to find such an all'antica pose. Tietze dated the painting in this period, while Suida and Wethey placed it after Titian's return from Rome in 1546, but Valcanover, who had earlier accepted a date in the early 1540s, recently placed it in the late 1530s on the grounds of the similarity in terms of colour between St. John and The Presentation in the Temple (Accademia, Venice), revealed by the recent cleaning of both pictures (Venice 1981).

G.R.

PROVENANCE
S. Maria Maggiore, Venice; 1808 destined for the Accademia when the church was secularised, but considered for removal to the Brera, Milan; 1812 recorded in the Accademia

EXHIBITIONS
Venice 1935, no. 35; Venice 1946, no. 230; Venice 1981[1], no. 15

REFERENCES
Brendel 1955, pp. 121–22; Crowe and Cavalcaselle 1877, II, p. 251; Dolce 1557, p. 54; Hope 1980, pp. 69–70; Mayer 1937, p. 178; Ricketts 1910, p. 114; Suida 1935, p. 125; Wethey 1969, I, pp. 136–37

119

120

120

Portrait of Gerolamo Melchiorre and Francesco Santo da Pesaro

91.5 × 77 cm
Signed slantwise and upside down at lower left: TF
Private Collection

This, one of the very few double portraits by Titian which is known to survive, ranks high among his sensitive portrayals of children. None but he could tune his young sitters to such a pitch. The presence of the painting in the gallery at Ca' Pesaro in 1797 implies the family of the sitters; while their ages and the style of painting leads to their identification, for no other pair of Pesaro brothers, so close in age, could have been portrayed thus in the 1540s.

Veronese, in part on the basis of portraits like this, although Veronese's style by that date is better indicated by the *Portrait of a Member of the Soranzo Family* (Cat. 141).

The format, with its direct presentation of the sitter against a neutral background, the brilliance of the colour and virtuosity in rendering the sitter's pearls and great jewel show the influence of Titian's portraits from the 1520s onwards. Since nothing is known about the sitter, dating is difficult. Veronese had begun to absorb Titian's principles in his earliest surviving portrait, that of *Francesco Franceschini* of 1551 (Ringling Museum, Sarasota). By the time of the *Count Giuseppe da Porto and his Son Adriano* (ex-Contini Bonacossi Coll., Florence) and its companion piece *Livia da Porto Thiene with her Daughter Porzia* (Walters Museum, Baltimore) of 1553–54, he overcame the hesitancy in the *contrapposto* of his earlier portrait. The directness of vision of the present portrait and of the closely related *Bella Nani* in the Louvre, Paris, can be related to the portrait-like figures introduced into the frescoes of the Sala dell' Olimpo at Villa Barbaro, Maser, which suggests that they should be dated to the end of the 1550s or the early 1560s.

R.C.

PROVENANCE
Collection of the Duc de Luynes; ceded to Mme Wagner; 1871 sold by her to the Musée de la Chartreuse

EXHIBITIONS
Venice 1939, no. 47; Paris 1965, no. 313

REFERENCES
Cocke 1980², p. 46; Pignatti 1976, p. 121, with full bibliography

139

139
Portrait of a Woman and Child with a Dog

115 × 95 cm
Musée du Louvre, Paris (inv. 1199)

Veronese's portraits range from a straightforward presentation of a sitter against a neutral setting, as in the Douai *Portrait of a Woman* (Cat. 138), to a more complex handling. In some cases he uses a strip of sky and landscape to one side, as in the present portrait, or in the marvellous *Portrait of a Man* in Budapest, in others he adds columns, curtains and chairs, as in the *Portrait of a Member of the Soranzo Family* (Cat. 141).

The present picture was in the Bevilacqua Collection in Verona, which was housed in the family palace on the Corso designed by Michele Sanmichele in the 1530s for Antonio and Gregorio Bevilacqua. The collection was started in the latter part of the sixteenth century by Mario Bevilacqua, who amassed an outstanding group of antiquities. There was a striking series of marbles (now in Munich), including a fine series of portrait heads, the *Dead Niobid* (acquired in Rome), a *Dionysus* and an *Aphrodite*. The finest piece was the *Adorante* (East Berlin), which had come to Venice from Rhodes in the early part of the sixteenth century and which entered the Bevilacqua Collection in 1570.

The paintings in the collection did not match the antiquities. They were assembled later as a representative group of works by local artists, including G. F. Caroto, Orlando Fiacco and Veronese, but the attributions were optimistic. Modern scholars attribute the small *Holy Family* (Louvre, Paris) to Brusasorci and the *Venus and Cupid* (Fogg Art Museum, Cambridge, Mass.) to Veronese's workshop, a fate shared by the *Venus* in Omaha. In the light of this it is interesting to compare the present portrait, which is more informal than the one in Douai and so probably dates from the later 1560s, with the other portraits in the exhibition.

R.C.

PROVENANCE
By 1648 in the Bevilacqua Collection, Verona; May 1797 removed on the orders of Napoleon; 1798 Musée du Louvre

EXHIBITIONS
Paris 1960, no. 1

REFERENCES
Blumer 1936, p. 269, no. 122; Franzoni 1970, pp. 56ff; Pignatti 1976, p. 121, with full bibliography

140
The Holy Family with St. John the Baptist and St. George

41 × 50 cm
The Visitors of the Ashmolean Museum, Oxford (inv. A863)

140

Veronese's great fresco cycle in Villa Barbaro, Maser, underlined the Christian faith of the patrons, Daniele and Marcantonio Barbaro, by including two lunettes of the Holy Family. The success of the cycle, which was finished by 1559, prompted a variant on the lunettes, the *Virgin and Child with St. Peter and an Unidentified Saint* (Museo Civico, Vicenza). The present canvas is a variant of the Vicenza painting, reduced to about half its size.

From the outset of his career Veronese fulfilled a demand for small versions of both religious and mythological paintings. The first datable canvas in the series is the *Madonna and Child with St. George, Santa Giustina and a Donor* (Girolamo Scrocchetto, in the Louvre). Scrocchetto is recognisable as the abbot who commissioned the *Feast* for S. Giorgio (Louvre), but here is shown as a much younger man, so this painting presumably dates from early in his first period of office as abbot, between 1551 and 1554. The small *Mystic Marriage of St. Catherine* at Christ Church, Oxford, precedes the Louvre painting, and the Montpellier version of this theme can be dated to 1568 on the evidence of a drawing. Other pictures of this type from the decade 1560–70 probably include the Verona *Deposition*, the Boston *Pietà*, the Detroit *Muse of Painting* and the Turin *Mars, Venus and Cupid*. The recently rediscovered and over-restored *Death of Procris* in a private collection in London probably dates from the 1570s.

Modern catalogues of Veronese's paintings include many more small paintings as autograph, but their claims need to be re-examined against this corpus. Some were produced with considerable workshop assistance, while others may have been painted by followers in the 1580s as a tribute to a style already in enormous demand. It is particularly instructive to be able to compare here the Oxford painting with the altarpieces from S. Francesco della Vigna and the Chrysler Collection (Cats. 133 and 135).

R.C.

PROVENANCE
Collection of Sir Richard Green Price; 1952 acquired by the Ashmolean Museum

REFERENCES
Pignatti 1976, p. 111, with full bibliography

141

Portrait of a Member of the Soranzo Family

184 × 113 cm
The Earl of Harewood
[*repr. in colour on p. 137*]

This notable portrait can be identified with one of a pair in the sale of the Flemish-born painter, Niccolò Renier. He lived and worked in Venice where his collection was sold after his death in 1666. G.15 of the sale catalogue was a portrait of a man shown 'seated in Roman style with, behind, architecture, a frame with touches of gold'. This fits with the Harewood painting, as do the dimensions of the companion picture, $11\frac{1}{2}$ by 8 *quarte* (196 × 136 cm).

Veronese had painted frescoes in the country villa of one branch of the Soranzo family in the early 1550s and was in contact with Francesco Soranzo in June 1584, discussing his spinach. The Soranzo are, however, a large patrician family with a number of branches, so that it is not possible at present to suggest a precise identification for the Harewood portrait.

The marvellously accomplished composition, based upon the diagonal running from top left to bottom right, must be understood as balancing that of the lost companion painting of the sitter's wife, which must have hung to the left of the present picture with the diagonal movement reversed. The handling of the costume retains the brilliance of the earlier portraits, but the contrasts are softened and there is a new sense of informality in the pose (although not in the choice of costume). This fits with portraits which, on external grounds, can be dated to the 1570s: they include the *Portrait of Alessandro Vittoria* (Metropolitan Museum, New York) probably of 1575, the *Portrait of Jacob König* in Prague, and the *Portrait of the Grand-Duke Francesco I Medici* in Kassel, which must date from after 1574.

Veronese's costume study for the present portrait was on the London art market in 1970. The handling of the black chalk on the blue paper has the almost abstract quality of his chalk preparatory sketches, but this is combined with accurate observation of the white highlights, which are followed closely in the painting, and of the fur, which he annotated with a 'P' (*pelliccia* means fur).

R.C.

PROVENANCE
1648 Reinst Collection; 1666 sale of Niccolò Renier's Collection, Venice, no. G.14; acquired by the 6th Earl of Harewood from the collection of Sir Charles Robinson.

EXHIBITIONS
Venice 1939, pp. 180–81

REFERENCES
Cocke 1984, cat. no. 77; Pignatti 1976, p. 153, with full bibliography; Savini-Branca 1965, pp. 96ff

142

Veronese developed the contrast between the main figures and the heavenly host in the votive picture of the battle painted for the Sala del Collegio in the Doge's Palace between 1577 and March 1578, which was commissioned by the Venetian naval commander Sebastiano Venier (see Cat. 108). This suggests that the Accademia painting was painted shortly after the battle.

R.C.

PROVENANCE
1664 S. Pietro Martire, Murano; 1812 Gallerie dell' Accademia

EXHIBITIONS
Venice 1939, no. 60

REFERENCES
Cocke 1984, cat nos. 61–63, 87; Gattinoni 1914, no. 13; Pignatti 1976, p. 133, with full bibliography

dimensions given for it in the 1682 inventory of the collection, 14 by 6½ *quarte* (238 × 110 cm), clearly differ from those of the present canvas.

143
The Resurrection of Christ

136 × 104 cm
Staatliche Museum, Gemäldegalerie, Dresden (inv. 235)
[*repr. in colour on p. 132*]

The Resurrection had been a popular theme in Venetian painting since Bellini's altarpiece for S. Michele in Isola (Dahlem Museum, Berlin). Titian's reworking of Bellini's design in his altarpiece in SS. Nazaro e Celso, Brescia, completed by 1522, was the starting point for Veronese's elegant painting. Titian heightened the asymmetry by his use of the dawn light behind the head of the standing soldier, and by the sweeping diagonal which runs through the landscape and is echoed in the poses of the soldiers. He balanced it by increasing the scale of the figure of Christ, which was based on a cast of the Laocoön.

Veronese retained the asymmetry, but used more dramatic gestures in the reactions of the soldiers. Christ is reduced in scale to match the other figures, but is isolated by the introduction of ruins, which symbolise the area that housed the sepulchre, and he stands out against a sky dominated by shades of green. The receding diagonal movement was developed by showing in the background the three Marys approaching the empty tomb guarded by an angel, the passage with which the account of the Resurrection in the Gospels opens. Christ appears suspended above the sepulchre, rather than bursting upwards; later Veronese improved on this in two altarpieces in which the Christ is developed from the figure in the present canvas. That from S. Giacomo, Murano (Westminster Hospital, London) can be dated to 1577–78, together with *The Visitation* from the same church now in the Barber Institute, Birmingham. The great altarpiece in S. Francesco della Vigna, which is often doubted and is in need of restoration, must date from before 1584, since it must be one of the two pictures in the church mentioned by Borghini in that year. The present painting must

142
Allegory of the Battle of Lepanto

169 × 137 cm
Gallerie dell' Accademia, Venice (inv. 136)

This painting is one of a series by Veronese celebrating the establishment of the Holy League and its defeat of the Turks at the Battle of Lepanto on 7 October 1571. The psychological impact of that victory for Christendom was enormous and outweighed any other considerations, including the loss of Cyprus.

The victory in the naval battle in the bottom half of the painting is attributed to divine intervention, indicated by the dramatic burst of light under the Virgin and by the angels throwing down flaming arrows through the storm clouds. The Virgin, as Queen of Heaven, receives the prayers of a group of saints: from left to right, Peter, who stands for the Papacy, James, who represents Spain, Giustina, on whose feast day the battle occurred, and Mark, the patron saint of Venice. The three saints who represent the members of the Holy League – Peter, James and Mark – also appear, throwing down palms of victory from the sky, in a highly finished drawing at Chatsworth. The absence of Santa Giustina from the drawing shows that it must celebrate the signing of the League in July 1571.

Ridolfi, writing in 1648, described another version of this subject in the collection of the Caliari family, in which the Virgin knelt in prayer before the Trinity, together with a personification of Venice between Mark and Giustina. The therefore have been painted either in the late 1560s or the early 1570s, at a moment when Veronese developed from the blue skies of his earlier paintings to the green ones used in many later works.

R.C.

PROVENANCE
1741 acquired by the Elector Frederick August III, Dresden; it was said to have come from the Imperial collection, Vienna, and may have been no. 559 in the 1737 Prague collection whose dimensions (2 *elen* 11 by 1 *elen* 15 [about 150 × 102 cm]) match the present painting

EXHIBITIONS
Venice 1939, no. 53

REFERENCES
Cocke 1980², pp. 90–91; Dresden 1929, no. 235; Köpl 1899, no. 559; Pignatti 1976, pp. 137–38, with full bibliography

144
The Crucifixion

102 × 102 cm
Musée du Louvre, Paris (inv. 1195)

This deeply moving canvas illustrates Veronese's ability to work on a small scale. The oblique setting of the crosses, with Christ seen from the side, and the dramatic sky, had been used slightly earlier in the large altarpiece of this subject which Veronese painted for S. Niccolò ai Frari in 1581–82 (Accademia, Venice).

Although there is less dramatic movement in this painting than in the Frari altarpiece, intensity of feeling is achieved through the swooning Virgin supported by St. John, and by the gesture of the Magdalen who hides her face in grief. The clouds roll over the sun to heighten the mood of mourning and to illustrate the passage in St. Matthew's gospel: 'Now from the sixth hour there was darkness over all the land unto the ninth hour.'

The composition was worked out in a drawing (Fogg Art Museum) which differs from the painting in many details. It was doubted by earlier critics, most notably the Tietzes, but the present writer believes that its free but controlled use of pen and ink and wash matches that of many autograph drawings from the last decade of Veronese's career.

R.C.

PROVENANCE
1683 Le Brun inventory of the French Royal Collection, no. 36

EXHIBITIONS
Venice 1939, no. 54

REFERENCES
Cocke 1980², p. 92; Cocke 1984, cat. 121; Engerand 1899, p. 93, no. 10; Pignatti 1976, p. 138, with full bibliography

144

145
Venus and Adonis

212 × 190 cm; originally 162 × 190 cm
Museo del Prado, Madrid (inv. 380)
[*repr. in colour on p. 134*]

In 1584 Borghini described Veronese's latest works: 'his most recent and exceptionally beautiful paintings are of Procris, and Adonis in Venus's lap, with nearly life-size figures'.

The *Venus and Adonis* and its companion *Cephalus and Procris* (Cat. 146) remained together in Venice, where they were acquired by Velázquez *c.* 1650 for the Spanish Royal Collection. The subsequent separation of the pair led to confusion in modern accounts of Veronese, in which they were said to have been commissioned for Rudolph II and the connection between the two canvases was overlooked, which is unfortunate, since they are linked with great care in both subject and composition. This was also masked by the additions at top and bottom of the present canvas, which have been revealed during the recent restoration and cleaning.

In the *Venus and Adonis* Veronese illustrates the passage from Ovid's *Metamorphoses*, X, 555ff, where the description of the lovers' idyll is a prelude to a warning about the dangers of hunting, tragically fulfilled in the *Cephalus and Procris*. Titian departed from this Ovidian text in his *poesia* of *Venus and Adonis* painted for Philip II in 1553–54, and invented a passionate leave-taking. This influenced Veronese's earlier version of this subject, now in Augsburg. That canvas, like many other mythologies, can be dated to the 1560s through its connection with the broad, sun-filled handling of the *Honor et Virtus* and *Omnia Vanitas* (Frick Collection, New York), painted for Albrecht V of Bavaria by 1567.

Borghini's admiration for the *Venus and Adonis* is justified by the marvellous handling of the blue brocade thrown over Venus's lap, the treatment of light and shade on the surface of her skin and the more abstract red of Adonis's cloak. In his *poesia* Titian exploited the naked female, to the evident satisfaction of contemporary voyeurs. Veronese, by contrast, suggests the psychological reality of love in the discreet gesture with which Venus fans her reclining lover and glances at Cupid, who restrains the dogs that will lure Adonis out to the hunt and so to his death. This is echoed in the dark sky behind the figures, which transforms the light-hearted mood of the paintings created in the 1560s into something more profound and striking.

R. C.

PROVENANCE
Before 1854 painted in Venice; *c.* 1650 acquired by Velázquez; 1666 Alcázar inventory no. 595; remained in the Alcázar until transferred to the Museo del Prado

REFERENCES
Bottineau 1958, p. 156; Borghini 1584, p. 563; Cocke 1980², p. 96; Lorente Junquera 1969, pp. 235ff; Pignatti 1976, p. 149, with full bibliography

146
Cephalus and Procris

162 × 190 cm
Musée des Beaux-Arts, Strasbourg (inv. 634)
[*repr. in colour on p. 135*]

This is the companion painting to the *Venus and Adonis* (Cat. 145) described by Borghini in 1584 as having been painted recently. Both were acquired for the Spanish Royal Collection by Velázquez *c.* 1650. By the beginning of the nineteenth century the connection had been forgotten and the present picture was looted by Joseph Bonaparte. An old engraving confirms its dimensions matched those of the *Venus and Adonis* before the eighteenth-century additions, which have been revealed in the recent restoration and cleaning.

The painting illustrates the tragic killing of Procris by Cephalus in Ovid's *Metamorphoses*, VII, 835ff. While out hunting Cephalus used to cry out to Aura (the breeze) and this innocent invocation led Procris to suspect him of marital infidelity. As she spied on Cephalus one day he mistook the rustling in the bushes for a wild animal, with the result that he killed his wife with the spear she had given him.

The legend was often included in woodcuts of the illustrated editions of Ovid, which were extremely popular in the sixteenth century. Veronese based the earlier, small version of *Cephalus and Procris* (private collection, London) on an illustration in the 1557 Lyons edition, with minor modifications and the addition of Cephalus's unfortunate invocation in the background. In the present painting the figures are enlarged, Procris is given a brocade dress to match that of Venus in the Madrid picture and the group is reversed to form a suitable complement to the *Venus and Adonis*.

Ovid's narrative continues with Cephalus tending his wife, who manages in her dying words to beg him not to let Aura take her place. Too late her husband realises the confusion that has led to the tragedy. This is conveyed in the grouping of the composition, with Procris stretched out on the ground and her husband leaning over in concern.

R. C.

PROVENANCE
By 1584 painted in Venice; *c.* 1650 acquired by Velázquez; 1666 Alcázar inventory, probably no. 601 (the dimensions fit but the subject is not mentioned); until at least 1784 remained in the Alcázar; by *c.* 1809 transferred to the Museo de Madrid in the Palacio de Buenvista; acquired by Joseph Bonaparte; 24 May 1845, Christie's sale (lot 69); 12 April 1851, William Coningham sale (noting the provenance from Joseph Bonaparte), Christie's sale (lot 59); G. Pulsford; 1912 acquired by the Musée des Beaux-Arts

REFERENCES
Borghini 1584, p. 563; Bottineau 1958, p. 157; Cocke 1980², p. 98; Lorente Junquera 1969, pp. 253ff; Pignatti 1976, p. 149, with full bibliography

147
San Pantaleone Healing a Child

277 × 160 cm
S. Pantalon, Venice

This altarpiece, painted for the main altar of S. Pantalon, was commissioned by the parish priest, Bartolommeo Borghi, in 1587. The church was later rebuilt and the picture moved to its present site on the second altar on the right of the nave in 1732. It is difficult to see *in situ*.

San Pantaleone's shrine at Ravallo became famous for healing people beyond conventional medicine; legends later grew up around the saint, who was believed to have been a court physician. In the painting he drives out a rather charming small devil from the possessed boy, who is held by Bartolommeo Borghi. The miraculous nature of the cure is underlined by his neglect of the medicine-box held by an assistant and by his upward glance at the angel bearing the martyr's palm. His charity is emphasised by the contrast between his rich cloak and the poverty of the setting, which reflects those used by Tintoretto in his cycle in the Scuola di San Rocco, Venice. The Christian character of the miracle is brought out by the contrast with the statue, which is intended to remind us of Asclepius, the pagan god of medicine, whose helplessness is symbolised by his lack of arms and legs. In the newly discovered preparatory drawing (Louvre, Paris; Cat. D82), the miracle is combined with the appearance of the Virgin and Child crowned by angels. Such a scheme could not fit into the proportions of the present altarpiece, but its emphasis on divine healing, as in other late paintings, carries an intimation that Veronese was aware of his own impending death.

R.C.

EXHIBITIONS
Venice 1939, no. 89; Venice 1971, p. 68

REFERENCES
Cocke 1980², p. 106; Cocke 1984, cat. 127; Pignatti 1976, p. 168, with full bibliography

147 *(before restoration)*

DRAWING IN VENICE

James Byam Shaw

The existing material of drawings by Venetian artists of the Renaissance is certainly less than that which survives of the Florentine School. Of the fifteenth century, I do not forget that there is a large collection of drawings by Pisanello and his followers in the so-called Vallardi Codex in the Louvre, and in the Louvre and the British Museum two precious volumes by Jacopo Bellini, the father of two great artists and father-in-law of a third. But these (which in any case are not within the scope of the present exhibition) have survived by lucky accident; drawings by the Bellini sons, Gentile or Giovanni, or their brother-in-law Mantegna, are not common even in the great museums; and of the later fifteenth and early sixteenth century only Carpaccio is really familiar as a draughtsman. And yet Venice was not quite without collectors of drawings; we know that Gabriele Vendramin, whose art treasures were seen and described by Marcantonio Michiel in 1530, owned for example at least one famous drawing by Raphael, and one might have expected such a collection to have included drawings by Giorgione and Titian. But in fact only one drawing, now at Rotterdam, is generally accepted as Giorgione's autograph, and drawings by Titian are decidedly rare by comparison with the surviving material of his Florentine contemporaries: Michelangelo, Fra Bartolomeo or Andrea del Sarto, only one of whom lived as long as he did. This may be due partly to accident; and it is no doubt also due to some extent to the emergence in Florence of great collectors of drawings in the sixteenth and seventeenth centuries: Vasari, the Medici family and Baldinucci, much of whose accumulations have been preserved. Nevertheless, it seems likely that Giorgione and Titian and other famous Venetians of the Renaissance, at least in the first half of the sixteenth century, were less interested in drawing than the Florentine artists, and less inclined to consider it an integral part of the process of producing a picture. Vasari, in the introduction to his *Lives of the Artists*, speaks of drawing as 'the father of our three arts, Architecture, Sculpture and Painting', and discusses at some length the processes and functions of drawing. I doubt whether most Venetian artists of the sixteenth century attached so much importance to it. There was never an *Accademia del Disegno* in Venice. A Venetian of Titian's generation preferred to draw with soft scumbling chalk or with the brush, a painter's medium, rather than with the pen or the hard chalk of the Florentines; and this applies to Carpaccio, a prolific draughtsman, and to most artists in the immediate circle of Titian, to Paris Bordone and the Bassano family particularly, if it is only partly true of Pordenone and Lotto. Those two important artists (of whom one was not strictly speaking Venetian, while the other worked much away from the capital) did use soft chalk in Titian's fashion; but also the pen

and wash technique to produce pictorial compositions, which might be *modelli* for paintings, or presentation pieces for friends or patrons (Cat. D23).

Of the few known drawings – about fifty at most – that modern authorities attribute to Titian himself, eight are exhibited here, and the majority of these – indeed the majority of all that are accepted generally as his – are studies in chalk or charcoal. The attribution to him of certain pen drawings, especially landscapes, though of early authority, is now much more generally disputed; and it may be thought, even from the one good example in the present exhibition (Cat. D69), that this was not the medium that suited Titian best. Was it to some extent forced upon him by the required practice, in his earlier days, of drawing upon a wood-block, so that a block-cutter could work upon a clear linear design, and so multiply and popularise his productions in the form of prints? With soft black chalk or a charcoal stick and some white, on his blue Venetian paper, he was certainly much better able to suggest form, even colour. Any painter, I suspect, would recognise the hand of a master in the splendid *Horse and Rider Falling* from Oxford (Cat. D73); fewer would feel the same enthusiasm for the drawing of the Duke of Urbino's armour (Cat. D71).

Giorgione's fashion of painting (and probably also drawing, though Vasari said that Giorgione never drew at all) is represented here not by any example by that rare master himself, but by one probable copy and two drawings by his little-known disciple, the engraver Giulio Campagnola (Cat. D9, D10 and D19), and also by one Giorgionesque subject attributed to Titian (Cat. D69). Titian's style in the pen and ink medium, in composing a 'landscape with figures', is represented not only by this drawing, which I believe to be by his own hand, but also in a drawing signed by a follower, Domenico Campagnola (Cat. D7), who was Giulio Campagnola's adopted son and pupil. The earliest of Domenico's landscapes, such as this, are close imitations of drawings by Titian himself. In later drawings, Campagnola debased this style of landscape into a kind of facile mannerism; nevertheless he furnished inspiration for Italian draughtsmen for generations to come, including Girolamo Muziano in the later Cinquecento, and Agostino and Annibale Carracci, and Domenichino and Grimaldi later still. But it was Titian's manner of drawing freely with chalks on blue paper, exemplified here by figure studies and the rare composition sketch for the *Battle of Spoleto* (Cat. D72), that was adopted by Jacopo Bassano and his sons' prolific studio, and by Paris Bordone and others of that generation – even occasionally by some (Lotto, Palma Vecchio, Pordenone) who were probably older than Titian himself.

Though Alvise Vivarini, Bartolomeo Montagna, Buon-consiglio and Boccaccio Boccaccino all outlived the turn of the fifteenth–sixteenth centuries, and are all represented by drawings in the exhibition here, they belong essentially to the tradition of Giovanni Bellini and his pupils; breaking away, as Bellini himself did, from the hard linear style of Mantegna, but still some way from the 'painter's style' of drawing as practised by Titian and his contemporaries. It may be noticed that the comparatively small representation of drawings in the exhibition – the selection of which, I may add, was not mine – is not proportionate to the number of known drawings by the artists included: there are, for instance, eleven by Pordenone and six by Lotto (who is not generally familiar as a draughtsman), whereas there are only six by Jacopo Tintoretto and seven by Paolo Veronese, both far better known in this respect. But there are good reasons for bringing lesser-known draughtsmen to wider recognition, and it was thought appropriate to emphasise here the work of Pordenone and Lotto, who spent most of their working lives away from Venice, but were leading artists of the Venetian *terraferma*.

We know far more drawings by Tintoretto than by Titian; and indeed of the great Venetians of the High Renaissance only Jacopo Tintoretto and Paolo Veronese were really prolific draughtsmen – with Domenico Tintoretto imitating his father in the second rank, and Palma Giovane following the example of both of them in this respect. Michelangelo's sculpture, according to Ridolfi, was almost a second master, after Titian, to Tintoretto; and there is a whole series of early studies by Tintoretto after plaster casts or small copies of Michelangelo's famous works in the Medici Chapel, more or less straightforward, but sometimes drawn in foreshortening or in artificial lighting. But I doubt whether Tintoretto's drawings in general, whatever Titian may have thought of them, would have much impressed Michelangelo. Tintoretto was of a different temperament, more extravagantly dramatic, perhaps more superficial in his aspirations so far as drawing was concerned. Ridolfi says too that he made little figure models in clay or wax, 'mannikins' of his own invention, and suspended them from the ceiling, artificially lit, in order to observe figures in sharp foreshortening and in different light effects. There are among his drawings numerous single figures, roughly drawn in chalk or charcoal, with unnaturally swelling contours, anatomically impossible, some nude, some in contemporary dress or armour; and many of these have been connected with the huge battle-pieces painted in Tintoretto's maturity – the Gonzaga *Triumphs* now in Munich, and those in the Doge's Palace in Venice. They are very different from the careful academic life-studies that the Florentines produced, often with details of hand or foot drawn at the side, as preliminaries to their paintings of the same period. Occasionally Tintoretto may have studied a static living model; but much more often his drawings are of struggling distorted figures in violent action – archers drawing their bows, soldiers brandishing swords or banners, falling horsemen – in poses such as no model could keep in the studio. More detailed studies might have been more useful to himself and to his pupils in carrying out their great works; but above all the *tempo* of violence had to be maintained; and where studies used in known paintings have been identified (see Cat. D62, D64, D67), they are studies of action or gesture rather than of the human body or of drapery or other details. Hardly any large sketches for whole compositions, like Titian's for the *Battle of Spoleto*, have survived; if Tintoretto made such sketches, we must suppose that they disintegrated because of their size, through use in the studio.

The distinction between the work of the master and that of his best pupils is often a matter of subjective judgement, and of disagreement among the experts; and this difficulty is particularly apparent in the Venetian School, where family studios were the rule, and several members of the family assisted the founder of the studio and drew more or less in his style.[1] Some small, dashing oil sketches on paper, once supposed to be by Jacopo Tintoretto, have turned out to be almost certainly by his son Domenico, who was born in 1560 and lived well into the next century (Cat. D60 of this exhibition may be as late as 1630); he and his sister Marietta both made drawings from an antique bust (the supposed *Vitellius*) which was among the studio properties and had been drawn by Jacopo himself in his younger days;[2] and Tintoretto's other son, Marco, and his son-in-law Sebastiano Casser must also have drawn in the 'Tintoretto' style.

Apart from Tintoretto's own family, and certainly more important than any of them, Palma Giovane (born in 1544) in his early figure studies comes very near to the Tintorettos in style and character. But Jacopo Tintoretto seems only very occasionally to have drawn in any medium but chalk or charcoal, heightened with white on blue paper; whereas Palma Giovane, though he sometimes imitated Tintoretto in this, used also pen and pale wash to great effect, imitating the method of free sketch practised so brilliantly by Paolo Veronese, who was nearer to him in age. Palma's earlier drawings in this medium have sometimes been mistaken for Paolo's; though in the latter part of his long life, in the early decades of the seventeenth century, Palma's handling of the pen became looser, his line more broken, his forms more mannered, and the influence of Paolo is less obvious.

Paolo Veronese was indeed not only a great painter, but a great draughtsman too, the best of the Venetians of the later Renaissance period. He did produce early in his career some figure-studies in the chalk manner of Titian, Bassano and Tintoretto; but the most characteristic of his drawings are of two quite different sorts, both represented by fine examples here: either finished compositions in pen and wash, carefully heightened with white bodycolour on grey or blue coloured paper – completely pictorial, like *modelli* for paintings, though apparently seldom used for that purpose by Paolo himself; or, more commonly, rough sketches made with a fine pen and a light touch, very lightly washed, of single figures or small groups, all confused together on the same large sheet of paper, which can often be identified as ideas for important paintings, sometimes two or three different subjects on the same sheet. From those swift notations there emerge beautiful rhythms, graceful combinations of figures in motion or in relationship to one another, that exceed in elegance and charm anything produced before in Venetian drawing of the sixteenth century. They set a fashion in drawing that was followed not only into the seventeenth century by Palma Giovane and others, but even into the eighteenth, in Venice by Sebastiano Ricci, and in England by Sir James Thornhill.

D6

D7

Landscape with Two Youths

185 × 274 mm
Pen and brown ink on white paper, laid down
Signed upper left in brown ink: *Dominicus/Campagnola*;
inscribed 76
The Trustees of the British Museum, London (1895–9–15–836)

The Tietzes assigned this work to a group of drawings
which they dated before 1517. The group, which includes
The Stigmatization of St. Francis (Weimar) and *Christ
Sleeping in the Boat* (University Library, Uppsala) shows no
trace of Titian's influence. All the drawings are somewhat
awkward in composition and, occasionally, in handling.
The dominating influences are those of Dürer and
Giorgione, and it is obvious that Domenico studied Dürer's
engravings: as the Tietzes observed, here the engraving tool
rules the pen.

D.E.S.

PROVENANCE
P. J. Mariette; Comte de Fries; Durand(?); Sir Thomas Lawrence;
A.C. (de) Paggi; J.C. Robinson (?); Malcolm;
1895 acquired by the British Museum

REFERENCES
Popham 1939, p. 322, repr.; von Hadeln 1927, pp. 16, 24, no. 48

D7

D8

D8
St. Mark Healing a Demoniac

242 × 316 mm
Pen and brown ink
Inscribed in the right-hand corner: *Dom/co Ca/gn. . .*
George Goldner Collection, Los Angeles

This is a characteristic example of a pen sketch by
Domenico; the attribution is supported by the inscription
(which may be a signature). The drawing was first
published by Julien Stock, who connected it to a bronze
relief of the same subject by Jacopo Sansovino, one of a
series made for San Marco, Venice, which was cast in 1537.
The sketch, which appears to be a study made after the
relief had been installed in the church, testifies to the impact
these works by Sansovino had on contemporary artists such
as Jacopo Bassano and Tintoretto. Although Campagnola
does not quite master the perspective arcading in the
background, in other respects this is a faithful copy.

B.B.

EXHIBITIONS
Sotheby's, London 18 November 1982, lot 6, p. 34

REFERENCES
Boucher 1976, pp. 560, 565; Stott 1982, pp. 370ff

Giulio Campagnola

Padua *c.* 1482 – Venice (?) *c.* 1515/18

Giulio Campagnola was born in Padua *c.* 1482. His father,
a learned man, attempted to place Giulio at the court of
Francesco Gonzaga at Mantua in 1497, in order that he
might work under Mantegna. Whether Giulio ever settled
there is not known, but he is recorded at the court of Ercole I
at Ferrara early in 1499, and in Venice in 1507. He is
mentioned in the will of Aldo Manuzio, the celebrated
printer, in January 1515; nothing certain is known about
Giulio thereafter. It is possible that one of his engravings
was completed by his pupil Domenico Campagnola
c. 1517–18, and it has been inferred from this that Giulio
was dead by that date.

Altogether, there are seven engravings signed by Giulio
Campagnola, and several more may be attributed to him
with confidence. Some show the influence of Mantegna,
while others contain passages copied directly from Dürer's
prints. However, the largest and best known group of
engravings is more closely related to the work of Giorgione:
these usually represent contemplative figures situated in
gentle landscapes with rustic buildings in the background.
In several of the engravings, Giulio achieved the sense of a
soft atmosphere by employing a dotted technique.

Contemporary accounts suggest that apart from working as a painter, Giulio was also a musician and well-versed in classical languages. Although various paintings, including the *Trial of Moses* and *Judgement of Solomon* (also attributed to Giorgione) in the Uffizi, Florence, have been ascribed to him, there are no attributions supported by documentary evidence.

D. McT.

REFERENCES
Fiocco 1915, pp. 137–56; Hind 1938–48, V pp. 189–205;
Kristeller 1907; Luzio 1888, pp. 184ff.;
Petrucci 1958, pp. 12ff.; Suida 1935–36, pp. 285–89;
Tietze and Tietze-Conrat 1944, pp. 132–37; Washington 1973, pp. 390–413

D9
Three Philosophers in a Landscape

183 × 274 mm
Pen and brown ink
Fondation Custodia (Coll. F. Lugt), Institut Néerlandais, Paris
(1978–T.21)

This characteristic example of a Giorgionesque landscape has only recently come to light. Although the drawing was attributed at auction first to Domenico Campagnola and later to the 'circle of Giorgione', James Byam Shaw has provided a detailed justification for attributing it to Giulio Campagnola. Of the various works associated with Giulio, only the engravings are securely attributed: Byam Shaw has indicated a number of compelling similarities between this drawing and Giulio's prints. These include the general similarity of subject matter to that of the engraving, *The Astrologer*, dated 1509 (Cat. P9); the analogous manner of

rendering foliage – in the bushes behind and to the right of the philosophers – in this drawing and in such prints as the *St. John the Baptist* (Cat. P10) and the *Stag at Rest* (Hind 1938–48, no. 14); and the related parallel lines of the sky in the prints *The Astrologer* (Cat. P9) and *Christ and the Woman of Samaria* (Hind 1938–48, no. 11).

The drawing also possesses numerous features frequently encountered in early sixteenth-century Venetian landscapes. Learned personages, who are not readily identifiable but often wear hoods or turbans and hold cryptic diagrams, appear in several other landscapes, most notably Giorgione's *Three Philosophers* in Vienna. The small reclining figures and the sheep at the right of the drawing, and the gabled rustic buildings in the background, are also elements repeatedly included in the idyllic landscapes produced in the Veneto at this time.

The vast majority of surviving landscape drawings from early sixteenth-century Venice are executed solely in pen and ink, and many, such as this example, suggest the hand of an engraver. However, other techniques were occasionally employed: a landscape drawing related to Giulio Campagnola's engraving of *St. John the Baptist* was executed with the point of the brush (Louvre, RF 1979; repr. Venice 1976¹, no. 2), while a landscape drawing attributed to Giorgione in Rotterdam is in red chalk.

D. McT.

PROVENANCE
21 November 1974, Sotheby's, London sale, (lot 4); R. Day;
anonymous collection; 29 November 1977, Christie's, London sale,
(lot 37); Frits Lugt, Fondation Custodia

EXHIBITIONS
London 1976, no. 5; Venice 1981², no. 37

REFERENCES
Byam Shaw 1983, p. 236, no. 231, pl. 264, with full bibliography

D9

D10

D11

DIO
Landscape with a Watermill

162 × 263 mm
Pen and brown ink
Gabinetto dei Disegni, Uffizi, Florence (no. 463P)

Traditionally ascribed to Marco Basaiti, this drawing was first attributed to Giulio Campagnalo by Kristeller in 1907, an attribution that has since received repeated support in discussions of Campagnola's drawings.

The corpus of Giulio's drawings has been established by analogies with his engravings and, although no exact relationships exist between this particular drawing and his engravings, a number of similarities are evident. Especially characteristic is the manner of rendering shrubbery, such as the bush on the bank in front of the buildings, so that the trunks radiate like the ribs of a fan and are silhouetted against shadow created by dense cross-hatching, while the leaves appear as schematic, flat areas. In contrast, the row of trees on the right represents a more unusual and particularly sensitive transcription of nature. Also typical is the picturesque variety of texture and outline in the buildings. Related to motifs in prints by northern artists, and to details in paintings by Giorgione and his circle, these buildings are made particularly distinctive by their steeply-pitched, hipped roofs – often with finials at the apexes – and by walls boarded with vertical planks.

This classic example of pastoral stillness and repose has been dated by Rearick (Florence 1976) to about 1512/14, while Oberhuber (Venice 1976) would evidently prefer a somewhat earlier date.

D. McT.

EXHIBITIONS
Florence 1961, no. 63; Florence 1976, no. 8;
Venice 1976, no. 4

REFERENCES
Florence 1976, p. 27; Venice 1976¹, p. 54, with full bibliography

Vittore Carpaccio

[Biography on p. 166]

DII
St. Augustine in his Study

277 × 427 mm
Pen and brown ink and brown wash
The Trustees of the British Museum, London (1934-12-8-1)

This study for the painting in the Scuola di S. Giorgio degli Schiavoni, Venice, was thought formerly to represent St. Jerome. According to legend, when St. Augustine was sitting in his study writing to St. Jerome, a miraculous light appeared announcing the latter's death.

Popham and Pouncey think that the drawing is preparatory to the painting, and not, as Muraro suggested,

a documentary drawing showing the 'state of play' of the picture. Pignatti has observed that Carpaccio was interested here in the use of light and shade, which give pictorial values to the composition as a whole, whereas in his earlier drawings (eg. *Prince Conan Taking Leave of his Father*; Chatsworth, Derbyshire) he concentrated on realistic details. One of the related scenes in the Scuola di S. Giorgio is dated 1502, and this drawing must belong to the first decade of the sixteenth century.

D.E.S.

PROVENANCE
P. & D. Colnaghi; 1934 presented by the National Art Collections Fund to the British Museum

REFERENCES
Pignatti 1972, no. 15; Popham and Pouncey 1950, no. 35

DI2

DI2
Head of a Bearded Man

197 × 141 mm
Black chalk, brush and brown wash
touched in places with the pen,
heightened with white, on faded brown paper (formerly blue?)
Verso: a draped left leg, a left foot and
the lower part of the drapery of a kneeling figure
Fondation Custodia (Coll. F. Lugt), Institut Néerlandais, Paris
(no. 5070)

As has often been observed, this head resembles that of an apostle in *The Calling of St. Matthew* in the Scuola di S. Giorgio degli Schiavoni, Venice, which is dated 1502. The drawings on the *verso* may be preparatory designs for *The Annunciation* from the Scuola degli Albanesi (now in the Ca d'Oro), datable *c.* 1504, as von Hadeln first suggested.

D.E.S.

PROVENANCE
Bonfiglioli Coll., Bologna; 1728/34 bought by Zaccaria Sagredo;
1763 John Udny; the Earls of Sunderland;
George Spencer Churchill, 8th Duke of Marlborough;
1883 Christie's, London sale; J. Heseltine;
1912 P. & D. Colnaghi and Obach; H. Oppenheimer,
1936 Christie's, London sale; Frits Lugt, Fondation Custodia

EXHIBITIONS
Rotterdam 1938, no. 447, pl. 23;
Paris, Rotterdam, Haarlem 1962, no. 36, pl. XXIX;
Nice 1979, no. 23, repr. (recto and verso);
Venice 1981¹, no. 28, repr.; London 1983, no. 79

REFERENCES
Byam Shaw 1983, I, no. 223; II, pls. 252, 253, with full bibliography

D13
Young Man in a Cap

265 × 187 mm
Black chalk, brush and a little pale brown wash,
heightened with white, on blue paper
The Governing Body, Christ Church, Oxford (no. 0282)

This drawing is generally thought to be of the same period
as the paintings for the Scuola di Sant' Orsola, Venice, now
in the Accademia. Although this sheet does not correspond
with any of the numerous portraits introduced into that
series, Byam Shaw considers that it can safely be dated
1495–1500, rejecting Ricci's attempt to identify the man
with one of the bystanders in the *Preaching of St. Stephen*
(1514) in the Brera, Milan.

D.E.S.

PROVENANCE
Sebastiano Resta; John, Lord Somers (?); Jonathan Richardson Senior;
Lansdowne MS. 803, R. 52, p. 28 (as Gaudenzio Ferrari);
Guise; Christ Church

REFERENCES
Byam Shaw 1976, no. 710, pl. 404, with full bibliography

D13

D14

Paolo Farinati

[Biography on p. 347]

D14
Virgin and Child in a Landscape

277 × 210 mm
Pen and brown ink and wash, heightened with white,
on blue paper
Inscribed in W. Gibson's hand: *P. Farinat. 5.2.*
Verso: study of a male figure holding an open book
and another figure, cut off; brush and brown wash
National Gallery of Scotland, Edinburgh (no. D. 1577)

A late drawing, datable in the 1580s according to Mullaly;
Andrews suggests the *verso* may relate to a decorative
scheme for a villa.

D.E.S.

PROVENANCE
Sir Peter Lely; Jonathan Richardson Senior; W. Gibson;
David Laing; Royal Scottish Academy;
1910 transferred to the National Gallery of Scotland

REFERENCES
Andrews 1968, p. 49, with bibliography

D15
Zephyr and Psyche

283 × 412 mm
Pen and brown ink and brown wash over traces of black chalk,
heightened with white (partly oxidised), on faded blue paper
Inscribed in the artist's hand in brown ink:
Zefiro vict [?]/porta psiche/isola al pa[lazzo]di chupido and *Borea
Capo de venti/rapise orithia sua diva/sua zovene cenza barba*; this
has been crossed out in the same hand; lower left: *piedi 6. Verso*
inscribed: *Zefiro che porta psiche la zovene cēza barbe cō le ale/
Venenere che spenachia lali a chupido cō cavezzo roto estrali/
favēdoli il carchaso tolto et favelle in ato schoriciato/e amore che
si dolia e patischa di tale ofeso fate da venere sua madre/
Merchurio che porta psiche col suo caduceo et alle al capelo e
piedi*; dated lower centre in the same hand: *Ultimi mazo 1588*:
inscribed lower right in W. Gibson's hand: *P. Farinato/8.2.*
Fitzwilliam Museum, Cambridge (no. 2956)

A similar drawing, inscribed *Mercurio porta psiche al cielo*,
also from the Lely, Gibson and Reynolds collections, is in
the Ashmolean Museum (Parker 1956, II, no. 223). Both
drawings are designs for octagonal ceiling paintings
illustrating the legend of Cupid and Psyche, reminiscent of
those by Giulio Romano in the Palazzo del Te at Mantua.
The elaborate contortion of the figures, heavy use of wash
and abundance of white highlights are characteristic of
Farinati's later work, this sheet being dated to the end of
May 1588.

D.E.S.

PROVENANCE
Sir Peter Lely; William Gibson (?); Sir Joshua Reynolds;
Dr H. Wellesley, 1886 Sotheby's, London sale (lot 529);
Sir James Knowles; 28 May 1908, acquired by G. T. Clough at
Sir James Knowles's sale, Christie's, London (part of lot 232);
1913 presented to the Fitzwilliam Museum

EXHIBITIONS
Cambridge 1960, no. 27; Cambridge 1980–81, handlist, pp. 11, 12

REFERENCES
Macandrew 1980, III, p. 261, no. 223

D16

D16
Design for a Fireplace

397 × 283 mm
Pen and brown ink and brown wash over black chalk,
laid down on a Mariette mount
Inscribed on the cartouche: J. BAPTISTA/ZELOTTI
Cabinet des Dessins, Musée du Louvre, Paris (no. 5598)

The former attribution to Zelotti cannot be sustained:
Pouncey observes that this is a characteristic example of
Farinati's draughtsmanship. Presumably it was intended as
a design for a fireplace in a country villa, since the caryatid
on the left sports hunting dress and a boot held in place by
a crescent moon – a symbol of Diana, goddess of the chase.
Above the fireplace are grouped several gods with their
attributes: Jupiter with his eagle, Mars with helmet and
shield, Cupid holding thunderbolts, Neptune with a trident,
standing on a dolphin, and Bacchus with his thyrsus. The
figures set on plinths flanking the architectural framework
each hold a spray of flowers.

D.E.S.

PROVENANCE
P. J. Mariette; 1775, Mariette's sale, Paris (lot 801)

EXHIBITIONS
Paris 1965, no. 246, repr.

REFERENCES
Tietze and Tietze-Conrat 1944, no. 2263 (as Zelotti)

D15

D17

D17
The Emperor Vespasian Standing in a Niche

394 × 270 mm
Pen and brown ink and brown wash over
black chalk, heightened with white
Inscribed upper right:
INP. CAES. VESPASIA / AVG. P.M.T.R.P.P.P.C / OS. III
Verso: the reverse of a medal with the inscription IVDEA CAPTA
SC and in Farinati's hand: *P[er] riverso di la medalia di vespisiano*
seli fa una palma arbore grāde aqu . . . / modo una dona asentata
tuta pensosa.e ū armado cō le mane ligate de di/[ētro] cone pregiō/
il drito di la medalia se li fa: IMP. CAES VESPA / AUG COS III/
Anche se lifa ū altro riverso luna figura cō unasta imano ch afronta
ū perchi/cō un albor di drio la qual figura sia p[er] dito vespasiano
caciatore over p[er]. . ./ meleagro
Her Majesty The Queen (no. 4995)

This is one of a group of eight drawings at Windsor
representing Roman emperors and antique heroes. Of these,
two are in architectural niches, and presumably formed part
of a project for the decoration of a palace. The inscription,
which is related to a hybrid silver coin dated AD 70, is taken
from Rovillius's *Prontuario,* the first edition of which was
published at Lyon in 1553, the first Italian edition appearing
the same year.

D.E.S.

REFERENCES
Popham and Wilde 1949, no. 300, pl. 174

Giovanni Battista Franco,
called il Semolei

Venice 1498–Venice 1561

Franco, a painter, etcher, engraver and prolific
draughtsman, was born in Venice and worked there before
moving to Rome, where he was much influenced by
Michelangelo and Raphael. He also worked in Florence and
Urbino, where he produced designs for majolica.

D.E.S.

D18

D18
Standing Figure of a Cloaked Man

260 × 126 mm, upper corners cut
Pen and brown ink and wash over black chalk
The Trustees of the British Museum, London (no. 5211–25)

A characteristic example of this prolific artist's work; the chalk underdrawing is freely handled whereas the penwork is similar to an engraver's technique. There are several pentimenti on the head. Popham suggested this might have been a study for one of the two philosophers in niches which, according to Vasari (VI, p. 586), were painted by Franco between the windows of the Libreria in Venice. Gere and Pouncey date the drawing between 1557 and 1561.

D.E.S.

PROVENANCE
R. Houlditch; W. Fawkener Bequest 1769

REFERENCES
Gere and Pouncey 1983, no. 114, pl. 103

D19

After Giorgione

D19
The Adoration of the Shepherds

227 × 194 mm, upper left-hand corner made up
Point of the brush and brown wash over black chalk, heightened with white, on blue paper
Her Majesty The Queen (no. 12803)

The Tietzes concluded that this drawing is a copy of a picture painted before the Allendale *Adoration of the Shepherds* (National Gallery, Washington D.C.), with part of which it corresponds, and that the Allendale panel was based on the earlier picture. Popham agreed that the drawing appears to be more primitive than the painting; he commented that the technique and appearance come very close to Carpaccio, but suggested that equally it might well be a translation of the Allendale picture by a draughtsman of an older generation into his own archaic idiom. However, Oberhuber regards this drawing as an original by Giorgione (Venice 1976).

D.E.S.

EXHIBITION
Venice 1976[1], no. 1, with full bibliography

REFERENCES
Popham and Wilde 1949, no. 343, pl. 162;
Tietze and Tietze-Conrat 1944, A719, with bibliography;
von Hadeln 1925[2], p. 32, pl. 1

Bernardino Licinio
[Biography on p. 174]

D20
Woman Holding a Vase

D20

214 × 147 mm
Black chalk, heightened with white, on blue-grey paper
Inscribed lower left in pencil: *A del Sarto*
Yale University Art Gallery (1961-65-46)

This drawing was first recognised as a work of Licinio by Rearick. His attribution is based on two representations of drawings in Licinio's painting *An Artist with Five Pupils* (Alnwick Castle, Northumberland). Most pertinent is a *Crouching Venus* in red chalk heightened with white on light blue paper. Of this he comments, 'while it is rather timid and tight in outline, its softly textured combination of chalks and the bland fidelity to appearance accord well with the style of the Licinio drawing at Yale'. Rearick notes that the artist used this drawing of a *Woman Holding a Vase* as the model for the Madonna in at least eight paintings. Several of these are dated, the earliest 1530 and the latest 1535, but two others, although undated, are considerably earlier; Rearick proposes that they are close

to 1520. While the figure in the drawing is never repeated exactly in any of these paintings, the pose is always similar.

The somewhat unusual idea of making a life study for the figure of the Madonna, using a simple vase as a stand-in for the Child, is, as Rearick points out, entirely compatible with the literal-minded simplicity of spirit that pervades all Licinio's work. The attribution to him is confirmed by the outline drawing on the *verso* of the painting of the *Virgin and Child between St. Joseph and St. Catherine* in Split, Yugoslavia (*Arte Veneta* 1980, pp. 151–53, fig. 4).

D.E.S.

PROVENANCE
Egmont; Sterling Memorial Library; Yale University Library;
1961 transferred to Yale University Art Gallery

REFERENCES
Haverkamp-Begemann and Logan 1970, no. 273, pl. 141;
Rearick 1967, pp. 382–83, pl. 22

D21

Lorenzo Lotto

[Biography on p. 175]

D21

Study for the Tarsia of Judith and Holofernes

315 × 246 mm
Pen and brown ink and brown wash, with traces
of white highlights
(the sheet has several old repairs, worm holes,
water stains and is somewhat faded)
Inscribed with extensive colour notes including
left to right, top to bottom:
nocte; veste di laca; biaco; nocte; laca; b[ianco]
Private Collection, London

Only two drawings relating to the *tarsie* in S. Maria
Maggiore, Bergamo have been identified: this sheet and the
drawing of *Samson Slaying the Philistine* in Janos Scholz's
collection, New York (Pouncey 1965, pl. 22). Whereas the
Scholz drawing is a compositional sketch, the *Judith and
Holofernes* is a detailed study for the intarsia: the contours
are carefully defined and internal details are indicated, an
elaborate wash and white highlights suggest the pictorial
and spatial distinctions and Lotto has added colour notes.
But this is not a fragment of a *modello* (it is slightly smaller
than the wooden panel); it must have immediately preceded
it.

In the creation of any design, either for a painting or a
tarsia, Lotto would have made use of various types of
drawings; this is a unique survivor of a category of drawing
which must have been fairly common in his work.

The work was in hand on 29 August 1527 and Lotto was
paid for it on 4 September (Rearick 1980).

D.E.S.

PROVENANCE
1957 acquired by the present owner

EXHIBITIONS
Edinburgh 1969, no. 42, pl. 5

REFERENCES
Chiodi 1962, p. 57, pl. 3; Pouncey 1965, pl. 20;
Rearick 1980, p. 31, fig. 15

D22

Sacra Conversazione

168 × 200 mm, the top slightly shaped
Pen and brown ink and grey wash, heightened with white,
squared with red chalk; slightly oxidised
Verso: list of accounts
Cabinet des Dessins, Musée du Louvre, Paris (no. 11.339)

D22

It is the superabundance of white and the subtlety with which Lotto uses this medium to indicate both movement and characterisation which astonishes in this enchanting drawing discovered by Pouncey. St. Anthony Abbot, identified by his pig, is led by an angel to the Infant Christ, who raises his hand in benediction. Berenson remarked of this drawing that it is 'by far the most interesting sketch for a composition by Lotto that has appeared yet. Pictorial to the last degree.' Pignatti dated it 1539 and related it to the *Madonna del Rosario*, but Pouncey followed Berenson in placing it between 1528 and 1530.

D.E.S.

EXHIBITIONS
Venice 1953, no. 8; Paris 1965, no. 97, repr.

REFERENCES
Berenson 1956, fig. 226; Pignatti 1953, p. 157;
Pouncey 1952, p. 325; Pouncey 1965, pl. 14

D23

An Ecclesiastic in his Study

165 × 199 mm
Point of the brush and brown wash over traces of black chalk
The Trustees of the British Museum, London (1951-2-8-34)

Popham (1951) first attributed this drawing to Lotto; Pouncey (1952) tentatively placed it *c.* 1530, a dating which seems preferable to Popham's suggestion of 1510–20 and which found favour with Berenson.

It is most interesting to compare Lotto's drawing with Carpaccio's *St. Augustine in his Study* (Cat. D11). Carpaccio was concerned with the overall composition while the personality of the saint was scarcely considered, but in Lotto's drawing the personality of the young prelate, 'so contented with his possessions', as Berenson observes, dominates the room, and he is in much closer communion with his lapdog than with the older man seated on the right.

D.E.S.

D23

D24

PROVENANCE
S. Woodburn; 1860 Christie's, London sale (lot 1087); Phillipps Fenwick;
1951 presented anonymously to the British Museum

REFERENCES
Berenson 1956, fig. 205; Fenwick catalogue 1935, p. 21, no. 1;
Popham 1951, p. 72 f.; Pouncey 1952, p. 32; Pouncey 1965, pl. 15

D24

Festivities in Honour of Padua

265 × 160 mm
Point of the brush and wash, heightened with white,
on white paper squared with red chalk for transfer
Inscribed: PADVA
Biblioteca Reale, Turin (no. 15909)

This drawing was recognised by Pouncey as an example of Lotto's draughtsmanship in its full maturity, close in date to the *Sacra Conversazione* (Cat. D22).

It is interesting to note how well the handling of the faces corresponds with that of the Leipzig drawing (Cohen 1975), all of which accord with the preliminary drawing in the

Rijksmuseum (Pouncey, fig. 7) for the *Double Portrait* (Cat. 44). But the closest correspondence is with the roundels of Lotto's altarpiece at Cingoli of 1539, which suggests a date that would coincide with the artist's stay in Venice from 1535 to 1538.

Pouncey argued that the illusionistic representation of the frame, including section drawings of its mouldings, shows that the drawing was a design for a painting of a fictive open doorway, and that the inscription, Padua, identifying the city represented in the little model carried by the man crowned with laurel, might imply that it was for a series illustrating the various cities under Venetian dominion, to be executed for some public room in the capital. The finished nature of the sheet, together with its squaring, shows it was intended as a model to be transferred to a larger scale.

Griseri has commented on the unpretentious manner, which is so characteristic of Lotto: 'Far from glorious is the trophy on the aching neck of the man bent in the effort to support it. As always, it is the humblest and most human attitudes with which Lotto identifies and by which he is most inspired.'

D.E.S.

REFERENCES
Bertini 1958, p. 32, no. 184 (as Girolamo del Santo); Cohen 1975²;
Griseri 1978, no. 35; Pouncey 1965, pl. 26;
Tietze and Tietze-Conrat 1944, no. 739, pl. 41

D25
Girls and Boys Singing

251 × 323 mm
Point of the brush and grey-brown wash, highlighted with white
(slightly oxidised), over traces of black chalk, on faded blue-grey
paper squared in black chalk
Gabinetto dei Disegni, Uffizi, Florence (no. 684E)

An old inscription on the *verso* attributes this drawing to Giorgione. Marini published it as an example of the finished draughtsmanship of Sebastiano Florigerio, comparing it to a drawing in Berlin for the head of Isaiah in S. Daniele del Friuli. Pouncey recognised the sheet, classed in the Uffizi as the work of Pordenone, as characteristic of Lotto's mature style and connected it in terms of technique, style and subject matter with the drawing of *Festivities in Honour of Padua* (Cat. D24). The sense of depth achieved by the grouping of the figures is particularly successful.

D.E.S.

REFERENCES
Marini 1956, pl. 7

D25

D26

PROVENANCE
Skippe; Mrs Rayner Wood; British Museum

REFERENCES
Berenson 1956, fig. 340; Popham 1938, p. 49;
Pouncey 1965, fig. 17; Tietze and Tietze-Conrat 1944, no. 766

Bartolomeo Cincani, called

Montagna

Vicenza (?) *c.* 1450 – Vicenza 1523

The exact date of birth of Bartolomeo Cincani (who at an early stage took the name Montagna by which he was subsequently always known) is not recorded, but there are reasonable grounds for placing it around, or perhaps a little before, the middle of the fifteenth century. Nor has it been established whether he was born in Vicenza, where the first documentary reference to him dates from 1459, or at Orzinovi in the province of Brescia, from where his father, Antonio, came.

Montagna is identified as a painter ('*pictor*') in documents from 1474 onwards, but we know that in 1469 he was living in Venice ('*in . . . civitate Venetiarum*'), undoubtedly while training in the studio of Giovanni Bellini. He is known to have been working in 1478 for the church of Piovene in the province of Vicenza, but even before then, already enjoying recognition as an outstanding artist ('*egregio maistro*'), he owned a workshop in the Berici hills that was patronised by a clientele of high social and cultural standing.

In 1482 Montagna was commissioned to execute two canvases – now lost – for the Scuola Grande di San Marco in Venice. Thereafter he monopolised the most important painting commissions in Vicenza and was summoned to work in other towns in the Veneto: firstly to Padua, where, with Pierantonio degli Abati and Benedetto Bordone, he contributed to the fresco decorations of the monastery of S. Giovanni di Verdara, begun in 1488, and to those in the upper hall of the new Bishop's Palace completed in 1506. He was to return to Padua after the events of the League of Cambrai, in about 1509, and remained there until 1514, executing, amongst other things, a fresco in the Scuola del Santo in 1512. Between 1504 and 1506 he painted the chapel of S. Biagio in SS. Nazaro e Celso, Verona.

From 1515 until his death it is evident that Montagna was slowing down his activities and his fame also declined. He can be considered one of the most original exponents on the Venetian mainland of Antonello da Messina's revolutionary style, as interpreted and enriched by Bellini.

L.P.

REFERENCES
Azzi Visentini 1980, pp. 5–10; Barbieri 1964, pp. 282–85;
Barbieri 1965, *passim*; Barbieri 1981, pp. 23–31; Gilbert 1967, pp. 184–88;
Mantese 1968–69, pp. 240–48;
Puppi 1962¹, *passim*, with earlier bibliography; Puppi 1964, pp. 194–204;
Puppi 1968², p. 219; Puppi 1975, pp. 23–29; Sambin 1962, pp. 104–08

D26

Study for St. Matthias

407 × 283 mm
Black chalk, heightened with white, on blue paper
squared in black chalk
Inscribed: *Lorenzo Lot l'opera è in Ancona*
The Trustees of the British Museum, London (1958–12–13–2)

This study for the *Virgin and Child Enthroned with St. Stephen, St. John the Evangelist, St. Matthias and St. Lawrence* (Cat. 53) is of great beauty, although, in Berenson's words, 'it sheds no light on the gestation of the figure for which it is a sketch'.

It does however tell much about Lotto's drawing technique. Popham first commented on the obvious northern influence: 'The cast of the drapery and its handling recalls not so much any contemporary Italian work as that of a German – Matthias Grünewald.' Pouncey notes how meticulously Lotto worked on his preparatory drawings in his old age, notwithstanding his long and experimental career. Even so, the translation from drawing to painting is not pedestrian, and although the basic pose is maintained there are several significant differences in the painted figures.

D.E.S.

D27

D27
Standing Figure of a Crowned Man

264 × 141 mm
Point of the brush and blue wash, heightened with white
on blue paper
The Visitors of the Ashmolean Museum, Oxford (Parker no. 25)

Previously attributed to Dürer, Parker recognised this
drawing as the work of Montagna, pointing out that the
technique was typically Venetian. He dated it fairly early
and remarked that the foreshortening has obvious analogies
to Mantegna's *sotto in sù*, which recalls Vasari's statement
that Montagna learnt to draw with Mantegna.

The purpose of the drawing is as uncertain as its subject:
Constantine, David and even Christ have been suggested.
The two vertical lines on either side of the figure may
indicate a niche; but in any case the figure would certainly
have been painted in a high position.

D.E.S.

PROVENANCE
Private collection, France; Private collection, United States of America;
1934 acquired by the Ashmolean Museum

EXHIBITIONS
Venice 1958, no. 9; Nottingham and London 1983, no. 9

REFERENCES
Macandrew 1980, III, p. 249, no. 25, Parker 1934, p. 8, pl. 9;
Parker 1956, II, no. 25, pl. X;
Puppi 1962¹, p. 149, fig. 75

D28
Three Standing Women

313 × 219 mm
Point of the brush and grey wash strengthened with pen and
brown ink and heightened with white, on faded blue-grey paper;
the two figures on the right are silhouetted, the outline of the
figure on the extreme right is strengthened in black chalk; laid
down; bordered on all sides by a line of brown ink
Inscribed in brown ink upper left:
Dosso da ferrara and *la duchessa*
Cabinet des Dessins, Musée du Louvre, Paris (no. 8224)

Morelli was the first to attribute this sheet to Montagna.
Both Borenius and Puppi have grouped it with his late
work, comparing it particularly with the group of women
on the right in the *Discovery of St. Anthony's Tomb* of 1512
in the Scuola del Santo, Padua, for which the present
drawing could be a discarded study. The handling of the
drapery and the figures can also be compared to the
altarpiece of *St. Mary Magdalene* in S. Corona, Vicenza,
and the woman on the right is close to a figure in *The
Mystic Marriage of St. Catherine*, formerly in the
Rothermere Collection. The subtly observed
characterisation is typical of Montagna's better work.

D.E.S.

PROVENANCE
Jabach; 1671 Louvre collections

EXHIBITIONS
Paris 1977–78, no. 5, with full bibliography

D28

Jacopo Palma il Giovane

[Biography on p. 192]

D29
The Agony in the Garden

415 × 188 mm
Pen and brown ink and brown wash, heightened with white,
over slight traces of black chalk on brown paper;
bordered on all sides by a line of brown ink
Signed (?) and dated lower left in brown ink: *giovine 1575*;
added in different ink: *Palma*
Fitzwilliam Museum, Cambridge (no. 3070)

The Tietzes dated this drawing *c.* 1600 or later on stylistic
grounds, taking the signature for a later inscription. The ink
used for the inscription *giovine 1575* is identical to that of
the drawing and there seems no reason to doubt that it is
genuine.

Another drawing of the same subject by Palma Giovane
is in the Albertina, Vienna (no. 1538), dated *c.* 1590 by Heil
(*Jahrbuch der Preussischen Kunstsammlungen*, Berlin,

1926, vol. 47, p. 60 ff.). The composition of both sheets
appears to derive from Veronese's painting of *Christ in the
Garden supported by an Angel* (Brera, Milan no. 241),
which Coletti has dated *c.* 1570, but which Pignatti placed
in the 1580s, at the very end of Veronese's career.

D.E.S.

PROVENANCE
Unidentified (Dutch?) collector;
Earl of Aylesford; acquired by G.T. Clough at sale of Earl of Aylesford;
1913 presented to the Fitzwilliam Museum

EXHIBITION
Cambridge 1980–81

REFERENCES
Tietze and Tietze-Conrat 1944, p. 201, no. 859

D30

D29

D30
Study for the Fall of the Rebel Angels

410 × 263 mm
Black oil and chalk, heightened with white oil,
on light brown paper (perhaps once blue?)
Inscribed below in an eighteenth-century hand: *Jacomo Tintoret*
The Trustees of the British Museum, London (1941-11-8-15)

Attributed to

Jacopo Sansovino

[Biography on p. 381]

D52

St. James the Greater

263 × 122 mm
Red chalk and red wash on buff paper squared in black chalk
National Gallery of Scotland, Edinburgh (no. D. 1896)

This drawing was catalogued by Andrews as the work of an anonymous north Italian artist who, Andrews suggested, had been 'remotely influenced by Titian'.

In a letter of 1975 to the National Gallery of Scotland Howard Coutts observed the relationship of this drawing to the figure by Sansovino on the upper left of the sacristy door of San Marco, Venice (Pope-Hennessy 1963). The door was modelled in 1546 and assembled in 1569, but not installed until 1572. The vitality of the drawing and the subtle modelling of the head in particular, together with its squaring, suggest that it was an original design for the door, rather than a later copy.

D.E.S.

PROVENANCE
Allan Ramsay?; Lady Murray;
1860 presented to the National Gallery of Scotland

REFERENCES
Andrews 1968, I, p. 150; II, ill. p. 180; Pope-Hennessy 1963[1], I, fig. 113

Andrea Schiavone

[Biography on p. 206]

D53

Cupid Presenting Psyche to the Gods

374 × 603 mm
Pen and brown ink and wash, heightened with white,
over traces of black chalk on brown washed paper
Metropolitan Museum of Art, New York, Rogers Fund 1963
(63.93)

The composition of this imposing drawing is based on Raphael's fresco (1518) of the same subject on the vault of the loggia of the Villa Farnesina, Rome. However, Schiavone has completely reversed Raphael's composition and the figures are altered throughout, both in pose and dress. Other parts of the composition, such as the seated man at the extreme left and the horse at the right, are additions.

According to a note on the old mount, the drawing was once ascribed to Parmigianino and, indeed, the proportions of Raphael's original figures have been modified to reflect Parmigianino's elegant figural types. The figure of Psyche herself reflects Francesco Salviati's Psyche on the ceiling of the Palazzo Grimani, Venice, and is still closer to the preliminary drawing of the figure in Budapest (Cheney 1963, fig. 5). However, Schiavone's own style is revealed in both the pen line, especially its use to define individual features, and the broad applications of wash.

The story of Psyche is told in the *Metamorphoses* of Apuleius (IV, 28–VI, 24). Raphael's frescoes of Psyche in the Farnesina were followed by numerous decorative cycles featuring the subject, including those by Perino del Vaga in the Castel Sant'Angelo and Giulio Romano in the Palazzo del Te. Battista Franco's treatment of *Cupid Presented to the Gods* in an oval format (Pierpoint Morgan Library, New York, no. IV, 73) was again derived from Raphael's fresco.

D52

D53

Richardson has suggested that the present drawing may have been made for one of Schiavone's lost ceiling paintings of Psyche, mentioned by Ridolfi (1648, I, p. 256), in the Castello di Salvatore near Susegano, Conegliano. The elongated oval format of the drawing was often used for Venetian ceiling paintings in the mid-sixteenth century. The drawing itself is usually dated to the 1540s (Richardson 1980). Paintings by Schiavone depicting the marriage of Cupid and Psyche are in the Palazzo Strozzi, Florence, and the Metropolitan Museum, New York.

D. McT.

PROVENANCE
C. R. Rudolf

EXHIBITIONS
London 1962, no. 62; New York 1965, no. 116

REFERENCES
Bean 1982, no. 236, with full bibliography; Richardson 1980, p. 129

D54

D54
The Annunciation

170 × 249 mm
Brush and yellow-brown wash, heightened with white,
over black chalk on yellow prepared paper
Cabinet des Dessins, Musée du Louvre, Paris (no. 9954)

This striking example of Schiavone's distinctive draughtsmanship has been realised with brush and black chalk alone; the conventional use of pen to define forms has been omitted altogether. Schiavone frequently used paper prepared in coloured washes, and the yellow paper of this drawing contributes significantly to the pictorial effect.

Originally classified among the anonymous sixteenth-century Italian drawings, this sheet was first attributed to Schiavone by Pouncey, and Châtelet related it to Schiavone's painting of the same subject in the church of the Carmini in Venice. Richardson, however, has suggested a possible connection with Schiavone's etching of *The Annunciation* (Bartsch 5).

D. McT.

PROVENANCE
During the French Revolution entered the Louvre collections

EXHIBITIONS
Paris 1964, no. 102

REFERENCES
Bacou and Viatte 1968, no. 62; Châtelet 1953, p. 90;
Richardson 1980, p. 131

Sebastiano del Piombo

[Biography on p. 209]

D55
Figure Studies for The Death of Adonis

275 × 425 mm
Black chalk and stump with traces of white chalk
worked into the stump
Recto: A River God; black and white chalk, red chalk and stump
Pinacoteca Ambrosiana, Milan (F.290, inv. no. 22)

The figure of Venus is a study for Sebastiano's painting of *The Death of Adonis*, c. 1512 (Uffizi, Florence). Despite earlier commentators' suggestions that the putto is a study for the same painting, Hirst has demonstrated convincingly that it relates to the Christ Child in the severely damaged *Adoration of the Shepherds* in the Fitzwilliam Museum, Cambridge.

The putto was drawn first and the figure of Venus was added later on top, and both studies are drawn with a freedom of handling and a pictorial use of chalk that show Sebastiano's Venetian origins, qualities which re-appear in his later drawings. The drawing after the antique on the *recto* is a study of the fragmentary torso of Hercules now in the Vatican collection, which was on the Quirinal in the mid-sixteenth century.

D.E.S.

EXHIBITIONS
Venice 1976[1], no. 9, with full bibliography

REFERENCES
Hirst 1981, p. 38, fig. 46

D56
Study for St. Agatha

354 × 189 mm
Black chalk, heightened with white, on blue paper
Cabinet des Dessins, Musée du Louvre, Paris (no. 10.816)

Pouncey first identified this sheet amongst the anonymous Italian drawings as a study for the principal figure of *The Martyrdom of St. Agatha* in the Palazzo Pitti, Florence. Hirst (1981) has shown that the painting, commissioned by Cardinal Ercole Rangone to celebrate his elevation to the cardinalate by Leo X on 1 July 1517, was completed by late 1519, and has observed that here Sebastiano was following 'Michelangelo's practice of making full-length studies for figures never planned to be depicted in entirety in the completed work'.

The figure is reminiscent of Michelangelo's design for the Christ in the *Flagellation* in the Borgherini Chapel, but Sebastiano obviously returned to a life-study in the drawing. The pentimento over the eyes appears to have been a preliminary idea for a blindfold, which was abandoned in the finished painting. The coagulations of white are very marked on the nude's left breast and the contour is heavily reinforced along the whole left flank of the body. The modelling of the torso is particularly subtle, with a soft and beautiful swell to the belly.

D.E.S.

PROVENANCE
E. Jabach; 1671 entered the Cabinet du Roi

D55

D56

EXHIBITIONS
Paris 1965¹, no. 100, repr.; New York 1974–75 and Paris 1975, no. 69;
Paris 1978, no. 12

REFERENCES
Bacou and Viatte 1968, pl. 31; Berenson 1961, II, no. 2497C;
III, figs. 101, 102; Hirst 1981, pp. 76–78, pl. 207; Pouncey 1952, p. 116;
Pouncey 1964, p. 291

D57
Study for St. James

237 × 444 mm
Black chalk and brown wash, heightened with white, on blue-grey
paper, squared in black chalk
The Trustees of the Chatsworth Settlement, Chatsworth,
Derbyshire

This is a study for the figure of St. James in Sebastiano's
Transfiguration in the Borgherini Chapel in S. Pietro in
Montorio, Rome. Pierfrancesco Borgherini commissioned
the chapel decoration in 1516. By November of that year
Sebastiano was working on cartoons of the prophets, and
work in the chapel seems to have begun in March 1517. The
Transfiguration in the half dome, for which this is a study,
was probably painted in 1519, and the chapel was unveiled
in 1524. Michelangelo provided sketches and detailed
studies for the *Flagellation*, and may have also helped with
the design of the *Transfiguration* (Hirst 1981, p. 59). Both
figures of the prophets derive from the prophets in the
Sistine Chapel, especially that on the right, which is based
directly on the prophet Joel.

This drawing is highly finished, and pictorial to a
remarkable degree; it was probably the final *modello* before
the preparation of the cartoon, a fragment of which – the
head of St. James – also survives (Hirst, pl. 87). Another
drawing for the *Transfiguration* is a study for the head of
St. Peter (British Museum, London). Of the surviving
drawings for the Borgherini project by Sebastiano, only the
recently discovered study for the left-hand prophet (Hirst,
pl. 82) has the same combination of vigour, pictorial

D57

D74
Study for The Angel of the Annunciation

422 × 279 mm, irregular
Black chalk and charcoal, heightened with white, on blue paper
faded to grey and stained
Verso: Study for a draped male figure; same technique
Gabinetto dei Disegni, Uffizi, Florence (no. 12903F)

Loeser published this drawing as a study for the Angel of
the Annunciation in Titian's altarpiece in S. Salvatore,
Venice, painted between 1559 and 1566. There are several
points of difference between the drawing and the finished
painting that have led Rearick (Florence 1976) to suggest
that the sheet is more closely related to the outside of the
lateral canvas of the *Assumption* in Dubrovnik Cathedral,
c. 1550.

Rearick has also related the drawing on the *verso* to the
1558 *Crucifixion* at Ancona. Noting a similarity in handling
between the draperies of the Virgin in the *Crucifixion* and
those of the drawing, he has ingeniously postulated that this
is a preparatory study for the figure of St. John to the right
of the cross. Certainly, the sheet is characteristic of Titian's
late style and a date of *c.* 1560 is more acceptable than
c. 1550.

The sense of weight in the moving draperies of the lower
section of the sheet, accentuated by the use of black chalk
and by the horizontal strokes of shading on the floor to the
right, is particularly successful. The white highlights are
sadly abraded, but a suggestion of tonal contrast is still
evident, and the softness of modelling in the wings is of the
greatest delicacy. Despite Rearick's *caveat*, it seems most
probable that this drawing is preparatory to the S. Salvatore
Annunciation.

D.E.S.

PROVENANCE
Fondo Mediceo-Lorenese (?)

EXHIBITIONS
London 1930, no. 670;
Florence 1976, no. 27, *verso* exhibited, figs. 31, 32, with full bibliography

REFERENCES
Pignatti 1979, no. 48; Venice 1976¹, figs. 26, 27

D75
A Couple in Embrace

252 × 260 mm
Charcoal and black chalk, heightened with white,
on faded blue paper
Fitzwilliam Museum, Cambridge (no. 2256)

The attribution of this drawing to Titian, made by Ricketts,
has been generally accepted. Fröhlich-Bum, Tietze and
Tietze-Conrat dated the drawing *c.* 1550–55. Jaffé has
proposed a considerably later date, *c.* 1570, comparing the
drawing with the x-rays of the painting of *Tarquin and
Lucretia* (Cat. 130) engraved by Cornelis Cort in 1571, and
with the unfinished painting of the same theme in the

D75

Akademie der bildenden Künste, Vienna, of *c.* 1570.

A copy of the present drawing (Louvre, inv. no. 5660)
was published in error as the original (*Kunstgeschichtliches
Jahrbuch der Zentralcommission*, III, 1909, p. 24, pl. III) by
Wickhoff, who suggested a date between 1510 and 1520.
That sheet, inscribed *Ti. . . Titiaen*, has now been
convincingly attributed to Jordaens by Meijer. Jordaens
was never in Italy and he derived any knowledge he had of
Titian's drawings from his contact with Rubens. This,
together with the existence of a free adaptation by Rubens,
c. 1617, of Titian's design of the embracing couple in his
so-called *Rape of the Daughters of Leucippus* (Alte
Pinakothek, Munich), points to the strong probability that
the Fitzwilliam drawing was once part of Rubens's
collection. The composition re-appears, modified and in
reverse, in the painting of *Mars and Venus* from the School
of Titian in the Kunsthistorisches Museum, Vienna
(no. 13). In the Jordaens copy there are much better
preserved areas of white highlight, which accord with the
faint traces of white in the Titian drawing. The sense of
weight in the woman's body and its abandoned sensuality
are the graphic equivalents of Titian's most voluptuous
painted nudes.

D.E.S.

PROVENANCE
Sir Peter Paul Rubens (?); Jonathan Richardson Senior;
Ricketts and Shannon;
1937 bequeathed to the Fitzwilliam Museum by Charles Haselwood
Shannon

EXHIBITIONS
London 1930, no. 669; London 1953, no. 56; Cambridge 1960, no. 54;
Venice 1976¹, no. 43, with full bibliography;
United States of America and Cambridge 1976–77, no. 45;
Cambridge 1979, no. 202; Cambridge 1980–81

REFERENCES
d'Hulst 1980, p. 361, fig. 1; Paris 1976, pp. 27–28, no. 16 (Meijer)

Paolo Caliari, called
Veronese

[Biography on p. 233]

D76
Five Studies of a Man

175 × 295 mm
Black chalk, heightened with white, on blue-grey paper
Cabinet des Dessins, Musée du Louvre, Paris (RF 38.932)

One of a group of ten drawings by Veronese acquired by
the Louvre in 1982 (see also Cat. D79 and D82), this sheet
came from a collection known as the 'Borghese Albums',
which was assembled by an unidentified collector, probably
in Venice, in the second half of the eighteenth century.

Four of the studies relate to *The Family of Darius before
Alexander* (National Gallery, London): the three on the left
are for the figure on the right – pointing to his comrade –
who is usually identified as Hephaeston, Alexander's
general. The second from the right is a study for Alexander
himself, his right hand on his chest and his left hand holding
his cloak on his hip. Roseline Bacou observes that the
second study from the left could have been used for the man
with outstretched arms in the foreground of *Christ in the
House of Levi* of 1573 (Accademia, Venice).

This elegant sheet reveals a remarkable analysis of
movement, and is new evidence for Veronese's style as a
draughtsman in black chalk. Pignatti has dated *The Family
of Darius c.* 1565, but the evidence of this new drawing and
its relationship to the painting in the Accademia, as noticed
by Bacou, supports Gould's dating on the grounds of the
style of the costume to *c.*1570 or later.

D.E.S.

PROVENANCE
'Borghese Albums' collection, numbered on the mount *P. no. 57(?)*;
acquired by the Musée du Louvre

REFERENCES
Bacou 1983, forthcoming publication

D77

D77
*Study for the Allegorical Figure
of Moderation*

211 × 227 mm
Black chalk, heightened with white, on blue paper
Inscribed upper right: *Moderatia*; lower right: *di Paolo Veronese*
The Trustees of the British Museum, London (1969-4-12-4)

This is a study for the figure of Moderation on the ceiling
of the Sala del Collegio in the Doge's Palace. Veronese was
commissioned to paint this ceiling in January 1575, and his
pictures were certainly finished by 3 March 1578.

The cycle of the ceiling glorifies Venice and includes eight
canvases of the Virtues. These are generally considered to
be in part by Benedetto, or from Veronese's workshop,
although Marini (1968) thought the figure of *Moderation*,

D76

[296]

depicted with an eagle, which she holds by the wing, was painted by Paolo with some studio assistance.

The drawing is characteristic of Veronese's use of chalk for studies of individual figures. White highlights are used to give the flesh a firm sense of modelling, despite the softness of the handling. Another study for one of the Virtues employing the same technique was acquired by the Louvre in 1982 (RF 38921); although not many of these preparatory drawings in chalk have yet been identified, it is clear that they must have been as regular a part of Veronese's studio practice as the more common pen and brown wash sketches and the finished *modelli*.

D.E.S.

PROVENANCE
27 March 1969, Sotheby's sale;
presented anonymously to the British Museum

REFERENCES
Pignatti 1976, I, no. 202; II, fig. 498

D78
The Martyrdom of Santa Giustina

470 × 240 mm
Pen and brown ink and point of the brush and brown wash, heightened with white, on greyish-blue paper squared in black chalk
The Trustees of the Devonshire Collection, Chatsworth, Derbyshire (no. 279)

This is a *modello* for the altarpiece in S. Giustina, Padua, commissioned from Veronese in 1575 and generally believed to have been painted in collaboration with Benedetto. It may have been the drawing mentioned by Carlo Ridolfi (1648, vol. I, p. 317), which was at that time kept in the rooms of the Abbot of S. Giustina.

The use of very elaborate highlighting with white is characteristic of Veronese's *modelli*, the luminous effect created giving a high degree of painterly finish. In the painting the two sections of the composition are closer together and the clouds are lower and heavier, to the detriment of the completed work. The figure to the left of Christ has been changed in the painting to John the Evangelist as opposed to John the Baptist who appears in the drawing.

D.E.S.

PROVENANCE
Lankrink; William, 2nd Duke of Devonshire;
Trustees of the Devonshire Collection, Chatsworth

EXHIBITIONS
United States and Canada 1962, no. 72 (Wragg)

REFERENCES
Pignatti 1976, fig. 470; Tietze and Tietze-Conrat 1944, no. 2056

D78

D79
Sheet of Studies for
The Adoration of the Magi

222 × 215 mm
Pen and brown ink and brown wash
Inscribed in the artist's hand in pen and brown ink upper left: numerals; near the soldier lower left: *tributa* (?); near the servant bending over lower left: *porta/una cassa*
Verso: drawn on the back of a letter which bears the address *Al Molto Mag^{co} S. Paolo Caliari Veronese Pictor ecl^{mo}*. . . .
Cabinet des Dessins, Musée du Louvre, Paris (RF 38.927)

D79

These are studies either for Veronese's *The Adoration of the Magi* (National Gallery, London) dated 1573, or for another similar painting of the same subject in S. Corona, Vicenza, generally dated *c.* 1575–80.

At the top of the sheet is a study for the group of the Virgin holding the Child, with St. Joseph near the column, and a study for one of the Magi kneeling in front of the Virgin. Behind the Virgin are little angels, and, on the right, children playing with a dog. The overall composition is

sketched below. Many changes occur between this preliminary study and the finished painting.

D.E.S.

PROVENANCE
'Borghese Albums' collection;
1982 acquired by the Musée du Louvre

REFERENCES
Bacou 1983, forthcoming publication

D80

D80
Study for a Seated Venus and Cupid with a Mirror

175 × 126 mm
Pen and brown ink and brown wash, the upper left hand
of the sheet squared in black chalk
Inscribed by the artist in brown ink:
spechio; traces of a further inscription below
The Trustees of the British Museum, London (1951-11-10-79)

Yapou observed, correctly, that this drawing was a
preliminary study for Veronese's painting of *Mars and
Venus* (National Gallery of Scotland, Edinburgh), dated by
Pallucchini and Pignatti to the late 1570s or 1580s.
Brigstocke rejects Cocke's theory, based on the evidence of
the drawing, that the painting was originally conceived as
a Venus with a mirror, or that the figure of Mars, which
fits awkwardly into the composition, was added later,
adducing evidence from x-ray photography that 'no
important change appears to have been made as work on
the picture progressed'.

D.E.S.

PROVENANCE
Colnaghi and Co.; 1951 acquired by the British Museum

REFERENCES
Brigstocke 1978, fig. 42; Cocke 1977, p. 122, fig. 6;
Pignatti 1976, vol. II, fig. 587; Yapou 1968, p. 3, no. 3, pl. 3

D81
Sheet of Studies for The Finding of Moses

308 × 210 mm
Pen, brown ink and brown wash
Inscribed in brown ink in the artist's hand upper left: *sonagi* (?);
centre left *strada*
Fitzwilliam Museum, Cambridge (PD 21-1977)

The drawing relates most closely to the *Finding of Moses*
(Galleria Sabauda, Turin) sent to Carlo Emmanuele I of
Savoy by Veronese together with the *Queen of Sheba before
Solomon* (Borghini 1584). The painting is generally
considered to be a workshop production after Veronese's
own design, and has usually been ascribed to the hand of
Benedetto Caliari (Pignatti 1976). Three sections of the
drawing are exactly repeated in the painting: the figure of
the woman, upper left, holding back a branch of a tree; the
figures of the dwarf and the mastiff, which occur twice on
the sheet; and the group of the maid handing up the infant
Moses to the daughter of Pharaoh.

The central group of the daughter of Pharaoh with her
attendants, part of which is repeated on the upper right, is
close, but not identical, to the painting. The sense of
movement evident in the stance of these figures – which
differ so markedly from those in the versions in Madrid,
Washington and Dresden – is maintained in the Turin
picture, dated by Cocke *c.* 1582. Cocke drew attention to
similarities with the drawing formerly in the Von Hirsch
Collection, which he related to the painting in the Walker
Art Gallery, Liverpool. He dated both the Liverpool and the
Turin paintings *c.* 1582 and added, 'the complete execution
of both pictures by different hands in the studio is a token
of Veronese's growing success in the last decade of his life'.

Cocke also noted that the pose of the standing woman
under the main group in this drawing anticipates the
Pharaoh's daughter worked out in the sheet in the Pierpont
Morgan Library, New York. He suggested (in a letter to the
Fitzwilliam Museum) that Veronese was working on the
Liverpool, Turin, Madrid and Washington paintings
simultaneously. The architectural studies have not yet been
related to any known painting by Veronese or his studio.

D.E.S.

PROVENANCE
Sir Peter Lely; Jonathan Richardson Senior; Sir Joshua Reynolds;
A. M. Champernowne; G. Bellingham-Smith; Tancred Borenius;
Captain N. Colville; 1977 accepted by Her Majesty's Treasury in lieu of
death duties and allocated to the Fitzwilliam Museum

EXHIBITIONS
Venice 1939, no. XII; Cambridge 1977, *hors catalogue*; Cambridge 1978;
Cambridge 1980–81

REFERENCES
Borenius 1921, pp. 54ff;
Cocke 1973, p. 142; Fiocco 1928, p. 208; von Hadeln 1926, no. 33;
Osmond 1927, p. 107; Pignatti 1976, A. 312, vol. I, p. 210; vol. II, fig. 986;
Tietze and Tietze Conrat 1944, p. 346, no. 2099

D81

D82
Sheet of Studies for San Pantaleone Healing a Child

214 × 245 mm, irregularly shaped
Pen and brown ink, brown wash
Inscribed in the artist's hand upper left: numerals
Verso: writing, undeciphered, visible when held to the light;
inscribed below on the backing paper in pen and brown ink:
Carletto Caliari
Cabinet des Dessins, Musée du Louvre, Paris (RF 38. 928)

In 1587, one year before his death, Veronese painted *San Pantaleone Healing a Child* (Cat. 147). Apart from the two little sketches of a standing Madonna holding the Child crowned by putti, the studies on this sheet are directly related to the painting. This drawing, dating from the very end of Veronese's career, is of remarkable freedom.

Roseline Bacou has noted that the reference to Carletto Caliari on the backing probably shows that the drawing belonged to the artist's son. In the old 'Borghese Album' collection it was misattributed to Carletto, whose initials, C.C., are again found in the double numbering system. It is generally accepted that Carletto played a small part in the execution of the S. Pantaleone painting.

D.E.S.

PROVENANCE
'Borghese Album'; 1982 acquired by the Musée du Louvre

D82

demonstrate how instructive the copying of Dürer's prints had been to Marcantonio's technique.

The richness of texture of this early impression might indicate that it was intended as a demonstration of Marcantonio's mastery of line engraving to rival Giulio Campagnola's stipple-engraving. This explanation seems more plausible if the print is compared to Giulio's *Venus Reclining in a Landscape* (Cat. P12); the figure in Giulio's print is very similar to that of the woman in the foreground here.

On the other hand, there are sufficient differences in the pose of the two figures to make it unlikely, in my view, that they are both copies of a lost work by Giorgione, as has been suggested. If a source is needed, one must look much further afield; the combination of a night scene, a burning town and small monsters are the trademark of Hieronymous Bosch, some of whose paintings (such as *The Martyrdom of St. Julia*, the shutters with *The Blessed* and *The Damned* and the altarpiece of the *Hermit Saints*, all of them incorporating these elements) were probably already in Venice. It is thus probable that Marcantonio put Giorgionesque figures in a Bosch-like landscape to show off his ability, and that the idea of reproducing another work of art, which so haunts art historians today, was far from his mind.

D.L.

Titian and an Anonymous Cutter

P16
The Triumph of Christ

385 × 2680 mm Woodcut from ten blocks
(Rosand and Muraro 1)
Inscribed along the top: *Nō pas a nous Seigneur / non pas a nous: mais a ton nom dōne la gloire. Ps. cxiij. Car il ny a nul aultre nom soubz le ciel dōne aux hōes: au q̄l no faille estre saluez. Et ny a point de salut en aulcū (aultre. Act, iiij.) Et aussy no as tu ouure*

toutes nos oeuures. Esa, xxvj. Car tu es celuy q par ton Sainct Esprit operez toutes choses en tous. j. Cor. xij.
Bibliothèque Nationale, Paris

The original of this very popular woodcut, which was copied several times, is known only from later impressions, such as the one exhibited here, printed in Antwerp around 1547. The first edition was issued either in 1508, as stated by Vasari, or around 1510/12 as most scholars now seem to believe; the point is not entirely academic because a polemic about the precedence of Titian over Raphael, or vice-versa, centres around it.

In the woodcut the figures of both St. Christopher and the Good Thief carrying the cross seem to be based on a figure in Michelangelo's lost cartoon of *The Battle of Cascina*, drawn copies of which were circulating in Italy at the time. Titian's figures, although related to Michelangelo's, are not, in my opinion, very close to it; they are much closer to a *Standard-Bearer* engraved by Marcantonio (Bartsch XIV, 357, 481). The crux of the problem is whether Marcantonio's print is after Titian's woodcut or after a lost drawing by Raphael – in other words, whether this type of figure, inspired by Michelangelo's cartoon, was conceived by the Venetian or the Umbrian, who was in Florence in 1508. I will not risk an opinion in this Raphael centenary year, in which several great experts in the field will publish their conclusions, and will add only that it should be borne in mind that Marcantonio's figure is facing in the same direction as Titian's and that we know that Marcantonio, when in Venice, had copied Dürer's woodcuts without reversing them.

Moreover, there is a drawing in Rome, attributed by Petrucci to Marcantonio, which shows the same figure reversed. Whether by Marcantonio or not, this drawing must be either a preparatory drawing for the engraving or a copy of such a drawing; on close examination it is evident that part of the outline is a tracing of Titian's figure and that where the model is not followed the drawing becomes much weaker. This would seem to exclude the possibility that the drawing in Rome is a copy of a lost study by Raphael, while it would naturally place it between Titian's woodcut and Marcantonio's engraving.

D.L.

P17

Giulio Campagnola
and Ugo da Carpi

P17
The Sacrifice of Abraham

790 × 1065 mm
Woodcut from four blocks (Rosand and Muraro 3)
Signed on a leaf at the bottom left of the top right block: UGO;
inscribed in the tablet top right: *In Venetia per Ugo da carpi /
Stampata per Bernardino/benalio: Cū privilegio [con]cesso/per Io
Illustrissimo Senato./Sul cāpo de san Stephano.*
Staatliche Museen Kupferstichkabinett und Sammlung der
Zeichnungen, East Berlin

The print is listed in the publisher Bernardino Benalio's
privilege of February 1515 and his name, together with that
of Ugo da Carpi, appears in the tablet on this, the only
known impression of the first state.

The attribution of the woodcut to Titian has been based
on its relationship to a drawing in New York, which, as
pointed out by Dreyer, is certainly a forgery (see p. 305),
and on the presence of Titian's name in the tablet, which,
however, occurs only in the third state printed decades
later. Whatever date is given to the print (those proposed
range between 1508 and 1518), there is no work by Titian
that can convincingly be compared with it; the composition
is unbalanced, the figures are too static and their faces

idiosyncratic and utterly different to those of Titian, the
borrowings from Dürer in the landscape are too many and
too literal. But the most obvious reason for rejecting
Titian's authorship for this woodcut is the total
dissimilarity between it and the magnificent *Submersion of
Pharaoh's Army in the Red Sea* (Cat. P19), an undoubted
autograph work.

Nor are the attributions of this *Sacrifice of Abraham* to
Palma Vecchio or Aspertini convincing. However, an
attribution to Giulio Campagnola, whose name has never
before been connected with a woodcut, might, in the view
of the present writer, be a better guess. We know very little
of Giulio's activity after *c.* 1510; the only document
referring to him after that date links him with the greatest
printer of the age, Aldo Manuzio, who, in his will of
January 1515, left dispositions for Giulio to finish cutting
the celebrated italic type Aldo had invented. Book
publishers were closely connected with the production and
sale of woodcuts, and it is possible that Giulio was also
responsible for two of the woodcut illustrations to the
Apocalypsis Ihesu Christi printed by Paganini in 1515/16,
which are stylistically very close to the figures in *The
Sacrifice of Abraham*. The three foreground figures in *The
Sacrifice* appear in reverse in a drawing in the Louvre, but
I do not believe it to be, as Dreyer proposed, by the same
hand as the forger of the Titian drawings, here identified
as Domenico Campagnola. The Louvre drawing is closer to
the preparatory drawing for Giulio's engraving of the
Shepherds in a Landscape (Cat. P7) and to *The Viola Player*
in the Ecole des Beaux-Arts, Paris, which is unanimously
attributed to Giulio.

PRINTS

If we accept the attribution of these woodcuts to Giulio, many other peculiarities could be explained: the borrowing from various prints by Dürer for the background of this *Sacrifice*, a typical feature of Giulio's work; the fact that Domenico, the adopted son of Giulio, had a hand in two other, much less successful, illustrations to the *Apocalypsis Ihesu Christi*; and the intriguing possibility that Domenico had access to the blocks of *The Sacrifice*, which he used to forge the so-called Titian drawing in the Metropolitan Museum of Art, New York, a crime of which he is accused in this catalogue.

D.L.

Titian and Ugo da Carpi

P18
St. Jerome

156 × 96 mm
Chiaroscuro woodcut from two blocks, greenish-grey and black
(Rosand and Muraro 6)

P18

Signed centre left: TICIANVS; bottom right: VGO
The Trustees of the British Museum, London

Most scholars agree that this woodcut is Ugo's first attempt at chiaroscuro, and that it should therefore be dated around 1516, when he applied for a copyright for the invention of this technique, which had, however, been invented in Germany about ten years earlier. It is certainly likely that the foremost contemporary painter was asked to share the glory of the first example in the new medium, and this might justify the almost excessive prominence given to the names. A much better effect was obtained when the names were printed in a very diluted ink (much lighter than the ink used for the rest of the key block), as in the early impressions in the Louvre and the Estense Library, Parma, which must have been experiments.

D.L.

Titian and an Anonymous Cutter

P19
The Submersion of Pharaoh's Army in the Red Sea

1225 × 2215 mm Woodcut from twelve blocks
(Rosand and Muraro 4)
Inscribed in the tablet bottom right:
La crudel persecuzione del ostinato Re, contro il populo tanto da Dio/amato, Con la sommersione di esso Pharaone goloso dil inocente / sangue. Disegnata per mano dil grande, et immortal Titiano. / In Venetia, p[er] domeneco dalle greche depentore Venitiano. / M.DXLIX
The Trustees of the British Museum, London

Arguably the greatest woodcut ever made, *The Submersion of Pharaoh's Army in the Red Sea* is mentioned in Benalio's application for a privilege to the Venetian Senate of February 1515, but it is known only in later impressions, printed by Domenico dalle Greche in 1549. It is also the largest Venetian figurative woodcut, Titian's extraordinary extrapolation from the monumentality of Jacopo de' Barbari's *Triumph of Men over Satyrs* (fig. 25) and his own *Triumph of Christ* (Cat. P16). The forerunner of all the large woodcuts shown here, its enormous size probably relates it very closely to *The Battle of Spoleto* (see Cat. D72) on which Titian was starting work at this time. As rightly pointed out by Siegfried and Oberhuber, this print became the natural outlet for the artist's ideas and studies for the large painting for the Sala del Gran Consiglio in the Doge's Palace, the commission for which seemed more than once in jeopardy between 1513 and 1516.

D.L.

P19

P20

Domenico Campagnola

Venice (?) *c.* 1500 – Padua after 1552

The son of a German artisan, Domenico was probably born in Venice and trained by his adoptive father, Giulio Campagnola. While still young, following Giulio's example, he turned his hand to painting, drawing, engraving and woodcutting and acquired great proficiency in all these media. After Giulio's death in about 1516, Domenico became for a few years Venice's foremost engraver, and his experiments at cutting woodblocks himself (rather than employing a professional woodcutter) were, albeit unsuccessful, very daring.

Domenico was a gifted draughtsman and also specialized in drawing landscapes, which were celebrated by his contemporaries and which he continued to produce all his life, selling them as finished compositions. His knowledge of the roller press (which he had used for printing his engravings), and of the flat press (used for woodcuts), and his expert draughtsmanship no doubt proved very useful for the forging of a group of Titian drawings intended to look like preparatory drawings for woodcuts. These forgeries might have been produced on one of Domenico's many trips to Venice, or even in the more secure tranquillity of Padua,

where he may have moved as early as 1520. He spent the rest of his life there as the city's busiest and most praised painter, although the reason for the praise escapes us today.

D.L.

P20

Landscape with Two Trees and a Group of Buildings

127 × 171 mm Engraving (Hind v, 214, 14)
Boymans-van Beuningen Museum, Rotterdam

Tentatively attributed to Domenico by Hind, this is probably one of the artist's first attempts at engraving. It shows an evident indebtedness to Giulio's landscapes, without sharing their refined technique, and might be considered the link between the still very crude *Youth Seated Contemplating a Skull* (catalogued by Hind as possibly by Giulio, Hind 20) and the signed *Venus Reclining in a Landscape* (Cat. P12; Hind 13) dated 1517. It should therefore be dated earlier.

D.L.

P21
Battle of Naked Men

218 × 226 mm Engraving (Hind v, 211, 4)
Signed and dated bottom left: DOMINICUS / CĀPAGNOLA / ·1517·
Bibliothèque Nationale, Paris

Although inspired by such examples as Titian's woodcut of
The Submersion of Pharaoh's Army in the Red Sea (Cat.
P19), Leonardo's *Battle of Anghiari* or Michelangelo's
Battle of Cascina, drawn copies of which were apparently
circulating widely in Italy at the time, Domenico's
treatment of the battle is confused and confusing, and it is
very difficult to make sense of the entanglement of bodies
and horses. The very tight cross-hatching and the
predominantly dark background of interlacing trees are also
to be found in Domenico's contemporary woodcut designs,
especially in those he is supposed to have cut himself.

D.L.

P22
The Assumption of the Virgin

284 × 198 mm Engraving (Hind v, 212, 3, 1)
Signed and dated bottom right:
DOMINICUS / CAMPA / GNOLA / 1517
The Trustees of the British Museum, London

This, Domenico's largest and most ambitious engraving, is
thought to reproduce an early idea by Titian for his
Assumption of the Virgin in the Frari, which was not
completed until the next year. Though prone to copying,
and probably even forging the great master's works (see
p. 305), I do not think that Domenico actually reproduced
any of them in his prints, for there is no direct correlation
between any of his prints and a Titian painting or drawing
– or, for that matter, any other known model.

D.L.

P21

P22

P23

St. Jerome

127 × 97 mm Engraving Hind v, 213, 10)
Signed top left: DOMINICUS / ·CAMP·; dated bottom left *1517*
Museum of Fine Arts, Boston, Harvey D. Parker Collection

This is Domenico's most successful engraving; it shows his
freest and most daring use of line. It should be compared
with *The Vision of St. Augustine* (Cat. P24), a woodcut of
similar dimensions probably cut by Domenico himself at the
same time as this engraving. Seeing them side by side is most
instructive; the image of the woodcut is more sharply
defined than that of the engraving, the line is thicker,
blacker, and more contrasted to the whiteness of the paper.

D.L.

P24

The Vision of St. Augustine

148 × 103 mm Woodcut (Rosand and Muraro 19)
Signed bottom left: .DO. CDO. CĀP.
The Trustees of the British Museum, London

Only one impression survives of this beautiful woodcut,
Domenico's masterpiece in the medium. As the Tietzes first
proposed and Rosand and Muraro confirmed, the artist
probably cut the block himself, for such a freedom and
energy is found in none of his other woodcuts, and certainly
not in those signed by a professional cutter, such as
Lucantonio degli Uberti. Together with the engraved *St.
Jerome* (Cat. P23), it can be regarded as an enthusiastic, if

P37

The cutting is different from that of any other woodcut by Campagnola and seems to me close only to the works of Antonio da Trento done for Parmigianino. It is possible that Antonio went to Venice in 1530 after escaping from Bologna where, according to Vasari, he had stolen all Parmigianino's drawings and prints. Such an attribution and date would fit well with the unusual medium: Antonio was probably one of the very few cutters in Italy at that time capable of making chiaroscuro woodcuts, which were becoming fashionable again in Venice under the auspices of Pordenone.

D.L.

Domenico Campagnola
and Antonio da Trento (?)

[Domenico: biography on p. 324]
Antonio: active *c.* 1527–1540 (?)

P38
Two Goats
at the Foot of a Tree

493 × 217 mm Chiaroscuro woodcut from two blocks,
light grey and black
(Rosand and Muraro 25)
Graphische Sammlung Albertina, Vienna

Among the group of woodcuts which were the result of a collaboration between the artist and a professional cutter, this is probably the most successful. The attribution to Domenico could hardly be questioned, after Caroline Karpinsky read his signature on the Budapest impression of the very similar *Landscape with Peasant and Dog.*

P38

P39

working methods are also recalled by the fact that in many cases each early impression is a new state: Schiavone seems to have gone back to some of his plates again and again, experimenting with techniques, tools, papers and inks in order to obtain new tonal effects.

D.L.

Andrea Schiavone

[Biography on p. 206]

P39
Moses and the Burning Bush

125 × 217 mm Etching and drypoint
(Bartsch XVI, 41, 3; Richardson 79, 3)
Graphische Sammlung Albertina, Vienna

Richardson, who has dated this print in the mid-1540s, has noted its indebtedness to the works of Giorgione, the early Titian and the prints of Giulio Campagnola, all of which seem to have deeply impressed the artist at this point in his career. The experimental quality of Giulio's engravings is recalled particularly in very early impressions, probably working proofs, such as this one.

The print demonstrates Schiavone's imaginative use of drypoint and the tonal effects created by its burr (for instance in the bushes and sheep on the left, and in Moses's hair or in the burning bush on the right), which call to mind, though not in terms of aesthetic achievement, Rembrandt's experimental printmaking. Rembrandt's

Polidoro da Lanciano (?) and an Anonymous Cutter

Polidoro: Lanciano 1515 – Venice 1565

P40
The Holy Family with the Infant St. John and St. Elizabeth in a Landscape

212 × 304 mm Woodcut (Rosand and Muraro 79)
Metropolitan Museum of Art, New York,
Harris Brisbane Dick Fund 1935

The number of painters in Venice who specialised in *Sacre Conversazioni* in the fourth and fifth decades of the century makes any attribution of a print such as this very difficult, particularly because it seems to be the only woodcut by this hand. But the setting of the figures in a wide landscape, the ruins on the left hung with peculiar vegetation, the rather eccentric faces and gestures all suggest Polidoro da Lanciano as the author. He was living in Venice in the late 1540s and was influenced by Giuseppe Porta Salviati, as is evident in this print. A further link with Salviati is the fact that, as noticed by Rosand and Muraro, the cutter of his *Crucifixion* was almost certainly responsible for this woodcut and probably also cut the landscapes in Vesalius's *De humani corporis fabrica*. This most gifted cutter then disappears as suddenly as he appeared at the beginning of the decade, leaving no clue to his identity.

D.L.

P40

which the foreground figures stand out prominently from the picture plane; his *Martyrdom of St. Mark* is especially close to Aspetti's *St. Daniel Dragged by a Horse*, while the sketchier background of *St. Daniel Nailed between Two Boards* may have been suggested by the treatment of architectural elements in the background of Sansovino's *St. Mark Healing a Demoniac*. Aspetti's figures, however, display an exaggerated fluidity closer in spirit to the reliefs of his uncle, Tiziano Minio, on the baptismal font of San Marco and in the Odeo Cornaro in Padua.

The authenticity of Aspetti's Paduan reliefs has recently been questioned by Olga Raggio, who claims that a second pair, acquired in 1970 by the Metropolitan Museum, New York, are the originals and that the Paduan bronzes are late aftercasts. But the Metropolitan reliefs have no known provenance before the early twentieth century, nor is there evidence to confirm that one set was substituted for another. In addition, the Metropolitan reliefs have untrimmed borders, which suggest that these reliefs were not made for the marble frames of the crypt altar; nor are they identical to the ones in Padua, as one would expect in the case of an original cast and an aftercast.

The most plausible explanation for the existence of the two sets is that they are both late sixteenth-century casts from Aspetti's original models, but made for different purposes. This would explain the numerous small discrepancies between the two pairs. The elaborate detail of the Metropolitan bronzes suggests that they were destined for a collector's cabinet, while the comparative lack of finish on the Paduan reliefs can be explained by their original setting: high finish and chasing would have been scarcely visible in the dark crypt. Aspetti's relief of the *Martyrdom of St. Lawrence* in S. Trinita, Florence, is similar in this respect.

B.B.

EXHIBITIONS
Padua 1976, nos. 121–22

REFERENCES
Benacchio 1931, pp. 123–28, 145; Brunetti in D.B.I., IV, 1962, pp. 418–22; Raggio 1982, with full bibliography

Girolamo Campagna

Verona 1549 – Venice c. 1625

Campagna was the son of a furrier and was probably apprenticed to Danese Cattaneo while the latter was at work on the Fregoso monument in Verona (c. 1562–65). On his death in 1572 Cattaneo left all his plaster casts and drawings to his disciple Campagna, who subsequently won a competition to complete the last relief in the shrine of St. Anthony in the Basilica del Santo, Padua, a commission originally won by his master. After an interval in Augsburg restoring antiquities for Hans Fugger, Campagna finally finished the relief, his first major work, in 1577; two years later he won another competition for the new high altar of the Santo. In the 1580s he provided allegorical statues for the tomb of Doge Niccolò da Ponte (1583) and for the Doge's Palace (1583–84), and completed his first large-scale Venetian altarpiece, the *Virgin and Child* for the Dolfin family in S. Salvatore (1585–90).

By 1590 Campagna was the major statuary sculptor in Venice, and was commissioned to carve seven statues for the balustrade of Sansovino's Library (1589–91) and one of two *Giants* for the Piazzetta entrance to the Public Mint (1590); he also made the bronze figures for the high altars of the Redentore and S. Giorgio Maggiore (1589–92), which are amongst the finest executed in Italy at that time. Later commissions included a marble *Virgin and Child* for S. Giorgio Maggiore (1595), the sculpture for the tomb of

S2

Doge Marino Grimani (1601–04) and statues of *St. Lawrence* and *St. Sebastian* for the high altar of S. Lorenzo (1615–17). Campagna's last major undertaking was the statues for the high altar of the Scuola Grande di S. Rocco (1613–20). The exact date of his death is not known, but he died before June 1625.

B.B.

REFERENCES

McTavish 1980; Timofiewitsch 1972; Timofiewitsch in D.B.I., XVII, 1974, pp. 300–06, with full bibliography

S3
Angel Holding a Candlestick

Bronze; 74 cm to tip of wing
Inscribed: HIER.ˢ CAMPAGNA. V.ˢ F.
S. Maria del Carmelo (I Carmini), Venice

S3

The first reference to this angel, one of a pair, appears in a guide-book of 1815. At that time both figures were in their present location – on the balustrade of the third altar to the right of the nave – but they are not mentioned in a guide-book of 1604. They have been variously dated from the early 1590s to the first decade of the seventeenth century. Timofiewitsch's suggestion of 1590–92 seems plausible, given the close similarity in pose to the *St. Mark* that Campagna made for the Redentore in 1588–90.

Together the angels create a sinuous *contrapposto* which owes much to the *Daniel* and *St. Catherine* made by Vittoria for S. Giuliano in the early 1580s. The complementary poses suggest that they were originally intended to flank a tabernacle or to form part of a retable. Apart from the elaborate wings, which may derive from northern woodcuts, they are distinctively Venetian in style.

B.B.

REFERENCES

Niero 1965, pp. 39–40; Timofiewitsch 1972, pp. 74–75, 255–56, no. 13, with full bibliography

S4
St. Agnes

Bronze; 93 cm
Inscribed on the base: FR. BALTHASAR. STELLA VENETUS/HIER. CAMPAGNA VERON. SCUL.
S. Maria Gloriosa dei Frari, Venice

The saint is paired with *St. Anthony of Padua* on the holy water stoups in the Frari. An inscription on the *St. Anthony* is dated 1609 and states that Friar Balthasar Stella commissioned the works from Campagna. Little attention has been given to the female figure, which has been identified as Innocence or Gentleness; Timofiewitsch correctly identified her as St. Agnes, the early Christian martyr whose attribute is a lamb, and drew attention to the fragment of a martyr's palm in her left hand. In addition, he has convincingly suggested that *St. Agnes* and *St. Anthony* were commissioned as a pair by Stella and that the traditional date of 1593 for *St. Agnes* can be discounted.

Although its patination has suffered from humidity, the *St. Agnes* is one of the finest small bronzes produced by Campagna in the manner of his master, Danese Cattaneo; it is also reminiscent of his own stucco *Virgin Annunciate* of 1582 in S. Sebastiano. While a date of 1609 for *St. Agnes* must be correct, the style has more in common with Campagna's early works and the pose may be based upon an earlier model.

B.B.

REFERENCES

Timofiewitsch 1972, pp. 286–87, no. 29, with full bibliography

S4

gifts are attested by his poem, *L'amor di Marfisa* of 1562. In Padua, too, he first gained fame as a portraitist with his bust of Bembo for the latter's tomb in 1547, and subsequently with that of the classical scholar Lazzaro Bonamico (Cat. S5). He also undertook major commissions in Verona, including the statue of the celebrated physician and poet Girolamo Fracastoro and the imposing Fregoso monument in Sant'Anastasia. While in Verona, Cattaneo probably took on Girolamo Campagna as an apprentice and collaborator; it was to Campagna that he bequeathed his collection of models and drawings.

Cattaneo's most notable works in Venice are the *Apollo*, originally on the well-head of the Public Mint and now at the Palazzo Pesaro, one each of a pair of atlantes and caryatids for the Doge's Palace (with Pietro da Salò), and busts of Gasparo Contarini and Giovanni Andrea Badoer in S. Maria dell'Orto and S. Giovanni Evangelista respectively. His last projects, the Monument to Doge Leonardo Loredan (d. 1521) in SS. Giovanni e Paolo and a relief for the Santo, Padua, were unfinished at the time of his death, but were completed by Campagna.

B.B.

REFERENCES

Burns 1980, pp. 165–66; Macchioni and Gangeni in D.B.I., XXII, 1979, pp. 449–56, with full bibliography; Rigoni 1970, pp. 217–37; Sansovino 1575, p. 18; Temanza 1778, pp. 269–83; Vasari (ed. Milanesi) 1878–85, VII, pp. 522–26

Danese Cattaneo

Carrara c. 1509 – Padua 1572

'A most cultivated poet, an excellent sculptor, and a person of great spirit, full of unadorned goodness.' So wrote Francesco Sansovino of his friend Danese Cattaneo. Cattaneo was born in the mountains of Carrara and studied sculpture under Jacopo Sansovino in Rome. In 1527 he followed his master to Venice and soon set up as an independent sculptor. His first works include a group of figures probably executed for Sansovino in San Marco. These no longer survive, but a statuette of *St. Jerome*, completed by 1530, remains in S. Salvatore. According to both Vasari and Francesco Sansovino, Cattaneo executed some of the sculptural decoration on the Library and the Loggetta.

Cattaneo also worked outside Venice. In Padua, he was involved in some projects for the shrine of St. Anthony, although little came of them. More significantly, while there he became a friend of Alvise Cornaro, Pietro Bembo, and Bernardo and Torquato Tasso, among others. His literary

S5

Lazzaro Bonamico

Bronze; 75.3 × 77.4 cm
Inscribed on the base: LAZ. BON. BAS.
Museo Civico, Bassano del Grappa
[*repr. in colour on p. 144*]

Bonamico (1479–1552) was an eminent classicist at the University of Padua who moved in the same intellectual circles as Cattaneo. On Bonamico's death, his heirs decided to erect a monument in the Paduan church of S. Giovanni di Verdara and commissioned a bust from Cattaneo, whose portrait of Pietro Bembo in the Santo was widely admired. The monument to Bonamico was, in fact, an exact copy of that of Bembo, the architectural design of which has recently been attributed to Cattaneo's friend, Andrea Palladio. It is probable that Cattaneo simply copied the design of the Bembo monument, substituting a bronze portrait for the marble bust. The bust and monument of Bonamico parted company when the church of S. Giovanni was demolished in 1818; the monument, with a stone copy of the bust, was re-erected in the second cloister of the Santo, while the bronze was acquired privately and subsequently given to the museum of Bonamico's native town of Bassano.

Cattaneo's excellence as a portraitist is evident in the refinement and sensitivity of this bust. It is the only bronze by the sculptor, and one of only four portraits securely attributable to him.

B.B.

PROVENANCE
S. Giovanni di Verdara, Padua; 1818 G. B. Roberti; 1841 Museo Civico

EXHIBITIONS
Venice 1946, no. 224; London 1961, no. 139, with bibliography;
Amsterdam 1961–62, no. 138

REFERENCES
Avesani in D.B.I, 1969, pp. 533–40; Burns 1979, pp. 19–20; Chiarelli 1909,
pp. 82–98; Planiscig 1921, p. 424

Desiderio da Firenze

Florence—active Padua 1532–45

Presumably of Florentine origin, Desiderio is first documented in Padua on 7 March 1532, when he received an advance payment for the bronze voting urn for the Maggior Consiglio of the Comune of Padua (Cat. S6). In these documents he is described as a sculptor and founder. The advance payment for the voting urn was dated four months before Riccio's death on 8 July 1532, at a time when he is known to have been too ill to work, and it has been conjectured by Moschetti that Desiderio was his assistant and was entrusted with the work because of his master's infirmity. But this theory cannot be substantiated: the style of the urn seems to owe little to Riccio, and can to a great extent be explained in Florentine terms.

Desiderio is next mentioned in a letter from Pietro Bembo to Giambattista Ramusio, dated 23 June 1537, in which Bembo recommended him as the best sculptor to execute the bronze cover for the baptismal font in San Marco, Venice, in such warm terms that it suggests Desiderio and Bembo were intimate friends. In fact, it was not until 18 April 1545 that Desiderio actually contracted to make the font cover in collaboration with the Paduan sculptor Tiziano Minio. The credit for the reliefs on it is conventionally given to Minio, but the respective roles of the two collaborators have never been established.

Attempts to ascribe other bronzes to Desiderio have enjoyed little success: a group of elaborately decorated handbells, ascribed to him by Planiscig, has been shown to be from the workshop of Vincenzo and Gian Girolamo Grandi, and of three statuettes of satyrs attributed to him by Planiscig one is signed by Adriano Fiorentino, the second is an autograph work by Riccio (see Cat. S21) and the third is derived from a Riccio model (see Cat. S24), while a sword hilt ascribed to him in the Armeria Reale, Turin, has also proved to be the work of Riccio. Desiderio may, nevertheless, have been responsible for certain bronze artefacts which seem to reflect the styles of both Riccio and Sansovino.

A.F.R.

REFERENCES
Cessi 1967, pp. 65–67; Jestaz 1975; Jestaz 1983, p. 39; Leithe-Jasper 1981;
Moschetti 1927, pp. 148–49; Planiscig 1921, pp. 396–403; Planiscig
1930–31; Pope-Hennessy and Radcliffe 1970, pp. 152–57; Radcliffe 1982,
pp. 415–18; Ronchi 1933–34, p. 310, note 1

S6

Voting Urn of the Maggior Consiglio of the Comune of Padua

Bronze, parcel-gilt; 51 cm
Museo Bottacin, Museo Civico, Padua (no. 370)

This urn, which is cast in three sections, bears the arms of the city of Padua on the three faces of the base and the lion of St. Mark three times on the bowl. Documents referring to its execution, published by Moschetti, show that it was already in progress by 7 March 1532, when an advance payment was made to Desiderio, and that it was finished by 8 February 1533, when Desiderio received a final payment. Although described as derivative from Riccio's style, the urn's general design and most of its decorative elements can be traced back to Florentine sources, most notably to Verrocchio.

A.F.R.

EXHIBITIONS
London 1961, no. 74; Amsterdam 1961–62, no. 71; Florence 1962, no. 70;
Padua 1976, no. 92

REFERENCES
Mariacher 1971, p. 34; Moschetti 1927, pp. 148–9; Moschetti 1938, p. 219;
Planiscig 1930–31, pp. 71–72

S6

plaque chased with a design analogous to that found on Venetian velvets. Szmodis-Eszláry dated the plaque 1550–1600, but the pattern is consistent with those found on textiles as early as the end of the fifteenth century.

Until recently the bust and its plaque were mounted in a pedimented wooden frame with flanking columns, bearing the inscription PROPRIO FILIO NON PEPERCIT, but the frame, which appeared to date from 1550–1600, was not necessarily made for the crystal, and the inscription is not therefore necessarily relevant to the subject.

A.F.R.

PROVENANCE
Wilhelm Gumprecht, Berlin; 1918 Wilhelm Gumprecht's sale Berlin (Cassirer), as Tullio Lombardo (lot no. 62); August Lederer, Vienna; private collection, Hungary; 1979 acquired by the Museum

REFERENCES
Kris 1929, pp. 42, 160; Planiscig 1921, pp. 245–48, 251; Szmodis-Eszláry, 1981

Antonio Minello

Active Padua 1484–Venice 1527/28

Born in Padua at an unknown date, Antonio was one of two sons of the sculptor Giovanni Minello. A document of 1484 suggests that one of Giovanni's sons was already working with him by that year, and this must have been Antonio

S11

since his only brother, Gerolamo, was not a sculptor but a tailor. Antonio is first documented by name in 1500 in a contract connected with the shrine of St. Anthony, when he and his father appear to have been working in partnership. His earliest independent work was probably the statue of *Santa Giustina* in one of the niches on the façade which forms part of the early decoration of the shrine; however, the overall scheme was supervised by his father. This figure is ascribed to Antonio by Marcantonio Michiel, and in terms of style the attribution seems to be correct.

In 1510, probably as a result of the War of the League of Cambrai, Antonio was in Bologna, where he worked on the great portal of S. Petronio begun by Jacopo della Quercia, carving the 15 panels of prophets for the archivolt with Antonio da Ostiglia. Returning to Padua he completed in 1512 his large narrative relief of *St. Anthony Receiving the Franciscan Habit* for the shrine in the Basilica del Santo, and in the same year had already begun his second relief for the chapel, *The Raising of the Child Parrasio*, which he abandoned after 1522 and which was finished in 1534 by Sansovino.

In 1525 Antonio left Padua for Venice, where he bought the contents of Lorenzo Bregno's workshop from his widow, undertaking to complete two works left unfinished by the sculptor. One of these was the altarpiece in S. Maria Materdomini, in which Minello's hand is clearly visible. His last dated work is the *Mercury* (Cat. S12) carved in 1527 for Marcantonio Michiel, and this is possibly also his last work, since documents published by Rigoni suggest that he died shortly before his father, whose death occurred in 1528. Other recorded works from his Venetian period were two colossal heads of *Hercules* and *Cybele* seen by Michiel in 1532 at the house of Andrea Odoni in Venice, but now lost. It is possible that Minello was also responsible for some of the small classicising marble reliefs generally associated with Antonio Lombardo and Mosca.

A.F.R.

REFERENCES
Frizzoni 1884, pp. 15–16, 155; Gonzati 1854, II, pp. xcv, xcix–c, civ; Paoletti 1893, p. 106; Pope-Hennessy 1952; Rigoni 1970, pp. 259–64; Sansovino 1663, p. 205; Sartori 1976, pp. 151–63; Supino 1914, pp. 29–30, 102; Venturi 1935, X, 1, pp. 410–19

S12

Mercury

Marble, inlaid with bronze; 76.8 cm
Inscribed: MERC. SIMULAC./ M. ANT. MICHAEL P.V./ ANN. VRB. VENET./ MC.VI.F.C./ CONSECRAVITQ./ ANT. MINELL. SCVLPT./ PATAVINVS./ XVI.KAL.MARTI. COEPTVM./ XVII.KAL. QVINT./ PERFECIT./ ANN. SAL./M.D.XXVII.
Victoria & Albert Museum, London (A.44-1951)

The inscription records that the statuette was commissioned by the Venetian patrician and humanist Marcantonio Michiel (1484–1552, the 'Anonimo Morelliano'); it was begun by Antonio Minello on 14 February 1527, and completed by him on 15 June of the same year. On the opposite side of the small altar from the

S12

inscription, a circular bronze plaque is inlaid; it is engraved with a diagram of the planets, showing the motions of Mercury, placed at the top, the relative positions of the planets on 15 June 1527, the date of the completion of the figure. It has been interpreted as a horoscope by Hartner and Pope-Hennessy, with some difference as to the precise time, which Hartner places at 8.04 a.m. and Pope-Hennessy at 11.46.40 a.m. Pope-Hennessy argues that this shows Mercury in a particularly favourable position as Lord of the Ascendant and of the Midheaven, also in conjunction with the Sun and Jupiter, and that the moment was therefore clearly chosen with great care and must have had some special significance for the career of Marcantonio Michiel. He explains this in terms of Michiel's repeated attempts to secure public office, with a particular desire to serve as ambassador, which were dashed in September 1525 as a result of a disgraceful conflict with a relative that caused him to be debarred from public office for a year. By February 1527, when the statuette was commissioned, Michiel was free once again to try for office. In that month

he married Maffea Soranzo, and began to scheme for election to the Senate, in which he was finally successful on 28 September 1527. The peculiarly favourable conjunction of Mercury on 15 June 1527 would therefore have been a good omen for him. This interpretation has since been questioned by Fletcher, and more recently Eade has brought into question the astrological status of the plaque. Observing that the earlier astrological calculations were wrong and that on 15 June 1527 Mercury was unfavourably positioned, Eade interprets the plaque not as a horoscope, but as a simple astronomical diagram showing the position of Mercury on 15 June 1527 in relation to the other planets.

The *Mercury* appears in the earliest inventory of Michiel's collection, probably compiled soon after his death in 1552, and in 1576 was in the possession of Michiel's grandson. As noted by Fletcher, who published the early inventory, the collection was housed in Michiel's palace at Santa Marina in Venice, where the *Mercury* appears to have been paired with a marble *Apollo* of similar scale and valued at the same amount. There is no indication as to whether the *Apollo* was a classical or a modern work. It was conjectured by Pope-Hennessy that the pose of the *Mercury* was based on a classical statue of Hypnos of a type represented in the Prado, Madrid, of which a number of examples survive. The Madrid *Hypnos* was at one time thought to represent Mercury.

A.F.R.

PROVENANCE
Acquired in London by Dr W. L. Hildburgh; 1951 presented by him to the Victoria & Albert Museum

REFERENCES
Cicogna 1861; Eade 1981; Fletcher 1973, p. 383; Fletcher 1981, pp. 465–66; Hartner 1955; Pope-Hennessy 1952; Pope-Hennessy 1964¹, no. 539

Giovanni Maria Mosca

Active 1507–1573

Mosca was probably born at Padua at an unknown date. His father, a boatman named Matteo Mosca, apprenticed him while still a youth to the Paduan stonemason, Giovanni Minello, in April 1507. After five years this contract was rescinded, and Mosca spent the last year of his apprenticeship with another Paduan stonemason, Bartolomeo Mantello, for whom he executed figures in stone, wax, clay and plaster, in exchange for food and clothing. He seems to have had a similar working relationship with the bronze-founder Guido Aspetti, called Lizzaro since a number of terracottas by Mosca were seen in Aspetti's workshop by the Venetian writer Marcantonio Michiel. One surviving work from this collaboration is the bronze relief of *The Decollation of the Baptist* made for the Paduan Baptistry in 1516.

Mosca's only major Paduan commission came in 1520 when he was assigned one of the marble reliefs for the new shrine of St. Anthony; his relief of *The Miracle of the Unbroken Glass* was almost complete by late 1528. The following year he agreed to carve the perspective backdrop for his relief, although he subsequently gave the remaining work to another sculptor, Paolo Stella. A second surviving Paduan work, *The Judgement of Solomon* (Cat. s14), was commissioned by the Paduan professor of philosophy, Giambattista Leone, at about the same time.

In the 1520s Mosca worked in Padua and Venice. Francesco Sansovino recorded a number of Mosca's Venetian works that cannot be traced, as well as two which are still *in situ*, the *San Sebastiano* and *San Pantaleone* on the high altar of the church of S. Rocco. Mosca's name has also been connected with the tombs of Giambattista Bonzio and Alvise Trevisan, both in SS. Giovanni e Paolo, but the attributions are not universally accepted.

Mosca did not enjoy conspicuous success in Padua or Venice and emigrated to Poland around 1530. There he entered the service of King Sigismund I and played a notable role in the development of Renaissance sculpture in eastern Europe. He was still alive in 1573.

B.B.

REFERENCES
Bialostocki 1976, pp. 53–57, 66–69; Fiocco 1965; Frizzoni 1884, pp. 16, 74–75, 77; Kozakiewiczowa 1964; Munman 1970; Paoletti 1893, pp. 240–41, 281; Planiscig 1921, pp. 259–78; Planiscig in Thieme-Becker, XXV, pp. 174–76; Rigoni 1970, pp. 127–28, 138; Sartori 1976, pp. 171–73

S13
Venus Anadyomene

Marble; 40.6 × 25.1 cm
Inscribed on the base: NVDA VENVS MADIDAS EXPRIMIT IMBRE COMAS
Victoria & Albert Museum, London (A.19-1964)
[*repr. in colour on p. 140*]

The inscription is taken from Ovid's *Ars Amatoria* III, 224, and the subject reflects descriptions of the lost *Venus Anadyomene* by Apelles. The relief has been ascribed to Antonio Lombardo (Pope-Hennessy 1964; Ruhmer 1974), but the large empty spaces in the background are uncharacteristic of Antonio, as are the full, sensuous forms of the body and face, which are closer to the female figures of his brother Tullio, as, for example, in his relief of *The Miracle of the Miser's Heart* in Padua (1520–25). Yet there is a softness in the handling, particularly of the hair, face and waves, which is alien to Tullio, whose carving was always crisp and clear, and the unbalanced composition is foreign to both brothers. These considerations point to a sculptor, perhaps of a younger generation, influenced by Tullio's mature style.

The obvious candidate is Mosca. Indeed, a close analogy to Venus is provided by the true mother in his relief of *The Judgement of Solomon* (Cat. s14), especially in the curiously unstable pose, the handling of the anatomy and the physiognomy. Even the lettering of the inscription corresponds exactly with that on Mosca's relief, to the extent that the letters 'V' and 'S' are rendered defectively in just the same way. It is also significant that Marcantonio Michiel saw several terracotta models by Mosca in the house of Guido Lizzaro in Padua, including one for *The Judgement of Solomon* (Cat. s14) and another of *Venus Emerging from a Shell*, which could well have been the

model for this relief. If so, the *Venus* probably originated in Padua in the circle of Giambattista Leone during the 1520s.

A.F.R.

PROVENANCE
Thomas, 8th Earl of Pembroke (1645–1732), Wilton House; by inheritance to successive Earls of Pembroke, Wilton House; 2 June 1964 bought by Wildenstein, Christie's, London sale (lot 98); 1964 acquired by the Victoria & Albert Museum, with the assistance of the National Art-Collectors Fund

REFERENCES
Frizzoni 1884, p. 74; Pope-Hennessy 1964¹, II, p. 465; Ruhmer 1974, pp. 63f

S14
The Judgement of Solomon

Marble; 60.2 × 59.5 × 15.5 cm
Inscribed on the background panels: QVIS DICET REG/ NON SAPIEN/ IVDI/CASSE/ CONT EMP ET A/MOR E DIIVDIC/ EST VER/ITAS; on the base: POSTHVMVS
Département des Sculptures, Musée du Louvre, Paris (no. 647)

The relief illustrates I *Kings* III, 16–28. The head of Solomon was stolen in 1874; both he and the false mother have lost their right arms. Inlaid panels, which once adorned Solomon's podium and the base on which the infant rests, have also been lost.

Marcantonio Michiel saw a terracotta model for a relief of *The Judgement of Solomon* in the workshop of the Paduan founder, Guido Lizzaro. Michiel noted that the marble version, commissioned by Giambattista Leone, was given by Leone to 'an English bishop'. Planiscig connected this *Judgement of Solomon* with Mosca's lost marble relief and Saxl noted that 'Posthumus', which is inscribed on the base, was one of Giambattista Leone's names.

A comparison of this work with Mosca's relief of *The Miracle of the Unbroken Glass* in the shrine of St. Anthony at the Basilica del Santo, Padua, confirms that they are by the same hand. Both reliefs share similar figure types, based upon the work of Antonio Lombardo, and the same schematic drapery patterns which bear no relationship to the forms beneath; both reflect the work of a sculptor of some talent but with a derivative manner and facile technique. The difference in quality between *The Judgement of Solomon* and the relief of *Mars* (Cat. s8), here attributed to Antonio Lombardo, illustrates Mosca's limitations as a sculptor: the executioner here appears to be based on Lombardo's *Mars*, or a common prototype, but his expression is less focussed, his curls lack the crispness of those of Mars, and the anatomy, particularly his right shoulder, is much less assured. The most accomplished figure, the true mother, is a softer version of a type found in the reliefs of Tullio Lombardo and may be compared with the *Venus Anadyomene* (Cat. s13).

The subject of the Judgement of Solomon was popular in Venetian art, but Mosca's presentation differs from the painting by Sebastiano (Cat. 97). Mosca presents the scene in the manner of a classical *adlocutio*, or exhortation by a Roman emperor to his troops, an idea that may have been

S14

suggested to him by Giambattista Leone. Leone was a professor of philosophy at Padua and belonged to a small group of intellectuals, including Pietro Bembo and Niccolò Leonico Tomeo, who were passionately interested in classical culture and encouraged contemporary artists to employ its styles and subjects. Leone commissioned the Paschal Candelabrum for the Santo from Riccio and may well have commissioned *The Judgement of Solomon* from Mosca after the sculptor was awarded the commission for *The Miracle of the Unbroken Glass* for the Santo in 1520. An approximate *terminus ante quem* for the relief can be taken from Leone's gift of the marble to the English bishop, who has been identified as the future Cardinal Reginald Pole. Pole was resident in Padua from 1521 to 1526 and studied philosophy with Leone. The relief was very likely executed during those years and given to Pole as a token of esteem by his former tutor.

B.B.; A.F.R.

PROVENANCE
Giambattista Leone, Padua; given by him to Cardinal Reginald Pole; *c.* 1800 acquired by Alexandre Lenoir in Paris, reputedly from a certain *marbrier* named Balleux, and incorporated in a fanciful reconstruction to his design of the monument of Michel de l'Hôpital in the Musée des Monuments Français by the sculptor Beauvallet

REFERENCES
Chastel and Klein 1969, pp. 15–19; Frizzoni 1884, pp. 74–75; Lenoir 1800–06, IV, pp. 111–12, no. 541; Planiscig 1921, pp. 262–63; Saxl 1938–39, pp. 354–55; Stechow 1960; Vitry 1922, p. 79

Maffeo Olivieri

Brescia 1484–Brescia 1543/44

Maffeo Olivieri seems to have passed his entire career in Brescia working as a bronze-founder and, in partnership with his brother Andrea, as a sculptor in wood. He is known by one identified work in each of these media: the signed and documented pair of bronze candelabra presented in 1527 to San Marco, Venice (Cat. S15), and a fully-documented, polychromed wooden altarpiece in the church of S. Maria at Condino (Trentino), commissioned in 1538 and completed by his brother in 1544–45 after Maffeo's death. The suggestion that Olivieri and his workshop – which appears to have been of some size – were responsible for the sumptuous monument of Marcantonio Martinengo (d. 1526), with its ambitious bronze reliefs (formerly in the church of the Corpo di Cristo, Brescia; now in the Museo Cristiano) is probably correct. Less acceptable are attempts to ascribe to Olivieri, on the basis of comparison with the figures on the candelabra, a variety of bronze statuettes in exaggerated poses; one case has now been proved to be wrong. However, the ascription to him of a group of medals, formerly assembled under the name of the 'Medallist of 1523', is more plausible. If this is correct, Olivieri was a medallist of considerable distinction. Apart from Gaspare de Olivieri Macri (active 1548–98), whose signed candlestick of 1551 is now in the Museo Poldi-Pezzoli, Milan, Olivieri is the only one of the many recorded members of the sixteenth-century bronze-founding industry which flourished in Brescia to have been identified so far.

A.F.R.

REFERENCES
Bode 1909²; Hill 1930, pp. 126–30; London 1975, no. 117; Morassi 1936; Planiscig 1921, pp. 306–08; Planiscig 1932¹; Rossi 1977

S15

Candelabrum

Bronze, inlaid with silver, on a marble base; 171.5 cm, 184 cm with base
Inscribed: MAPHEVS OLIVERIVS BRIXIANVS FACIEBAT, and
ALTOBELLVS AVEROLDVS BRIXIANVS EPIS. POLEN. VENET. /
APOSTOLICVS DEO OPT. MAX. DEDICAVIT.
Basilica di San Marco, Venice

The candelabrum is one of a pair which differ only in the allegorical figures seated in the niches on the central register. Identical inscriptions appear on each candelabrum on two inlaid bands of silver set just below the socket and directly above the ring of male statuettes in the centre of the upper section of the stem. They record that the candelabra were made by Maffeo Olivieri of Brescia, and that they were commissioned by Altobello Averoldo of Brescia, Bishop of Pola and Apostolic Legate in Venice. Marin Sanuto noted in his diary on 24 December 1527 that on that day Averoldo had presented to San Marco two large candelabra which were placed before the high altar. Averoldo had been appointed Legate to Venice in 1526, and the gift would thus appear to have been connected with his appointment. Among the medals which have been ascribed to Olivieri is one of Averoldo. The inscription on this medal also describes him as Apostolic Legate to Venice, so it would seem likely that the medal was commissioned at much the same time as the candelabra.

The allegorical figures in the niches on the middle register of one of the candelabra, all female, are identifiable as the

S15

Virtues Charity, Prudence, Temperance and Fortitude. Of the figures on the other candelabrum, three of which are female and one male, two of the female figures represent Faith and Hope, while the other two figures remain enigmatic.

A.F.R.

REFERENCES

Bode 1909; Hill 1930, no. 486; Planiscig 1921, pp. 306–08; Planiscig 1932[1]

Andrea Briosco, called

Riccio

Trent (?) 1470 – Padua 1532

Andrea Briosco, known as Riccio (Curly-head) was born in 1470, one of the six sons of the goldsmith Ambrogio di Cristoforo Briosco; his family was Milanese by origin, but had more recently settled at Trent. Riccio may have been born at Trent, although his father worked in Padua before his birth and settled there soon afterwards. Riccio was trained as a goldsmith in his father's workshop, but he abandoned the profession to learn the art of sculpture, in bronze and terracotta, from the Paduan sculptor Bartolommeo Bellano, a former assistant of Donatello.

His first documented activity was the completion in 1498 of Bellano's monument to Pietro Roccabonella in S. Francesco, Padua, after Bellano's death in 1496/97. In July 1506 he received the commission for two bronze reliefs of the *Story of Judith* and the *Transport of the Ark* which were to complete Bellano's cycle of reliefs of Old Testament subjects on the choir screen of the Basilica del Santo. These were finished and installed by March 1507, and in the same month he received the contract for the great bronze Paschal Candelabrum for the Santo, his most important work, finally installed only in 1516 because of interruptions caused by the war. Shortly afterwards he executed another major work, the monument to Girolamo and Marcantonio della Torre for S. Fermo Maggiore, Verona (Cat. S17, S18), and in 1520 one of his most important works in terracotta, a life-size statue of the seated Virgin and Child, was installed on the altar of the Scuola del Santo. His last recorded work was a life-size group in polychromed terracotta of the *Lamentation over the Dead Christ*, modelled for the church of S. Canziano in 1530, from which only the figure of the dead Christ survives in the church, while the upper halves of the statues of the two Marys are in the Museo Civico, Padua. Riccio was on intimate terms with the leading scholars of his day at the University of Padua, and this is reflected in the learned character of his work. It must have been largely for them that he made his bronze statuettes, a genre in which he excelled, and which he used as a vehicle for the expression of profound human insights.

A.F.R.

REFERENCES

Gonzati 1852, I, pp. 139–47; Planiscig 1927; Rigoni 1970, pp. 217–20, 230–31; Radcliffe 1983; Sartori 1976, pp. 198–230

S16

The Victory of Constantine

Bronze, parcel-gilt; 38.5 × 50.5 cm
Galleria Giorgio Franchetti alla Ca d'Oro, Venice

This relief, which depicts the victory of Constantine the Great over Maxentius at the Battle of the Milvian Bridge in 312, is one of a series of four reliefs with subjects from the *Legend of the Cross*. The other three represent *The*

S16

Finding of the Crosses, *The Proof of the True Cross*, and *Constantine's Vision of the Cross*. The reliefs come from the church of S. Maria dei Servi in Venice (suppressed in 1812), where they were built into the altar of the Holy Cross, an altar with a tabernacle which housed a relic of the True Cross in a cruciform reliquary of jasper, enclosed in a silver casket. The tabernacle was closed by a pair of bronze doors modelled in relief with a scene representing the *Glorification of the Cross*, with *The Deposition* and *The Entombment* below. The bronze doors are now in the Ca d'Oro, along with the four narrative reliefs.

The relic was presented to the church in 1492 by the Venetian diplomat Girolamo Donato (1454–1511). However, there is no contemporary record for the construction of the altar, first mentioned only in 1581 by Francesco Sansovino, who gave no information as to its origin. As a result, the dating of the four reliefs and the tabernacle door has been the subject of considerable debate. It was assumed by Planiscig and other writers that the altar and its bronze reliefs were commissioned by Donato himself, although there is no documentary evidence for this. Since Donato died destitute, the commission could hardly date from the end of his life, or have been provided for in his will, as has been suggested. Planiscig, noting that Donato was active in Venice principally between 1501 and 1509, dated the bronze reliefs within these years, thus making them roughly contemporary with the two bronze reliefs by Riccio for the choir screen of the Basilica del Santo, which are documented to 1506–07. Draper has recently argued that the reliefs are stylistically more evolved than those in the Santo, and has dated them to *c.* 1507–10. However, Pope-Hennessy had already come to the opposite conclusion, seeing the reliefs as less evolved than those in the Santo, and therefore to be dated to not long after the gift of the relic, probably to the years 1495–1500, a dating supported by Cessi and, more recently, by Radcliffe. The tabernacle doors, with their scarcely assimilated references to Mantegna and Bellano and architectural features inspired by Pietro Lombardo, must themselves be a very early work by Riccio, probably made only shortly before the four narrative reliefs, since there are very close correspondences in handling, particularly in the treatment of the architectural elements.

A.F.R.

PROVENANCE

Church of S. Maria dei Servi, Venice; 1812 transferred to the Accademia di Belle Arti; later transferred to the Museo Archeologico in the Palazzo Ducale

REFERENCES

Cessi 1965², pp. 56–60; Draper 1978, pp. 170–71, 180, note 14; Planiscig 1927, pp. 211–20; Pope-Hennessy 1963¹, p. 18; Radcliffe 1972, p. 43; Radcliffe 1983, p. 44; Sansovino 1581, p. 57b

S17 & S18

The Illness of the Professor
The Soul of the Professor in the Fortunate Woods

Bronze; each 37 × 49 cm
Département des Objets d'Art, Musée du Louvre, Paris

These two reliefs belong to a series of eight removed in 1796 from the tomb of Girolamo and Marcantonio della Torre in the church of S. Fermo Maggiore, Verona, all of which are now in the Louvre. The tomb, largely intact except, apparently, for six bronze figures of putti missing from the top of the sarcophagus, still stands today in the Cappella Turriana in S. Fermo Maggiore; the reliefs have been replaced by modern copies.

The tomb commemorates Girolamo della Torre (d. 1506), a distinguished physician who taught medicine at the University of Padua, and one of his sons, Marcantonio, also a distinguished professor of medicine, an anatomist, collaborator of Leonardo da Vinci and classical scholar, who died in 1511. Riccio's authorship of the tomb is attested in a document discovered by Morelli in the archive of S. Agostino, Padua; it contains a draft epitaph for Riccio's own tomb by Fra Desiderio dal Legname, which cites the tomb along with Riccio's other major masterpiece, the Paschal Candelabrum. This was rejected in favour of the more elegant epitaph by Girolamo del Negro, which mentions only the Candelabrum.

No other documents relating to the tomb have been discovered, and its date is therefore problematic. It was dated by Planiscig to the years 1516–21; that is, between the completion of the Paschal Candelabrum and the commencement of Riccio's next documented work in bronze, the bust of Antonio Trombetta. Saxl assumed that the scenes depicted in the narrative reliefs relate exclusively to the life of Girolamo della Torre, rather than to that of his son Marcantonio as well, and for that reason Pope-Hennessy has proposed that the tomb must have been commissioned before the death of Marcantonio in 1511. However, the scenes depicted are in no way specific to the father or the son, and could apply equally well in general terms to either of them. They show a medical professor teaching, his illness and his death and the subsequent progress of his soul. The protagonist, a conventional bearded classical type, is in no way characterised, and resembles neither Girolamo nor Marcantonio as they appear in the casts from their death-masks on the top of the tomb, or in their medals.

It seems unlikely that so ambitious a project could have

S17

S18

been begun during the War of the League of Cambrai, and the years 1516–21, proposed by Planiscig, would appear to be the most appropriate period in Riccio's career for these reliefs. Such a dating would make absolute sense in terms of Riccio's stylistic development. It is to be presumed that the tomb was commissioned by the three surviving brothers of Marcantonio della Torre: Giulio, the jurist and distinguished amateur medallist, Giambattista, the philosopher and astronomer, and Raimondo, the essayist. It seems likely that they would have devised, or at least contributed to, its complex programme.

The reliefs from the tomb, in particular those of the death scene and of a pagan sacrifice, may be explained in part in terms of the writings of Girolamo Fracastoro, a close friend of the brothers della Torre (Saxl 1938–39). However, the clue to the meaning of four of the eight reliefs, which Saxl failed to grasp, is contained in a work to which he refers in another context, the dialogue *Alverotus* by Niccolò Leonico Tomeo, the Paduan philosopher. This describes a birthday party at the house of Francesco Alvarotti, the jurisconsult, at which Giambattista Leone, the patron and friend of Riccio, recites the account of the wanderings of the soul in the sixth book of Virgil's *Aeneid*; it is then discussed by the whole party. It is clear that Riccio followed the text in great detail, and that the reliefs which follow the death scene therefore depict the fortunes of the soul of the professor (whether Girolamo or Marcantonio, or indeed both) in pagan terms.

The eight reliefs in the series can now be seen to tell the following story:

1] A medical professor teaches in front of a statue of Minerva, while behind him stand figures of Hygea and Apollo.
2] The professor is taken ill. At the left stand the Fates, and Atropos prepares to cut the thread of his life (Cat. s17).
3] The professor dies, surrounded by his mourning friends, and his soul, in the form of a winged boy carrying a book and a palm frond, runs away in the foreground.
4] A pagan sacrifice to Aesculapius is performed in front of a classical temple in order to secure the passage of the soul of the deceased to heaven (Saxl).
5] A classical purification ceremony is conducted before the della Torre tomb. This is taken from Virgil's description of the funeral of Misenus in the sixth book of the *Aeneid*.
6] The soul of the professor, still in the form of a winged boy and identified from other souls by the book he carries, enters the underworld and is welcomed by Charon into his boat. Under the great tree are all the ghastly figures which, in Virgil's description, haunt the entrance to Hades; the Furies, hunger, fear, poverty, old age, sleep, and death together with the centaurs, harpies and chimaera.
7] This relief (Cat. s18) depicts three episodes: the wandering soul of the professor, still carrying his book, is welcomed into the company of carefree dancers in the Fortunate Woods (left foreground); he kneels and drinks the waters of the river Lethe, which will erase his memory and prepare him to return to earth a second time (right background); finally the professor, once more restored to his original earthly form and identified by the book at his feet, sits sleeping in company with

other restored souls waiting to return to earth, while Fame crowns him with a wreath (right foreground).
8] The final relief depicts the triumph of earthly fame over death: the figure of Fame (recognisable from the previous relief) strides over the globe, while Death shrinks away to the right; to the left Pegasus strikes the ground with his hoof and creates Hippocrene, the fountain of the Muses.

The wholly pagan character of the reliefs, and of the tomb itself, which is devoid of any Christian imagery, is in line with the views of Marcantonio and his brothers and friends, who, as thoroughgoing humanists, seem to have had little interest in conventional religion, in contrast with their father Girolamo, who, though a humanist, appears to have been a devout Christian. As Pope-Hennessy has observed, the tomb has no precedent. It amounts to a direct expression of the humanist thinking of the younger generation of the Paduan *scuola* of the first half of the sixteenth century, and as such is unique in the visual arts.

A.F.R.

PROVENANCE
S. Fermo Maggiore, Verona; 1796 removed to Paris and incorporated by Percier and Fontaine in the doors below the gallery in the Salle des Caryatides, in the Louvre

REFERENCES
Morelli 1800, p. 94; Planiscig 1927, pp. 371–400, 479, nos. 43–50; Pope-Hennessy 1971, p. 333; Saxl 1938–9, pp. 354, 355–9

s19
Curete Milking the Goat Amalthea (The Nourishment of Jupiter)

Bronze, parcel-gilt; 26 cm
Museo Nazionale del Bargello, Florence (no. 392)
[*repr. in colour on p. 143*]

This work is first recorded in 1588 in the inventory of the Grand Duke Francesco I, and formed part of a collection of bronzes in his gallery in the Casino di San Marco in Florence. There are substantial traces of gilding on the hair of the young man and on the remaining fleece of the partly shorn goat, corresponding with the inventory description '*velj e capelli tocchi d'oro*'; which proves that the bronze was never more than partially gilded. The bronze, which now stands on a figured marble block, was mounted until the present century on a moulded oval socle of partly-gilded chestnut wood set with hardstones. This typically Florentine late sixteenth-century socle is of a kind commonly used for statuettes in Francesco I's collection, and can still be seen on one or two old Medici bronzes in Florence which escaped resocling, such as the version of the *Ignudo della Paura* on deposit at the Uffizi (Florence 1980, no. 643).

The bronze was reproduced in the fresco of *April* by Falconetto in the Palazzo d'Arco at Mantua, datable to 1520, and it must therefore have been made before that date (Buddensieg). Pope-Hennessy and Ciardi Duprè related it to the reliefs of the della Torre tomb (see Cat. s17, s18) and consequently dated it to 1516–20. However, it is intimately related to the figure of a *victimarius* preparing a goat for sacrifice in the bottom right-hand corner of the relief of *The Transport of the Ark* (1506–07) on the choir screen of the Basilica del Santo, and in terms both of style and facture it would appear to belong to the same phase in Riccio's career (Planiscig). The figure is unique amongst Riccio's surviving bronze statuettes in being parcel-gilt; this finish occurs only in the two reliefs of the choir screen and the four reliefs of the *Legends of the Cross* from S. Maria dei Servi, which must be dated even earlier (see Cat. s16). The use of parcel-gilding may therefore perhaps be taken as supporting evidence for an early date for this statuette.

Planiscig, who was under the false impression that the two statuettes shared a common provenance from the Carrand Collection, conjectured that the figure had at one time formed a group with the figure of '*Abundance*' (Cat. s25), which is a Carrand piece. He interpreted this figure as catching milk in the shell which she holds in her outstretched right hand. However, the handling and facture of the two bronzes differ, and there is no warrant for any iconographical connection between them (Pope-Hennessy). Furthermore, it is not possible to integrate them physically in any satisfactory manner, and the '*Abundance*' appears to belong to a much later phase in Riccio's development.

The subject was identified by Buddensieg as a Curete milking the goat Amalthea to nourish the infant Jupiter. In Falconetto's fresco in Mantua a small child kneels on all fours on the ground and drinks from the udder. However, in a drawing (Musée du Louvre, no. 10730) that is clearly after this bronze, there is no such figure of a child and the Curete directs the milk into a shallow bowl lying on the ground. It would thus seem unlikely that the bronze ever had an adjunct figure: if it did, it was lost by 1588, since there is no mention of it in the S. Marco inventory.

The drawing in the Louvre has been ascribed to Gianfrancesco Penni, and Buddensieg has conjectured that it may have been made by Penni in Mantua during his stay there in early 1528. Jestaz notes that the bronze is reproduced again in the stucchi of the Galleria dei Mesi in the Palazzo Ducale, Mantua, completed in 1573. This would seem to argue that either this bronze or another version of it was available and well-known in Mantua in the mid-sixteenth century. The only other known versions are obvious forgeries of recent date, and this work itself on superficial examination appears to be a direct cast, and therefore probably unique, like many of Riccio's finest bronzes. Circumstantial support for a Mantuan provenance can, perhaps, be found in the fact that in the inventory of the Gallery of the Casino di San Marco the bronze appears with the fine early cast of Antico's *Mercury*, now also in the Bargello, which could only have come from Mantua.

A.F.R.

PROVENANCE
Francesco I de'Medici, Grand Duke of Tuscany, Galleria del Casino di San Marco, Florence; 1637 Guardaroba Granducale; Gallerie degli Uffizi

EXHIBITIONS
London 1961, no. 56; Amsterdam 1961–62, no. 53; Florence 1962, no. 52; Florence 1980, no. 647 (Conti)

REFERENCES
Buddensieg 1963; Ciardi Duprè 1966; Jestaz 1983, p. 51; Planiscig 1927, pp. 193–96, 259–61, 480, no. 60; Pope-Hennessy 1971, p. 333

S20

S20

Walking Boy (Tobias?)

Bronze, black-brown varnish and dark green oxidation over natural brown patina; 12.8 cm
Kunsthistorisches Museum, Sammlung für Plastik und Kunstgewerbe, Vienna (inv. no. Pl. 5514)

The boy wears a tunic gathered up over tight trousers; leaves and fruit decorate his belt, and on his back hangs a bowl, possibly a container for a whetstone. In his right hand is an unidentifiable object, which is only partially preserved. The left hand, which has been restored, is stretched out and slightly raised, as is the head. The position of the hand and the direction in which the figure is looking suggest that the statuette was probably originally conceived not as an independent work of art, but as part of a group in which the boy was holding out his hand to another person (assuming that the hand is correctly restored). This led Bode to identify him as the young Tobias, though this is not supported by the boy's trappings, which seem to point to an ancient pagan cult, though they provide insufficient evidence to justify Planiscig's identification of the youth as the young Mercury. Old inventories describe the figure as a servant at a sacrifice, or as a genius of the harvest or the wine-gathering. Thus Ciardi Duprè may be right in seeing the boy as a participant in a mystery cult. The chronology of Riccio's work, and hence a dating of the statuette, has not been satisfactorily established.

M.L.-J.

PROVENANCE
1821 first definitely recorded in the inventory of Imperial coin and antique cabinet (p. 209, no. 50); 1880 transferred to the Kunsthistorisches Museum

REFERENCES
Bode 1906, I, pl. XXXVI; Bode 1922, pl. 45, p. 44 (wrongly said to be in Berlin); Ciardi Duprè 1966, II, no. 299; Planiscig 1924, p. 21, no. 28; Planiscig 1927, p. 199; Planiscig 1930, p. 18

S21

Satyr Drinking

Bronze, black-brown varnish over brown patina; 21.7 cm
Kunsthistorisches Museum, Sammlung für Plastik und
Kunstgewerbe, Vienna (inv. no. Pl. 5539)

The satyr is seated, his legs slightly spread. With his right
hand he raises a cup to his mouth, while his left hand rests
on his left knee. The body is powerfully modelled, the
hammered surface creating a lively effect, and the details of
the face and the hair are executed with extreme care; yet
the figure is characterised not by dynamic tension, but, like
many of Riccio's best statuettes, by a poetic expression of
relaxed contentment. It can no longer be determined
whether the figure – probably a late work – was conceived
as an independent statuette or perhaps as the crowning
glory of some more important piece.

Two replicas, each with slight variations, are in the
Museo Civico, Padua, and the Louvre, Paris.

M.L.-J.

PROVENANCE
By 1863 in the Imperial coin and antique cabinet; 1880 transferred to the
Kunsthistorisches Museum

REFERENCES
Bode 1906, I, Pl. LXIII (wrongly stated to be in the Wallace Collection);
Bode 1922, p. 47; Ciardi Duprè 1976, no. 244; Jestaz 1975, pp. 159f; Jestaz
1983, pp. 33ff; Planiscig 1921, p. 401; Planiscig 1924, no. 157 (as Desiderio
da Firenze); Planiscig 1927, pp. 343f (as Riccio)

S22

S22

Shouting Horseman

Bronze; 33.5 cm
Victoria & Albert Museum, London (A.88-1910)

This bronze is severely damaged, and was partially repaired
whilst in the collection of Frédéric Spitzer in Paris in the late
nineteenth century. The three legs on which the horse
stands are largely restorations, and the tail, which is itself
original, has been broken off and refixed at an angle which
is probably incorrect. The crest of the rider's helmet is
missing, as is the blade of the sword, the hilt of which he
still holds in his right hand. The rider's left hand is drilled
to hold a fixture that is now lost, clearly a shaft, probably
of a spear. The entire surface was heavily repatinated after
the repairs were carried out.

This is universally accepted as an autograph work by
Riccio. The horse is unique, but versions of the rider occur
on a variety of different horses of widely varying scales and
types (Staatliche Museen, Berlin; Liechtenstein Coll.,
Vaduz; Beit Coll., Russborough; Musée Jacquemart-André,
Paris; Wernher Coll., Luton Hoo; formerly Pierpont
Morgan Coll., London and New York). In all these cases
the rider is a modern copy (in some cases elaborated) of the

S21

Francesco Segala

Active Padua 1559–Padua 1592

Segala, unusual among sixteenth-century sculptors in coming from a middle-class family, was the son of an advocate and the son-in-law of a professor of Latin. The earliest reference to him records his marriage in 1559, by which date he would have finished his apprenticeship as a sculptor. The name of his master is not known, but given his style and his membership of Alvise Cornaro's circle in Padua, the most likely candidates are Agostino Zoppo or Tiziano Minio. Segala appears to have inherited the role of sculptor to Cornaro after the death of Minio in 1552, and Cornaro introduced Segala to other Venetian patrons. His earliest documented work is the bronze statuette of *St. Catherine* made for a holy-water stoup in the Basilica del Santo, Padua in 1564. Segala promised it to the Santo in exchange for the torso of a marble figure by Zoppo and some wax figures by Minio, then in the church's possession. Shortly afterwards Segala obtained a more significant commission for eleven stucco figures for the Oratory of San Prosdocimo in S. Giustina (1564–65); the ten surviving saints reflect a mixture of the styles of Zoppo, Minio and, to a lesser degree, Danese Cattaneo.

Segala's contact with Cattaneo came through the recommendation of Cornaro, and the elder sculptor stood surety for Segala's contract to make a bronze figure of *St. John the Baptist* for the baptismal font of San Marco in Venice in 1565. Eight years later Segala competed unsuccessfully against Girolamo Campagna for the commission for the last relief for the shrine in St. Anthony at Padua. His letter to the authorities on that occasion refers to unspecified works for the Patriarch of Aquileia, Giovanni Grimani, and to his portrait busts. Though none of these are named, several busts in Paduan churches can be ascribed to Segala. The most important example is on the tomb of the scholar Tiberio Deciano in the church of S. Maria del Carmine, a work already underway in 1579. Other portraits include those of Girolamo Michiel in the Santo (c. 1560) and Sperone Speroni in the cathedral, which was completed by Girolamo Pagliari after Segala's death in 1592. His skill as a portraitist in coloured wax is attested by the miniature of the Archduke Ferdinand of Tyrol (c. 1579).

Segala was a better sculptor in stucco than in stone. Among his finest achievements are the allegorical figures and busts in stucco made for the Sala dei Marchesi in the Palazzo Ducale, Mantua, around 1579. Their proportions are far more graceful than his contemporaneous marble statues such as the *Abundance* and *Justice* on the Deciano monument, or the *Charity* and *Abundance* on the Scala d'Oro of the Doge's Palace (c. 1581). Two 'bronzed' stucco saints made for the Santo in 1591 disappeared in the seventeenth century. His will of 1592 mentions several works in wax, small bronzes, three busts of Speroni and four 'quadri di Donato', which would have been plaster copies of Donatello's Santo reliefs; none of these have been traced.

B.B.

REFERENCES
Pietrogrande 1942–54, 1955, 1961; Planiscig 1921, pp. 550–55; Sambin 1966, pp. 328–29; Sartori 1976, pp. 215–19

S34

S34
Omphale

Bronze; 72 cm
Museo Civico, Padua (no. 89)

Omphale and a companion statuette of *Hercules* were originally ascribed to the Tuscan sculptor Bartolomeo Ammannati, but an attribution to Francesco Segala has been proposed more recently by Ciardi Duprè on the suggestion of Middeldorf. An identical pair of bronzes in Berlin was recognised as the work of Segala on the basis of comparisons with other works by the sculptor. *Omphale* is virtually identical with a *St. Catherine* which Segala made for the Basilica del Santo in 1564, and both figures depend stylistically upon models like Sansovino's bronze *Peace* from the Loggetta and even the Virgin in the Thyssen *Annunciation* (Cat. S29). Similarities with the *St. Catherine* would suggest a date in the mid-1560s for the *Omphale*. This was the period in which Segala entered Sansovino's circle and in which Sansovino exerted a strong influence upon the young sculptor.

B.B.

EXHIBITIONS
Florence 1962, no. 109; Padua 1976, no. 114

REFERENCES
Ciardi Duprè 1962, p. 64; Lauts 1936; Moschetti 1938, I, p. 224

Severo Calzetta, called
Severo da Ravenna

Active Ravenna 1496–Ravenna 1525/43

Severo's father, Domenico Calzetta, is described in a document as Ferrarese and Severo himself, when first recorded in Ravenna in 1496, was described as '*de Feraria*'. However, in documents relating to his activity in Padua from 1500, he is invariably described as '*da Ravenna*', and it is clear that he was well established as a sculptor before 1500 in Ravenna, where he owned property. In 1500 he contracted in Padua to carve the marble statue of *St. John the Baptist* for one of the niches above the arcade of the shrine of St. Anthony. This was finished by 1502, and from that date until early 1509 he lived and worked in Padua. He seems to have left Padua in June 1509, when the intellectual and artistic life of the city was interrupted by the War of the League of Cambrai, and in 1511 he was once again in Ravenna, where he is recorded as making statues for the visit of Pope Julius II. From 1511 until 1525, when we have the last notice of him, Severo was living and working in Ravenna. A document of 1543 concerning his son Niccolò, also a sculptor and master of a workshop in Ravenna, refers to Severo as dead. Pomponius Gauricus in 1504 described Severo as an 'outstanding sculptor in bronze and in marble, chaser, wood-carver, modeller and painter'. The *St. John the Baptist* in Padua is the only marble by him which has so far been identified, but two signed bronze statuettes have come to light which have made it possible to assign to his workship an extensive group of bronze statuettes and vessels. These suggest that Severo's sculpture foundry was the most prolific in Italy in the first half of the sixteenth century. Severo's style is related to that of Pietro Lombardo, and it is possible that he had some experience in the Lombardo workshop.

A.F.R.

REFERENCES
Avery and Radcliffe 1983; Bernicoli 1914, pp. 555–56; Chastel and Klein 1969, p. 263; Middeldorf 1977, p. 290; Planiscig 1935; Ricci 1905, p. 18; Sartori 1976, pp. 36–37

S35
St. John the Baptist

Bronze; 26 cm
The Visitors of the Ashmolean Museum, Oxford
(Fortnum Bequest 1899)

This statuette was tentatively ascribed to Antonio Lombardo by Bode, who associated it with a small bronze figure of *St. Jerome* (versions in the Victoria & Albert Museum, London, and the Museo Cristiano, Brescia) and with the bronze reliefs from the Barbarigo Altarpiece (Ca d'Oro). But Planiscig ascribed it to Filippo da Gonzate on the strength of a supposed resemblance to Filippo's bronze statues of the Evangelists in Parma Cathedral (1508).

While Bode's view has some merit, Planiscig's is demonstrably wrong. Pope-Hennessy recognised the close

S35

connection of the statuette with Severo Calzetta's signed and documented marble statue of *St. John the Baptist* in one of the niches above the arcade on the façade of the shrine of St. Anthony in Padua, and attributed it to Severo. That the statuette is indeed by Severo, rather than a reduction by another hand from the marble, has been conclusively proved by recent radiography at the Victoria & Albert Museum, which has shown it to be wholly consistent in facture with the technically idiosyncratic bronzes that are certainly products of Severo's foundry. The marble *Baptist* was commissioned on 19 June 1500 and completed by 1502. Avery and Radcliffe, who group the bronze statuette with a very similar statuette of *St. Sebastian* in the Louvre and with a bronze of the *Crucified Christ* in the Cleveland Museum of Art, have proposed that all three are early Paduan works by Severo, probably contemporary with the marble *Baptist*. They further comment that it is of the same notably high quality as the two known signed bronzes by Severo, and is therefore probably autograph, unlike the many replications of varying degrees of debasement demonstrably from his workshop. Although the statuette is not by the same hand as the Barbarigo reliefs and the statuettes of St. Jerome, Bode's observations are valid to the extent that the figure is deeply imbued with the influence of the Lombardo.

A.F.R.

PROVENANCE
Charles Drury E. Fortnum, Stanmore; 1899 bequeathed to the Ashmolean Museum

EXHIBITIONS
London 1961, no. 88; Amsterdam 1961–62, no. 81; Florence 1962, no. 80

REFERENCES
Avery and Radcliffe 1983; Baldoria 1891; Bode 1907–12, I, p. 39, pl. LXXVII; Frizzoni 1884, p. 17; Planiscig 1929; Planiscig 1930, p. 24, pl. CXII, fig. 195; Pope-Hennessy 1963², p. 22; Sartori 1976, p. 36

Alessandro Vittoria

Trent 1525–Venice 1608

Alessandro was the son of a tailor, Vigilio Vittoria della Volpe. It may be assumed that in his home town of Trent he was apprenticed to the sculptors Vincenzo and Gian Girolamo Grandi from Padua. He arrived in Venice on St. James's Day (25 July) 1543, and entered the studio of Jacopo Sansovino, then the leading sculptor and architect. Following a quarrel with his master, Alessandro retired from Venice and spent the years 1551–53 in Vicenza, where he first encountered the work of north Italian mannerists, such as Parmigianino and Giulio Romano, which was to prove decisive for his future career. Through the offices of Pietro Aretino, he was reconciled with Sansovino and returned to Venice where, after the death of Titian in 1576 and Sansovino in 1570, he became the dominant figure in the artistic life of the city, both as sculptor and decorator, playing a role analagous to that of his contemporary, Giambologna in Florence. He practised as a sculptor, architect and painter and his influence endured until the eighteenth century. Little is known of his studio and pupils.

In addition to the great stucco decorations – the Scala d'Oro of the Doge's Palace and the Libreria Marciana – his major works include the altars of S. Francesco della Vigna, S. Maria Gloriosa dei Frari, S. Giuliano and S. Salvatore. Vittoria occupied a unique position as a portraitist, equal to that of the greatest Venetian painters, and as a sculptor he had no rival.

The finest examples of Vittoria's bronzes are the *Diana* in Berlin, the *Jupiter* (Cat. s36), the allegorical figure of *Winter* in Vienna and the so-called '*Fugger Altarpiece*' (Cat. s42).

M.L-J.

REFERENCES
Cessi 1960–62; Cessi 1965[1]; Giovanelli-Gar 1858; Leithe-Jasper 1963; Planiscig 1921, pp. 435ff; Serra 1921; Temanza 1778, pp. 475ff; Vasari (ed. Milanesi) 1881, VII, pp. 518ff

S36

Jupiter

Bronze traces of black varnish, brown patina; 71.1 cm
Signed:ˆAˆVˆEˆ
Musée National de la Renaissance, Ecouen (inv. no. 23)

The naked god is set diagonally on a small rectangular base. The balance of mass is striking: the upper part of the body leans slightly backwards, turning over the right leg which is drawn forwards and bears no weight. The head is slightly raised and turned to the left. Jupiter holds a thunderbolt in his left hand, which is raised against his chest, while the right hand is held behind him, resting on the right buttock. Though the body of the god is heavy and muscular, the composition lends it the airy grace of a dancer. This is matched by the extraordinarily soft modelling of the surface, which is fresh and spontaneous, especially in such details as the face, hair and nails.

As the statuette is not mentioned in the early sources, it can only be dated by means of stylistic comparison. This type occurs frequently in Vittoria's work, and the freshness of the modelling would suggest a date in the early 1560s when he was occupied on the great stucco decorations of the staircases of the Doge's Palace and the Libreria Marciana. It contrasts, however, with the series of statuettes of the gods, probably completed only slightly earlier, which can be connected with the statue of *Mercury* on the façade of the Doge's Palace of 1558; these are all more generously proportioned and smoother in modelling.

It is not until two decades later, in the 1580s, that one finds comparable stylistic features in Vittoria's work. By then the figures are somewhat stockier, the modelling softer and the pathos more marked. The question of dating cannot be decided until the completion of a technical analysis which is now underway. The statuette is unpublished; the first detailed publication is being prepared by the author of this entry.

M.L-J.

PROVENANCE
1980 acquired by the Musées nationaux for the Musée National de la Renaissance, Ecouen, at an auction in Nantes

S36

S37
St. Sebastian (Marsyas?)

Bronze; black varnish, dark brown patina; 54 cm
Signed on the base: ALEXANDER' VICTOR' T(RENTINUS)' F
The Metropolitan Museum of Art (inv. no. 40.24)
[*repr. in colour on p. 138*]

The naked youth leans against a tree-stump; his body is turned vigorously to the right and his right hand appears to be bound to the tree behind his back, while his left hand is held behind his head, which is turned to the right. The figure is mounted on a round base.

Vittoria drew inspiration for this figure from both Michelangelo's *Slaves* for the tomb of Julius II and, in particular, Carpaccio's picture of *The Martyrdom of the Ten Thousand* of 1515, which was copied by the young Tintoretto. Vittoria first used the pose for his *St. Sebastian* for the Montefeltro altar in S. Francesco della Vigna of 1563–64. The New York bronze and its variant in Los Angeles are to be seen as further developments of that figure; the turning of the body is more pronounced and derives only indirectly from the original prototypes.

On 14 December 1566 Vittoria recorded payments for the casting by Maestro Andrea (da Brescia) of a figure of St. Sebastian. He mentioned it again on 7 November 1570 in his third will, making the interesting remark that the statuette, if suitably adapted, could be used for both a St. Sebastian and for a figure of Marsyas. On 16 May 1575 Vittoria paid Orazio, the son-in-law of Maestro Andrea, for casting a second figure of St. Sebastian. Both figures are again mentioned in Vittoria's fifth will dated 6 March 1584, and in this the first variant (now referred to as Marsyas) is described as a signed piece. The Los Angeles bronze is unsigned. It is uncertain whether the St. Sebastian or the Marsyas figure came into the possession of Mario Bevilacqua, as stipulated in the will; it is at all events not mentioned again by Vittoria. The second bronze is still mentioned in the wills of 1595 and 1608, where it is even stated that it is to be offered for sale to an interested prince or gentleman. According to Temanza, Bartolomeo della Nave owned a *St. Sebastian* by Vittoria (see Cat. 70). The extraordinary artistic success of this composition by Vittoria is attested to by the numerous representations of the figure in paintings by Italian and Netherlandish artists. The model was known by the Augsburg silversmiths of the seventeenth century, as is proved by a statuette in the church of Mergentheim in Germany.

M.L-J.

PROVENANCE
Mr and Mrs Edwin S. Bayer; Glendenin J. Ryan; 1940 acquired by the
Metropolitan Museum of Art, Lee Fund

REFERENCES
Cessi 1960, p. 47; Gerola 1925, pp. 346, 353–54; Goldsmith-Philipps 1940,
pp. 126ff; Leithe-Jasper 1963, p. 118; Predilli 1908, pp. 132, 135, 225;
Temanza 1778, p. 495; Valentiner 1942, pp. 149ff; Valentiner 1950,
pp. 224 ff.; Valentiner 1951, p. 172, no. 66; Weihrauch 1965, p. 279

S38
Benedetto Manzini

Marble; 72 cm
Signed on right-hand edge: ALESSANDRO 'VITORIA' 'F'
Galleria Giorgio Franchetti alla Ca d'Oro, Venice

Benedetto Manzini wears a high-necked tunic with a folded cloak over the shoulder. The head is turned sharply to the right, the right shoulder being pulled somewhat forward, emphasising the movement which gives the portrait such immediacy and expressiveness.

The bust of Benedetto Manzini, who was the parish priest of S. Geminiano from 1545, was originally situated between two columns on the right-hand wall of the choir of the church, which was completed by Jacopo Sansovino during his incumbency. The church was demolished in 1807 to make way for the Napoleonic wing of the Procuratorie. Manzini's gaze is fixed on the altar so that he participates, as it were, in the eucharist. This is one of Vittoria's early portraits. It must have been made before 1568, since it is mentioned by Vasari. It was praised by contemporaries for its life-like quality and vivid expression. In this work, if not before, Vittoria showed himself to be a portraitist comparable to Titian, Tintoretto and Veronese.

M.L-J.

S38

pp. 105–220.

E. MUIR, *Civic Ritual in Renaissance Venice*, Princeton, 1981.

MUNICH 1930, *Sammlung Schloss Rohoncz: Plastik und Kunstgewerbe*, exhibition catalogue, Neue Pinakothek, Munich, 1930.

R. MUNMAN, 'Two lost Venetian Statues', *The Burlington Magazine*, CXII, 1970, pp. 386–87.

R. MUNMAN, 'The Lombardo Family and the Tomb of Giovanni Zanetti', *Art Bulletin*, LIX, 1977, pp. 28–38.

M. MURARO, *Carpaccio*, Florence, 1966.

M. MURARO and D. ROSAND *see* VENICE 1976²

E. MUSATTI, *Storia della Promissione Ducale*, Padua, 1888.

G. NAGLER, *Die Monogrammisten*, Munich, 1858–79

A. NAVAGERO, *Opera Omnia*, Venice, 1754.

A. NÉOUSTROÏEFF, 'I quadri italiani nella collezione del Duca G. N. von Leuchtenberg di Pietroburgo', *L'Arte*, VI, 1903, pp. 329–46.

J. NEUMANN, *Titian: The Flaying of Marsyas*, London, 1965.

E. NEWTON, *Tintoretto*, Bristol, 1952.

NEW YORK 1926, *Early Italian Paintings at the Duveen Galleries*, catalogue by W. R. Valentiner, New York, 1926.

NEW YORK 1963, *Venetian Paintings of the Sixteenth Century*, exhibition catalogue edited by R. L. Manning, Finch College Museum of Art, New York City, 1963.

NEW YORK 1965, *Drawings from New York Collections, The Italian Renaissance*, exhibition catalogue edited by J. Bean and F. Stampfle, New York, 1965.

NEW YORK and LONDON 1969–70, *Italian Drawings from the Ashmolean Museum, Oxford*, exhibition catalogue by D. Sutton and K. Garlick, Wildenstein, New York and London, 1969–70.

NEW YORK 1971, *The Richard H. Rush Collection*, exhibition catalogue introduced by R. L. Manning, Finch College Museum of Art, New York, 1971.

NEW YORK and PARIS 1974–75, *Italian Renaissance Drawings from the Musée du Louvre*, exhibition catalogue edited by R. Bacou and F. Viatte, Metropolitan Museum, New York; Musée du Louvre, Paris, 1974–75.

G. NICCO FASOLA, 'Lineamenti del Savoldo', *L'Arte*, XLIII, 1940, pp. 51ff.

NICE 1979, *L'art religieux à Venise, 1500–1600*, exhibition catalogue edited by P. Provoyeur, Musée National Bibliothèque Marc Chagall, Nice, 1979.

G. NICODEMI, *La Pinacoteca Tosio-Martinengo*, Bologna, 1927.

M. NICOLLE, *Le Musée de Rouen. Peintures*, Rouen, 1921.

B. NICOLSON, 'The Winter Exhibition at the Royal Academy – II', *The Burlington Magazine*, 1962, pp. 109–10.

A. NIERO, *La Chiesa dei Carmini*, Venice, 1965.

A. NIERO, *La Chiesa di S. Giacomo dall'Orio*, Venice, 1979.

NORFOLK 1967–68, *Italian Renaissance and Baroque paintings from the Collection of Walter P. Chrysler, Jr.*, exhibition catalogue edited by R. L. Manning, Norfolk Museum of Arts and Sciences, Norfolk, Virginia, 1967–68.

NOTTINGHAM and LONDON 1983, *Drawing in the Italian Renaissance Workshop*, exhibition catalogue by F. Ames-Lewis and J. Wright, University Art Gallery, Nottingham, and Victoria & Albert Museum, London, 1983.

V. NOVOTNY, *I Maestri del Colore. I Capolavori della Galleria Nazionale di Praga*, Prague, 1960.

V. OBERHAMMER and F. KLAUNER, *Die Gemäldegalerie des kunsthistorischen Museums in Wien. Malerei der romischen Länder*, Vienna, 1960.

V. OBERHAMMER, F. KLAUNER and G. HEINZ, *Kunsthistorisches Museum, Wien, Katalog der Gemäldegalerie, I Teil, Italiener, Spanier,*

Franzosen, Englander, Vienna, 1965.

K. OBERHUBER, *Graphische Sammlung Albertina – Renaissance in Italien*, Vienna, 1966.

K. OBERHUBER, *Rome and Venice – Prints of the High Renaissance*, Cambridge, Mass., 1974.

K. OBERHUBER, 'Titian Woodcuts and Drawings – Some Problems', *Tiziano e Venezia*, Vicenza, 1980, pp. 523ff.

L. OBERZINER, *Il Ritratto di Cristoforo Madruzzo di Tiziano*, Trent, 1900.

F. ONGANIA, ed., *La Processione del Doge nella Domenica delle Palme incisa in Venezia per Mattio Pagan 1556–69*, Venice, 1880.

P. A. ORLANDI, *Abecedario Pittorico*, Venice, 1753.

S. ORTOLANI, 'Di Giangirolamo Savoldo', *L'Arte*, XXVIII, 1925, pp. 163ff.

F. B. P. OSMASTON, *The Art and Genius of Tintoret*, 2 vols., London, 1915.

P. OSMOND, *Paolo Veronese, his career and work*, London, 1927.

H. OST, *Tizians Kasseler Kavalier*, Cologne, 1982.

L. OZZOLA, *Il Museo d'Arte Medievale e Moderna del Palazzo Ducale di Mantova*, Mantua, 1954.

O. PÄCHT, *Italian Illuminated Manuscripts from 1400 to 1550*, Oxford, 1948.

PADUA 1976, *Dopo Mantegna: Arte a Padova e nel territorio nei secoli XV e XVI*, Palazzo della Ragione, Padua, 1976.

F. PAGLIA, *Il Giardino della Pittura*, ms. of 1663–75, edited by C. Boselli, Brescia, 1967.

A. PALLADIO, *I Quattro Libri dell'Architettura*, Venice, 1570.

R. PALLUCCHINI, 'Sculture della R. Galleria Estense', *Emporium*, LXXXIV, 1936, pp. 301–08.

R. PALLUCCHINI, 'Vicende delle ante d'organo di Sebastiano del Piombo per San Bartolomeo a Rialto', *Le Arti*, 1941, pp. 448–56.

R. PALLUCCHINI, *La pittura veneziana del Quattrocento*, 2 vols., Novara, 1944 [1944¹].

R. PALLUCCHINI, *La pittura veneziana del Cinquecento*, 2 vols., Novara, 1944 [1944²].

R. PALLUCCHINI, *Sebastian Viniziano*, Milan, 1944 [1944³].

R. PALLUCCHINI, *I capolavori dei musei veneti*, Venice, 1946.

R. PALLUCCHINI, 'Veneti alle mostre di Brescia e di Genova', *Arte Veneta*, I, 1947, p. 148.

R. PALLUCCHINI, 'La Mostra di Feltre', *Arte Veneta*, II, 1948, p. 171.

R. PALLUCCHINI, *La giovanezza del Tintoretto*, Milan, 1950.

R. PALLUCCHINI, 'Veneti alla Royal Academy di Londra', *Arte Veneta*, V, 1951, p. 219.

R. PALLUCCHINI, *Tiziano*, Bologna, 1952–53.

R. PALLUCCHINI, *Giorgione*, Milan, 1955.

R. PALLUCCHINI, 'Jacopo Bassano e il Manierismo', *Studies in the History of Art dedicated to William E. Suida*, London, 1959.

R. PALLUCCHINI, *I Teleri del Carpaccio in San Giorgio degli Schiavoni*, Milan, 1961.

R. PALLUCCHINI, *I Vivarini*, Venice, 1962.

R. PALLUCCHINI, *L'Arte di Lorenzo Lotto*, University of Padua publication, 1965–66.

R. PALLUCCHINI, 'Due concerti bergamaschi del Cinquecento', *Arte Veneta*, XX, 1966, pp. 87–97.

R. PALLUCCHINI, *Tintoretto*, Florence, 1969 [1969¹].

R. PALLUCCHINI, *Tiziano*, 2 vols., Florence, 1969 [1969²].

R. PALLUCCHINI, 'Il Tintoretto di Newcastle-upon-Tyne', *Arte Veneta*, XXX, 1976, pp. 81–97.

R. PALLUCCHINI, *Jacopo Bassano e il Manierismo*, University of Padua publication, 1977–78.

PALLUCCHINI 1978 *see* VENICE 1978.

R. PALLUCCHINI, *La pittura veneziana del Seicento*, Milan, 1981.

R. PALLUCCHINI, 'Note carianesche', *Arte Veneta*, XXXVI, 1982 [1982¹].

P. PALLUCCHINI, *Jacopo Bassano*, 1982 [1982²].

R. PALLUCCHINI and G. MARIANI CANOVA,

L'Opera completa del Lotto, Milan, 1975.

R. PALLUCCHINI and F. ROSSI, *Giovanni Cariani*, Bergamo, 1983 (forthcoming publication).

R. PALLUCCHINI and P. ROSSI, *Tintoretto, Le Opere sacre e profane*, 2 vols., Milan, 1982.

A. PALOMINO DE CASTRO Y VELASCO, *El museo Pictórico*, 1724; reprinted Madrid, 1947.

G. PANAZZA, *I Musei e la Pinacoteca di Brescia*, Bergamo, 1959.

G. PANAZZA, 'La presenza a Bergamo di Alessandro Bonvicino detto il Moretto', *I Pittori Bergamaschi. Il Cinquecento*, III, Bergamo, 1979.

E. PANOFSKY, *Problems in Titian, mostly Iconographic*, New York, 1969.

P. PAOLETTI, *L'architettura e la scultura del Rinascimento in Venezia*, 3 vols., Venice, 1893.

P. PAOLETTI, *Raccolta di documenti inediti per servire alla storia della pittura veneziana nei secoli XV e XVI*, Padua, 1894.

A. PAOLUCCI, 'Rassegna dei Restauri', *Arte Veneta*, XXXIV, 1980, p. 285.

PARIS 1935, *Exposition de l'art italien de Cimabue à Tiepolo*, exhibition catalogue, Petit Palais, Paris, 1935.

PARIS 1960, *Exposition de 700 tableaux tirés des reserves du Louvre*, exhibition catalogue, Paris, 1960.

PARIS 1962¹, *Dessins du Louvre*, Musée du Louvre, Paris, 1962.

PARIS 1962², *Le dessin italien dans les collections hollandaises*, exhibition catalogue, Paris, Rotterdam and Haarlem, 1962.

PARIS 1964, *Dessins de l'Ecole de Parme*, exhibition catalogue edited by R. Bacou, Paris, 1964.

PARIS 1965, *Le seizième siècle européen. Dessins du Louvre*, exhibition catalogue edited by R. Bacou, Musée du Louvre, Paris, 1965.

PARIS 1965–66, *Le seizième siècle européen. Peintures et Dessins dans les collections publiques françaises*, catalogue edited by P. Rosenberg, M. Laclotte and A. Cacan, Paris, 1965–66.

PARIS 1967, *Le cabinet d'un grand amateur, P.-J. Mariette, 1694–1774. Dessins du XVe siècle au XVIIIe siècle*, exhibition catalogue, Paris, 1967.

PARIS 1976, *Hommage à Titien*, exhibition catalogue edited by B. Meijer, Institut Néerlandais, Paris, 1976.

PARIS 1977–78, *Collections du Louis XIV*, exhibition catalogue edited by R. Bacou, Orangerie, Paris, 1977–78.

PARIS 1978, *Nouvelles attributions*, handlist to exhibition, Musée du Louvre, Paris, 1978.

K. T. PARKER, 'Alvise Vivarini: Studies of Hands. Coll. Mr. Frits Lugt, Maartengdijk, Holland', *Old Master Drawings*, I, 1926, p. 6.

K. T. PARKER, *North Italian Drawings of the Quattrocento*, London, 1927.

K. T. PARKER, 'Bartolomeo Montagna', *Old Master Drawings*, IX, 1934, p. 8.

K. T. PARKER, *Catalogue of the Collection of Drawings in the Ashmolean Museum*, 2 vols., Oxford, 1956.

A. PERISSA, 'Scuola dei Sartori', in Gramigna, Perissa and Scarabello, *Scuole di Arti Mestieri e Devozione a Venezia*, Venice, 1981.

A. PERTUSI, 'Quedam regalia insignia', *Studi Veneziani*, VII, 1965.

A. PETRUCCI, 'Interpretazione di Giulio Campagnola', *L'Arte*, 1958, pp. 12ff.

A. PETRUCCI, *Panorama dell'Incisione Italiana – Il Cinquecento*, Rome, 1964.

PHILADELPHIA 1941, *John G. Johnson Collection. Catalogue of Paintings*, Philadelphia, 1941.

C. PHILLIPS, 'Some portraits by Cariani', *The Burlington Magazine*, XXIV, 1913, pp. 157–64.

G. PICCININI, *Guida di Reggio Emilia*, Reggio Emilia, 1921.

C. PIETRANGELI, 'Nuovo lavori nella più antica Pinacoteca di Roma', *Capitolium*, XXVI, 1951, pp. 59–71.

L. Pietrogrande, 'Francesco Segala', *Bollettino del Museo Civico di Padova*, xxx–xliii, 1942–54, pp. 111–35; xliv, 1955, pp. 99–119; l, 1961, pp. 29–58.

A. Pigler (ed.), *Museum der Bildender Künste Szépmüvészeti Muzeum Budapest, Katalog der Galerie Alter Meister*, i, Tübingen, 1968.

T. Pignatti, *Pittura veneziana del Cinquecento*, Bergamo, 1947.

T. Pignatti, 'Gli inizi di Andrea Riccio', *Arte Veneta*, vii, 1953, pp. 25–38.

Pignatti 1963 *see* Lauts 1962.

T. Pignatti, 'La pianta di Venezia di Jacopo de' Barbari', *Bollettino dei Musei Civici Veneziani*, ix, 1964, pp. 9–49.

T. Pignatti, *Giorgione*, Venice, 1969; second edition 1978; English edition 1971.

T. Pignatti, *Vittore Carpaccio*, Milan, 1972.

T. Pignatti, *Veronese: l'opera completa*, 2 vols., Venice, 1976.

T. Pignatti, *Tiziano. Disegni*, Florence, 1979.

Pignatti 1979–80 *see* Los Angeles 1979

A. Pinetti, *Il conte Giacomo Carrara e la sua galleria secondo il catalogo del 1796*, Bergamo, 1922.

A. Pinetti, *Inventario degli oggetti d'arte d'Italia. Provincia di Bergamo*, Rome, 1931.

P. Pino, *Dialogo della Pittura*, Venice, 1548; another edition edited by R. Pallucchini, Venice, 1946.

E. Piot, 'La sculpture à l'exposition rétrospective du Trocadéro', *Gazette des Beaux-Arts*, xviii, 1878, pp. 576–660.

M. Pittaluga, *Il Tintoretto*, Bologna, 1925.

P. Piva and G. Pavesi, 'Giulio Romano e la chiesa abbaziale di Polirone; documenti e proposte filologiche', *Studi su Giulio Romano*, Accademia Polironiana, San Benedetto Po, 1975, pp. 53–119.

Piva 1980 *see* Venice 1980¹.

L. Planiscig, *Die Estensische Kunstsammlung, I. Skulpturen und Plastiken des Mittelalters und der Renaissance*, Vienna, 1919.

L. Planiscig, *Venezianische Bildhauer der Renaissance*, Vienna, 1921.

L. Planiscig, *Die Bronzeplastiken, Kunsthistorisches Museum in Wien*, Vienna, 1924.

L. Planiscig, *Andrea Riccio*, Vienna, 1927.

L. Planiscig, 'Bronzeplastiken der da Gonzate', *Pantheon*, iii, 1929, pp. 43–47.

L. Planiscig, *Piccoli Bronzi italiani del Rinascimento*, Milan, 1930.

L. Planiscig, 'Desiderio da Firenze: Dokumente und Hypothesen', *Zeitschrift für Bildende Kunst*, lxiv, 1930–31, pp. 71–78.

L. Planiscig, 'Maffeo Olivieri', *Dedalo*, xii, 1932, pp. 34–55 [1932¹].

L. Planiscig, 'Alessandro Vittorias Verkundigungsrelief für Hans Fugger', *J.K.S.W.*, n.f. vi, 1932, pp. 155ff [1932²].

L. Planiscig, 'Severo da Ravenna (der "Meister des Drachens")', *J.K.S.W.*, n.f. ix, 1935, pp. 75–86.

L. Planiscig, 'Pietro, Tullio, und Antonio Lombardo', *J.K.S.W.*, n.f. xi, 1937, pp. 87–115.

J. Pope-Hennessy, 'A statuette by Antonio Minelli', *The Burlington Magazine*, xciv, 1952, pp. 24–28.

J. Pope-Hennessy, *Italian Renaissance Sculpture*, London, 1958; second edition, 1971.

J. Pope-Hennessy, *Italian High Renaissance and Baroque Sculpture*, 3 vols., London, 1963 [1963¹].

J. Pope-Hennessy, 'Italian bronze statuettes', *The Burlington Magazine*, cv, 1963, pp. 14–23, 48–71 [1963²].

J. Pope-Hennessy, *Catalogue of Italian Sculpture in the Victoria and Albert Museum*, 3 vols., London, 1964 [1964¹].

J. Pope-Hennessy, 'Sculpture for the Victoria and Albert Museum', *Apollo*, lxxx, 1964, pp. 458–65 [1964²].

J. Pope-Hennessy, *Italian High Renaissance and Baroque Sculpture*, London, 1970.

J. Pope-Hennessy, assisted by A. Radcliffe, *The Frick Collection: an illustrated catalogue*, iii, *Sculpture: Italian*, New York, 1970.

J. Pope-Hennessy, 'The Relations between Florentine and Venetian Sculpture in the Sixteenth Century', *Florence and Venice: Comparisons and Relations, II. Cinquecento*, edited by S. Bertelli and others, Florence, 1980, pp. 323–35.

A. E. Popham, *Catalogue of the Phillipps Fenwick Collection of Drawings*, London, 1935.

A. E. Popham, 'Lorenzo Lotto', *Old Master Drawings*, xii, 1938, p. 49.

A. E. Popham, *A Handbook to the Drawings and Water Colours in the Department of Prints and Drawings*, British Museum, London, 1939.

A. E. Popham, 'A drawing attributed to Lorenzo Lotto', *British Museum Quarterly*, xvi, 1951, pp. 72ff.

A. E. Popham, 'Two Drawings of Correggio', *British Museum Quarterly*, xix, 1954, p. 34.

A. E. Popham, *Italian Drawings in the Department of Prints and Drawings in the British Museum. Artists working in Parma in the Sixteenth Century*, 2 vols., London, 1967.

A. E. Popham and P. Pouncey, *Italian Drawings in the Department of Prints and Drawings in the British Museum. The Fourteenth and Fifteenth Centuries*, London, 1950.

A. E. Popham and J. Wilde, *The Italian Drawings of the XV and XVI centuries in the collection of His Majesty the King at Windsor Castle*, London, 1949.

O. Popovitch, *Catalogue des peintures du Musée des Beaux-Arts de Rouen*, Paris, 1967; another edition, Paris, 1978.

Portland 1956, *Paintings from the Collection of Walter P. Chrysler, Jr.*, exhibition catalogue edited by B. Suida Manning, Portland Art Museum, Oregon, 1956.

P. Pouncey, 'A study by Sebastiano del Piombo for the Martyrdom of St. Agatha', *The Burlington Magazine*, xciv, 1952, p. 116.

P. Pouncey, 'Girolamo da Treviso in the service of Henry VIII', *The Burlington Magazine*, xcv, 1953, pp. 208–11.

P. Pouncey, 'Aggiunte a Girolamo da Treviso', *Arte Antica e Moderna*, 1961, pp. 209–10 [1961¹].

P. Pouncey, 'A drawing by Pordenone', *British Museum Quarterly*, 1961, p. 27 [1961²].

P. Pouncey, Review of B. Berenson 'I Disegni dei Pittori Fiorentini', *Master Drawings*, ii, 1964, p. 291.

P. Pouncey, *Lotto Disegnatore*, Vicenza, 1965.

R. Predelli, ed., 'Le carte e le memorie di Alessandro Vittoria', *Studi Trentini*, 1908.

G. Previtali, 'Il bernoccolo del conoscitore (a proposito del presunto "Ritratto di Gian Girolamo Albani" attribuito al Moroni)', *Prospettiva*, 24, 1981, pp. 24–31.

P. Prodi, 'The Structure and Organisation of the Church in Venice: Suggestions for Research', *Venetian Studies*, edited by J. Hale, London, 1972, pp. 409–30.

A. Puerari, *Boccaccino*, Milan, 1957.

L. Puppi, *Bartolomeo Montagna*, Venice, 1962 [1962¹].

L. Puppi, 'Maestri italiani del colore nella Galleria Nazionale di Praga', *Emporium*, cxxxv, 1962, pp. 147–58 [1962²].

L. Puppi, 'Qualche novità montagnesca', *Emporium*, lxx, 1964, pp. 194–204.

L. Puppi, ed., *Paolo Farinati, Giornale*, Florence, 1968 [1968¹].

L. Puppi, 'Postilla montagnesca: una questione di Metodo', *Arte Veneta*, xxii, 1968, p. 219 [1968²].

L. Puppi, *Michele San Micheli architetto di Verona*, Padua, 1971.

L. Puppi, 'Per Tullio Lombardo', *Arte Lombarda*, xvii, i, 1972, pp. 100–03.

L. Puppi, 'Un'integrazione al catalogo e al regesto di Bartolomeo Montagna', *Antichità Viva*, xiv, 1975, pp. 23–29.

Puppi 1980 *see* Venice 1980.

L. Puppi and L. Olivato Puppi, *Mauro Codussi e l'architettura veneziana del Primo Rinascimento*, Milan, 1977.

A. Quintavalle, 'Jacopo Palma il Giovane nel modenese e nel reggiano', *Arte Veneta*, x, 1957, pp. 129–42.

A. Quintavalle, *La Galleria Estense di Modena*, Genoa, 1959.

A. Radcliffe, *European Bronze Statuettes*, London, 1966.

A. Radcliffe, 'Bronze oil lamps by Riccio', *Victoria and Albert Museum Yearbook*, iii, 1972, pp. 29–58.

A. Radcliffe, 'A portrait of Georg Vischer', *Apollo*, xcix, 1974, pp. 126–31.

A. Radcliffe, 'Ricciana', *The Burlington Magazine*, cxxiv, 1982, pp. 412–24.

A. Radcliffe, 'A forgotten masterpiece in terracotta by Riccio', *Apollo*, cxviii, 1983, pp. 40–48.

L. Ragghianti Collobi, *Il Libro de' Disegni del Vasari*, Florence, 1974.

O. Raggio, 'Tiziano Aspetti's Reliefs with Scenes of the Martyrdom of St. Daniel of Padua', *Metropolitan Museum Journal*, 1982, pp. 131–46.

C. G. Ratti, *Istruzione di quanto può vedersi di più bello in Genova in pittura, scultura ed architettura*, Genoa, 1780.

P. Ravaglia, 'Un quadro inedito di Sebastiano del Piombo', *Bollettino d'arte*, i, 1921–22, p. 474.

W. R. Rearick, 'A drawing by Bernardino Licinio', *Master Drawings*, v, 1967, pp. 382–83.

Rearick 1976 *see* Florence 1976.

W. R. Rearick, 'Early Drawings of Jacopo Bassano', *Arte Veneta*, xxxii, 1978, p. 161.

W. R. Rearick, 'Lorenzo Lotto, The Drawings, 1500–25', *Atti del Convegno Internazionale di Studi per il V Centenario della Nascita di Lorenzo Lotto*, Asolo, 1980.

W. R. Rearick in *Italian Paintings XIV-XVIII Centuries from the Collection of the Baltimore Museum of Art*, Baltimore, 1981, pp. 131–47.

Reggio Emilia 1955, *Catalogo della Mostra dei quadri . . . della Cassa di Risparmio di Reggio Emilia*, Reggio Emilia, 1955.

Q. Van Regteren Altena, *Les dessins italiens de la reine Christine de Suède*, Stockholm, 1966.

S. Reinach, *Répertoire de peintures du Moyen Age et de la Renaissance (1280–1580)*, Paris, 1918.

A. Ricci. *Memorie Storiche delle Arti e degli Artisti della Marca d'Ancona*, Macerata, 1834.

C. Ricci, *Raccolte artistiche di Ravenna*, Bergamo, 1905.

C. Ricci, *La Pinacoteca di Brera*, Bergamo, 1907.

E. P. Richardson, 'Two Bronzes by Jacopo Sansovino', *Art Quarterly*, xiii, 1950, pp. 3–9.

F. Richardson, *Andrea Schiavone*, Oxford, 1980.

G. M. Richter, *Giorgio da Castelfranco called Giorgione*, Chicago, 1937.

C. Ricketts, *Titian*, London, 1910.

C. Ridolfi, *Vita di Giacopo Robusti detto il Tintoretto . . .*, Venice, 1642.

C. Ridolfi, *Le Maraviglie dell'Arte*, Venice 1648; another edition edited by D. von Hadeln, 2 vols., Berlin, 1914, 1924.

P. Righetti, *Descrizione del Campidoglio*, 2 vols., Rome, 1836.

F. Rigon, *Tiziano – Iconografia Tizianesca al Museo di Bassano*, Bassano, 1976.

F. Rigon, 'Taccuino Bassanesco', *Arte Veneta* xxxii, 1978, pp. 174–81.

E. Rigoni, *L'arte rinascimentale in Padova: Studi e documenti*, Padua, 1970.

Rijksmuseum 1961, *Rijksmuseum Amsterdam, Catalogue of Paintings*, Amsterdam, 1961.

Rijksmuseum 1976, *All the Paintings in the Rijksmuseum. A completely illustrated*

Catalogue, by G. Schwarz and others, Amsterdam, 1976.

G. ROBERTSON, *Vincenzo Catena*, Edinburgh, 1954.

G. ROBERTSON, 'The Giorgione Exhibition in Venice', *The Burlington Magazine*, XCVII, 1955, p. 272.

G. ROBERTSON, 'New Giorgione Studies', *The Burlington Magazine*, CXIII, 1971, p. 475.

M. C. RODESCHINI, 'Note sulle due pale del Moretto a Bergamo' *Notizie da Palazzo Albani*, X, 1981, pp. 23–34.

M. R. RODGERS and O. GOETZ, 'A Masterpiece of Italian Renaissance Sculpture', *Bulletin of the Art Institute of Chicago*, XXXVII, i, 1943.

S. ROMANIN, *Storia documentata di Venezia*, 10 vols., Venice, 1853–61.

ROME 1945, *Mostra d'arte italiana a Palazzo Venezia*, catalogue edited by E. Gagliardi, Rome, 1945.

ROME 1976, *Immagini da Tiziano*, exhibition catalogue edited by M. Catelli Isola, Rome, 1976.

O. RONCHI, 'La casa di Pietro Bembo a Padova', *Atti e memorie della R. Accademia di Scienze, Lettere ed Arti in Padova*, XL, 1933–34, pp. 285–329.

A. RONCHINI, 'Delle relazioni di Tiziano coi Farnesi', *Atti e memorie delle RR. deputazioni di storia patria per le provincie modenesi e parmensi*, II, 1864, pp. 129–46.

D. ROSAND, 'Palma il Giovane as Draughtsman. The early career and related observations', *Master Drawings*, II, 1970, pp. 148–61.

D. ROSAND, *Painting in Cinquecento Venice: Titian, Veronese, Tintoretto*, New Haven and London, 1982.

D. ROSAND and M. MURARO, *Titian and the Venetian Woodcut*, exhibition catalogue Washington, 1976.

T. ROSCOE, *Life of Lorenzo de' Medici*, 2 vols., second edition, London, 1796.

M. ROSKILL, *Dolce's 'Aretino' and Venetian Art Theory of the Cinquecento*, New York, 1968.

F. ROSSI, 'Maffeo Olivieri e la bronzistica bresciana del '500', *Arte Lombarda*, n.s., XLVII–XLVIII, 1977, pp. 115–34.

F. ROSSI, *Accademia Carrara. Catalogo generale dei dipinti*, Bergamo, 1979.

F. ROSSI, 'Pittura a Bergamo intorno al 1500. Ricostituzione di un patrimonio scomparso', *Atti dell'Ateneo di Scienze, Lettere e Arti*, 1980.

F. ROSSI, 'Bergamo e Palma il Vecchio. Un rapporto dialettico', *Serina a Palma il Vecchio*, Bergamo, 1981.

P. ROSSI, *Tintoretto: I ritratti*, Venice, 1974.

P. ROSSI, *I disegni di Jacopo Tintoretto*, Florence, 1975.

P. ROSSI 1982 *see* PALLUCCHINI and ROSSI 1982

ROTTERDAM 1938, *Meesterwerken uit vier eeuwen, 1400–1800*, exhibition catalogue, Museum Boymans-van Beuningen, Rotterdam, 1938.

ROVILLIUS, *Prontuario*, Lyon, 1553.

J. ROWLANDS, 'Two unknown works by Palma Vecchio', *Pantheon*, XXIV, 1966, pp. 372–77.

O. RUCKELSHAUSEN, 'Typologie des oberitalienischen Porträts im Cinquecento', *Giessener Beiträge zur Kunstgeschichte*, III, 1975, pp. 63–137.

U. RUGGERI, review of G. Mariacher, 'Palma il Vecchio', *Arte Lombarda*, XIV, 1969, pp. 166–67.

H. RUHEMANN, 'The Cleaning and Restoration of the Glasgow Giorgione', *The Burlington Magazine*, XCVII, 1955, p. 278.

E. RUHMER, 'Antonio Lombardo: Versuch einer charakteristik', *Arte Veneta*, XXVIII, 1974, pp. 39–73.

G. A. RUSCONI, *Della architettura . . . secondo i precetti di Vitruvio . . . libri 10*, Venice, 1590.

M. SABELLICUS, *De Venetae Urbis Situ*, Venice, 1502.

E. SACCOMANNI, 'Domenico Campagnola: gli anni della maturità', *Arte Veneta*, XXXIV, 1980,

pp. 63ff., pp. 147ff.

E. SAFARIK, 'Giovanni Busi detto il Cariani', in *D.B.I*, XV, pp. 527–29.

R. SALVINI, *La Galleria Estense di Modena*, Rome, 1955.

R. SALVINI, *La Galleria degli Uffizi*, Florence, 1956.

R. SALVINI, 'Noterelle su Romanino e Dürer', in *Festschrift Ulrich Middeldorf*, Berlin, 1968, pp. 319–23.

P. SAMBIN, 'I testamenti di Alvise Cornaro', *Italia medioevale e umanistica*, IX, 1966, pp. 295–385.

P. SAMBIN, 'Nuovi documenti per la storia della pittura in Padova dal XIV al XVI secolo . . .', *Bollettino del Museo Civico di Padova*, LI, 1, 1972, pp. 99–126.

F. J. SÁNCHEZ CANTÓN, *Museo del Prado, Catalogo de los cuadros*, Madrid, 1949.

F. SANSOVINO, *Delle cose notabili che sono in Venetia*, Venice, 1565.

F. SANSOVINO, *Ritratto delle più nobili et famose città d'Italia*, Venice, 1575.

F. SANSOVINO, *Venetia città nobilissima et singolare*, Venice, 1581; another edition edited by G. Martinioni, Venice, 1663.

A. SANTAGIUSTINA PONIZ, 'Disegni tardi di Domenico Campagnola 1552–1564', *Arte Veneta*, XXXV, 1981, pp. 62ff.

M. SANUTO, 'Vita dei Dogi', *Rerum Italicarum Scriptores*, XXII, Milan, 1733.

M. SANUTO, *I Diarii*, 58 vols., edited by R. Fulin and others, Venice, 1879–1903.

M. SANUTO, *De Origine, situ et Magistratibus Urbis Venetae ovvero La Città di Venetia (1493–1530)*, edited by A. Caracciolo Aricò, Milan, 1980.

A. SARTORI, 'Il S. Giovanni Battista nel Deserto del Bassano, *Arte Veneta*, XII, 1958, pp. 200 ff.

A. SARTORI, *Documenti per la storia dell'arte a Padova*, Vicenza, 1976.

S. SAVINI-BRANCA, *Il Collezionismo Veneziano nel '600*, Padua, 1965.

F. SAXL, *Costumes and Festivals of Milanese Society under Spanish Rule*, British Academy Annual Italian Lecture, 1936; Oxford, 1938.

F. SAXL, 'Pagan Sacrifice in the Italian Renaissance', *Journal of the Warburg and Courtauld Institutes*, II, 1938–39, pp. 346–67.

F. SAXL, *Lectures*, London, 1957.

V. SCAMOZZI, *Idea dell'Architettura Universale*, Venice, 1615.

A. SCHAFFER, W. VON WARTENEGG and H. DOLLMAYR, *Kunsthistorische Sammlungen des Allerhöchsten Kaiserhauses. Führer durch die Gemäldegalerie. Alte Meister. I. Italienische, Spanische, und Französische Schulen*, Vienna, 1894.

J. SCHLOSSER, *Werke der Kleinplastik in der Skulpturensammlung des Allerhöchsten Kaiserhauses, I. Bildwerke in Bronze, Stein und Ton*, Vienna, 1910.

J. SCHLOSSER, 'Aus der Bildnerwerkstatt der Renaissance: III. Eine Reliefserie des Antonio Lombardi', *Jahrbuch der Kunstsammlungen des Allerhöchsten Kaiserhauses in Wien*, XXXI, 1913, pp. 87–100.

W. SCHMIDT, 'Zur Kenntnis Giorgione', *Repertorium für Kunstwissenschaft*, 1908, p. 155.

J. SCHULZ, 'Pordenone's Cupolas', in *Studies in Renaissance and Baroque Art presented to Anthony Blunt*, London and New York, 1967.

J. SCHULZ, *Venetian Painted Ceilings of the Renaissance*, Berkeley and Los Angeles, 1968.

J. SCHULZ, *The Printed Plans and Panoramic Views of Venice (1496–1799)*, Venice, 1970.

J. SCHULZ, 'Jacopo de' Barbari's view of Venice. Map Making, City Views and Moralized Geography before the year 1500', *Art Bulletin*, LX, 1978, pp. 425–74.

J. SCHULZ, 'Tintoretto and the first competition for the Ducal Palace "Paradise" ', *Arte Veneta*, XXXIII, 1980, pp. 112–26.

W. SCHUPBACH, 'Doctor Parma's Medical Macaronic', *Journal of the Warburg and Courtauld Institutes*, XLI, 1978, pp. 147–91.

G. SCHUTZ-RAUTENBERG, *Kunstlergraber des 15. und 16. Jahrhunderts in Italien*, Dissertationnen zur Kunstgeschichte 6, Cologne–Vienna, 1978.

S. SERLIO, *Tutta l'opera d'architettura et prospettiva di Sebastiano Serlio Bolognese*, Venice, 1619.

L. SERNAGIOTTO, 'Discorso sopra il celebre pittore Bonifacio Veneziano', *Atti della Reale Accademia di Belle Arti in Venezia*, 1883, pp. 5–53.

L. SERRA, *Alessandro Vittoria*, Milan, 1921.

L. SERRA, 'Un dipinto del Savoldo', *Rassegna Marchigiana*, II, 1923–24, pp. 266–68.

U. SERVOLINI, *Ugo da Carpi*, Florence, 1977.

S. SETTIS, *La 'Tempesta' Interpretata: Giorgione, i committenti, il soggetto*, Turin, 1978.

C. SEYMOUR JR., *Art Treasures for America. An anthology of painting and sculpture in the Samuel H. Kress Collection*, New York, 1961.

V. SGARBI, *Palladio e la maniera. I pittori vicentini del Cinquecento e i collaboratori del Palladio 1530–1630*, exhibition catalogue edited by V. Sgarbi, 1980.

V. SGARBI, 'Giovanni De Mio, Bonifacio De' Pitati, Lamberto Sustris: indicazioni sul primo tempo del manierismo nel Veneto', *Arte Veneta*, XXXV, 1981, pp. 52–61.

V. SGARBI, '1518: Cariani a Ferrara e Dosso', *Paragone*, 389, 1982, pp. 3–18.

F. R. SHAPLEY, *Paintings from the Samuel H. Kress Collection, Italian Schools XVI–XVIII Century*, New York, 1973.

F. R. SHAPLEY, *Catalogue of the Italian Paintings in the National Gallery of Art, Washington*, Washington, 1979.

W. S. SHEARD, 'Sanudo's List of Notable Things in Venetian Churches and the Date of the Vendramin Tomb', *Yale Italian Studies*, I, 1977, pp. 219–68.

W. S. SHEARD, *Antiquity in the Renaissance*, Smith College Museum of Art, Northampton, Mass., 1978 [1978¹].

W. S. SHEARD, ' "Asa Adorna": The Prehistory of the Vendramin Tomb', *Jahrbuch der Berliner Museen*, N.F., XX, 1978, pp. 117–56 [1978²].

J. SHEARMAN, 'Le seizième siècle européen', *The Burlington Magazine*, CVIII, 1966, pp. 59–67.

J. SHEARMAN, *The Early Italian Paintings in the Collection of Her Majesty the Queen*, Cambridge, 1983.

I. SHOEMAKER AND E. BROUN, *The Engravings of Marcantonio Raimondi*, Spencer Museum of Art, Lawrence, Kansas, 1981.

S. SINDING-LARSEN, 'Christ in the Council Hall. Studies in the Religious Iconography of the Venetian Republic', *Institum Romanum Norvegiae. Acta ad Archaeologiam et Artium Historiam Pertinentia*, V, Rome, 1974.

R. A. SKELTON, Introduction to the facsimile edition of Bordone's *Isolario (1528)*, Amsterdam, 1966.

J. SMIRNOVA, *Jacopo Bassano*, Moscow, 1976.

P. SOHM, 'The Staircases in the Venetian Scuole Grandi by Mauro Codussi', *Architectura*, VIII, 1978, pp. 125–49.

P. SOHM, *La Scuola Grande di San Marco 1437–1550: The Architecture of a Venetian Lay Confraternity*, Johns Hopkins, Baltimore, Doctoral Thesis; University Microfilms International, Ann Arbor, Michigan, 1981.

A. SOMOF, *Ermitage impérial, Catalogue de la Galerie des Tableaux. Première Partie, les Écoles d'Italie et d'Espagne*, St. Petersburg, 1899.

M. S. SOPHER, *Sixteenth Century Prints*, Claremont, Ca., 1978.

R. SOPRANI, *Vite de' pittori, scultori, ed architetti genovesi*, edited by C. G. Ratti, 2 vols., Genoa, 1768–69.

A. SPAHN, *Palma Vecchio*, Leipzig, 1932.

W. Stechow, 'The Authorship of the Walters "Lucretia" ', *Journal of the Walters Art Gallery*, XXIII, 1960, pp. 73–85.

J. Steer, *Alvise Vivarini: His Art and Influence*, Cambridge, 1982.

Stockholm 1962–63, *Konstens Venedig*, exhibition catalogue, National Museum, Stockholm, 1962–63.

R. Stone, 'Tullio Lombardo's *Adam* from the Vendramin Tomb: A New Terminus ante Quem', *Marsyas*, XVI, 1972–73, pp. 87–88.

R. Stone, 'Antico and the development of bronze casting in Italy at the end of the quattrocento', *Metropolitan Museum Journal*, XIV, 1982, pp. 87–116.

D. Stott, 'Fatte a Sembianza di Pittura: Jacopo Sansovino's Bronze Reliefs in S. Marco', *The Art Bulletin*, LXIV, 1982, pp. 370–88.

D. Strom, 'Desiderio and the Madonna Relief in Quattrocento Florence', *Pantheon*, XL, 1982, pp. 130–35.

S. A. Strong, *Chatsworth Drawings*, London, 1902.

W. Suida, *Genua*, Leipzig, 1906.

W. Suida, 'Beiträge zu Lorenzo Lotto', *Belvedere*, 1932, pp. 170–73.

W. Suida, *Tiziano*, Rome, 1933; French edition, 1935.

W. Suida, 'Tizian, die beiden Campagnola und Ugo da Carpi', *Critica d'Arte*, I, 1935–36, pp. 285–89.

W. Suida, 'Spigolature giorgionesche', *Arte Veneta*, VIII, 1954, p. 153.

W. Suida, *The Samuel H. Kress Collection*, Birmingham, 1959.

I. Supino, *Catalogo del R. Museo Nazionale di Firenze*, Rome, 1898.

I. Supino, *Le sculture delle porte di S. Petronio in Bologna*, Florence, 1914.

B. Sweeny, *Johnson G. Johnson Collection. Catalogue of Italian Paintings*, Philadelphia, 1966.

E. Szmodis-Eszláry, 'Relief en cristal de roche d'un maître vénitien du début du XVIe siècle', *Bulletin du Musée Hongrois des Beaux-Arts*, 56–57, 1981, pp. 97–104.

M. Tafuri, *Jacopo Sansovino e l'architettura del 500 a Venezia*, Padua, 1969; another edition, 1972.

Tafuri 1980 see Venice 1980.

F. M. Tassi, *Vite de' pittori, scultori e architetti bergamaschi*, Bergamo, 1793.

B. de Tauzia, *Notice des dessins de la collection His de la Salle*, Paris, 1881.

T. Temanza, *Vite dei più celebri architetti e scultori veneziani che fiorirono nel secolo Decimosesto*, Venice, 1778.

A. Tempestini, 'Un inedito di Sebastiano Florigerio', *Scritti d'amici per Maria Cionini Visani*, Turin, 1977, pp. 81–3.

A. Tempestini, *Martino da Udine*, Udine, 1979.

D. Teniers the Younger, *Theatrum Pictorium*, Antwerp and Brussels, 1660.

M. Thausing, 'Giorgione', in *Wiener Kunstbriefe*, Leipzig, 1884.

W. Thomas, *The History of Italy 1549*, edited by G. Parkes, Ithaca, 1963.

H. Tietze, *Tizian*, 2 vols., Vienna, 1936.

H. Tietze, *Tintoretto. The Paintings and Drawings*, London, 1948.

H. Tietze, *Titian, Paintings and Drawings*, London, 1950.

E. Tietze-Conrat, 'A drawing by Paris Bordone, not Titian', *The Burlington Magazine*, LXXII, 1938, p. 189.

E. Tietze-Conrat, 'The so-called "Adulteress" by Giorgione', *Gazette des Beaux-Arts*, XXVII, 1945, p. 189.

E. Tietze-Conrat, 'Titian's design for the Battle of Cadore', *Gazette des Beaux-Arts*, II, 1948, ii, pp. 237–42.

H. Tietze and E. Tietze-Conrat, 'Contributi critici allo studio organico dei disegni veneziani del cinquecento', *Critica d'Arte*, II, 1937, pp. 77–88.

H. Tietze and E. Tietze-Conrat, 'Titian's Woodcuts', *The Print Collector's Quarterly*, XXV, 1938, pp. 332ff. and pp. 464ff.

H. Tietze and E. Tietze-Conrat, 'Domenico Campagnola's Graphic Art', *The Print Collector's Quarterly*, XXVI, 1939, pp. 311–33, 445–65.

H. Tietze and E. Tietze-Conrat, *The Drawings of the Venetian Painters in the XVth and XVIth Centuries*, New York, 1944.

W. Timofiewitsch, *Girolamo Campagna – Studien zur venezianischen Plastik um das Jahr 1600*, Munich, 1972.

A. Tofanelli, *Descrizione delle sculture e pitture che si trovano in Campidoglio*, Rome, 1818; another edition, edited by Frency, 1820.

C. Torre, *Il ritratto di Milano*, Milan, 1674.

R. Tozzi, 'Disegni di Domenico Tintoretto', *Bollettino d'Arte*, 1937, pp. 19–31.

G. Trecca, *Paolo Veronese a Verona*, Verona, 1940.

W. Tressider, *The Classicism of the early work of Titian: its Sources and Character*, dissertation, University of Michigan, 1979.

F. Trevisani, 'Osservazioni sulla mostra del "Lotto nelle Marche, il suo tempo, il suo influsso"', *Arte Veneta*, XXXV, 1981, pp. 275–88.

E. Trincanato, *Venezia Minore*, Milan, 1948.

E. Trincanato and U. Franzoi, *Venise au fil du temps. Atlas historique d'urbanisme et d'architecture*, Boulogne-Billancourt, 1971.

E. G. Troche, 'Giovanni Cariani', *J.K.P.K.*, LV, 1934, pp. 97–125.

K. Tscheuschner, 'Über den Tizian no. 172, der Dresdener Galerie', *Repertorium für Kunstwissenschaft*, XXIV, 1901, pp. 292–93.

Udine 1939, *Mostra del Pordenone e della pittura friulana del Rinascimento*, exhibition catalogue, edited by B. Molajoli, Udine, 1939.

United States 1969, *Chatsworth Drawings II*, International Exhibitions Foundation, catalogue edited by J. Byam Shaw, 1969.

United States and Cambridge 1976–77, *European drawings from the Fitzwilliam*, International Exhibitions Foundation, five museums in United States and The Fitzwilliam Museum, catalogue edited by M. Jaffé, Cambridge, 1976–77.

United States and Canada 1962–63, *Old Master Drawings from Chatsworth*, International Exhibitions Foundation, seven galleries in the United States and Canada, catalogue edited by T. Wragg, 1962–63.

U. Vaglia, 'Sant'Antonio di Padova nei dipinti del Romanino esposti alla Mostra di Brescia', *Il Santo*, 1965, pp. 143–48.

F. Valcanover, *Museo Civico di Feltre*, Vicenza, 1954.

F. Valcanover, 'Il ritratto veneto da Tiziano al Tiepolo', *Arte Veneta*, X, 1956, pp. 240–44.

F. Valcanover, *Tutta la pittura di Tiziano*, Milan, 1960.

F. Valcanover, *L'opera completa di Tiziano*, Milan, 1969.

F. Valcanover, 'La Pala Pesaro', *Quaderni della Soprintendenza . . . di Venezia*, VIII, 1979, pp. 57–72.

W. R. Valentiner (ed.), *Unknown Masterpieces*, London, 1930.

W. R. Valentiner, 'Alessandro Vittoria and Michelangelo', *Art Quarterly*, 1942, pp. 149–57.

W. R. Valentiner, *Studies of Italian Renaissance Sculpture*, London, 1950.

W. R. Valentiner, *Gothic and Renaissance Sculptures in the collection of the Los Angeles County Museum*, Los Angeles, 1951.

W. R. Valentiner, *Catalogue of Paintings. Raleigh, North Carolina Museum of Art*, Raleigh, 1956 (1956[1]).

W. R. Valentiner, 'The Raleigh Museum's First 220 Paintings: notes on the collection', *Art News*, IV, 1956 (1956[2]).

R. van Marle, 'A Landscape painted by Titian about 1530', *International Studio*, XCVI, 1930, pp. 118ff.

G. Vasari, *Le vite de' più eccellenti architetti, pittori et scultori*, Florence, 1550.

G. Vasari, *Le vite de' più eccellenti pittori, scultori, ed architetti*, edited by G. Milanesi, 9 vols., Florence, 1875–85.

Venice 1935, *Mostra di Tiziano*, catalogue edited by N. Barbantini, Venice, 1935.

Venice 1937, *Mostra del Tintoretto*, exhibition catalogue, edited by N. Barbantini, Venice, 1937.

Venice 1939, *Mostra di Paolo Veronese*, exhibition catalogue by R. Pallucchini, Venice, 1939.

Venice 1945, *Cinque secoli di pittura veneta*, exhibition catalogue by R. Pallucchini, 1945.

Venice 1946, *I capolavori dei musei veneti*, exhibition catalogue edited by R. Pallucchini, Venice, 1946.

Venice 1953, *Mostra di Lorenzo Lotto*, exhibition catalogue edited by P. Zampetti, Venice, 1953.

Venice 1955, *Giorgione e i Giorgioneschi*, exhibition catalogue edited by P. Zampetti, Venice, 1955.

Venice 1957, *Jacopo Bassano*, exhibition catalogue edited by P. Zampetti, Venice, 1957.

Venice 1958, *Disegni Veneti di Oxford*, exhibition catalogue edited by K. T. Parker, Fondazione Giorgio Cini, Venice, 1958.

Venice 1959, *La pittura del Seicento a Venezia*, exhibition catalogue by G. Mariacher, Venice, 1959.

Venice 1963, *Vittore Carpaccio*, exhibition catalogue by P. Zampetti, Venice, 1963.

Venice 1971, *Arte a Venezia, dal Medioevo al Settecento*, exhibition catalogue edited by G. Mariacher, Venice, 1971.

Venice 1976[1], *Disegni di Tiziano e della sua cerchia*, exhibition catalogue by K. Oberhuber and H. Goldfarb, Fondazione Giorgio Cini, Venice, 1976.

Venice 1976[2], *Tiziano e la silografia veneziana del Cinquecento*, exhibition catalogue by M. Muraro and D. Rosand, Venice, 1976.

Venice 1978, *Giorgione a Venezia*, exhibition catalogue, Venice, 1978.

Venice 1979, *Venezia e la Peste 1348–1797*, exhibition catalogue, Venice, 1979.

Venice 1980[1], *Architettura e Utopia nella Venezia del Cinquecento*, exhibition catalogue, Venice, 1980.

Venice 1980[2], *Disegni veneti di collezioni inglesi*, exhibition catalogue edited by J. Stock, Fondazione Giorgio Cini, Venice, 1980.

Venice 1981[1], *Da Tiziano a El Greco. Per la storia del Manierismo a Venezia*, exhibition catalogue edited by R. Pallucchini, Venice, 1981.

Venice 1981[2], *Disegni veneti della Collezione Lugt*, exhibition catalogue by J. Byam Shaw, Fondazione Giorgio Cini, Venice, 1981.

A. Venturi, *Il Museo e la Galleria Borghese*, Rome, 1893.

A. Venturi, 'Jacopo Tintoretto. L'esordio', *L'Arte*, XXI, 1928, pp. 178–86.

A. Venturi, *Storia dell'arte italiana: IX La pittura del Cinquecento*, I–VII, Milan, 1925–34.

A. Venturi, *Storia dell'arte italiana: X La scultura del Cinquecento*, I–III, Milan, 1935–37.

L. Venturi, *Le origini della pittura veneziana*, Venice, 1907.

L. Venturi, 'Saggio sulle opere d'arte italiana a Pietroburgo', *L'Arte*, XV, 1912, pp. 306–09.

L. Venturi, *Giorgione e il giorgionismo*, Milan, 1913.

L. Venturi, 'A traverso le Marche', *L'Arte*, XVIII, 1915, pp. 1–28, 172–208.

L. Venturi, *Italian Paintings in America*, 3 vols., Milan and New York, 1933.

R. Venuti, *Accurata e succinta descrizione di Roma moderna*, 4 vols., Rome, 1767.

G. Verci, *Notizia intorno alla vita e alle opere de' Pittori . . . della Città di Bassano*, Venice, 1775.

VERONA 1980, *Palladio and Verona*, exhibition catalogue edited by R. Marini, Verona, 1980.
L. VERTOVA, 'Bernardino Licinio', *I Pittori Bergamaschi: Il Cinquecento*, I, Bergamo, 1975.
L. VERTOVA, 'Bianca Vertova Puella e Santa', *Antichità Viva*, XV, 1976, pp. 6–10.
G. VEZZOLI, 'Incontro di S. Angela Merici con l'Arte', in *Studi in onore di Luigi Fossati*, Brescia 1974, pp. 391–96.
VIENNA 1966, *Katalog der Sammlung für Plastik und Kunstgewerbe*, II, *Renaissance*, Kunsthistorisches Museum, Vienna, 1966.
P. VITRY, ed., *Musée National du Louvre: Catalogue des sculptures du Moyen Age, de la Renaissance et des Temps Modernes, I. Moyen Age et Renaissance*, Paris, 1922.
C. VOLPE, 'Primitives to Picasso' (review), *Arte Antica e Moderna*, Jan–March, 1962, pp. III–IV.
E. VON DER BERCKEN, *Die Gemälde des Jacopo Tintoretto*, Munich, 1942.
H. M. VON ERFFA, 'Der Nurnberger Stadtpatron auf italienischen Gemälden', *Mitteilungen des Kunsthistorisches Instituts in Florenz*, XX, 1976, pp. 1–12.
D. VON HADELN, 'Zum Oeuvre Paris Bordones', *Repertorium für Kunstwissenschaft*, XXXI, 1908, pp. 544–55.
D. VON HADELN, 'Beiträge zur Tintoretto-forschung', *J.K.P.K.*, XXXII, 1911, pp. 1–58 [1911¹].
VON HADELN 1911² *see* LUDWIG 1911.
VON HADELN 1914, 1924 *see* RIDOLFI 1914, 1924.
D. VON HADELN, *Handzeichnungen des Giacomo Tintoretto*, Berlin, 1922.
D. VON HADELN, 'Drawings by Palma Vecchio', *The Burlington Magazine*, XLIII, 1923, pp. 168–73.
D. VON HADELN, *Zeichnungen der Tizian*, Berlin, 1924; English edition, London, 1927.
D. VON HADELN, 'Notes on Savoldo', *Art in America*, XIII, 1925, pp. 72ff. [1925¹]
D. VON HADELN, *Venezianische Zeichnungen der Hochrenaissance*, Berlin, 1925 [1925²].
D. VON HADELN, *Venezianische Zeichnungen der Spätrenaissance*, Berlin, 1926.
D. VON HADELN, *Paolo Veronese, aus dem Nachlass des Verfassers herausgegeben vom Kunsthistorischen Institut in Florenz*, edited by G. Schweikhart, Florence, 1978.
S. VSEVOLOJSKAIA, *La peinture italienne xiii⁰–xviii⁰ siècles*, Musée de L'Ermitage Leningrad, 1982.
G. WAAGEN, *Works of Art and Artists in England*, 3 vols., London, 1838.
G. F. WAAGEN, *Treasures of Art in Great Britain*, 3 vols., London, 1854; reprinted London, 1970.
J. WALKER, *Bellini and Titian at Ferrara*, London, 1956.
P. WARD-JACKSON, *Italian Drawings in the Victoria and Albert Museum*, 2 vols., London, 1979.
O. WARNER, *Great Sea Battles*, London, 1963.
G. F. WARNER and J. P. GILSON, *Catalogue of Western Manuscripts in the Old Royal and King's Collections in the British Museum*, London, 1921.
WASHINGTON 1951, *Paintings and Sculpture from the Kress Collection*, National Gallery of Art, Washington D.C., 1951.
WASHINGTON 1961–62, *Art Treasures for America*, exhibition catalogue, National Gallery of Art, Washington, 1961.
WASHINGTON 1973, *Early Italian Engravings from the National Gallery of Art*, exhibition catalogue by J. Levenson, K. Oberhuber and J. Sheehan, Washington, 1973.
WASHINGTON 1976 *see* ROSAND and MURARO
WASHINGTON 1981–82, *The Drawings of Andrea Palladio*, exhibition catalogue by D. Lewis, Washington, 1981–82.

WASHINGTON, FORT WORTH, ST. LOUIS, 1974–75, *Venetian Drawings from American Collections*, exhibition catalogue edited by T. Pignatti, The National Gallery of Art, Washington, Kimball Art Museum, Fort Worth, The St. Louis Art Museum, 1974–75.
WASHINGTON, LOS ANGELES, NEW YORK 1979, *The Heritage of Titian*, exhibition catalogue edited by E. Fahy, Washington, Los Angeles and New York, 1979.
E. K. WATERHOUSE, 'Paintings from Venice for seventeenth century England: some records of a forgotten transaction', *Italian Studies*, VII, 1952, pp. 1–23.
E. K. WATERHOUSE, *Giorgione*, Glasgow, 1974.
A. J. WAUTERS, 'Une Ambassade Flamande', *Revue de Belgique*, IV, 1904, pp. 290ff.
H. B. WEHLE, *The Metropolitan Museum of Art. A Catalogue of Italian, Spanish and Byzantine Paintings*, New York, 1940.
H. R. WEIHRAUCH, *Studien zum bildnerischen Werke des Jacopo Sansovino*, Strasbourg, 1935.
H. R. WEIHRAUCH, 'Italienische Bronzen als Vorbilder deutscher Goldschmiedekunst', *Festschrift für Theodor Müller*, Munich, 1965, pp. 263ff.
H. R. WEIHRAUCH, *Europäische Bronzestatuetten, 15.–18. Jahrhundert*, Brunswick, 1967.
P. P. WEINER, *Les chefs d'oeuvre de la Galerie de tableaux de l'Ermitage à Petrograd*, Munich, 1928.
D. WESTPHAL, *Bonifazio Veronese*, Munich, 1931.
H. WETHEY, *The Paintings of Titian: I The Religious Paintings; II The Portraits; III The Mythological and Historical Paintings*, London 1969, 1971, 1975.
A. WETHEY and H. WETHEY, 'Titian: Two Portraits of Noblemen in Armor and their Heraldry', *Art Bulletin*, LXII, 1980, pp. 76–96.
H. WETHEY 1982, 'Tiziano e la decorazione della Sala del Maggior Consiglio nel Palazzo Ducale di Venezia' *Atti del XXIV Congresso Internazionale di Storia dell'Arte*, X, Bologna 1982, pp. 177–83.
F. WICKHOFF, 'Der Saal des grossen Rathes zu Venedig in seinem alten Schmucke', *Repertorium für Kunstwissenshaft*, VI, 1883, pp. 1–37.
F. WICKHOFF, 'Les Écoles Italiennes au Musée Impérial de Vienna', *Gazettes des Beaux-arts*, IX, 1893, pp. 130–47.
J. WILDE and others, *Katalog der Gemäldegalerie*, Vienna, 1928.
J. WILDE, 'Widergefundene Gemälde aus der Sammlung des Erzherzogs Leopold Wilhelm', *J.K.S.W.*, N.F. IV, 1930, pp. 245–66.
J. WILDE, 'Ein unbeachtetes Werk Giorgiones', *J.K.P.K.*, LII, 1931, pp. 91–100.
J. WILDE, 'Die Probleme um Domenico Mancini', *J.K.S.W.*, N.F VII, 1933, pp. 97ff.
J. WILDE, 'Die Mostra del Tintoretto zu Venedig', *Zeitschrift für Kunstgeschichte*, VII, 1937, pp. 140–53.
J. WILDE, *Venetian Art from Bellini to Titian*, Oxford, 1974.
S. WILK, 'Tullio Lombardo's "Double Portrait" Reliefs', *Marsyas*, XVI, 1972–73, pp. 67ff.
S. WILK, *The Sculpture of Tullio Lombardo: Studies in Sources and Meaning*, New York and London, 1978.
C. WILLARD, 'Walter P. Chrysler, Jr. exhibits his Personal History of Art', *Look*, March 6, 1956.
E. WIND, *Bellini's Feast of the Gods*, Cambridge, Mass., 1948.
C. WINTER, *The Fitzwilliam Museum*, Cambridge, 1958.
E. WINTERNITZ, *Musical instruments and their significance in Western Art*, London, 1967.
R. WITTKOWER, 'Transformations of Minerva in Renaissance Imagery', *Journal of the Warburg*

and Courtauld Institutes, II, 1938–39, pp. 194–205.
R. WITTKOWER, *Architectural Principles in the Age of Humanism*, third edition, New York, 1971.
W. D. WIXOM, *Renaissance Bronzes from Ohio Collections*, Cleveland Museum of Art, Cleveland, Ohio, 1975.
K. WOERMANN, *Die Italienische Bildnismalerei der Renaissance*, Esslingen, 1906.
Y. YAPOU, *Drawings of the sixteenth century School of Verona in the Department of Prints and Drawings, British Museum*, unpublished M.A. report, Courtauld Institute, University of London, 1968.
P. ZAMPETTI, *Lorenzo Lotto nelle Marche*, Urbino, 1953.
ZAMPETTI 1955 *see* VENICE 1955.
P. ZAMPETTI, *Jacopo Bassano*, Rome 1958.
P. ZAMPETTI, in *Kindlers Malerei Lexikon*, I, Zurich, 1974.
P. ZAMPETTI, *L'opera completa di Giorgione*, introduction by V. Lilli, Milan, 1968.
P. ZAMPETTI, *Lorenzo Lotto. Il Libro di Spese Diverse (1538–1556)*, edited by P. Zampetti, Venice and Rome, 1969.
P. ZAMPETTI, 'Andrea Previtali', in *I Pittori Bergamaschi: Il Cinquecento*, I, Bergamo, 1975.
P. ZAMPETTI and N. IVANOFF, 'Giacomo Negretti detto Palma il Giovane', in *I Pittori Bergamaschi: Il Cinquecento*, III, Bergamo, 1979.
ZAMPETTI 1980 *see* LORETO 1980.
A. ZANETTI, *Descrizione di tutte le pubbliche pitture della città di Venezia ... o sia Rinnovazione delle Ricche Minere di Marco Boschini ...*, Venice, 1733.
A. ZANETTI, *Della pittura veneziana e delle opere pubbliche de' veneziani maestri*, Venice, 1771.
V. ZANETTI, *Del Monastero della Chiesa di S. Maria degli Angeli*, Venice, 1863.
F. ZANOTTO, *Il Palazzo Ducale di Venezia*, 3 vols., Venice, 1853.
F. ZANOTTO, *Nuovissima guida di Venezia e delle isole della sua Laguna*, Venice, 1856.
Z. ZARETSKAIA and N. KOSSARÉVA, *La Sculpture de l'Europe occidentale à l'Ermitage*, Leningrad, 1970.
F. ZAVA BOCCAZZI, 'Tracce per Girolamo da Treviso il Giovane in alcune xilografie di Francesco De Nanto', *Arte Veneta*, XII, 1958, pp. 70–78.
F. ZAVA BOCCAZZI, *La Basilica dei Santi Giovanni e Paolo in Venezia*, Venice, 1965.
F. ZERI, *Italian Painting in the Walters Art Gallery*, Baltimore, 1976 [1976¹].
F. ZERI, 'La percezione visiva dell'Italia e degli italiani nella storia della pittura', in *Storia d'Italia Einaudi*, VI, Turin, 1976 [1976²].
H. ZERNER, 'Giuseppe Scolari' *L'Oeil*, 1965, I, pp. 25ff.
V. ZIPPEL, 'Un busto ignoto del Vittoria', *L'Arte*, XXIX, 1926, pp. 73–74.
G. ZORZI, *Le opere pubbliche e i palazzi privati di Andrea Palladio*, Venice, 1965.
G. ZORZI, *Le chiese e i ponti di Andrea Palladio*, Venice, 1967.
G. ZUCCOLO PADRONO, 'Miniature manieristiche nelle commissioni dogali dei Cinquecento presso il Museo Correr', *Bollettino del Musei Civici Veneziani*, XIV, 1969, pp. 4–18.
A. P. ZUGNI TAURO, 'La presenza di quattro artisti in Feltre: Ludovico Pozzoserato, Andrea Palladio, Giannantonio Selva, Tranquillo Orsi', *Arte Veneta*, XXXII, 1978, pp. 255–61.
ZURICH 1948–49, *Kunstschätze der Lombardei*, exhibition catalogue by C. Baroni and G. A. Dell'Acqua, Zurich, 1948–49.
P. ZURLA, *Di Marco Polo e degli altri viaggiatori veneziani più illustri*, Venice, 1818.

INDEX OF LENDERS

Also owners who prefer to remain anonymous

ROYAL ACADEMY TRUST

*The Trustees and Appeal Committee of the Royal Academy Trust
wish to express their gratitude to the many companies and individuals
who have already given their support to the appeal.
Among many others they would like to extend their thanks to:*

THE FRIENDS OF THE ROYAL ACADEMY

PATRON
H.R.H. The Duke of Edinburgh, KG, KT

The Friends of the Royal Academy receive the following privileges
FRIENDS £18.00
FRIENDS (Concessionary)
£15.00 annually for full-time
Museum Staff and Teachers
£12.00 annually for Pensioners and
Young Friends aged 25 years and under
Gain free and immediate admission to all
Royal Academy Exhibitions with a guest or
husband/wife and children under 16.
Obtain catalogues at a reduced price.
Enjoy the privacy of the Friends' Room
in Burlington House.
Receive Private View invitations to various
exhibitions including the Summer Exhibition.
Have access to the Library and Archives.
Benefit from other special arrangements,
including lectures, concerts and tours.

COUNTRY FRIENDS £10.00 annually for Friends
living more than 75 miles from London.
Gain free and immediate admission to
Royal Academy Exhibitions on 6 occasions
a year with a guest or husband/wife
and children under 16.
Receive all the other privileges offered to Friends.

ARTIST SUBSCRIBERS £30.00 annually
Recieve all the privileges offered to Friends.
Receive free submission forms for the
Summer Exhibition.
Obtain art materials at a reduced price.

SPONSORS £500 (corporate),
£150 (individually) annually
Receive all the privileges offered to Friends.
Enjoy the particular privileges of reserving the
Royal Academy's Private Rooms when
appropriate and similarly of arranging
evening viewings of certain exhibitions.
Receive acknowledgement through the inclusion
of the Sponsor's name on official documents.

BENEFACTORS £5,000 or more
An involvement with the Royal Academy
which will be honoured in every way.

*Further information and Deed of Covenant
forms are available from
The Friends of the Royal Academy,
Royal Academy of Arts, Piccadily,
London W1V 0DS*

BENEFACTORS
Mrs. M.G.T. Askew
Mrs. Hilda Benham
Lady Brinton
Mr. and Mrs. Nigel Broackes
Keith Bromley, Esq.
The John S. Cohen Foundation
The Colby Trust
Michael E. Flintoff, Esq.
The Lady Gibson
Jack Goldhill, Esq.
Mrs. Mary Graves
D.J. Hoare, Esq.
Sir Antony Hornby
George Howard, Esq
Irene and Hyman Kreitman
The Landmark Trust
Roland Lay, Esq.
The Trustees of the Leach Fourteenth Trust
Hugh Leggatt, Esq.
Mr. and Mrs. M.S. Lipworth
Sir Jack Lyons, CBE
The Manor Charitable Trustees
Lieutenant-Colonel L.S. Michael, OBE
Jan Mitchell, Esq.
The Lord Moyne
Mrs. Sylvia Mulcahy
G. R. Nicholas, Esq.
Lieutenant-Colonel Vincent Paravicini
Mrs. Vincent Paravicini
Richard Park, Esq.
Phillips Fine Art Auctioneers
Mrs. Denise Rapp
Mrs. Adrianne Reed
Mrs. Basil Samuel
Eric Sharp, Esq., CBE
The Revd. Prebendary E.F. Shotter
Dr. Francis Singer
Lady Daphne Straight
Mrs. Pamela Synge
Harry Teacher, Esq.
Henry Vyner Charitable Trust
Charles Wollaston, Esq.

CORPORATE SPONSORS
Bankers Trust Company
Barclays Bank International Limited
Bourne Leisure Group Limited
The British Petroleum Company Limited
Christie Manson and Woods Limited
Citibank
Consolidated Safeguards Limited
Courage Charitable Trust
Delta Group p.l.c.
Esso Petroleum Company Limited
Ford Motor Company Limited
The Granada Group
Arthur Guinnes and Sons PLC
Guinness Peat Group
House of Fraser plc
Alexander Howden Underwriting Limited
IBM United Kingdom Limited
Imperial Chemical Industries PLC
Investment Company of North Atlantic
Johnson Wax Limited
Lex Service Group PLC
Marks and Spencer p.l.c.
Mars Limited
Martini & Rossi Limited
The Worshipful Company of Mercers
The Nestlé Charitable Trust
Ocean Transport and Trading Limited (P. H. Holt
Ove Arup Partnership
Philips Electronic and Associated Industries Limite
The Rio Tinto-Zinc Corporation PLC
Rowe and Pitman
The Royal Bank of Scotland plc
J. Henry Schroder Wagg and Company Limited
The Seascope Group
Shell UK Limited
W. H. Smith & Son Limited
Thames Television Limited
J. Walter Thompson Company Limited
Ultramar PLC
United Biscuits (U.K.) Limited

INDIVIDUAL SPONSORS
The A.B. Charitable Trust
Abdulah Ben Saad Al-Saud
Ian Fife Campbell Anstruther, Esq.
Mrs. Ann Appelbe
Dwight W. Arundale, Esq.
Edgar Astaire, Esq.
Miss Margaret Louise Band
Godfrey Bonsack, Esq.
Peter Bowring, Esq.
Mrs. Susan Bradman
Cornelis Broere, Esq.
Jeremy Brown, Esq.
Simon Cawkwell, Esq.
W. J. Chapman, Esq.
Major A. J. Chrystal
Henry M. Cohen, Esq.
Mrs. Elizabeth Corob
Mrs. Yvonne Datnow
Raymond de Prudhoe, Esq.
Raphael Djanogly, Esq. JP
Mrs. Laura Dwyer
Mrs. Gilbert Edgar
Aidan Ellis, Esq.
Robert S. Ferguson, Esq.

Graham Gauld, Esq.
Victor Gauntlett, Esq.
Lady Gibberd
Peter George Goulandris, Esq.
J. A. Hadjipateras, Esq.
Mrs. S. Halliday
A. Herbage. Esq.
Mrs. Penelope Heseltine
H. J. Holmes, Esq.
Norman J. Hyams, Esq.
Roger Hughes, Esq.
Mrs. Manya Igel
J. P. Jacobs, Esq.
Mrs. Christopher James
Alan Jeavons, Esq.
Irwin Joffe, Esq.
S. D. M. Kahan, Esq.
Peter W. Kininmonth, Esq.
Bruce Lloyd Esq.
Owen Luder, Esq.
Mrs. Graham Lyons
Ciarán MacGonigal, Esq.
Dr. Abraham Marcus
Peter Ian McMean, Esq.
Princess Helena Moutafian, MBE

Raymond A. Parkin, Esq.
Mrs. Olive Pettit
Mrs. M. C. S. Philip
Cyril Ray, Esq.
Mrs. Margaret Reeves
The Rt. Hon. Lord Rootes
The Hon. Sir Steven Runcim
The Master, The Worshipfu
    Company of Saddlers
Sir Robert Sainsbury
R. J. Simia, Esq.
Christina Smith
Steven H. Smith, Esq.
Thomas Stainton, Esq.
Cyril Stein, Esq.
James Q. Stringer, Esq.
Mrs. A. Susman
Mrs. G. M. Susman
The Hon. Mrs. Quentin Wa
Sidney S. Wayne, Esq.
Frank S. Wenstrom, Esq.
David Whithead, Esq.
Brian Gordon Wolfson, Esq
Lawrence Wood, Esq.

There are also anonymous Benefactors and Sponsors